THE CONQUEST AND COLONIZATION
OF HONDURAS

THE CONQUEST AND COLONIZATION OF HONDURAS

1502–1550

ROBERT S. CHAMBERLAIN

1966
OCTAGON BOOKS, INC.
New York

Originally published 1953 by
Carnegie Institution of Washington
as Publication No. 598

*Reprinted 1966 by special arrangement with
Carnegie Institution of Washington*

OCTAGON BOOKS, INC.
175 FIFTH AVENUE
NEW YORK, N.Y. 10010

LIBRARY OF CONGRESS CATALOG CARD NUMBER: 66-28383

Printed in U.S.A. by
NOBLE OFFSET PRINTERS, INC.
NEW YORK 3, N. Y.

Contents

Illustrations

Introduction

THIS STUDY of the Spanish conquest and colonization of Honduras, like my history of the occupation of Yucatan, grew out of my original intention to write a biography of Francisco de Montejo, one of the great but lesser known conquistadores. As my research in the Archivo General de Indias de Sevilla and other Spanish archives progressed, several unexpected elements came to light.

First, Montejo's activities in Yucatan and in Honduras, although interlocked, in reality constituted two separate careers. The second element was the extremely close relationship between Spanish occupation of Yucatan and the final conquest of Honduras, a relationship which centered not only in the person of Montejo, but also in plans which he conceived for personal aggrandizement and for development of the two provinces. The third factor was the surprising revelation through many original documents that half a decade of the history of Honduras (from mid-1539 to the spring of 1544) had hitherto never been recorded in historical writings: five years which brought significant constitutional developments, extension of conquest and settlement, and economic progress through the discovery of new and rich deposits of precious metals. The story of these years was lost to the chroniclers by 1600, if not before.

The wealth of documents made it possible to give a technical, detailed picture of the combination of policy and practical actions through which, step by step, conquest and colonization were begun, carried forward, and made permanent. The territorial compactness of the Province of Honduras especially lent itself to such clinical analysis.

In this study the earliest years of Honduras, which from the first was a meeting-place for cross-currents of Spanish expansion, are merely summarized as background. Here, analysis begins in 1534, when trends which were to determine the pattern of final conquest and settlement were set in motion.

The history of Honduras to 1550 is extremely complex and is the story of one of the most perpetually turbulent provinces of the Indies for the first two decades of its history. Its remoteness from other centers of colonization gave wide scope for individual action, to governors and colonists alike. The fact that thrusts of Spanish expansion from several directions (over from Santo Domingo, down from Mexico, and up from Panama) met there, created rivalry and violence among the Spaniards from the first. The close connection which later developed between nearby Guatemala and Honduras, and the interrela-

I

tion between the conquest of Yucatan and that of Honduras caused further jurisdictional confusion.

It is no exaggeration to say that rivalry and bloodshed among captains and governors so engaged the efforts of the Spaniards that they were long diverted from their main purpose. Although the province was discovered in 1502, conquest did not begin until 1524. Yet only as late as 1539 did the Spaniards achieve definitive dominion, and it was five years more before the royal government was able finally to bring order to the province, through installation of the *audiencia,* a commission system of government.

The story of the founding of Honduras necessarily includes a large element of constitutional and institutional history, as well as an account of the conquest and peopling of the province. The implanting of government within the colony and the fixing of its place within the broader framework of Spanish overseas administration bulk large.

The constitutional story involves not only the first rivalries of newly arrived captains, but also later conflicts between powerful conquistador-governors— men of high standing in their own rights—and at the close of the period covered by this study, jurisdictional competition between the highest agencies of government in the northern sections of the Spanish Indies, the Viceroy and Audiencia of New Spain on the one hand and the Audiencia of Santo Domingo on the other. The trend of this governmental evolution in Honduras is symbolic of the broader evolution of Castilian overseas administration, even though, because of its exceptional turbulence, the province represents an exaggerated case.

I have included a number of detailed passages on petitions, recommendations, and protests which governors, local authorities, ecclesiastics, and colonists presented to the Crown in Castile and to higher agencies of government in the New World at various times, as well as passages from other legal documents drawn up by individuals or groups, which set forth the views of both officials and citizens on issues which concerned the colony. In the absence of extensive private documents, such as letters, autobiographies, memoirs, and diaries, documents such as these are the only ones available to show the "public opinion" of the colonists. These petitions, recommendations, and protests of the authorities, notably those of the municipal councils, or *cabildos,* expressed in correspondence or through procurators (*procuradores*) show what the officials and citizens, or segments of both, believed should be done to benefit the colony, whether the province as a whole or their own towns, at various stages.

Petitions or recommendations of groups or of individuals contrary to the acts or policies of the authorities represent what can be called an "opposition party." Likewise the views of the municipal councils and citizen body—local interests within the colony—are frequently at variance with each other. Minority groups completely at odds with the provincial authorities or with the majority of the colonists would not infrequently designate their own representatives to carry their particular views to Court in Castile or to higher New World organs of government. The cabildos, annually elected, stated the official viewpoint, or that of the group in power. But at times the elections to the cabildos, and therefore the actions of their members, were closely controlled by the governors. It was especially under such circumstances that opposition groups would name their own agents as the only means of obtaining a hearing before the Crown or highest agencies of government in the Indies.

The most spectacular, but by no means uncommon, statements were called forth by royal policies and legislation which the colonists, whether officials or private citizens, considered inimical to their personal interests or the good of the colony as a whole. Neither authorities nor colonists had the slightest hesitation in protesting to the Crown or higher organs of New World government under such circumstances. Much less did they hesitate to protest the acts of a governor, or to make recommendations to him regarding his policies. There was in Honduras much reflection of earlier Castilian democracy and of the rugged individual attitudes of colonists of a truly frontier province, constitutionally expressed, as well as of lawless disorder and turmoil.

In this way legally stated petitions, recommendations, and protests, even when they failed to produce results, are valuable as one of the few means available to determine the opinion of the colonists at any given time and to ascertain what they considered to be the policies best calculated to promote the welfare of the colony and its members.

The American diplomat and scholar E. G. Squier has left us a mid-nineteenth-century description of Honduras, which, combining general accuracy and feeling for the region, well serves to set the scene geographically:

The aspects of nature in Honduras are varied and striking. The conditions of conformation of coast, of elevation and consequent temperature, the amount of rain falling upon the respective declivities of the Cordilleras, all contribute to diversify the forms under which vegetable life presents itself to the eye of the traveler. The three great features, nevertheless, are the coast alluvions, generally densely wooded, the elevated valleys of the interior, spreading out in broad savannas, and the high plateaus of the mountains, sustaining an unending forest of scattered pines, relieved by occasional clumps of oak.

Upon the northern coast, in the broad plain through which the Ulua and Chamelicon find their way to the sea, the country is so low as occasionally to be overflowed for considerable distances. Here grow immense forests of cedar, mahogany, ceiba, India-rubber, and other large and valuable trees, thickly interspersed with palms, whose plumes rise through every opening, and fringe the bases of the hills. The smaller streams are arched over with verdure, and completely shut out from the sun, while the large rivers gleam like silver bands in fields of unbroken emerald. But even here, where the land is lowest, spread out broad grassy meadows, the retreats of innumerable wild-fowl, and during the dry season, when the grass on the hills becomes sere and withered, offering abundant support for herds of cattle. . . .

Further to the eastward, on the same coast, the heavy forests are confined chiefly to the valleys proper of the rivers, and give place, at little distances inland, to sandy savannas, covered with coarse grass, and clumps of pines and acacias. But the plain country of the coast is everywhere narrow. The spurs or dependent ridges of the mountain groups of the interior often come down to the very shore. Immediately back of Omoa, within cannonshot of its fortress, the mountains begin to rise abruptly, and speedily attain the height of nine thousand feet, looking down majestically upon their shadows in the clear waters of the beautiful Bay of Amatique. Such also is the case at the port of Truxillo. The peaks of Congrehoy, and the Mountains of the Holy Cross or Poyas, form gigantic landmarks for the mariner in his approach to the coast of Honduras.

The alluvions of the Pacific coast are also densely wooded, but not extensive. At short distances inland they give place to numerous savannas and *jicarales,* . . . . These savannas are studded with clumps of acacias (gum-arabic bushes), and covered with grass; but the pine does not appear on this side of the continent, except upon the slopes of the hills at an altitude of about twelve hundred feet.

The valleys of all the rivers, on both coasts, are heavily wooded and covered with *lianes,* or vines; but as they are ascended toward the interior, vegetation diminishes, and is reduced to a narrow fringe of trees and bushes upon their immediate banks. These valleys, in the high interior country, often expand into broad and beautiful plains, half savanna, half woodland, the common grounds where the products of the tropics and of the temperate zone, the palm and the pine, flourish side by side. Such are the plains of Espino and Comayagua on the Humuya, of Otoro on the Sta. Barbara, Sesenti on the Ulua, La Florida on the Chamelicon, Olancho on the Aguan, and Yoguare on the Cholulteca. In some of these, as in that of Comayagua, the variant forms of cactus become distinguishing features, frequently attaining to gigantic size, and almost taking the character of forests. . . . Here, too, the agave appears, with its dense green cluster of spiny-edged leaves, shooting up its tall stem, to flower but once. . . .

The mountains which rise around these valleys are ascended by terraces, crowned with forests of pines and oaks, and carpeted with grass. The summits of the mountains sometimes run up in peaks, but generally constitute broad table-lands, more or less undulating, and often spreading out in rolling savannas, traversed with low ridges of verdure, and green belts of trees, which droop over streams as bright and cool as those of New England. Here the familiar blackberry is indigenous, and the bushes which impede the traveler are covered with fruit. Wheat-fields, billowing beneath the cool mountain winds, and orchards of peach and apple trees . . . give to these districts all the aspects of the temperate zone. . . .

Upon the higher mountain crests, where the short and hardy grass betokens a temperature too low for luxuriant vegetation of any kind, the air-plants . . . disappear, and the pines and gnarled oaks are draped in a sober mantle of long gray moss, which waves mournfully in the wind, like frayed and dusty banners from the walls of old cathedrals. . . .

The geological features of Honduras are equally marked and impressive. Starting from the Gulf of Fonseca and advancing northward, we leave behind us the volcanic coast-range, with its high, grassy peaks of scoriae, and reach at once vast masses of white and rose-colored rock, the outliers of the great sandstone nucleus of the central plateaus. Viewed from a distance, they appear like cliffs of trap or basalt, and take a thousand castellated forms with the changing positions of the traveler. Among these we find occasional beds of blue limestone, and ribs of quartz and greenstone are here and there boldly protruded through the superincumbent rocks, richly veined with ores of silver and of gold.

As we proceed farther inland, the mountains rise by a succession of terraces, deeply furrowed by streams descending to the sea. These terraces prove to be a succession of vast stratified sandstone deposits or beds, presenting abrupt edges, up which the sure-footed mule toils painfully and with difficulty. But when the ascent is accomplished, the traveler finds spread out before him extensive savannas, interspersed with groves of pines, and clumps of oaks and bushes. Often the layer of soil is thin, and a scant vegetation strives in vain to divest nature of its savage aspect. . . .

Suddenly the plateau along which he is journeying breaks away in a few rapid terraces, and reveals, almost beneath his feet, a wide and level plain, mottled with savanna and forest, threaded with bright streams, and dotted with villages. . . .

In the western part of Honduras, among the mountains of Corquin, the outline of the country is exceeding bold and diversified. The rivers, collecting their waters in interior basins, break through the porphyritic mountains and hills which surround them in deep valleys or gorges, with steep and precipitous sides. Yet in these fissures, whose bottoms are only reached by dangerous zigzag paths, are found strips of alluvial soil, where the Indian builds his hut, and the necessary plantain has a luxuriant growth, beneath high and frowning cliffs, bristling with peaks, like gigantic sentinels, along their rocky ramparts.

A greater variety of trees and abundance of verdure cover the hills and mountains of the northern coast, which have, in consequence, a less rugged aspect than those on the Pacific declivity, where the rains are not so constant. The hills are more swelling, and the mountains, though equally elevated, have a softer and more harmonious outline. They present few cliffs or rocky crests, and in their denser forests afford more congenial retreats to the multitudinous forms of animal life which are nurtured in the genial tropics.

Birds of brilliant plumage sparkle in the foliage of the trees, and crowds of monkeys troop among their branches. The tapir, the peccary, and the ant-eater live in their shade, and the puma and the cougar lurk in their recesses. Here, too, are found the boa, the bright corral, and the deadly tamagas, the vanilla hangs in festoons from the limbs, and the sarsaparilla veins the earth with its healing root. And while silver, imprisoned in flinty quartz or crumbling greenstone, tempts men to labor with the promise of rich reward on the other slope of the continent, here gold glitters in the sands of almost every stream.

It is thus that Nature, lavish of her gifts, has comprised within the comparatively narrow limits of Honduras a variety of scenery, as well as of climate and production, unsurpassed by any equal portion of the earth. . . .[1]

As was the case for my study on the conquest and colonization of Yucatan, on completing this work on Honduras, I wish to acknowledge my deep indebtedness to those who inspired my interest in the pre-Columbian peoples and civilizations of the New World and in the Spanish Empire, who trained me for my work, and who encouraged me to complete it. I also wish to express appreciation to Mr. Frederick G. Fassett, Jr., of Massachusetts Institute of Technology, for counsel in the preparation of my manuscript; and to Mrs. W. H. Harrison, Editor of the Department of Archaeology of Carnegie Institution of Washington, who, with Mrs. Elinor Snoddy, provided excellent editing. I likewise owe a very great debt to my wife, who patiently and carefully read my manuscript and offered cogent suggestions and criticisms on its organization and presentation. My mother, too, over many years has encouraged and inspired my efforts in the historical field.

ROBERT S. CHAMBERLAIN

Alexandria, Virginia

[1] Squier, 1855, pp. 152–59.

I
The Conquest and Colonization
of
Honduras and Higueras
to
1537

1

Honduras and Higueras to 1534

THE DISCOVERY

IT WAS the great Admiral of the Ocean Sea, Christopher Columbus, who discovered and first claimed Honduras for the Crown of Castile during the initial stages of his final voyage. Columbus sailed from Cadiz early in May 1502, and toward the close of June arrived off the Isla Española, or Santo Domingo, then center of Spanish colonization in the New World. After preparing his ships for the voyage of new discovery at an outlying port, in mid-July Columbus sailed on in quest of the rich Indies which he felt must lie somewhere westward and to which he hoped to find a strait.[1] At the end of July the admiral reached Guanaja, one of the Bay Islands just off the northern coast of Honduras. There the Spaniards found natives who seemed of somewhat higher type than those in the West Indies. Soon a great native trading dugout appeared carrying a large number of rowers and women and children passengers. An Indian of superior mien was in charge. The natives were dressed in excellently woven cotton, and the canoe carried well wrought articles which figured in the highly developed trade of the region, including axes and other utensils of copper and pottery. The appearance of this canoe heightened Columbus' hopes that the rich and populous lands which he sought were near.

The admiral then sailed directly across to a point jutting from the mainland, where he dropped anchor and went ashore on August 14. Columbus named this the Punta de Caxinas after a type of edible fruit which abounded in the region. This point later came generally to be known as the Cabo de Honduras. The admiral next sailed east along the coast and came to the mouth of a river, where he again landed. The natives greeted the Spaniards in friendly fashion. Because some of these Indians had the lobes of their ears greatly distended, Columbus quaintly called the region the Costa de las Orejas, or

[1] The summary of the discovery and early history of Honduras, which is intended only to provide the background for developments after 1534, is based on the following secondary works, early histories, chronicles and primary sources: Bancroft, 1883–87; Díaz del Castillo, 1904 and 1933–34; Fuentes y Guzmán, 1882–83; Helps, 1900–04; Herrera, 1601–15; Juarros, 1857; Milla and Gómez Carillo, 1879–97; Morrison, 1942; Oviedo, 1851–55; Scholes and Roys, 1948; Strong, 1935; Valle, 1948; Fifth Cortés *Carta de Relación* (Gayango's edition, 1866); *Relación* of Alonso Dávila, 1533; *Colección de documentos inéditos . . . de Indias*, 1864–84; 14:97 ff.; Montejo *v*. Alvarado, 1533, Archivo General de Indias de Sevilla, Justicia 1005-3-1. The *Colección de documentos inéditos . . . de Indias*, 1864–84, will hereafter be cited as DII; the Archivo General de Indias de Sevilla will be cited as AGI. All references in footnotes are to materials listed in sections E (Manuscript Sources), F (Published Documents), and G (Chronicles, Early Histories and Secondary Works) of the Bibliography.

Coast of the Ears. The admiral formally took possession of the land for the sovereign of Castile, naming the river off which his ships lay the Río de la Posesión, and then continued eastward.

Almost a month of gales, headwinds, and thunderstorms now placed Columbus' flotilla in peril, but the admiral finally doubled the eastern point of Honduras, sailed on to calmer seas and followed the low-lying Mosquito Coast southward. The grateful Spaniards gave thanks to God for their delivery from troubled seas by naming the eastern point of Honduras Cabo Gracias a Dios.

Although in bad health and low spirits, Columbus continued his great mission, which took him to Panama and eventually led to many months of shipwreck and utmost hardship off Jamaica. He and his men were tardily rescued in mid-1504 and sailed from Santo Domingo in September for Castile, his unparalleled career of discovery at an end.

Two decades elapsed between Columbus' discovery of Honduras and the beginnings of Spanish occupation. Then expeditions arrived from several directions almost simultaneously, for by that time the Spaniards had discovered, explored, and conquered wide lands both to the north and south of Honduras.

To the south, Spanish efforts concentrated in the region of Panama, or Castilla del Oro, where after a halting start colonization had become permanent. Vasco Núñez de Balboa had in 1513 discovered the vast Pacific, and the old crafty and rapacious Pedrarias Dávila, who came out as governor of Castilla del Oro in 1515, had with relentless energy sent out expeditions of discovery and conquest in all directions. Also, from the newly founded City of Panama the *Contador* of Española, Gil González Dávila, and Andrés Niño in 1522–23 sailed northward along the coast. They explored the western part of Nicaragua and its great lake, finding a large native population of some wealth and cultural attainment. González Dávila and Niño sailed as far as the great bay to the south of Honduras, which they named the Bahía de Fonseca in honor of Juan Rodríguez de Fonseca, Bishop of Burgos and royal minister of the Indies.

Although González Dávila and Niño had made their voyage at their own expense and with direct royal authority, Pedrarias immediately sought to turn their achievements to his own advantage and gain Nicaragua for himself, especially since the appointment of his successor in Castilla del Oro was already in the offing. Pedrarias therefore placed every possible obstacle in González Dávila's path, seeking to prevent him from leaving Panama, and sent an expedition of his own into the Pacific side of Nicaragua under Francisco Hernández de Córdoba, not the explorer of the same name who had discovered Yucatan in 1517.

Hernández de Córdoba founded the town of Bruselas on the Gulf of Nicoya and moved to the Freshwater Sea, or Lake Nicaragua, on the western shores of which he founded a city, Granada. Farther north he founded another city, León. Thereafter he sent out various expeditions, one of which moved northward into Honduras. Spanish colonization in Nicaragua remained concentrated along the Pacific. Since access to the Caribbean was more feasible northward by way of the ports on the Bay of Honduras than eastward, officials and colonists of Nicaragua long looked to Honduras rather than the eastern shores of their own province for contact with the West Indies and Castile, a fact which led to rival jurisdictional claims between the early governors of Honduras and Nicaragua.

Meanwhile González Dávila had escaped Pedrarias and made his way back to Española. He then besought the Crown to grant him authority over the districts of Nicaragua which he had explored, and hastened to prepare an expedition to return there. He sailed from Santo Domingo in the first part of 1524. His objective was the Caribbean coast of Nicaragua, from which he intended to make his way westward to the Freshwater Sea. His actual course, however, took him to the northern shores of Honduras where a storm struck his ships. Because Dávila had to throw a number of horses overboard to lighten the vessels, the Spaniards gave the name Puerto de Caballos to the spot which was to figure largely in the subsequent history of Honduras.

González Dávila next sailed farther west to the region of the Bay of Amatique and the Río Dulce, outlet of the great inland Golfo Dulce. He formally took possession of this territory and founded a town, San Gil de Buenavista. He then voyaged back along the coast with a portion of his men, landed at a point east of the Cabo de Honduras, and pushed inland toward Nicaragua. The colonists of San Gil de Buenavista soon fell into difficulties, however, and, in search of a more hospitable region, moved to the then important Indian pueblo of Nito, near the mouth of the Río Dulce.

In Nicaragua, Pedrarias' captain, Hernández de Córdoba, heard of Spaniards to the north and forthwith sent out a company under Hernando de Soto to learn who the newcomers were. By this time González Dávila had penetrated a considerable distance inland and soon he and de Soto met in a district known as Toreba. As neither had the slightest intention of giving way, fighting ensued. González Dávila was the victor but, since he did not feel strong enough to confront Hernández de Córdoba's main forces, he returned to Puerto de Caballos, where he learned that still other Spaniards had recently arrived from New Spain. As he soon found, this new expedition was led by Cristóbal de Olid, who had been sent to Honduras by Hernán Cortés, conqueror of the Aztec Empire, but who had renounced Cortés' authority and intended to possess the province for himself.

OLID, LAS CASAS, AND THE BEGINNINGS OF COLONIZATION

While initial Spanish occupation of Central America was expanding from Panama and Santo Domingo, much more spectacular and important events were occurring far to the north. Yucatan and its Maya civilization had been discovered in 1517 by an expedition from Cuba under the other Francisco Hernández de Córdoba. In the next year Juan de Grijalva followed up this momentous discovery by sailing along the coast of Yucatan and Mexico as far as the Río Panuco. Grijalva's expedition revealed the existence of the rich, far-flung empire of Montezuma, with its great population, large cities, and its capital, Tenochtitlan, far back in the mountains of the interior. The amazing conquest of this vast Aztec Empire by the incomparable Cortés between 1519 and 1521 followed with breath-taking swiftness.

After Cortés had made himself master of lands of the fallen Aztec Empire, which came to be known as New Spain, and had been confirmed as governor by the Crown, he turned toward new conquests. Since Guatemala and Honduras were said to be great and wealthy, he prepared a large expedition at Vera Cruz to take possession of Honduras and to search for a strait believed to exist between the Atlantic and Pacific oceans. He placed one of his most trusted and able captains of the conquest of Mexico, Cristóbal de Olid, in command of this enterprise. Cortés had additional supplies for the expedition made ready in Cuba, which Olid was to gather before he sailed for Honduras.

Olid sailed for La Habana in January 1524. In Cuba enemies of Cortés, foremost among them the governor Diego Velázquez, under whose authority Cortés had sailed for Mexico in 1519 but whose jurisdiction he had immediately renounced, persuaded Olid, who was far from devoid of personal ambition, to serve Cortés as that great conqueror had served Velázquez. Olid carefully kept his intention of taking Honduras for himself from Cortés' faithful followers.

Olid sailed from Cuba and arrived off the coast of Honduras some leagues east of Puerto de Caballos early in May. He took possession of the land in Cortés' name, but the official records indicate Olid's true resolve. Without delay he founded a town which he named Triunfo de la Cruz, and soon thereafter openly revealed his intention to renounce Cortés' jurisdiction. The majority of his men accepted him as their leader, whereupon he next hastened westward into the interior. The Spaniards soon found the Valley of Naco to be "the best land in that province, level, fertile, spacious, and surrounded by mountains, with broad roads, many flowers, fruits, and very delicious plants, almost equal to Valencia. . . ." [2]

There were now four claimants to jurisdiction over Honduras: González Dávila by virtue of royal authority, Pedrarias by right of Hernández de Córdoba's and de Soto's expeditions, Cortés because he had sent Olid to take possession in his name, and Olid himself. Eventually there was a fifth claimant, the Audiencia of Santo Domingo, then highest organ of royal government in the New World, which sought to establish direct political control. These contending interests, as might be expected, produced confusion, treachery, violence, and civil war. Situations of this kind were to recur many times during the next two decades, to the serious detriment of the development of the province.

When reports of Olid's intention finally reached Cortés, he sent another able captain, Francisco de las Casas, in whom he had special confidence because they were related by marriage, to force his rebellious subordinate once again to acknowledge his authority. Cortés assigned only about 150 men to las Casas, to whom he felt certain a large number of Olid's soldiers would immediately rally.

The new captain arrived off Triunfo de la Cruz just as Olid was preparing to strike at González Dávila, who was now in the Valley of Naco. At first neither of the latter had desired an open break and they had therefore come to a momentary accommodation; but Olid, whose men outnumbered those of González Dávila, was merely awaiting a chance to dispose of his rival with a minimum of effort, for González Dávila had trustingly divided his forces. Olid now sent a lieutenant named Briones to surprise one section of González Dávila's men while he himself planned to sail along the coast to strike at other groups. Briones acted quickly and weakened González Dávila's position by capturing about half his men. Olid was about to set sail when las Casas' ships appeared off Triunfo de la Cruz.

Understandably, Olid was wary of the new expedition and he not only sought to prevent it from landing but also sent a hasty message recalling Briones. The ships of Olid and las Casas soon fired on each other, to the discomfiture of Olid, who then proposed a truce and offered to recognize Cortés' authority on condition that las Casas should not come ashore until final terms had been agreed upon. By this means Olid hoped to hold off attack until supported by Briones, who, however, unknown to Olid, had been approached by las Casas and offered rewards for support against Olid. On receiving las Casas' promises, Briones played a waiting game, hoping to serve

[2] Herrera, 1601–15, Decada 3, Libro 5, Capítulo 12 (hereafter cited by numerals only, e.g. 3-5-12).

his own interests. But Olid was rescued from this uncertain situation by a sudden storm, which wrecked las Casas' ships and killed a number of his men, placing the survivors entirely in Olid's hands.

Olid next moved to the Valley of Naco to complete González Dávila's discomfiture and established himself in the pueblo of Naco. One of his captains soon surprised González Dávila and the force remaining with him in the vicinity, and took them back to Naco as Olid's prisoners. Meanwhile Briones, who feared Olid's vengeance, gave allegiance to Cortés.

Olid dealt liberally with González Dávila and las Casas, treating them more like honored guests than prisoners. His magnanimity ultimately betrayed him, for his captives and others plotted his death, anticipating support from Briones. The conspirators found their opportunity one evening when they set upon Olid and wounded him gravely. Although he managed to escape for the moment and sought shelter in an Indian hut, he was soon found, tried, and beheaded.

The conspirators now proclaimed Cortés' authority, with las Casas as his representative, and all colonists forthwith accepted this new dispensation. As master of the colony in Cortés' name, las Casas first consolidated his position and then, especially since the harbor of Triunfo de la Cruz was inadequate, decided to move the town to another place and change its name to Trujillo. He designated a cabildo for the new town, which he intended should have some eighty citizens. Las Casas' original desire was to set up the new town of Trujillo at Puerto de Caballos, an excellent harbor. He himself was by this time eager to return to New Spain, so he named Juan López de Aguirre as his lieutenant and empowered him to effect the transfer of the town. Then, taking González Dávila with him, las Casas set out for New Spain overland, by way of Guatemala, in the conquest of which Pedro de Alvarado and his subordinates were now engaged. On his march las Casas encountered Briones, whom he hanged for his treachery.

Left in command in Honduras, López de Aguirre moved westward from Triunfo de la Cruz to Puerto de Caballos, but rejected the region as unsuitable for colonization and decided to turn far eastward to the Cabo de Honduras, beyond Triunfo de la Cruz, where Columbus had first touched the mainland of Honduras. He based this decision on reports brought by Spaniards who had arrived at Puerto de Caballos by sea and who described the district of the Cabo de Honduras in favorable terms.

López de Aguirre then sailed to the cape with about half his men on this recently arrived ship, while the remainder marched overland. Rather than await the arrival of the land party, however, López de Aguirre sailed away, not to return. When the group who had come by land reached the cape, they were greatly disconcerted by his desertion but nevertheless founded Trujillo, or Trujillo del Pinar, in May 1529, selecting as their leader an *alcalde,* or municipal officer of justice, named Medina, whom las Casas had designated as one of the town's chief authorities.

The Audiencia of Santo Domingo, as highest representative of royal government in the Indies, had been gravely concerned by the turbulent course of events in Honduras and now decided to interpose its weighty authority to end blighting strife among the Spaniards and advance the major task of colonization. The high tribunal therefore sent its *Fiscal,* or Crown Attorney, Pedro Moreno, to Honduras to assert its superior jurisdiction over the province. Moreno arrived shortly after the establishment of Trujillo, and Medina pleaded with him for support for the depleted colony. There were now left in northern Honduras only about forty citizens in Trujillo, lacking arms and supplies, and a few more at Nito, the remnants of González Dávila's efforts at settlement in the region of the Río Dulce. The plight of the Spaniards at Nito was even worse than that of the citizens of Trujillo.

Moreno promised aid if the Spaniards of Trujillo would exchange Cortés' authority for that of the Audiencia of Santo Domingo. Under his terms the colonists were also to accept one of Olid's former officers, Juan Ruano, as chief magistrate. Medina and the citizens of Trujillo accepted these conditions, for they had little choice. The name of Trujillo was now changed to Ascensión. Moreno also sent messages to Hernández de Córdoba in Nicaragua to persuade him to throw off Pedrarias' authority and likewise accept that of the Audiencia of Santo Domingo. He soon returned to Santo Domingo, promising to send help for Honduras. In a sudden reversal, the colonists of Ascensión now once more proclaimed adherence to Cortés, expelled Ruano, and again adopted the name of Trujillo.

Further proof of the concern which the Audiencia of Santo Domingo felt for Honduras is found in efforts to support González Dávila and his earlier colony. Sometime during this strife-torn period the tribunal sent reinforcements under command of Pedro de Garro, a veteran of the Spanish armies which fought in Italy. Garro, eventually a citizen of Santiago de Guatemala, later told of this.

Roughly twenty years ago [he wrote] I, Pedro de Garro came to that land and province of Honduras and Naco as a captain commissioned by the president and judges of Santo Domingo, with forty-three horsemen and fifty-seven foot soldiers to bring help to Gil González Dávila, who was in the province of Naco, and to carry out this expedition I myself purchased a ship. . . .[3]

[3] Probanza of Pedro de Garro, 1541, Archivo General del Gobierno, Guatemala, Papers from the Archivo Colonial. The Archivo General del Gobierno, Guatemala, will henceforth be cited as AGG.

CORTÉS MOVES TO HONDURAS

While the Spaniards of Honduras were fighting among themselves, Cortés, who received intermittent reports of developments, became thoroughly impatient. Anxious for new achievements and hoping to find gold, he determined to go to Honduras, definitely establish his authority there, and explore and subdue the vast unknown territories between New Spain and that province. Cortés then organized an expedition of about 140 Spaniards and 3000 Mexican allies and set out in the latter part of 1524 from the Spanish town of Espíritu Santo on the gulf coast of the Isthmus of Tehuantepec.

After a long march across low-lying Tabasco, southern Campeche, and northern Peten, the Spaniards entered a desolate range, which they called the Mountains of Flint. Their stony roughness caused the utmost hardships to both men and horses, and many valuable mounts were lost. Rains, swollen streams, and lack of food brought further trials to the Spaniards after they had finally crossed the mountains, but at length they arrived at the Río Dulce. There, in the spring of 1525, they came upon the remnants of González Dávila's now desperate colonists at Nito. Thus Cortés completed a hazardous and incredibly difficult march across the vast unknown lands between New Spain and Honduras, one of the most spectacular of his many great deeds.

Cortés was joyfully acclaimed by the weak and almost starving colonists of Nito, who had lacked strength to venture far from their settlement even to search for the bare necessities of life. They had, in fact, been laboriously repairing a vessel in which to sail away when Cortés and his men arrived. Cortés now sent out parties to gather supplies, and, fortunately, a ship also arrived with provisions.

As the Spaniards as a whole looked upon Nito and its region as unhealthful and unsuited for permanent settlement, Cortés decided to transfer the harassed colonists elsewhere. He sent some of them south into the rich Valley of Naco which his able lieutenant Gonzalo de Sandoval soon pacified. Cortés decided to explore the region of the Golfo Dulce before he himself moved southward. With forty or so Spaniards and a number of Indians he ascended the Río Dulce in an improvised brigantine and canoes and came out on the Golfo Dulce. At first he hoped that it would prove to be the long-sought strait between the North Sea, or Caribbean, and the South Sea, but he soon realized his error.

After arriving at the western end of the Golfo Dulce, he penetrated inland and engaged in some fighting with the Indians, especially at the large town of Chacujal. The impressive buildings of Chacujal were compared by the Spaniards with those of the Maya Chontal capital of Acalan, and even with those of the great Nahua cities of Mexico. Cortés found large stores of food at this town and sent his brigantine back to Nito, laden with supplies. Rafts were constructed to transport more of the provisions. Cortés and a few men then went downstream to Nito on the rafts, while most of his soldiers went back overland. Cortés had a brush with the natives on the return to Nito, to which the swift waters of the Río Dulce returned him in an unbelievably short time. The provisions he had gathered during the Golfo Dulce expedition and those garnered in the district of Nito stood the Spaniards in good stead, for those who had remained at Nito again badly needed supplies.

There were widely credited reports in Mexico that Cortés and his men had perished during their long, hard march. The anxious Pedro de Alvarado in Guatemala had sent out expeditions to search for his former commander, and when Cortés was in the territory beyond the Golfo Dulce it is likely that the two companies were not very far apart.

Cortés was ready to move farther into Honduras immediately after his return from the Golfo Dulce and was now prepared to abandon entirely the region of Nito as an attempted center of Spanish colonization. Therefore, he sailed with the whole company to Puerto de Caballos, to which some of those whom he had earlier sent southward from Nito had already moved.

At Puerto de Caballos, now also known as the Puerto de San Andrés, Cortés founded a town, Natividad de Nuestra Señora, since the harbor was well protected and the region round about seemed inviting. Diego de Godoy was placed in command of the new municipality of fifty citizens, and Cortés sailed on to Trujillo. Contrary to expectations the area proved pestilential, and within a brief period about half the Spaniards of Natividad de Nuestra Señora succumbed to disease. With Cortés' permission the remainder then went to the fertile and healthful Valley of Naco, where Sandoval was securely established.

At Trujillo things had gone surprisingly well after the departure of the Fiscal of the Audiencia of Santo Domingo, Pedro Moreno, the ensuing expulsion of Juan Ruano, and the return of the town to allegiance to Cortés, who forthwith assumed superior jurisdiction. He set himself to the task of placing Honduras on a truly firm footing, sending a report of his activities to the Audiencia of Santo Domingo in the hope of obtaining their recognition. He also sent ships to Cuba and Jamaica for domestic animals, plants for cultivation, and additional provisions.

With Cortés absent, self-seeking enemies in New Spain, heartened by reports of his death, had temporarily gained control in the City of Mexico, and the government fell into disorder. So Cortés, though greatly desiring to complete his work in Honduras and create lasting stability there, appointed his relative, Hernando de Saavedra, as his lieutenant in Honduras, and made ready to sail back to New Spain, while Gonzalo de Sandoval was to return overland through Guatemala.

Circumstances forced Cortés on several occasions to delay sailing for New Spain. Contrary to plan, he not only remained in Honduras for a time longer but recalled Sandoval. Although Cortés was now in ill health because of disease contracted on the fever-laden tropical coast of Honduras, he nevertheless governed with characteristic foresight and vigor.

In the interim Saavedra had moved inland under Cortés' instructions and had brought a number of populous districts under control, even though he met with resistance in some places. *Caciques,* or native lords, now came before Cortés from a wide area to give willing allegiance. Indeed, his prestige among the natives mounted everywhere, for the Indians felt assured of considerate treatment and consequently regarded him as a protector. Through a skillful combination of force and moderation Cortés made Spanish control over Honduras more secure than ever before.

JURISDICTIONAL STATUS

Meanwhile, the jurisdictional status of the Central American provinces as a whole had become more complicated. In Nicaragua, Hernández de Córdoba, motivated by personal ambition, sought to cast off Pedrarias' authority and accept that of the Audiencia of Santo Domingo in accordance with the Fiscal Moreno's recommendations. He consequently planned to obtain recognition of his authority over Nicaragua as being independent from that of Pedrarias, even though some of his more important subordinates opposed such a course. In an effort to expand his territories, Córdoba sent a new expedition northward into land between Nicaragua and Honduras over which Cortés claimed jurisdiction. The captain in charge, apparently meeting with resistance from the Indians, began to ravage the district and to enslave its inhabitants. The harassed natives called on Cortés for protection, and he sent Sandoval to warn Hernández de Córdoba's company away, whereupon they returned to Nicaragua for further instructions.

Hernández de Córdoba then sent another company into Honduras and with it letters for the Crown and the Audiencia of Santo Domingo designed to advance his personal interests. His captain was to seek an adequate port on the North Sea to serve Nicaragua and was also probably to try to arrange an understanding with Cortés regarding jurisdiction.

Sandoval encountered and captured this second expedition, sending some of its members back to Cortés at Trujillo. From these prisoners Cortés learned of their leader's plan to make himself governor of Nicaragua. Cortés then sent presents and courteous messages to Hernández de Córdoba and offered him aid to obtain supplies through Honduras, but at the same time recommended that he should not break with Pedrarias.

Hernández de Córdoba soon met serious opposition in Nicaragua itself from some of his officers and a considerable number of colonists. Fearing to lose control of the situation and anticipating eventual vengeance from the hard-bitten Pedrarias, he then besought the powerful Cortés to move southward and personally take over the government. Cortés seems to have welcomed the invitation, for he had come to believe that Nicaragua was a wealthy province. In fact, unknown to Hernández de Córdoba, he may even have insinuated to some of that captain's subordinates that he desired authority there, thus to prepare the way for immediate acceptance.

Cortés now ordered Sandoval to organize an expedition for Nicaragua and might well have taken over the province had not his followers in New Spain sent him urgent appeals to return. His party in New Spain had tenuously redressed the balance there in his favor after learning that reports of his death were false. Cortés therefore finally sailed for New Spain late in April 1526, leaving instructions for his lieutenant, Hernando de Saavedra, for the advancement of colonization in Honduras.

The great conqueror of Mexico thus left Honduras never to return. He had done much for the province, temporarily stopping dissension among the Spaniards, extending and stabilizing the area of Spanish control, and checking northern expansion of the territorial claims of both Hernández de Córdoba and Pedrarias. Honduras would undoubtedly have been spared many future trials and dangers had Cortés been able to remain longer to give the province the benefits of his military and political genius.

After the great conqueror had left, but acting on his instructions, Saavedra sent the *Contador,* or Comptroller, of Honduras, Bartolomé de Celada, southward to found a town in the Valley of Olancho—disputed territory between Honduras and Nicaragua. Celada founded this town in May 1526, naming it the Villa de la Frontera de Cáceres, but it proved short-lived.

Turning once again to Nicaragua, Pedrarias at length moved up from Panama, took direct control of the province, and executed the rebellious Hernández de Córdoba. Also, Pedrarias lost no time in projecting his jurisdictional claims northward. He not only claimed Honduras, but sent expeditions into· the Valley of Olancho. Natives reported these incursions to Saavedra, who demanded that Pedrarias' men withdraw, to which Pedrarias returned an outwardly conciliatory answer and even indicated a desire to come to an agreement with Cortés himself concerning rival claims. The Audiencia of Santo Domingo was to be the final arbiter of the proposed arrangement.

Meanwhile, however, Pedrarias instructed his captains in the Valley of Olancho to attack adherents of Cortés. Doing this treacherously, they captured a number of Cortés' followers and moved on toward the north coast, intending to occupy Puerto de Caballos in order to give Nicaragua its needed port. Saavedra soon learned of these developments and sent a superior force to oppose Pedrarias' company. After a parley both groups agreed to retire, but Pedrarias' captains failed to keep their word and one of them continued toward Puerto de Caballos. The other moved back to the Valley of Olancho to safeguard it for Pedrarias and founded a settlement there. Harsh mistreatment of the Indians of this valley ensued, and they soon rose in widespread revolt, destroying the settlement which Pedrarias' men had set up and killing many Spaniards, including the captain. The survivors sought refuge with a cacique who had not joined the revolt.

At about the same time rebellious natives in overwhelming numbers attacked a few Spaniards at Cortés' former town of Natividad de Nuestra Señora at Puerto de Caballos and forced them to take refuge in a natural stronghold close by. This little party held off the Indians and sent an urgent appeal for help to Saavedra, but he was in no position to give it at the time, and the group of Pedrarias' men who were moving toward the coast now turned back to join their comrades in the Valley of Olancho rather than continue to Puerto de Caballos. So the little garrison of Natividad de Nuestra Señora had to wait until help arrived or until they could break the siege themselves. When Pedrarias' company got back to the Valley of Olancho, they found, of course, that their fellow Spaniards there had met disaster. After they joined the refugees the combined groups could maintain only a precarious foothold on which Pedrarias could still base jurisdiction over the area.

As Cortés' lieutenant, Saavedra vigorously protested Pedrarias' acts but did not feel strong enough to attack his forces in the Valley of Olancho. Pedrarias, thus encouraged to press his claims over Honduras more aggressively than ever, sent emissaries to demand submission of Saavedra and the cabildo of Trujillo; but before these emissaries reached the city the situation in Honduras had been altered fundamentally through the arrival of a governor appointed directly by the Crown.

LÓPEZ DE SALCEDO AS ROYAL GOVERNOR

While these developments were taking place in Honduras, the Crown had made decisions of vital importance to the province. The Crown wished to bring its newly acquired Indies under effective direct control quickly and was persistently expanding the mechanism of absolute government through creating agencies, such as the Audiencia of Santo Domingo and royal governors, to replace individuals who, like Cortés, for example, could act with a great degree of personal initiative. It wanted order and stability in the colonies and an end to strife among Spaniards, which could do nothing but impede the development of new overseas possessions.

A new governor, Pedro de los Ríos, was now named to replace Pedrarias in Castilla del Oro, and, late in 1525, Diego López de Salcedo was appointed by the Crown as royal governor of Honduras. The Spaniards of this and the neighboring provinces were ordered to cease their bickering; López de Salcedo was instructed to investigate affairs and take measures necessary to bring order.

López de Salcedo sailed from Santo Domingo for Honduras early in September 1526, with two ships and a considerable number of soldiers. One ship was laden with provisions and clothing for sale to the colonists. Detained at Jamaica for a full month by unfavorable winds, López de Salcedo arrived off Cabo Camarón, east of Trujillo, on October 24 and soon anchored before the town.

The transfer of authority from the absent Cortés and his lieutenant Saavedra to the new royal governor was not effected without delay and lengthy negotiation, which all but broke over into civil strife, for there were shows of force on both sides. Saavedra, whose men outnumbered those of López de Salcedo, was resolved to defend Cortés' authority to the last, and it was not until he and the cabildo of Trujillo were convinced beyond doubt that López de Salcedo's commission came directly from the Crown and not merely from the Audiencia of Santo Domingo, high tribunal though it might be, that the newcomers were permitted to disembark without fighting. The opposing parties at first watched each other "as though we were Moors and Christians" and negotiated haughtily and without any good will. Then Saavedra gave way, threatened with punishment from the Crown by López de Salcedo, who announced his determination to land, ready for action. López de Salcedo then came ashore with all his soldiers, carrying aloft the royal standard of Castile, and "without harm to either party and through the will of God" was at length formally received as governor.[4]

The new chief magistrate now brought legal action against Saavedra and others, including members of the cabildo of Trujillo, and sent them off for Santo Domingo to be tried further by the audiencia. En route, however, the prisoners seized control of the ship and sailed to Cuba in search of sanctuary. Installation of López de Salcedo as governor furthered the establishment of

[4] López de Salcedo to the Crown, Trujillo, December 22, 1526, AGI, Guatemala 39.

royal absolutism, but the process was not complete until 1544, when the newly created Audiencia de los Confines took office as the supreme governing agency in all the Central American provinces.

Farther south, Pedro de los Ríos arrived in Panama at the close of July 1526 to replace the harsh and aged Pedrarias, who stepped aside, but not without vigorous protest to the Crown. De los Ríos claimed jurisdiction over Nicaragua as a part of Castilla del Oro, just as had Pedrarias.

After López de Salcedo was installed as governor of Honduras, the emissaries whom Pedrarias had earlier sent northward to demand submission of Saavedra and the cabildo of Trujillo finally arrived at the Honduran city. Since they found there a royal governor instead of Cortés' representative, they did not dare present Pedrarias' demands. Nevertheless, López de Salcedo had them thrown into prison.

The Crown had not fixed territorial limits for the province when it appointed López de Salcedo governor of Honduras. Because of this and the removal of Pedrarias as governor of Castilla del Oro, López de Salcedo now reversed the entire process with respect to jurisdictional claims. Basing his pretensions on González Dávila's and Cortés' activities, he contended that Nicaragua was rightly within his jurisdiction as governor of Honduras and set out for the southern province at the head of 150 men to make good his authority there. He left Francisco de Cisneros as his representative in Trujillo, with a few citizens to guard the city.

On his southward march López de Salcedo imposed the harshest kind of burdens on the unhappy Indians of the Valley of Olancho, hanged certain native lords who were involved in the recent attack on the Spaniards at Natividad de Nuestra Señora, and had an unsuccessful brush with rival Spaniards still in the Valley of Olancho. His demands on the Indians for supplies and service aroused such fear and bitter hatred among them that they burned their pueblos, destroyed their crops, and fled to the mountains. This hostility spread far westward into the populous, fertile Valley of Comayagua and south into Nicaragua, where it caused anxiety among the colonists of León. Under such conditions the expedition suffered great lack of provisions and constant danger from widespread native hostility.

Nevertheless, López de Salcedo reached León in the spring of 1527. Miguel de Estete, the lieutenant whom Pedrarias had placed in the city, and the cabildo showed little hesitation in accepting his authority; but his ill-calculated acts of government soon created dissatisfaction among the Spaniards and goaded the already restless Indians of northern Nicaragua into open revolt. Naturally, the state of the province soon became precarious.

Meanwhile, de los Ríos was moving into Nicaragua in defiance of López de Salcedo's claims to jurisdiction. Even though the latter's administration there had been anything but satisfactory, the municipal councils of the province refused to accept de los Ríos, whom López de Salcedo ordered to leave. On his way back to Panama, de los Ríos was courteously received by the town of Bruselas, which Hernández de Córdoba had founded on first entering the province, whereupon López de Salcedo took petty revenge by disestablishing the town.

Pedrarias, now in Panama, protested his removal as governor of Castilla del Oro so vehemently that the Crown before long compensated by appointing him governor of Nicaragua, thus detaching that province from Castilla del Oro. López de Salcedo, now cut short in Nicaragua, prepared to return to Honduras with his followers, but authorities and colonists alike, led by Miguel de Estete, turned on him and proclaimed their allegiance to Pedrarias. They prevented López de Salcedo from leaving the province and seized his officials. Hastening from Panama, Pedrarias arrived at León in March 1528, and was everywhere received as governor. He dealt with López de Salcedo summarily, throwing him in prison and citing a royal cedula providing that authorities of other provinces should not intervene in the affairs of Nicaragua. He also ignored López de Salcedo's request to return to Honduras. Held in prison for the better part of a year, López de Salcedo broke in health and in spirit. Mediators finally arranged for a settlement whereby López de Salcedo's jurisdiction was to be restricted to a region lying along the north coast from Cabo Gracias a Dios on the east to Puerto de Caballos on the west and projecting into the interior in triangular fashion. He was to renounce all territory

from León to the Port of Natividad, one hundred leagues from north to south, and from Chorotega, called Fonseca by another name, to Puerto de Caballos, seventy leagues from north to south, and one hundred leagues along the North Sea, along with an equal stretch along the South Sea and whatever else may be discovered [in those regions]. . . . [5]

On these terms he was released and returned to Honduras early in 1529.

The agreement thus imposed settled in a practical way the question of jurisdiction between the governors of Honduras and Nicaragua. Dissension was to arise over the territory along the South Sea from the Río de Lempa, which separated San Salvador from San Miguel, and over lands to the eastward and north of the Bahía de Fonseca, but since it was Pedro de Alvarado and his captains who effectively expanded Spanish colonization down from Guatemala

[5] Herrera, 1601–15, 4-3-2.

in that direction, it was with them rather than with the governors of Nicaragua that the early chief magistrates of Honduras were henceforth to fall into territorial disputes.

While López de Salcedo was attempting to gain authority over Nicaragua, matters went badly in Honduras. His lieutenant, Francisco de Cisneros, was unable to maintain order among the depleted but unruly citizen body and was soon thrust to one side, letting the province lapse into administrative chaos. From Nicaragua, López de Salcedo detailed Diego Méndez de Hinostrosa to restore order, but an opposing faction soon threw him into prison and placed a *regidor,* or municipal councilman, of Trujillo, Vasco de Herrera, in authority. The new chief magistrate, enjoying adequate support for a time, sent an expedition to subjugate the Valley of Olancho, but this led to further harassment and ruthless enslavement of the natives, without any permanent benefit for the colony.

When López de Salcedo returned early in 1529 he was too weakened to restore his authority as governor. Incapable of quelling the struggle for power between his lieutenant Méndez de Hinostrosa and the usurping regidor Vasco de Herrera, he earned the contempt of most of the colonists.[6] Hoping to overcome their deep discontent, he finally organized a considerable expedition once again to attempt colonization of the rich Valley of Naco, where, in addition to its known attractiveness, gold was now persistently reported; but the ill-starred governor died in the first days of 1530 and this enterprise was deferred.

CEREZEDA AS ACTING GOVERNOR

López de Salcedo had named an official of the royal treasury of the province, Andrés de Cerezeda, as his interim successor. Although his name figures large in the history of Honduras for the next few years, Cerezeda was so far from being a forceful man that a typical period of administrative anarchy and deadly contest for power followed López de Salcedo's death. Vasco de Herrera, again supported by the cabildo of Trujillo, and Méndez de Hinostrosa, claiming that his authority as López de Salcedo's lieutenant was still valid, contested Cerezeda's acting governorship. Nevertheless, a nominal compromise was finally reached whereby Cerezeda and Vasco de Herrera were to act as joint administrators and Méndez de Hinostrosa was to be eliminated. Vasco de Herrera was too strong for partnership, however, and although Cerezeda continued nominally as one of the two chief magistrates, it was his colleague who actually wielded authority, staunchly supported by the municipal council. Quarrels

[6] There was still a small group which strongly supported the governor, however. Undoubtedly at López de Salcedo's instance the *Hijosdalgo, conquistadores* and *pobladores* of Trujillo sent a letter, dated August 20, 1529, to the Crown in support of the governor (AGI, Guatemala 9).

between the two inevitably arose, especially after the cabildo drew up a secret request to the Crown that Vasco de Herrera be appointed governor, a move of which Cerezeda learned.

Meanwhile the expedition which López de Salcedo had prepared to move westward just before his death finally entered the Valley of Naco and started a town, Nuestra Señora de la Encarnación. Like all previous efforts to found settlements to the westward, this one eventually failed. About the same time, another company under Alonso Ortiz pacified an unruly district not far from Trujillo. When Ortiz first entered the region the natives fled before him, but this captain displayed such understanding and moderation that he was able to bring them back peacefully to their homes—a notable accomplishment, especially at this time.

Vasco de Herrera's control of the province proved tenuous, for there were too many factions to permit him to rest secure. Cerezeda and Méndez de Hinostrosa both sought opportunity to assert themselves, and discontent among the colonists increased, if anything. Vasco de Herrera therefore again turned to the ever-hopeful possibility of saving the situation by colonization elsewhere, even though he might have to abandon Trujillo in the process. Fearing that this plan would bring the colony down in irrevocable ruin, Cerezeda did what he could to oppose it. But a revolt of overtaxed Indians in the mines close to Trujillo, during which several Spaniards were killed, gave Vasco de Herrera his opportunity. He organized an expedition for the nominal purpose of subduing the rebellious Indians, but actually he marched into the interior in an attempt at colonization.

With Cerezeda temporarily absent from Trujillo at this time and with Vasco de Herrera also gone, Méndez de Hinostrosa made preparations to usurp authority. He organized a following and appeared before the cabildo, demanding that a single chief magistrate be named and that order be maintained. When Vasco de Herrera at length returned from the fruitless expedition, leaving a company in the interior, and took action against him, Méndez de Hinostrosa presented his commission as lieutenant, given him by López de Salcedo, and claimed recognition. But Vasco de Herrera pronounced the death penalty against Méndez de Hinostrosa, who hastily sought sanctuary in a church, from which his followers soon rescued him, since for the moment they outnumbered Vasco de Herrera's men in Trujillo. Those whom Vasco de Herrera had left in the interior had gone on to the Valley of Olancho to subdue rebellious natives and could not be quickly recalled.

Cerezeda, though vacillating and weak, had the good of the colony at heart and sought to act as mediator to restore some measure of stability throughout this quarrel. Suddenly taking matters into their own hands, Vasco de Herrera's opponents killed him and threw their full support to Méndez de Hinostrosa. Cerezeda now feared for his own life and sought to escape, but Méndez de Hinostrosa trapped him and demanded that Cerezeda recognize him as governor. In this crisis Cerezeda for once stood firm and refused, despite threats of assassination.

Méndez de Hinostrosa then went ahead with his plans to seize sole power, despite Cerezeda's convocation of the cabildo in a secret meeting to find a solution, and compelled the citizens to recognize him. He next appointed a new cabildo and ordered Cerezeda to cease any further attempts to exercise authority. He also sent messages asking support from the company in the Valley of Olancho, now commanded by Diego Díaz de Herrera, brother of the dead Vasco, and succeeded in winning the soldiers over to his party. Cerezeda sought too late to bring Diego Díaz De Herrera and his men back to Trujillo to support him.

Méndez de Hinostrosa's position now seemed strong. But in defiance Cerezeda organized his own followers, struck swiftly, and after sharp fighting captured his opponent, whom he beheaded. Cerezeda also took action against his victim's followers. Thus, after a year and more of intrigue, assassination, and fighting, Cerezeda emerged as sole acting governor, finally fulfilling his selection for that office by López de Salcedo.

Cerezeda had not long exercised his authority when, toward the close of October 1532, Diego Alvítez, whom the Crown appointed to succeed López de Salcedo as chief magistrate of Honduras, arrived off the coast. In appointing Alvítez, the Crown had responded to reports of anarchy and urgent appeals for the designation of a new royal governor. The flotilla which brought Alvítez and his party was wrecked some leagues from Trujillo, but he finally arrived and assumed office. Advanced in age and weakened by exposure, Alvítez saw death close at hand and, with it, the need for a successor. Therefore, on November 12, 1532, he chose Cerezeda as acting governor, as had López de Salcedo before him, and died soon thereafter. Honduras was again without a governor who enjoyed the prestige which direct royal appointment alone could bring.

Cerezeda again assumed the acting governorship. Despite his sincere desire to serve the colony, he proved as incompetent and vacillating as before. Factions again formed and enemies, among them Diego Díaz de Herrera, plotted to depose him; he was able to maintain his position only with the utmost difficulty. The need to allay discontent and factionalism, as well as the obligation to advance colonization, now caused Cerezeda to evolve extensive schemes for conquest and settlement. He planned to establish a town on the route from the north coast of Honduras to Nicaragua, provide secure communications with that province, and to attempt once more colonization of the Valley of Naco. To carry out the first objective he sent a captain and sixty men southward, intending to follow with more, but his departure was delayed by unexpected news that Spaniards were approaching Trujillo along the coast from the west. They were led by Alonso Dávila, a principal lieutenant of Francisco de Montejo, *Adelantado* of Yucatan, who was then engaged in the conquest of that province. From Salamanca de Campeche, on the west coast, Montejo had in 1531 sent Dávila inland to start another town. In search of an appropriate region, Dávila had pushed on southeastward until he crossed the entire peninsula of Yucatan and reached the Bahía de Chetumal, where he founded a town. Stubborn native resistance caused abandonment of this town in 1532. Since the entire region behind Dávila was in revolt and he was therefore cut off from Montejo, his expedition proceeded along the Caribbean coast toward Honduras by canoe, with a view to re-establishing the town at a favorable site. None was found until Dávila reached the area of Puerto de Caballos and the Río de Ulua. By this time months of untold hardship and danger had reduced his expedition to the utmost straits. He sent an urgent appeal to Trujillo for aid, to which Cerezeda responded by sending out a column to carry supplies for his desperate countrymen—and also to learn their purpose. With this aid, Dávila's exhausted men finally reached Trujillo early in 1533.

Dávila hoped to return to the region of the Río de Ulua and Puerto de Caballos to establish a town in Montejo's name, but that was impossible without support from the authorities of Trujillo. Since the area he proposed to colonize lay in territory claimed by Cerezeda for Honduras he could not, of course, divulge his true purpose to that official. Cerezeda, though not aware of Dávila's real intention, refused the support, pointing out, in all truth, that the situation in Honduras was too precarious for such extensive aid.

With dissension so rife in Trujillo, it was inevitable that Dávila should become deeply involved in the current intrigues, especially with his hope of founding a town in Montejo's name to the westward. To this end he plotted with Diego Díaz de Herrera but in vain. Finally realizing the futility of his plan, he contracted with the master of a ship which arrived at Trujillo to carry him and the majority of his men back to the west coast of Yucatan to rejoin Montejo. A small group of Dávila's company remained to join the citizenry of Trujillo.

Dávila's unplanned arrival in Honduras foreshadowed events to come, for it was Montejo, under whose authority Dávila acted, who was to emerge as the final conqueror of Honduras.

After Dávila's departure the situation in Honduras continued to deteriorate.

Although Cerezeda finally set out to join the captain whom he had sent inland to establish a town on the route to Nicaragua, he soon found it necessary to turn back, for he received word that, in his absence, Diego Díaz de Herrera planned to desert Trujillo with the remaining colonists. Cerezeda hastened back to prevent this, and his efforts to colonize the southern interior therefore came to naught. Discontent, factionalism, and instability had by this time reached proportions which threatened the existence of the colony, now in a most abject state. Lack of everything the Spaniards needed heightened the danger.

Although many captains and hundreds of men—more than Pizarro needed to overthrow the vast, populous, and fabulously rich Inca Empire—had come to Honduras since the beginnings of colonization, the Spaniards had so dissipated their strength in internecine quarrels that Trujillo, with less than 200 citizens, alone was left of the many efforts at settlement. Slave raids and brutal warfare wrought havoc among the natives but failed utterly to achieve the real conquest of any territory beyond a restricted area about Trujillo itself. There were great decreases in the Indian population in all regions where the Spaniards remained for any length of time, except in the rich Valley of Naco. Native life had been disrupted wherever the invaders went. Many Indians were carried off as slaves to the West Indies, where the native population was rapidly disappearing and there was great need of labor. Governors who did not themselves participate in this slave traffic condoned it for others. In 1533 pestilence swept away a large number—half, it is said—of the Indians who still remained in the area of Spanish control.

The district of Trujillo and regions to the south had been ruthlessly exploited to the point of exhaustion; little was left to hold the Spaniards. No rich mines of gold or silver and very little treasure had been found. The *encomienda* system, with its tributes and services upon which the Spaniards depended in great degree for their maintenance, could not function adequately under the circumstances. Such encomiendas as did exist were now very weak in tribute-paying Indians and in produce. After almost a decade Trujillo and its surroundings were closer to abandonment than ever; many of its citizens threatened to leave in search of greener fields. Stories of the unmeasured riches of Peru heightened discontent, just as in every province which the Spaniards found poor and unattractive.

Desperately seeking means to hold the disintegrating colony together, Cerezeda early in 1534 returned to his plan for conquest and settlement in the Valley of Naco. This time the decision to move westward was destined to bring permanent results and, after many anxious moments, was to change the entire history of Honduras and give the colony a new and brighter aspect.

2

Cerezeda and the Beginnings of Permanent Colonization in Honduras

EARLY DELIMITATION OF HIGUERAS

BY THE TIME the acting governor Andrés de Cerezeda prepared to move westward from Trujillo in 1534, territorial expansion of Honduras had again been given official recognition, despite the restrictive agreement between Pedrarias and López de Salcedo. The region along the coast toward the Golfo Dulce and inland, including the area of the Río de. Ulua and the Valley of Naco, was officially called Higueras, which, united with Honduras, was considered to make up the "Provincia de Higueras e Cabo de Honduras." [1] Thus Honduras for a time meant only the eastern districts of the combined province, the territory westward from Cabo Camarón, including Trujillo, to a point some leagues west of Trujillo itself; Higueras extended along the coast west and north to an undefined point in the Río Dulce–Golfo Dulce region and toward the vague boundaries of Guatemala and Yucatan. The Valley of Olancho, behind Trujillo, was included in Honduras, and all territory westward from the coast of the "North Sea," or Caribbean, south to Nicaragua, San Salvador, and San Miguel was encompassed by Higueras. In 1540, after the town of San Pedro had been founded southwest of the mouth of the Río de Ulua and near Puerto de Caballos, a treasurer of Honduras-Higueras, Diego García de Celís, roughly defined the territory:

. . . the last section of the governmental jurisdiction of this province toward Yucatan, which is Higueras, extends thirty leagues and more along the coast beyond this town [of San Pedro] and Puerto de Caballos; and from this Puerto to the City of Trujillo there are about forty-three leagues along the coast, and from the port of Trujillo to Cabo Camarón, where we place the final limits of the province in the direction of Nombre de Dios, there are another thirty-five or forty leagues along the same coast. . . . [2]

[1] For instance, the cedula of April 22, 1535 (AGI, Guatemala 402) by which the Crown announced to Cerezeda the administrative union of the Province of Honduras and Higueras and the Province of Yucatan was addressed to "andres de cerezeda nro. gor. dlas. provincias de higueras e cabo de honduras." The cedula went on: "como vereys por las provisiones q. enbiamos al adelantado don franco. de montejo avemos acordado de juntar esa provincia de cabo de honduras a la provincia e governacion de youcatan . . . y le avemos encomendado el cargo desa provincia como quien . . . tiene mucha esperiencia de aquellas ptes. e es persona de quen. confiamos mirara en todo nro. servicio e bien desa repuca. . . ."

The cedula of March 1, 1535, by which the Crown appointed Montejo governor of Honduras and Higueras (AGI, Guatemala 402) began: "Don Carlos etc. por quanto y por fallecemiento de do. lopez de salzedo nro. governador que fue de la provincia de higueras y cabo de honduras. . . ."

Hitherto the term Honduras alone has been used in the text for purposes of simplification, but henceforth the hyphenated term Honduras-Higueras will be employed in referring to the province as a whole.

[2] Diego García de Celís to the Crown, San Pedro, 1540, AGI, Indiferente General 1206.

In the latter 1520's Honduras-Higueras was removed from the authority
of the Audiencia of Santo Domingo and placed under the new Audiencia
of New Spain for superior judicial affairs, but in 1534 the province was returned
to the older audiencia.[3]

Initial failures to colonize Higueras not only made its limits vague but put
even its jurisdictional status potentially in question. In 1532, to foster the
economic development of Guatemala and give it a much needed port on the
North Sea, the Crown authorized Pedro de Alvarado, as governor of that
province, to conquer and colonize territory lying within the general area of
Higueras. Less than a year later, Diego Alvítez, then governor of Honduras-
Higueras, was specifically given royal license to subjugate and settle the Valley
of Naco and the region of Puerto de Caballos. Close upon this measure, in
1533, followed a grant of the governorship of the vast territory from the western
limits of Tabasco to the Río de Ulua, to Francisco de Montejo, Adelantado of
Yucatan, with permission to conquer and people the region of the Río de Ulua,
Puerto de Caballos, and the Valley of Naco, should neither the aforementioned
governors nor their lieutenants have colonized those districts under earlier
royal cedulas.[4] Further complicating this already confused situation, and almost immediately after assigning Montejo the territory from the Río de Copilco to the Río de Ulua, the Crown reaffirmed the authority it had already
conferred on Alvarado to act in Higueras. In this confirmation, however, the
Crown instructed him not to encroach on territories already colonized by, or
under the effective control of, governors of Yucatan and Honduras-Higueras.
The royal cedulas just described had an important influence on the history
of Honduras-Higueras from 1536 until the establishment of the Audiencia
de los Confines in 1544, since they gave authority to the governors of Honduras-Higueras, Guatemala, and Yucatan to colonize the same general territory under specified circumstances. Conditions in Higueras and its environs
were for a long period such that each of the three governors could interpret
these royal measures pretty much as he chose.[5]

STATE OF NATIVE CULTURE

Honduras-Higueras is said to have been heavily peopled when the Spaniards first came. Many towns of considerable size were found, especially in
the Valleys of Comayagua and Naco, and in the region of the Río de Ulua,

[3] Cedula of March 22, 1534, AGI, Guatemala 402; Residencia of Montejo for Honduras-Higueras, 1544,
AGI, Justicia 300.
[4] The cedulas concerned are found in the following register books: AGI, Guatemala 393 and 402 and
México 2999.
[5] *Ibid.*

but little is now known of the native groups. It seems clear, however, that there were a number of stocks of varying degrees of culture, some quite advanced. Fine pottery was made in the region about Lake Yojoa, between the coast and the mountains, and Indians of the highlands had displayed great engineering skill in the construction of strong stone fortifications. Agriculture was highly developed, with cotton and the great New World staple, maize, produced in large amounts. From the cotton the Indians wove good textiles.[6]

Extensive commerce was conducted with the Maya of Yucatan, notably from the area of the Río de Ulua, and with Aztec merchants northwestward through Tabasco. Such trade was carried in large canoes across or along the Bay of Honduras, thence by trails and rivers through the Peten, home of the Itza Maya. Exchange between Higueras and Yucatan had existed for centuries and still continued. Columbus had seen impressive evidence of this commerce, as we have noted.

Cacao from fine, carefully cultivated groves was a principal product of the Río de Ulua area, which received in return fine Yucatecan cotton cloth from the north. Yucatan Maya caciques maintained trading posts and agents in the southern region, such value did they place on this commerce.

Points of highest culture seem to have been the rich Ulua valley and the fertile and somewhat higher Valley of Comayagua. It is not surprising that there should have been centers of advanced culture in Higueras, for Copan, one of the greatest and most ancient cities of the brilliant Maya "First Empire," though now long decadent, lay near by to the west. Some of the Indians of Higueras, indeed, may have been related to the Maya.

The natives of the coastal area of Honduras proper seem in the main to have been less civilized than those of Higueras and were on the whole more easily subdued or pushed to one side. But natives of the hinterland, especially those of the Valley of Olancho, were warlike. The Indians of the mountainous interior of the entire Higueras section and of the Valley of Comayagua were of stern make-up, as well as high culture. They were spirited, liberty-loving and warlike, and had not been seriously affected by earlier Spanish incursions into their territory or by Spanish attempts to colonize. They were ready and willing to offer the strongest kind of resistance to any invader. Although the cultured Indians of the populous Valley of Naco and the Río de Ulua accepted the Spaniards without persistent hostility when they first came, they too proved determined to preserve their liberties when Spanish colonization threatened to become permanent.

[6] For a brief description of the native cultures of Honduras-Higueras see Roys, 1943, pp. 113-21.

OCCUPATION OF HIGUERAS UNDER CEREZEDA

In planning the colonization of Higueras in 1534, Cerezeda, who was now contador of the royal treasury of the province as well as acting governor, had the full support of the lesser authorities and of the more thoughtful colonists of Honduras. Having no intention whatsoever of abandoning Trujillo and the Honduras section of the province, he set apart fifty citizens, mostly those who had neither health nor spirit for rigorous enterprise, to maintain the city and took about 130 into the new area.[7]

Cerezeda divided the company destined for Higueras into two groups. One group, about sixty horsemen and footmen, marched overland, driving live-stock with them; the other, led by Cerezeda himself, went by sea at the close of March. The expedition was carefully prepared, for it was one of conquest as well as of exploration and colonization.[8] On reaching Higueras the two companies united at the pueblo of Naco, well known to the Spaniards, where they remained for a considerable period. When forced to move on because of lack of supplies, Cerezeda returned to the Valley of Sula, along the lower Río de Ulua. In a region inhabited by Indians known to them as the Chontales, the Spaniards founded the Villa de Buena Esperanza in token of the better things for which they were searching. The site was three leagues from the native town of Quimistan, seven from Naco, and twenty-three from the excellent harbor of Puerto de Caballos. Cerezeda then ordered columns into the surrounding area to conquer it and to explore for gold and silver.[9] With such westward expansion, the political and economic center of Honduras-Higueras shifted from Honduras to Higueras as the more important section. This was later confirmed by the intervention of Alvarado in 1536, the final conquest of Higueras by Montejo from 1537 to 1539, and the later creation of the Audiencia de los Confines.

[7] Oviedo, 1851–55, 31-36; Herrera, 1601–15, 5-9-9; Cerezeda to the Crown, Buena Esperanza, August 31, 1535, AGI, Guatemala 39; Cabildo of Gracias a Dios to the Crown, December 21, 1536, AGI, Guatemala 44; Francisco de Barrientos to the Crown, Trujillo, July 25, 1534, AGI, Guatemala 49; Diego García de Celís to the Crown, Puerto de Caballos, June 20, 1534, AGI, Guatemala 49; Fiscal v. García de Celís, 1537, AGI, Justicia 1035-3-1; Oviedo, 1851–55, 31-36; Herrera, 1601–15, 5-9-9. Haring, 1947, pp. 298, 300, provides the following descriptions of the duties and position of the Royal Treasury Officials:

"The collection of the revenues with few exceptions was in charge of individuals styled specifically the Royal Officials (oficiales reales de hacienda, or simply oficiales reales). In the beginning there were four in each colony, a treasurer, a comptroller (contador), a business manager (factor), and an inspector (veedor). The duties of treasurer and comptroller are fairly obvious. The factor disposed of the tribute in kind received from the natives, made purchases for the authorities, and in general attended to any commercial transactions in which the king's monies were involved. The veedor was overseer of the exchequer's interests at the mines and assay offices where the bullion was refined and the quinto subtracted from it. . . .

"In Habsburg times the crown always separated clearly the political and military functions of government from the administration of finances. Consequently the oficiales reales, although of inferior rank to the governors, were in their own sphere of co-ordinate authority with them; and in some cases they might oppose actions which controverted their instructions or involved extraordinary expenditures. . . ."

[8] Ibid.
[9] Ibid.

While Cerezeda was attempting to spread Spanish sovereignty from Honduras, an expedition of about forty men led by Cristóbal de la Cueva penetrated Higueras from Guatemala. This company had been sent out by the acting governor of Guatemala, Jorge de Alvarado (brother of Pedro, who was then absent on his celebrated expedition to distant Quito), to find a satisfactory harbor, as royal authority had sanctioned, and to establish a road between the prospective port and the City of Santiago de Guatemala. Jorge de Alvarado had also heard that the Indians of Honduras-Higueras were at war, and he therefore also contemplated the pacification of that area.[10]

Cerezeda feared that de la Cueva's arrival meant encroachment on land under his jurisdiction, so he sent to ascertain the Guatemalan captain's intention. The two then conferred personally, taking as a basis of discussion the royal cedulas authorizing the governors of Guatemala and Honduras-Higueras to conquer and settle the coast of the North Sea and Guatemala's need for a port of supply. They reached an agreement providing that, since Cerezeda had occupied the region first, de la Cueva's men were to be placed under his command. He was to lead them and the colonists of Buena Esperanza in campaigns of exploration, conquest, and settlement along the coast and back into the hinterland. De la Cueva gained the concession that the much needed road of supply be established from the North Sea to Guatemala and that a port be set up.[11]

The original plans under this agreement seem to have called for the founding of the port either near the Golfo Dulce, at the site of abandoned San Gil de Buena Vista where Gil González Dávila had met with failure a decade before, or at Puerto de Caballos, where previous efforts had likewise failed. This would have fulfilled de la Cueva's principal objective, but for some reason he abandoned it and suggested colonization inland, midway between the North and South seas.[12] Cerezeda at first assented to de la Cueva's proposal but later advanced objections. Dissension developed, augmented by the fact that after a time de la Cueva's men refused to recognize Cerezeda's authority, despite the agreement between the two leaders. De la Cueva thereupon gave up any further attempts at collaboration and led his men toward the South Sea. There he apparently refounded, or at least invigorated, the town of San Miguel, just northwest of the great Bahía de Fonseca, which had been founded

[10] Herrera, 1601–15, 5-9-9; Cerezeda to the Crown, Buena Esperanza, August 31, 1535, AGI, Guatemala 49; Montejo to the Crown, Gracias a Dios, June 1, 1539, DII, 24:250–97, passim; Pedraza to the Crown, Gracias a Dios, May 18, 1539, AGI, Guatemala 9; Probanza of Melchor Hernández, 1556, AGG, Papers from the Archivo Colonial, Section of San Salvador, leg. 193, exped. 1; Probanza of Gonzalo de Armenta, 1565, AGG, Papers from the Archivo Colonial; Probanza of Miguel de Trujillo, 1548, AGG, Section of San Salvador, leg. 121, exped. 21. See also Chamberlain, 1947a.
[11] Ibid.
[12] Ibid.

by one of Pedro de Alvarado's captains but which, largely through having furnished a great proportion of its men to Alvarado for his expedition to Quito, had become almost entirely depopulated.[13]

De la Cueva and his followers had remained in Higueras for some time, and they and Cerezeda's colonists must have penetrated into many parts of the province, exploring, conquering, and searching for gold. Whatever they may have done, no permanent advantage resulted. The leaders had planned ably and commanded enough men, but dissension had again blighted the effort. Had they worked harmoniously, they might well have brought many improvements not only to Higueras but also to Guatemala. As it was, the province of San Miguel alone benefited, although it indeed urgently needed new colonists.[14]

The re-establishment of San Miguel by de la Cueva brought that district once again within the control of Guatemala. Cerezeda and the other authorities of Honduras-Higueras, regarding San Miguel as their own territory, vigorously protested to the Crown. The area remained in dispute for a number of years between the governors of the two provinces.[15]

Following these events, Cerezeda did his utmost to expand Higueras with his own resources and nominally established control over the Naco and Sula areas. The cacique Ciçumba, who ruled extensive and populous territories along the lower stretches of the Río de Ulua and who had many warriors at his command, was the principal enemy. Along the river this Indian ruler had formidable fortresses which he considered impregnable; he was confident and defiant. Cerezeda attacked him while de la Cueva was still in Higueras and gained an ephemeral triumph, but as soon as the Spaniards left, the resolute cacique not only took up arms again but also sought to organize resistance among all Indians of the area who were resolved to oppose the invaders.[16] Cerezeda speedily divided the territory he had penetrated among the citizens of Buena Esperanza in encomienda. Now the long-rumored gold and silver deposits came to light and, to the great satisfaction of the colonists, promised them future wealth.

Notwithstanding many shortcomings as a chief magistrate and military leader, Cerezeda was by no means devoid of vision and a desire for the colony's welfare, as his earlier attempts to mediate between quarreling factions in Trujillo and his agreement with de la Cueva testify. He recognized that Higueras had great commercial possibilities, especially in light of the recent

[13] *Ibid.*
[14] *Ibid.*
[15] *Ibid.*
[16] Cerezeda to the Crown, Buena Esperanza, August 31, 1535, AGI, Guatemala 39.

conquest of rich and heavily peopled Peru. He now contemplated the establishment of a route across the province from Puerto de Caballos to the Bahía de Fonseca to carry trade and supply between Castile and the West Indies, the Central American provinces, and the colonies of the South Sea, especially Peru, with its bullion. This avenue of commerce was to supplant the shorter but difficult and pestilential route across Pànama. In view of this plan, Cerezeda's interest in San Miguel takes on real purpose. Other parts of his broad developmental project looked to the founding of a town at Puerto de Caballos, the establishment of a city at the inland pueblo of Maniani on the route between Puerto de Caballos and the Bahía de Fonseca—a city intended as a center of trade for a wide area—and the construction of connecting roads within Higueras. He may likewise have returned to the idea of re-establishing a port town at San Gil de Buena Vista.[17]

It is not altogether clear whether these farseeing commercial designs were originated solely by Cerezeda or whether they were partly inspired by de la Cueva or the treasurer of Honduras-Higueras, Diego García de Celís. Nevertheless, they seem to have received the first definite form from Cerezeda, who also made them known to the Crown. His agreement with de la Cueva may, in fact, have looked ahead to these undertakings as well as to the immediate needs of Honduras-Higueras and Guatemala.[18]

Pedro de Alvarado later recognized the merits of this design and took it over.[19] When Montejo became governor of Honduras-Higueras he expanded its concepts until it became the keystone of his policies there.[20]

DISCONTENT UNDER CEREZEDA

Despite promising beginnings, it soon became apparent that colonization would not of itself remedy the situation into which Honduras-Higueras had fallen. After Cerezeda and the majority of its citizens had moved westward, Trujillo declined, for most of the citizens left there were old, infirm, ill or dispirited. Food, clothing, and all other necessities grew so scarce that continued existence of the city again became doubtful. Lacking real leadership and hopelessly discouraged, the citizens of Trujillo resented the prospect of eclipse of Trujillo and Honduras should colonization in Higueras prove permanent. Moreover, they quite mistakenly believed that Cerezeda favored aban-

[17] *Ibid.;* Chamberlain, 1946b.

[18] *Ibid.* See also Pedraza to the Crown, Gracias a Dios, May 18, 1539, AGI, Guatemala 9.

[19] *Ibid.;* Fiscal *v.* Alvarado, 1537, AGI, Justicia 1035-2-2. Alvarado's decision to found a city, Gracias a Dios, inland between the North and South Seas in the same general region in which Cerezeda wished to establish a town, demonstrates Alvarado's interest in the plan.

[20] Montejo to the Crown, Naco, July 28, 1537, AGI, Guatemala 9; Montejo to the Crown, Gracias a Dios, June 1, 1539, DII, 24:250–97 *passim;* Pedraza to the Crown, Gracias a Dios, May 18, 1539, AGI, Guatemala 9.

donment of their city. It is not surprising that they sent despairing appeals to the Audiencia of New Spain and Santo Domingo and to the Crown for material aid and for a governor appointed directly by the Crown.[21]

In Higueras, Cerezeda's inherent shortcomings were intensified by illness, and, as time passed, he proved not only incapable of enlarging the area he had superficially conquered but also unable to exploit such potential elements of permanence and stability as did exist. The Spaniards' ruthless mistreatment of the Indians, enforced arduous labor, and enslavement rapidly produced their usual effects. The original heavy population tended to decrease, Indians fled beyond the reach of the Spaniards, and the natives who remained under Spanish control displayed growing resentment and hostility. Many refused to serve their encomenderos. All these were serious matters, since the colonists depended on large numbers of Indians for food and service. Ciçumba was the natural leader of this mounting resistance.[22]

With the weakness of the province and its leader everywhere apparent, Ciçumba's opposition became more and more effective; an ever-increasing number of warriors rallied to him, and districts which had been but sketchily subdued rose in arms. Areas nominally subjugated were lost, and expansion of the conquest was out of the question. It was not long, therefore, before the Spaniards were pinioned to a small area about Buena Esperanza, in constant fear that a mass uprising would bring the Indians down on them in overwhelming numbers.[23]

Discontent among the colonists of Buena Esperanza, now but a hollow name, each day became more intense, for they were short of supplies in a rich and fertile area, since the already weakened and unwilling encomienda towns failed to supply their needs. They saw ever-growing numbers of hostile Indians pressing in from all sides. Contemptuous of Cerezeda's incompetence, they flouted his authority whenever they saw fit. Rivalry and personal friction now arose between Cerezeda and his fellow official, the treasurer Diego García de Celís, second in rank in the colony. García de Celís was a man of irascible temperament, short patience, and considerable vigor; he refused to heed Cerezeda whenever they disagreed. The two thus became avowed enemies, seri-

[21] Francisco de Barrientos to the Crown, Trujillo, July 25, 1544, AGI, Guatemala 49; Cabildo of Trujillo to the Crown, March 12, 1540, AGI, Guatemala 44; Relación of Alonso Dávila, 1533, DII, 14:197 ff.

[22] Fiscal v. Alvarado, 1537, AGI, Justicia 1035-2-2; Cerezeda to the Crown, Buena Esperanza, December 1, 1535, AGI, Guatemala 39; Cerezeda to the Crown, Puerto de Caballos, August 14, 1536, AGI, Guatemala 39; Cabildo of Gracias a Dios to the Crown, December 1, 1536, AGI, Guatemala 44; Fiscal v. Diego García de Celís, 1537, AGI, Justicia 1035-3-1; Pedraza to the Crown, Gracias a Dios, May 18, 1539, AGI, Guatemala 9; Cedula of January 30, 1538 concerning enslavement of Indians, AGI, Guatemala 402; Pedraza v. Montejo, 1539, AGI, Justicia 129-2; Montejo to the Crown, Gracias a Dios, June 1, 1529, DII, 24:250 ff.; Herrera, 1601–15, 5-9-8 and 6-1-8.

[23] Ibid.

ously dividing the loyalty of the colonists. Chaos was the inevitable result. The colony was without unity of purpose when it was most needed.[24]

Of the colonists who had gone to Higueras, many considered the move a failure and wished to leave; some forty or fifty actually drifted away. News of the conquest of Peru, with all its wealth, continued to exercise its disrupting influence. Even the existence of precious metals close at hand produced no desire to remain since the rebellious Indians made mining impossible. Absence of strong, united leadership and lack of a true colonizing motive among most of the settlers spelled destruction for Buena Esperanza unless effective help came from elsewhere.[25]

Cerezeda, despite his other weaknesses, roundly refused to evacuate the region. But not wishing to admit utter incompetence, he at first was content passively to await whatever aid might turn up. In contrast, García de Celís recognized that only rapid, positive measures could save the colony and sought to arouse Cerezeda to action but without avail. Cerezeda stubbornly permitted personal pride to stand in the way, even though he himself now desired that a royal governor replace him.[26]

APPEALS FOR ALVARADO TO TAKE COMMAND

García de Celís, with the support of the more steadfast municipal authorities and colonists, decided to appeal for aid to the powerful Pedro de Alvarado, Adelantado and Governor of Guatemala, who had recently returned from his adventurous expedition to Quito, to other officials of Guatemala, and to members of the Audiencia of New Spain. Cerezeda perforce fell in with his plans, largely to maintain the fiction of his authority before the officials of Guatemala and New Spain. The two leaders and the municipal officials of Buena Esperanza then drew up a communication describing their disastrous situation and urgently pleading for support until the Crown could take measures to remedy conditions.[27]

García de Celís now moved one step further. He resolved to go to Guatemala in the name of all those determined to seek immediate help, to present their appeals personally. Accompanied by a party of ten soldiers, he set out from Buena Esperanza early in October 1535. He planned to return within two months, and it was agreed that Cerezeda and the municipal officers would

---

[24] *Ibid.* Charges were placed against García de Celís for insubordination when he went to Castile in 1536–37 (Fiscal *v.* Diego García de Celís, 1537, AGI, Justicia 1035-3-1) and the Crown ordered that he and Cerezeda henceforth cease their quarreling (Cedula of November 13, 1537, AGI, Guatemala 402).
[25] *Ibid.*
[26] *Ibid.*
[27] *Ibid.*

not sanction the abandonment of Higueras before then.[28] After a trying march, García de Celís reached Santiago de Guatemala late in November.[29] They found Pedro de Alvarado absent, preparing a new South Sea expedition at the port of Acajutla. Alonso Maldonado, an *oidor,* or judge, of the Audiencia of New Spain, who had been sent to Guatemala by that tribunal to investigate the administration of Pedro de Alvarado and his lieutenants, had just departed for the City of Mexico.[30]

García de Celís also learned that the Crown, in March 1535, had appointed Montejo governor of Honduras-Higueras.[31] He may likewise have been informed of the Crown's action which united Honduras-Higueras and Yucatan into a governmental and fiscal unit.[32] Since García de Celís had come to Guatemala to obtain Alvarado's support, news that Montejo had been appointed governor of Honduras-Higueras greatly disturbed him.[33]

That Maldonado was still within reach was to García de Celís' advantage, however, since it gave him opportunity to make his mission thoroughly known to an influential member of the powerful Audiencia of New Spain sooner than otherwise would have been possible. He could also reckon in advance with Montejo's eventual arrival in Honduras-Higueras and deal with Maldonado regarding the complications which Montejo's appointment might bring. García de Celís therefore hastened to inform Maldonado of the perilous situation in Higueras and to request him to make it known to the Audiencia of New Spain. He also told Maldonado of his intention to seek direct aid from Alvarado and the other authorities of Guatemala, enclosing pleas to be despatched to the newly arrived Viceroy of New Spain, Antonio de Mendoza, to the audiencia, and to Montejo. His letter to Montejo indicated recognition of that official as governor of Honduras-Higueras in view of his royal appointment.[34]

Maldonado answered immediately and promised full compliance with these requests. He also urged García de Celís to prevail upon the officials and colonists of Higueras not to abandon their province until sufficient time elapsed to permit the higher authorities of New Spain to send help.[35] Nevertheless, the urgency of the situation led García de Celís to communicate directly with Alvarado, who because of his proximity to Higueras could act more rapidly than any other. He forwarded the despatches brought from Buena Esperanza

[28] *Ibid.*
[29] Fiscal *v.* Diego García de Celís, 1537, AGI, Justicia 1035-3-1; Fiscal *v.* Alvarado, 1537, AGI, Justicia 1035-2-2; Diego García de Celís to the Crown, Isla Terceira, March 5, 1537, AGI, Santo Domingo 168.
[30] *Ibid.*
[31] Cedula of March 1, 1535, AGI, Guatemala 402.
[32] Cedula of April 13 and April 22, 1535, AGI, Guatemala 402.
[33] Fiscal *v.* Diego García de Celís, 1537, AGI, Justicia 1035-3-1; Diego García de Celís to the Crown, Isla Terceira, March 5, 1537, AGI, Santo Domingo 168.
[34] *Ibid.*
[35] *Ibid.*

and in his own letters implored Alvarado to move to Higueras with the least possible delay so that the colony could be held together until Montejo arrived as royal governor. He declared that if support were not forthcoming immediately, the province would be abandoned before Montejo could get there.[36]

An understandable reluctance made Alvarado ponder this difficult task. He was organizing an armada for a kind of enterprise that had long appealed to his restless nature, a quest for greater glory and riches in the Spice Islands, and his preparations were well advanced. Since the entire system of conquest was based on tangible rewards for the conquistadores within the lands they subjugated, careful thought was necessary before incurring the heavy expenses of an expedition to succor a restive province which might in the end offer insufficient wealth. Moreover, the Crown already vested the governorship of Honduras-Higueras in Montejo, who, it seemed, would eventually reap whatever rewards and prestige might materialize from the labors of Alvarado and his followers. However, Alvarado's intervention could bring to his own province of Guatemala its long-desired outlet on the North Sea, and deposits of precious metals were already known to exist in Honduras-Higueras, although their full extent was not yet revealed.[37]

Alvarado's reluctance to heed the despairing call from Higueras caused García de Celís, on December 23, formally to demand ("require," as it was termed in Castilian law) that he do so. He presented this "requirement" in name of the authorities and colonists of Honduras-Higueras and as their chosen representative. He fully understood Alvarado's hesitancy and in a prophetic message to the Crown he expressed fear that should Alvarado intervene, only to be followed by Montejo as governor, discontent, dissension, and friction among officials and colonists would inevitably follow. Undeterred, he continued efforts to persuade Alvarado to help.[38]

[36] *Ibid.* Fiscal *v.* Alvarado, 1537, AGI, Justicia 1035-2-2.

[37] Fiscal *v.* Alvarado 1537, AGI, Justicia 1035-3-1; Pedraza *v.* Montejo, 1539, AGI, Justicia 129-2; Montejo *v.* Alvarado, 1541, Justicia 134-3-1.

[38] *Ibid.*

3

The Aspirations of Montejo and their Relation to the History of Honduras-Higueras

MISRULE IN HONDURAS-HIGUERAS

DURING the early years of Spanish expansion in the New World, before the strong hand of Castilian absolutism imposed everywhere the direct will of the sovereign, the acts and aspirations of vigorous, resolute, and ambitious conquistadores of high station frequently determined the course of events in wide regions. Thus, from 1535 to 1539, and even afterward, the personal ambitions of Francisco de Montejo, Adelantado of Yucatan and later Governor of Honduras-Higueras, shaped the history of the latter province and established him as its true conqueror.[1]

Even before 1535, the Crown had assigned to Montejo the government of the wide region extending from the western boundaries of the province of Tabasco southeastward to the Río de Ulua, including parts of the littoral of Higueras.[2] But in this year it appointed him Governor of Honduras-Higueras and united this province and Yucatan into an administrative and fiscal unit under Montejo's superior authority.[3]

The factors which led to the Crown's actions of 1535 were multiple and complex. It is readily understood that the chronic anarchy and instability of Honduras-Higueras should long have been a cause of concern to the Crown and the higher agencies of royal government in the New World. Officials and colonists alike had many times petitioned for a thorough-going solution of the problem. In the spring of 1533 the cabildo of Trujillo, certain citizens, and the harassed Cerezeda himself, as acting governor, sent a series of appeals to the Audiencia of New Spain, within whose jurisdiction Honduras-Higueras lay at that time. They described the precarious situation and emphasized the need for a governor designated by the Crown, enjoying the respect and prestige which direct royal appointment alone could carry. The audiencia conveyed the content of these messages to the Crown, with an accompanying admission

---

[1] For Montejo's personal design for a greatly expanded Adelantamiento of Yucatan and greater territorial limits for Yucatan see: Montejo to the Crown, Veracruz, April 20, 1529, DII, 13:86–91; Montejo v. Alvarado, 1533, AGI, Justicia 1005-5-1; Residencias of Montejo for Honduras-Higueras, Chiapas, Tabasco and Yucatan, 1544, 1550, AGI, Justicia 244 and 300; Chamberlain, 1948.

[2] Cedulas of December 19, 1533, AGI, México 2999.

[3] See Cedulas of March 1, April 13 and April 22, 1535, AGI, Guatemala 402.

that even this high tribunal was incapable of maintaining order in the distant, turbulent province.[4]

After Cerezeda had shifted the colony's center of gravity to Higueras in 1534, the resentful, dissatisfied cabildo and citizenry of Trujillo reported their plight directly to the Crown. They again petitioned that, to prevent the depopulation of the city, "a governor of authority" be appointed, that additional colonists be sent, and that the province be transferred from the jurisdiction of the Audiencia of New Spain to that of Santo Domingo, since the island tribunal was considered more accessible. At the same time, they accused Cerezeda of having abandoned Trujillo and Honduras to its fate.[5] To these recommendations were added those of a treasury official of the province, the veedor, Francisco de Barrientos. He urged the sovereign to appoint as governor "a real man and a man of the Indies" who could command respect and would understand the colonists' point of view, since he considered such an appointment fundamental to order in the province.[6]

Such recommendations contributed not only to the formation of over-all Crown policy, but also to the gradual adoption of a series of specific measures designed to improve the situation of the province. One of the most important was the return, in 1534, of Honduras-Higueras to the judicial authority of the Audiencia of Santo Domingo.[7] The Crown also considered the appointment of a fitting royal governor. The last one had been the unfortunate Diego Alvítez. Fray Alonso de Guzmán, a Jeronomite who was still in Castile, had already been designated Bishop of Honduras, in order to bring the secular Church of the province to full organization as soon as possible, so the Crown considered it practical that he also become chief magistrate. But he did not proceed to Honduras-Higueras, leaving the province still without either royal governor or bishop of its own.[8]

MONTEJO'S TRAINING AS A CONQUEROR

At this juncture Montejo seemed to the Crown, in distant Castile, almost providentially placed to offer a lasting solution for the vexing problems of Honduras-Higueras. He had made a distinguished record in the New World and he was in high favor at Court. As a lesser nobleman already of mature

[4] See Audiencia of New Spain to the Crown, August 5, 1533, AGI, México 68; Relación of Alonso Dávila, 1533, DII, 14: 197 ff.; Cedula of March 1, 1535 designating Montejo governor of Honduras-Higueras, AGI, Guatemala 402; Juan de Ruano to the Crown, Trujillo, April 14, 1533, AGI, Guatemala 49; Cerezeda and Juan de Ruano to the Crown, Trujillo, June 14, 1533.

[5] See Herrera, 1601–15, 5-9-9 and 6-1-8; references to earlier despatches in Cabildo of Trujillo to the Crown, March 12, 1540, AGI, Guatemala 44; Francisco de Barrientos to the Crown, Trujillo, July 25, 1534, AGI, Guatemala 49.

[6] Francisco de Barrientos to the Crown, Trujillo, July 25, 1534, AGI, Guatemala 49.

[7] Cedula of March 22, 1534, AGI, Guatemala 402.

[8] See cedula designating Montejo governor of Honduras-Higueras, March 1, 1534, AGI, Guatemala, 402.

years he had gone first to the Indies with Pedrarias in 1514.[9] After serving as captain in one of the expeditions which Pedrarias sent to northern South America, Montejo went to Cuba in search of more promising fields. There he became a friend of the chief magistrate, Diego Velázquez, and was assigned Indians and haciendas on the north coast just west of La Habana. Already planning for discovery and conquest in his own right, Montejo developed his holdings to financial advantage in preparation for whatever opportunity might arise.

His first chance came in 1518. As a captain, he participated in Grijalva's expedition of 1518, which sailed beyond Yucatan to Mexico. The next year Montejo went to Mexico with Cortés as one of his captains. He was designated an alcalde of Villa Rica de la Vera Cruz when Cortés founded that first Spanish municipality in Mexico. Shortly afterward Cortés named him one of two representatives to carry to Castile the gold, silver, and other rich treasure already amassed on the coast for presentation to the King-Emperor Charles. Montejo was also to represent Cortés before the Crown. He was to work for recognition of Cortés as governor of Mexico and defend him against the charges which Velázquez, whose authority Cortés had renounced in undertaking the conquest of Mexico, brought against him before the Crown.

For several years Montejo ably served Cortés in Castile. His work led to official recognition of Cortés as governor of the Mexican lands he had conquered, now known as New Spain. Returning to the Indies, Montejo became a citizen of the new City of Mexico and received rich recompense from Cortés. In 1524 Montejo was again called to return to Castile to represent both Cortés and the municipalities of New Spain at Court.

With each step forward, Montejo's personal ambition, stimulated by Cortés' unparalleled success, rose to new heights. His knowledge of Yucatan and its Maya civilization had convinced him that the "island" of Yucatan was strategically situated across developing trade lanes and could therefore become a great commercial province. This was colonial expansion in the truest sense. Impressed by the high culture of the natives and believing that their land held much treasure and natural wealth, he regarded Yucatan as holding great promise for the independent career he had long planned.

By now Montejo had attained both considerable wealth and favor and influence at Court. Taking advantage of a propitious time while with the Court at Granada late in 1526, he successfully petitioned the Crown for authority to conquer and colonize the "Isles of Yucatan and Cozumel." This royal patent gave Montejo the high title of adelantado, which was hereditary, and the offices of governor and captain-general, which were for life.

[9] For Montejo's career outside Honduras-Higueras see Chamberlain, 1948.

THE OCCUPATION OF YUCATAN

Organizing a large and well-equipped expedition at Seville, Montejo sailed for the New World in mid-1527. After halting at Santo Domingo for final preparations, he continued to the east coast of Yucatan to begin the conquest. This initial effort proved extremely costly, and probably late in 1528 Montejo found it necessary to go to New Spain to gather reinforcements. While there he obtained authority over the colony of Tabasco, which was on the verge of disintegration. In 1529, he moved to Tabasco with new forces raised in Mexico and recalled his troops from Yucatan. After restoring Spanish control in Tabasco and saving that colony from abandonment, he renewed the conquest of Yucatan in 1530–31.

Using Tabasco as a base, Montejo occupied the west coast of Yucatan, establishing a town at Campeche. Then, in 1531 and 1532, he sent out expeditions to conquer and settle the north coast and interior. One of these expeditions was that commanded by Alonso Dávila, described in Chapter I in connection with the acting governorship of Andrés de Cerezeda. Another expedition had founded a municipality amid the ruins of the ancient Maya city of Chichen Itza.

By the summer of 1533, despite Dávila's failure in the isolated extreme southeast, Montejo and his colonists sincerely believed that the conquest of the greater part of Yucatan had been achieved and its colonization and progress were assured. Both the Crown and the Audiencia of New Spain were convinced by reports from Yucatan that Montejo had attained brilliant success. His prestige was consequently of the highest. His later appointment as governor of Honduras-Higueras and the administrative union of that province and Yucatan stemmed from his apparent success and personal aspirations. Once launched on his career as a high royal official, he evolved a tremendously ambitious personal design to gain authority over territory far wider than Yucatan.

When Montejo received his royal grant in 1526 he still believed the province to be an island with definite limits fixed by bodies of water. He found that this was not so during a voyage in 1528 into the Bahía de Chetumal. From there he sailed along the coast of the Bay of Honduras around to the area of the Río de Ulua. He was deeply impressed with the littoral and became especially interested in the rich, fertile region of the Río de Ulua. This was the beginning of his concept of a wider Yucatan. Upon return to New Spain from the east coast of Yucatan, he became convinced that the province of Tabasco, with its rivers and ports just to the southwest, was essential for the conquest and occupation of Yucatan and should be assigned to his jurisdiction.

Montejo's concept, now rapidly developing to its full proportions, was first stated to the Crown in a despatch from Vera Cruz in April 1529. He claimed that Tabasco and all territories southward and southeastward to and including Higueras and a belt of land extending across Higueras to the South Sea at the Bahía de Fonseca, with the province of San Miguel, were in actuality lands of his jurisdiction as Adelantado of Yucatan. The large province of Chiapas, south of Tabasco, he also considered territory of Yucatan. Chiapas was at this time under the authority of his former fellow captain under Cortés, Pedro de Alvarado, as part of his lands as Governor of Guatemala.

Montejo thus planned to gain authority over wide, contiguous territories and, with eventual royal approval, to weld them into a vastly expanded adelantamiento of Yucatan. Endowed by his sovereign with vested privileges and full civil and military authority, he hoped to govern this great adelantamiento as a cohesive unit. Its economic development, both internally and through commerce with other colonial areas and Castile, was an important element of the program. His design, now the object of all his thought and energy, became the motivating force of his life.

This plan was important in causing the Crown to name Montejo royal governor of Honduras-Higueras and thus influenced the history of that province. When in mid-1533 Montejo was certain that he had achieved the conquest and permanent colonization of most of Yucatan proper, he placed his claims for an expanded adelantamiento before the Crown in great detail, with special emphasis on the essential territorial unity of the province of Tabasco, the lands which lay west of the Río de Ulua and north and east of the frontiers of Guatemala, and the peninsula of Yucatan.

Dávila's recent return from Trujillo provided Montejo with added weight for his arguments with respect to the area of the Ulua. Not only did Montejo claim that region, he prepared an expedition, in anticipation of royal approval for his petitions, to establish a colony there. Furthermore, while Dávila was in Trujillo, Cerezeda's opponents had requested him to make it known to Montejo and the Crown that they desired Montejo, with the prestige he enjoyed, to become their governor by royal appointment, believing that united with Yucatan, Honduras could become strong and stable. Thus, although Montejo himself did not claim the area of Trujillo as part of his adelantamiento, but only the coastal area west of the Río de Ulua, events played into his hand as a candidate for the governorship of the entire province of Honduras-Higueras.

MONTEJO'S APPOINTMENT TO HONDURAS-HIGUERAS

Beginning late in 1533 the Crown began the series of moves which brought Montejo decisively into the course of events in Honduras-Higueras. In December of that year he was designated governor of the lands between the Río de Copilco—that is, the western limits of the province of Tabasco—and the Río de Ulua. The eastern stretches of this territory included the coastal area of Higueras. In making this grant the Crown tentatively incorporated these vast territories into the Adelantamiento of Yucatan. Montejo fully anticipated that the Crown would soon definitely confirm such an incorporation and henceforth took the unwavering legal position that these lands were, by royal action, part of his adelantamiento and that he was to govern them accordingly. One of the concomitants of this royal grant was specific authorization for Montejo to colonize the region of the Río de Ulua.[10]

Then, on March 1, 1535, in answer to the need of Honduras-Higueras for a royal governor, the Crown appointed Montejo, to hold office at the sovereign's will.[11] A few weeks later came the administrative union of Yucatan and Honduras-Higueras.[12] In giving the two provinces a common government, the Crown believed that they were in close communication, that under Montejo's authority Honduras-Higueras would derive strength from what was thought in Castile to be permanently occupied Yucatan, and that over a period of years both provinces would profit by mutual support and development.

These measures, on the surface, carried Montejo's personal design far on the road toward fulfillment, but actually his governmental position was extremely complex. The Crown had been careful to keep his appointment to the governorship of Honduras-Higueras entirely separate from the provisions of the original royal grant of authority over Yucatan. Even the union of Yucatan and Honduras-Higueras under his administration did not connote that he held the same status in Honduras-Higueras that he did in Yucatan.

In Yucatan he was hereditary adelantado and lifetime governor and captain-general by special royal patent. In Honduras-Higueras he was governor and also, with that office, captain-general, by normal royal appointment, his tenure of office entirely at the will of the sovereign. Honduras-Higueras had not been made part of Yucatan nor of Montejo's adelantamiento; it remained a separate jurisdictional area. As chief magistrate of both provinces, Montejo's position was dual. The Crown intended that he should govern Yucatan under one dispensation (the terms of his royal patent of 1526), while in Honduras-

[10] Cedulas of December 19, 1533, AGI, México 2999.
[11] Cedula of March 1, 1535, AGI, Guatemala 402.
[12] Cedulas of April 13 and April 22, 1535, and November 13, 1537, AGI, Guatemala 402.

Higueras he was to act under an entirely different one (his appointment as royal governor in 1535). Under the royal measures of 1535 he could not govern in Honduras-Higueras as adelantado, governor, and captain-general of Yucatan, and likewise he could not administer Yucatan as governor and captain-general of Honduras-Higueras. This separate status of the two provinces was emphasized by the fact that in superior judicial affairs Yucatan lay within the power of the Audiencia of New Spain, with its seat in the City of Mexico, whereas Honduras-Higueras was under the Audiencia of Santo Domingo. Montejo, of course, hoped that eventually the Crown would make Honduras-Higueras an integral part of his hereditary adelantamiento of Yucatan.

Despite the intention of the Crown to preserve Yucatan and Honduras-Higueras as separate provinces, the grant to Montejo of the governorship of the territory between the Río de Copilco and the Río de Ulua in 1533 complicated the territorial situation. This grant was not abrogated, and as a result Montejo personally considered that his status in the coastal regions of Higueras rested on a different basis than did his position in the deep interior of Higueras itself and in the eastern section of the province of Honduras-Higueras as a whole, that is, Honduras proper. As already explained, he regarded the littoral of Higueras—the coast of the territory of Honduras-Higueras west of the Río de Ulua—as already incorporated in his adelantamiento of Yucatan by action of the Crown.

These overlapping grants of authority, combined with confusion and dualism in jurisdictional limits and governmental status, arising to a great degree from Montejo's personal design and his determination to consummate it, were to complicate the history of Honduras-Higueras for almost an entire decade after 1535.

Belief that he had permanently assured Spanish control in Yucatan had motivated the Crown's appointment of Montejo as governor of Honduras-Higueras and the administrative union of the two provinces. Meanwhile the situation had undergone a complete reversal: sudden and stark disaster had befallen Montejo in Yucatan.

Not long after Montejo, in mid-1533, had in his supreme confidence in the future, sent his comprehensive claims for an expanded adelantamiento before the Crown, the Maya of the interior of Yucatan rose in determined mass revolt. The Spaniards on the coast at Campeche lost control of the land behind them; those in the city at Chichen Itza were, after a long siege, forced to withdraw to the north coast. Montejo and his captains painfully reconquered part of the lost territory and might yet have succeeded had not the colonist-soldiers deserted Yucatan in ever-increasing numbers. They had found no readily acquired riches in the province and were dissatisfied, believing that rewards in the form of encomiendas were not sufficient to justify the continued danger, toil, and hardship. By contrast, news of the wealth of Peru stimulated discontent, just as it had in Cerezeda's colony in Higueras, and most of the Spaniards in Yucatan determined to seek more profitable fields. Despite all his efforts, Montejo could not hold his men in the peninsula, and he was unable to obtain reinforcements or aid from any quarter, not even from the Audiencia of New Spain. With bitter resentment he was forced to abandon Yucatan with his remaining men late in 1534 or early in 1535, and return to New Spain.

Thus the entire set of postulations on which the Crown had acted in appointing Montejo governor of Honduras-Higueras and in uniting that province and Yucatan administratively disappeared in fact. Because of inevitable slowness in communications the Crown, when adopting these measures, had been entirely unaware of the fundamental change in Montejo's position. Nevertheless, the actions of the Crown provided a point of departure for Montejo to renew his career on its original bases when he at length recovered from his disaster in Yucatan. This career was for the next ten years to center about Honduras-Higueras, was to lead to the final conquest of that province, and was to play its part in creating the beginnings of the colony's orderly development.

4

The Intervention of Pedro de Alvarado

THE NEGOTIATIONS BETWEEN MONTEJO AND ALVARADO

MONTEJO returned to the City of Mexico in 1535 so disheartened by his failure in Yucatan that for the moment he had no thought of future plans. Time revived his ambitions, however, and he began to seek means of recouping his losses in Yucatan. He intended to return to the west coast of the peninsula, or perhaps to make a new start on the southeastern stretches of its Caribbean shores. Honduras-Higueras, for the time being, seemed remote and not a primary objective; Yucatan was first. So when his appointment to the governorship of Honduras-Higueras came, instead of being an advantage in his design to erect a greater adelantamiento, as it would have been had he succeeded in Yucatan, it meant little to him, for it would involve a change in his renewed plans.[1] His efforts in Yucatan had been costly, financially as well as spiritually. He was heavily in debt, and each successive expedition in Yucatan had left him more deeply committed than ever. He was using every means at his disposal—his holdings in New Spain and more loans—to organize his new Yucatan enterprise.[2]

Montejo was conversant with conditions in Honduras-Higueras, from both direct and indirect reports. He knew that bringing order to the province would require heavy expenditures, prolonged efforts, and rapid action to avert immediate dissolution. For the time being, he was prepared to undertake none of these things, especially in such a distant area. Therefore, shortly after receiving his cedula of appointment, he petitioned the Crown for permission to decline the governorship. He protested lack of resources for such a difficult undertaking and suggested that other officials in the Indies were in a much better position than he to take over the government of such a precariously sustained region.[3]

Late in 1535, the first Viceroy of New Spain, Antonio de Mendoza, consulted with Montejo regarding Honduras-Higueras, for he was well aware of the problem. In these conversations the two men reviewed Montejo's position, particularly his finances, and explored the political implications. The

[1] See Montejo v. Fiscal concerning removal from office in Yucatan, 1552, AGI, Escribanía de Cámara 1006A, and Chamberlain, 1948, passim.
[2] Ibid.
[3] Ibid.

tempo of the discussions was quickened upon Alonso Maldonado's return from Guatemala with the despatches from Cerezeda, García de Celís, and the other authorities of Honduras-Higueras, telling of their appeal to Alvarado for aid.[4] Since Honduras-Higueras needed assistance at the earliest possible moment and since Alvarado's resources and proximity made him the best man to give it, it was now decided that Montejo should renounce the governorship in Alvarado's favor. In return Montejo was to seek authority over Alvarado's province of Chiapas, adjacent to Tabasco, which he had claimed as part of his adelantamiento as early as 1529. Mendoza, who undoubtedly offered to facilitate negotiations for such an exchange, had become convinced that Montejo was for the time being unable to assume the financial or military burdens of the governorship of Honduras-Higueras and so suggested the next best solution to the problem.[5]

In informing Alvarado of the proposals, Mendoza emphasized the advantages which permanent occupation and stable conditions in Honduras-Higueras would bring to Guatemala and the fact that Chiapas could well serve Montejo in his revived plans for conquest and colonization of Yucatan. He also promised his good offices with the Crown in arranging such a transfer.[6] In letters to Alvarado, Montejo likewise urged the desirability of such an exchange. He also guaranteed to Alvarado that, should circumstances dictate his own eventual acceptance of the governorship of Honduras-Higueras, he would delay departing thither until Alvarado had made known his decision. In order that García de Celís might guide himself accordingly, Montejo also offered to advise that official directly of the final decision and of his conviction that Alvarado alone could save Honduras-Higueras.[7]

At the same time, Mendoza and Montejo also sent despatches to the Crown in which they reviewed the entire situation, told of their negotiations with Alvarado, and requested that Montejo be permitted to renounce the governorship of Honduras-Higueras. The viceroy, as promised, either asked the Crown itself specifically to sanction the proposed exchange of Honduras-Higueras for Chiapas, or petitioned authority for himself to approve any mutually satisfactory transfer of other territories between Montejo and Alvarado.[8] Alvarado announced to Mendoza and Montejo his willingness to make the exchange

[4] *Ibid.*; Cedulas of October 8, 1535 and May 26, 1536, AGI, Guatemala 402; Fiscal *v.* Diego García de Celís, 1537, AGI, Justicia 1035-3-1.

[5] *Ibid.*; Fiscal *v.* Diego García de Celís, 1537, AGI, Justicia 1035-3-1; Fiscal *v.* Alvarado, 1537, AGI, Justicia 1035-2-2; Montejo to Alvarado (City of Mexico, late 1535 or early 1536), DII, 14:300–01; Pedraza *v.* Montejo, 1539, AGI, Justicia 129-2; Montejo *v.* Alvarado, 1541, AGI, Justicia 134-3; Cedula of May 26, 1536, AGI, Guatemala 402; Diego García de Celís to the Crown, Isla Terceira, March 5 and April 30, 1537, AGI, Santo Domingo 168.

[6] *Ibid.*

[7] *Ibid.*

[8] *Ibid.*

and to abide by any decision which Mendoza might take, pending final action by the Crown. This Mendoza also reported to the Crown.[9]

Alvarado now regarded intervention in Honduras-Higueras differently than he had earlier. He could now consider that he had complete authority to aid that province without anticipating later claims over it from Montejo. Furthermore, Alvarado was increasingly aware of the many advantages to Guatemala from the exchange. Honduras-Higueras could contribute much more to the economic development of Guatemala than could Chiapas because the former province had a port on the North Sea and valuable mineral deposits.

Even more important from a long-range point of view was a growing conviction in both Guatemala and Honduras-Higueras that the two provinces were in reality one, and should be a jurisdictional unit under the governor of Guatemala. In Guatemala this feeling was, of course, closely related with the recognized need for a port on the North Sea; in Honduras-Higueras it sprang from a desire to survive, since Guatemala, governed by one of the most vigorous officials in the Indies, was stable and could lend strength to its weak neighbor. Advocates of this union considered Honduras-Higueras incapable of separate existence, an opinion first officially expressed by García de Celís early in 1536. It was, of course, contrary to Montejo's long-range projects and to the recently decreed unification of Yucatan and Honduras-Higueras. García de Celís, furthermore, became increasingly convinced that only Alvarado and the Guatemalan authorities could permanently sustain Honduras-Higueras, and that Montejo could never overcome the province's many difficulties, especially since his withdrawal from Yucatan. García de Celís almost certainly argued thus in his efforts to persuade Alvarado.

All these considerations induced Alvarado early in 1536 to support Higueras, and he so informed Montejo and the viceroy, although no clear-cut understanding had yet been reached regarding Chiapas.[10]

Meanwhile Montejo's request for permission to renounce the governorship of Honduras-Higueras had called forth impatient royal cedulas, ordering him to assume office notwithstanding his objections or prevailing local conditions. Cedulas instructed the viceroy to "require" (legally demand) that Montejo accept the governorship even should he persist in refusing. These royal decrees reached the City of Mexico after the passage of correspondence between the viceroy, Montejo, and Alvarado and inevitably confused matters.[11]

[9] *Ibid.*

[10] Fiscal *v.* Alvarado, 1537, AGI, Justicia 1035-2-2; Fiscal *v.* Diego García de Celís, 1537, AGI, Justicia 1035-3-1; Pedraza *v.* Montejo, 1539, AGI, Justicia 129-2; Montejo *v.* Alvarado, 1541, AGI, Justicia 134-3; Diego García de Celís to the Crown, Isla Terceira, March 5 and April 30, 1537, AGI, Santo Domingo 168. See also Alvarado to the Crown, Santiago de Guatemala, November 20, 1535, AGI, Guatemala 9.

[11] Montejo to the Crown, Gracias a Dios, June 1, 1539, DII, 24:250-97; Montejo to the Crown, Gracias a Dios, December 26, 1545, AGI, Guatemala 9; Montejo *v.* Fiscal over removal from office in

In the face of these commands, Montejo, according to his own statement, felt obliged to assume authority over Honduras-Higueras against his desire and better judgment. Moreover, his tentative understanding with Alvarado must have caused him concern. He may have protested to the Crown, and he certainly again conferred with Mendoza, still seeking release; but no alternative was found. Following royal instructions, the viceroy apparently actually "required" him to accept his now unwelcome office.[12] Mendoza and Montejo notified the Crown that Montejo would comply as soon as possible.

These developments came too late to permit notification to Alvarado before he left for Higueras. Later, the viceroy and Montejo sent him additional letters, advising that Montejo was preparing to take office in Honduras-Higueras, but they received no reply from Alvarado, who had already been in Higueras for a considerable period.[13]

There were even further complications. The Crown now altered its original decision that Montejo assume office in Honduras-Higueras, but too late to affect immediate events. This change was motivated by the despatches from Mendoza and Montejo while their negotiations with Alvarado were still in progress and was made before news of Alvarado's intervention and Montejo's final acquiescence could reach Castile. Under new instructions the Crown told Mendoza that, in case Montejo still insisted on release from the governorship after being "required" to accept it, the viceroy himself should name a substitute because of the province's urgent need. A cedula of appointment, with a blank space for the name of the man whom Mendoza would designate, accompanied these orders. Some time afterward the Crown sanctioned an exchange of territory between Alvarado and Montejo,[14] wherein the viceroy should act as mediator, with authorization to approve any transfer that he considered expedient and in the best interests of the Crown.[15] These cedulas were to be of the greatest significance to both Montejo and Alvarado several years later.

Yucatan, Escribanía de Cámara 1006A; Cedulas of October 8, 1535, and May 26, 1536, AGI, Guatemala 402; Residencia of Montejo for Honduras-Higueras, 1544, AGI, Justicia 300.

[12] *Ibid.*

[13] *Ibid.*

[14] Cedula of May 26, 1536, AGI, Guatemala 402.

[15] Cedula of May 25, 1538, AGI, Guatemala 393. The text of this important cedula follows: "La Reyna: Don antonio de mendoza nro. visorrey y governador de la nueva españa e presidente de la nra. abdiencia y chancilleria real q. en ella reside don po. de alvarado nro. adelantado governador y captain general de la provincia de guatimala nos ha hecho relacion ql. conquisto y poblo el puerto de cavallos qs. en la provincia de higueras y cabo de honduras cuya governacion como sabeis tenemos encomendada al adelantado don franco. de montejo han platicado en trucar este puerto de caballos pr. la cibdad real de los llanos de chiapa y q. tambien platicaron de trocar otras cosas de sus governaciones por q. ambos les estava bien e me ha suplicado mandase tener por bueno el dho. trueco q. entre el y el dho. adelantado montejo hiziere del dho. puerto de caballos e la dha. cibdad real de los llanos de chiapa o otra qualquier cosa q. troquen d. las dhas. dos governaciones y lo mandase confirmar y aprobar o como la mi md. fuere lo ql. visto por los del nro. consejo de las yndias. y concertado con el empr. mi sor. fue acordado q. devia mandar dar esta mi cedula pa. vos e yo tuvelo por bien por ende yo vos mando q. si los dhos. adelantado don po. de alvarado y don franco. de montejo se concertaren de trocar algun pueblo o pueblos

The chronology of the correspondence between Mendoza, Montejo, Alvarado, and the Crown is difficult to establish. Communications were perforce delayed, so that the Crown was always far behind actual developments. After Alvarado had once set out for Higueras it was almost impossible to reach him in any reasonable time.

These factors must be considered in connection with a deadly quarrel which arose between Montejo and Alvarado in 1539. Alvarado went to Higueras in the honest belief that Montejo had renounced the governorship; finding that Montejo later assumed office, Alvarado believed that he had been deliberately misled. He held Montejo guilty of subterfuge, attacked his integrity, and maintained that Montejo had gone to Honduras-Higueras with cool calculation to reap the rewards of his efforts. We have seen that Montejo had acted in good faith and was wholly sincere in accepting office, for he did so under inflexible orders from his sovereign. That these misunderstandings should have given rise to deep-seated antagonism between Montejo and Alvarado and should have led to a crisis when they at length came face to face in Honduras-Higueras was just as inevitable as it was unfortunate. This quarrel brought evil results for the province itself.[16]

Once compelled to accept the governorship of Honduras-Higueras, Montejo readjusted his thinking accordingly. Exercise of authority over the region was an important part of his long-range plans, to the fulfillment of which he could now return. Upon marshalling his resources in New Spain, he must also have concluded that he could, after all, meet the financial demands of office in Honduras-Higueras, and he undoubtedly looked to additional revenues there, for the Spaniards literally "lived off the country" both during and after conquest.[17]

Furthermore, the Crown had already ordered Alvarado's residencia for Guatemala. The same oidor Alonso Maldonado, who had earlier carried out an investigation of the government of that province, had been designated to conduct this judicial review of Alvarado's administration and assume the interim governorship. There had been complaints against Alvarado from a number of quarters, and Montejo may have believed that Alvarado's governorship in Guatemala and Chiapas was nearing its close. If such proved the case,

o otra qualquier cosa de la una governacion e la otra pareciendos ql. tal concierto estara bien a entrambos governaciones y a la conformidad de los dhos. governadores les deys licencia y facultad p. q. puedan hazer e hagan el dho. concierto y trueco y otorgar sobre ello qualesquier escripturas q. sobre ello fueren necesarias las quales confirmareis en nro. nonbre q. confirmandolas vos yo por la presente las confirmo y apruevo fha. en vallid. a XXV dias del mes de mayo de 1538 años yo la Reyna Fda. de Juan vazquez y señalado de beltran y carvajal y bernal y velazaquez."
[16] See Pedraza v. Montejo, 1539, AGI, Justicia 129-2.
[17] See Residencia of Montejo for Honduras-Higueras, 1544, AGI, Justicia 300.

it could well be to Montejo's advantage in the southward expansion of his adelantamiento.[18]

THE SITUATION IN HIGUERAS BEFORE ALVARADO'S ARRIVAL

Meanwhile conditions had deteriorated in Higueras. After the departure of García de Celís disintegration of the colony was accelerated. Cerezeda still could not impose the slightest vestige of control. No individual or group of citizens came forward to support his efforts to preserve the colony until help should arrive.[19]

When no word came from García de Celís within the two months set for his return, deepest despair fell on everyone, for he apparently could not get through any report of his successful mission and Alvarado's coming. No aid had turned up from any other quarter, as Cerezeda had seemed to hope, and the colonists saw no prospect of support.

The Indians of the region, toward whom the Spaniards had throughout shown harshness and cruelty upon every opportunity, each day became more of a menace. Encouraged by their success in compressing their enemies in an ever-decreasing area about Buena Esperanza, a number of caciques, led and inspired by the redoubtable Ciçumba, planned to overwhelm and destroy the colony. Cerezeda learned of this dangerous conspiracy and, goaded by the life-and-death emergency, he and the colonists mustered sufficient strength to forestall the attack by seizing and executing certain of the leaders, although Ciçumba escaped.

A Spanish renegade, Gonzalo Guerrero, who had been held captive by the Maya of Yucatan and who had not only chosen to remain among them but had risen to high position because of his military talents, participated in this plot. He crossed the Bay of Honduras with fifty canoes of picked warriors to aid the Indians of Higueras against his former countrymen. He had already caused great harm to Montejo and Alonso Dávila in Yucatan between 1527

---

[18] Cedula of October 27, 1535, AGI, Guatemala 393; Residencia of Alvarado, 1535–37, AGI, Justicia 295–96.

[19] Except where otherwise indicated, the account of the situation in Higueras before Alvarado's arrival, his rescue of the colony, campaigns, and plans for colonization is based on the following sources: Alvarado to the Crown, Santiago de Guatemala, November 20, 1535, AGI, Guatemala 9; Fiscal v. Diego García de Celís, 1537, AGI, Justicia 1035-3-1; Fiscal v. Alvarado, 1537, AGI, Justicia 1035-2-2; Montejo v. Pedraza, 1539, AGI, Justicia 129-2; Montejo v. Alvarado, 1541, AGI, Justicia 134-3; Residencia of Montejo for Honduras-Higueras, 1544, AGI, Justicia 300; Cerezeda to the Crown, Puerto de Caballos, August 14, 1536, AGI, Guatemala 39; Cabildo of Gracias a Dios to the Crown, December 21, 1536, AGI, Guatemala 44; Diego García de Celís to the Crown, Isla Terceira, March 5 and April 30, 1537, AGI, Santo Domingo 168; Gerónimo de San Martín, San Pedro, April 24, 1537, AGI, Guatemala 49; Pedraza to the Crown, Gracias a Dios, May 18, 1539, DII, 24:250-97; Alonso de Caceres to the Crown, Gracias a Dios, September 5, 1539, AGI, Guatemala 43; Probanzas of Gonzalo de Alvarado, 1548 and 1555, AGI, Patronato 58-4; Probanzas of Gaspar Xuárez de Avila, 1552 and 1560, AGI, Patronato 53-11; Herrera, 1601–15, 6-1-8 and 6-3-19.

and 1535. Guerrero and his warriors apparently arrived too late to join the conspiracy against Buena Esperanza, but he was to return at a crucial time.

Buena Esperanza was thus saved from sudden assault, but the basic situation failed to improve. Sentiment for abandonment of Higueras became overwhelming, now that almost everyone had given up hope for timely aid. The citizens became openly mutinous. They accused Cerezeda of "not having charity or concern with regard to the bringing in of men and teams of slaves for the mines" and declared that "many noblemen die of hunger and fall into debt, and others scrape and sow the ground with their own hands, something which has never before been seen in the Indies." They said further, "the governor . . . has caused all this, for which reason he should at once, and without delay, ride away and go off to the City of Trujillo, where he is governor, taking with him those who might want to go with him" so that the remainder could go to other provinces.[20] The cabildo of Buena Esperanza, on May 5, 1536, voted to abandon Higueras. Cerezeda, who still stubbornly opposed abandonment, perforce gave his formal but meaningless approval, as his position as nominal head of the colony required. The colonists were thereupon authorized to disperse as they saw fit, with one provision. To prevent massacre at the hands of the Indians, the colonists were to band together in groups of not less than twenty in going out. Certainly no better evidence of their utter insecurity could be found.

Cerezeda intended to return to Trujillo, which, despite its unhappy situation, survived, again potentially the only Spanish settlement in the entire province. It is significant that neither the authorities nor citizens of Buena Esperanza considered a return to Trujillo by the entire group, notwithstanding the fact that some of them had demanded such action a short time before.

The evacuation of Buena Esperanza, now a name of only bitter memories, was begun amid tumult and disorder. More helpless than ever because now very ill, Cerezeda not only was shamefully insulted by the departing Spaniards, but feared that they might kill him. He painfully fled to the pueblo of Naco, one of the few places where a Spaniard could find refuge among friendly natives. Such was the state of affairs when, on May 9, García de Celís returned to report that Alvarado was nearby with help.

ALVARADO'S CAMPAIGNS IN HIGUERAS

Once having decided to rescue Higueras, Alvarado, with characteristic vigor, set an expedition on foot. With heavy personal expenditure, he gathered eighty

---

[20] Lunardi, 1946b, p. 84.

well-armed Spaniards, horse and foot, and over 3000 Indian auxiliaries, and started from Santiago de Guatemala late in February. Alvarado's brother Gonzalo, Juan de Chávez, and Gaspar Xuárez de Avila were the principal subordinate captains. The able treasurer of Guatemala, Francisco de Castellanos, also accompanied the expedition, as did García de Celís. The large number of native auxiliaries were not only to serve in war but to be settled among the inhabitants of Higueras as allies of the Spaniards. Many were of a fierce, warlike stock known to the Spanish as the Achies, or Aches, who spread terror among other Indians. Since the expedition was designed to advance colonization, the Spaniards drove livestock with them. They also took *cuadrillas,* or teams of Indian and negro slaves, each headed by an experienced miner, to search for and exploit deposits of precious metals. These cuadrillas were owned by officials and citizens of Guatemala and San Salvador, among them Alvarado and the treasurer Castellanos.

Alvarado took a route far inland and through the region in which stood a strong, rocky eminence known to the Spaniards as the Peñol of Cerquin, which in the following months was to play a decisive role in the final conquest of Higueras. The warlike Indians of this region concentrated at this stronghold to defy the invaders. Although Alvarado would ordinarily have accepted this challenge eagerly, he knew that the rescue of Buena Esperanza was imperative and, seeing the strength of the native fortification, he passed by and pressed on toward the disintegrating settlement.

Alvarado came upon the scene at the most critical juncture. Hearing that he was near, Cerezeda immediately sent messages hailing him as the savior of the province and beseeching him to take over the administration. Alvarado's arrival immediately halted the exodus of the colonists, and many returned at once. They had literally had "their feet in the stirrups," and in only a few more days Alvarado's arrival would have been too late. Cerezeda's own words best describe the situation:

. . . the land was depopulated four days ago and everyone was mutinous. They threw me out of the town, even though I was bed-ridden because of a tumor between my legs. . . . They drove me from my house with the greatest joy in the world, despite [my infirmities]. . . . [They told me] to go off toward the sea and that they would give me men to go with me to Trujillo, so that they could carry off with them unimpeded all the Indians who served them in this region, thus to continue the [illegal enslavement] which they had begun before they expelled me from the town. To prevent them from killing me I drew strength from my very weakness and remained hidden and deserted in my house, and then went to Naco, where I received word [of your arrival]. I am returning with intolerable effort as rapidly as I can, but because of riding horseback I doubt that I shall recover my strength within three months.[21]

Alvarado accepted authority over the province. Cerezeda, García de Celís, and the cabildo of Buena Esperanza, which was again called together, installed him in office as *justicia mayor,* or chief officer of justice, and captain-general of all Honduras-Higueras, pending confirmation by the Crown or the appointment of another governor. Cerezeda continued as contador.

With his usual decision and firmness, Alvarado began to reconstitute the colony and bring about order. With the counsel of Cerezeda and García de Celís he drew up a comprehensive plan of pacification and settlement, following the farseeing projects which Cerezeda had already envisaged. Alvarado's vigorous leadership transformed the spirit of the colonists overnight. They turned from despair to confidence. Casting aside their factiousness, they rallied behind him, now determined on permanent occupation. Such a radical change of attitude proves that the ills which plagued the province for so long had resulted primarily from the absence of an able governor. The effect of Alvarado's prestige and power on the Indians was no less significant. The ruthlessness of "Toniatiuh," the Indian name for Alvarado, was well known. Many of the natives looked upon him with fear and awe, although such feelings did not hinder the more determined, especially Ciçumba, from resolve to meet the Spaniards in battle.

After consolidating control over the area about Buena Esperanza and in the Valley of Naco, Alvarado established a temporary base at the pueblo of Tencoa from which to extend his dominion. Buena Esperanza was not immediately disestablished, but continued for several years as a secondary place before giving way completely to new towns founded after Alvarado's arrival.

To further his plans of colonization, Alvarado sent his capable and trusted lieutenant, Juan de Chávez, southward into the interior at the head of forty or fifty Spaniards from among the men he had brought from Guatemala and those who had been at Buena Esperanza, with 1500–2000 native auxiliaries. He instructed Chávez to explore and conquer the rugged mountainous interior, search out an advantageous site, and there found a city. The city was intended to be the capital of the province, as its projected *ciudad,* or city, status makes clear. It was originally proposed that this place be founded on a good route of communication between Higueras and Guatemala, the establishment of which was a part of Chávez' mission.

[21] Cerezeda to Alvarado in Lunardi, 1946b, pp. 197–98.

After Chávez had set out inland, Alvarado himself went to the plains of the lower Río de Ulua, which were heavily populated with many important pueblos. He then prepared to strike directly against the fountainhead—Ciçumba—of native resistance in the whole region, knowing that if the cacique were overcome, the remainder of the coastal territory would speedily fall into Spanish hands. Ciçumba haughtily defied the renowned Toniatiuh just as he had Cerezeda, relying on the strength of a great fortress he had prepared on the banks of the Río de Ulua. Furthermore, the Spanish apostate, Gonzalo Guerrero, with chosen Maya warriors, had added strength to Ciçumba's forces. Ciçumba's confidence in his own strength was short-lived. In a brief but decisive campaign Alvarado took his great fortress by launching a daring attack from canoes. He captured Ciçumba and a large number of his lords and warriors, and dispersed the once formidable native army. Guerrero's strange and adventurous life was brought to an end in this battle by an arquebus ball. After the fight the Spaniards found him among the dead, dressed in scanty native clothing and covered with war paint in Maya style.

This important victory over Ciçumba broke the backbone of native resistance throughout the valley of the Río de Ulua, for it had indeed been Ciçumba who had "caused all the harm to the Spaniards" in that region.[22] A series of native strongholds now rapidly fell one after the other, making Alvarado soon master of the entire littoral.

Alvarado then led his forces to the district of the pueblo of Choloma, some leagues from Puerto de Caballos. There, on June 26, 1536, he founded the town of San Pedro. Thirty-five Spaniards were designated *vecinos,* or citizens, of the new municipality.[23] Alvarado assigned 200 of his own slaves to labor in the construction of the new town and in the surrounding fields. Next the Spanish leader pushed expeditions into outlying areas under his brother Gonzalo and other captains, to extend the conquest, make San Pedro militarily secure, and obtain supplies. Fixing the limits of the district to be allotted the new town, he assigned its pueblos in *repartimiento* to the citizens. In carrying out this repartimiento he declared null and void all encomienda grants previously made in the area by Cerezeda.

Meanwhile, Juan de Chávez and his men had run into serious difficulties in the mountains of southern Higueras. After a wearing march up from the Valley of Naco, through hostile territory all the way, they had come before the lofty, inaccessible, rocky, and mesa-like Peñol of Cerquin. This natural stronghold had been skillfully fortified by the Indians, who had gathered in

---

[22] Cedula of July 30, 1537, AGI, Guatemala 402.
[23] Documents regarding the founding and repartimiento of San Pedro and Gracias a Dios, 1536, AGI, Patronato 20-4-6. The documents concerning Gracias a Dios are dated July 20.

great numbers from the surrounding territory, fully set against giving way before Chávez. The Indians of this area were perhaps led by a remarkable young cacique, Lempira, later the leader in the great revolt against Montejo. Whether or not Lempira led the resistance at this time, the peñol-fortress of Cerquin commanded the whole of southern Honduras and was a most formidable obstacle for Chávez.

The Spanish captain attempted to take the place by storm but was unable even to reach its base. He then began a siege, but he was direly short of supplies, since the gathering of natives at the peñol left none to provide food for the Spaniards, who had suffered all the way up from the Valley of Naco. Now their situation was even worse. Seeing that the peñol and its region could be conquered only after prolonged effort, most of the force wished to return to Guatemala, where they had homes, encomiendas, and other holdings. They first became impatient, then almost mutinous. They declared that Chávez should "let the peñol go to the devil, since the land was no place for them, and they wanted nothing more to do with it, and that he should permit them to go with God to their homes in Guatemala." [24]

Chávez, a good and loyal captain who wished to carry out his assignment from Alvarado, at first turned a deaf ear to these protests, but after a time was forced to give heed and draw off from the peñol. He did not intend to withdraw finally or to go back to Guatemala, but rather to gather supplies and encourage his soldiers with more easily won success elsewhere before again leading them against the stronghold.

Chávez now marched eastward, through the mountains, into the Valley of Maniani, just north of the Valley of Comayagua, exploring and searching for a site at which to found his city—and meanwhile permitting the Indians around the peñol to plant their crops, so that the Spaniards could use the harvest when renewing the war against them. In connection with Chávez' advance into the Valley of Maniani, it should be remembered that Cerezeda had proposed the erection of a municipality in that region, which lay on the best route between the North and South Seas, as part of his plans for the economic development of Higueras. It seems likely that the place tentatively selected for the city was either at or near the town of Maniani itself. Chávez must have sent full reports of his plans and the course of his campaign to Alvarado, along with geographical information on the district which the city was intended to control, for Alvarado on July 20, 1536, issued from San Pedro formal instruments giving legal existence to the city, now officially designated Gracias a Dios. He appointed a cabildo, naming his brother Gonzalo as one of

[24] Pedraza to the Crown, Gracias a Dios, May 18, 1539, AGI, Guatemala 9.

the two *alcaldes ordinarios,* and commissioned Chávez his *alcalde mayor* and lieutenant governor. Almost 100 officials and soldiers were listed as citizens. At the same time he drew up new instructions for Chávez and prepared the repartimiento of the district of Gracias a Dios, abrogating, as in the case of San Pedro, any encomienda grants Cerezeda might have made therein.[25]

Alvarado proposed to reinforce Chávez and intended that a number of men still with him and his captains on the coast should be included among the citizens of the new city. He chose his brother to take these reinforcements. Gonzalo de Alvarado was then in the "Valley of Oloma, Citaguana, Ciguatepeque, Río Tinto," exploring, extending the conquest, and gathering supplies for San Pedro, which badly needed food until the season's plantings in its vicinity should ripen. With twelve or so horsemen and fourteen or fifteen footmen, accompanied by Indian auxiliaries, he had pacified a considerable area and had sent back substantial amounts of maize, beans, and other foodstuffs to San Pedro. Pedro de Alvarado now sent Gaspar Xuárez de Avila with about ten soldiers to join Gonzalo and take him the documents which gave Gracias a Dios legal existence and established the repartimiento of its district. Xuárez de Avila was designated Gonzalo's principal lieutenant for the expedition.

Formal notification of the residencia which the Crown had ordered taken of Alvarado for his governorship in Guatemala now arrived from Maldonado. He was to conduct Alvarado's residencia and to act as interim governor of Guatemala. By this time Alvarado had also received the information that Montejo had finally accepted the governorship of Honduras-Higueras and was preparing to depart from the City of Mexico to assume control. For some time Alvarado had desired to go to the Castilian Court to advance his interests, especially in connection with projects for South Sea exploration, and also to defend himself against charges concerning his official acts, which, over several years, had been presented from various sources and seriously threatened his position. The investigation of his administration of Guatemala by Maldonado and Maldonado's acting governorship there seemed to menace his future. Montejo's eventual acceptance of office in Honduras-Higueras, of which Alvarado now considered himself the savior, also roused him. He had indeed saved the colony of Higueras and strengthened the province. His belief that a large part had been thoroughly conquered and that permanent colonization had been assured in San Pedro and Gracias a Dios convinced him that his task was largely completed and his right to governorship of the entire province proved. In mid-August 1536, therefore, he sailed for Castile, accompanied

---

[25] Documents regarding the founding and repartimiento of San Pedro and Gracias a Dios, 1536, AGI, Patronato 20-4-6. See Chamberlain, 1946a and references there, and Lunardi, 1946b, for accounts of the founding of Gracias a Dios.

by García de Celís and two procuradores designated by the municipal authorities and citizens of San Pedro to represent them at Court, Francisco Cava and Nicolás López de Yrarraga.

Cava and López de Yrarraga were instructed by the colonists to make clear to the Crown the importance of Alvarado's services in Higueras and their wish that he should be governor. The two delegates were to request the sovereign to return Alvarado to Honduras-Higueras until complete stability had been established. They were also to petition the Crown to sanction a number of measures for the political and economic advancement of the province. García de Celís, too, both in his independent position as a royal treasury official and on behalf of the colonists, was to work for these objectives.

Despite sincere belief to the contrary, Alvarado actually left for Castile with his work only superficially done, as was to become clear a year later. He had subjugated a considerable area, his captains had penetrated deeply in many directions, and caciques from far-outlying regions had come to him and his subordinates to give homage when summoned with the *requerimiento,* or official summons to obedience, the issuance of which was required by law. According to legal definitions, therefore, Alvarado could claim that he had conquered a wide area. But few of his conquests were enduring, and it was only his campaigns in parts of the Valley of Naco and along the lower Río de Ulua that brought lasting results. The situation of Gracias a Dios proved nebulous, although Alvarado was not aware of that fact when he left. He still thought that Chávez was accomplishing his mission, even though he must have learned that Chávez had to withdraw from the Peñol of Cerquin. Furthermore, although Alvarado had rescued Higueras, he seems to have taken no effective steps to strengthen Trujillo, which remained in just as lamentable state as before.

Many caciques from whom Alvarado had wrung obedience by force of arms, as well as those who gave allegiance voluntarily but insincerely, were encouraged to rise in rebellion when the awe-inspiring Toniatiuh sailed away. Also, Alvarado had permitted harsh treatment of the Indians, including extensive enslavement and sale of resisting natives, and thus created deep resentment and sowed the seeds of future revolt.

Other troublesome problems were connected with the repartimientos, or assignments of native pueblos in encomienda, made by Alvarado in the districts of San Pedro and Gracias a Dios. He had prepared these partitions hastily and without adequate information regarding the numbers of inhabitants or the resources available for tribute. Place names were confused and erroneous. Alvarado, Chávez, and other captains had gathered much intelligence from direct observation and from reports of native rulers and other Indians, but it was both insufficient and inaccurate. Districts which the Spaniards had never actually entered, or at best had passed through rapidly, were included in Alvarado's partitions. The result was that names of rivers and mountains were thought to be those of pueblos, and that the same towns were assigned two or more times under different names. It appears that some encomenderos did not receive the cedulas of encomienda which the law required, and many others did not take formal possession of their encomiendas in the semifeudal ceremony demanded by law, a ceremony akin to investiture. Following the customary practice of high officers, Alvarado had taken some of the most important towns for himself. He also assigned towns to officials and colonists of Guatemala. All these factors created many complications and much dissatisfaction, especially after Montejo arrived, since encomiendas adequate to maintain the conquistador-encomenderos were important to the stability of any new province.[26]

[26] It is difficult to explain the importance of the repartimiento-encomienda system in a few words and almost impossible even roughly to define the repartimiento-encomienda as an institution in brief space. The constitutional forms, usages and customs on which this New World institution was based went far back into Castilian history where, over and above the institutions of the attenuated type of feudalism which existed in Castile, there were other unique forms and practices which grew out of the Spanish reconquest of Moorish lands in the Iberian Peninsula.

The terms repartimiento and encomienda are inseparably linked. Repartimiento in the connotation used here had two meanings: (1) the act of partition of the Indians and native pueblos of a given area among the Spaniards upon its first conquest or occupation, and (2) the Indians or pueblos assigned in encomienda during the first partition of a new region to conquistadores and *pobladores,* or first colonists who had not actually participated in military operations. The Spaniard who received a grant of Indians or a native pueblo, or pueblos, under this system was an encomendero. As the institution became formalized under royal legislation, in the technical legal sense, Indians or pueblos assigned in the first partition of an area in repartimiento in the meaning of the act of division were repartimientos. They became encomiendas upon being assigned to a second encomendero following the death of the original grantee, or loss by him of his grant for cause stipulated by law. However, in practice the term repartimiento in the sense of the Indians or pueblos assigned to encomenderos and the term encomienda were interchangeable in the earlier period.

The normal repartimiento and encomienda consisted in the right to enjoy the tributes and, until toward the mid-sixteenth century, the labor services of a designated number of Indians or of the inhabitants of a specifically named pueblo, or pueblos, which were assigned to an encomendero as a reward for his services in the conquest and colonization of the region in which his repartimiento-encomienda lay. Until about the middle of the sixteenth century, encomenderos could, entirely at their own will and whenever they wished, determine the tributes and services which their encomienda Indians were to give them. This freedom of action led to such great abuses and worked such hardships on the natives that the Crown sought to legislate the eventual abolition of the encomienda system through the celebrated New Laws of 1542–1543, but this effort raised such a storm of protest throughout the Indies that the Crown had to give up the idea of eventual elimination of the system. Nevertheless it began to impose more strict control over the institution and progressively formalized it through continuing legislation.

Among the most important of the measures to bring the encomienda within the framework of royal government, some of which were adopted even before the promulgation of the New Laws, were those which provided that Crown officials should establish fixed amounts and types of tributes for encomienda Indians and pueblos in accordance with the population, activities of the natives, and resources of the area which they inhabited, and those designed to eliminate labor service of encomienda Indians for their encomenderos. Tributes were now to be given only at specifically designated periods. Collection of tributes was henceforth carried out either by civil officers themselves, who assigned the encomenderos their return, or under strict supervision of such officers, who required the encomendero to limit collection to the amounts and types of tribute which had been fixed by official taxation.

The right to conduct repartimientos, in the sense of the act of partition, and to assign Indians in encomienda was an exclusive royal prerogative, since the natives of the New World were the direct vassals of the Crown of Castile. The sovereign delegated this prerogative to specifically designated high officials or superior agencies of colonial government, notably audiencias, who in turn could delegate such

THE FOUNDING OF GRACIAS A DIOS

Meanwhile the forces which Pedro de Alvarado had set in motion for the conquest of the interior before his departure for Castile were at work. As soon as Gonzalo de Alvarado received the documents which gave legal existence to Gracias a Dios and his brother's instructions to reinforce Chávez, he

---

power to specifically named lesser officials. Only with such authorization could Indians or pueblos be granted in repartimiento and encomienda. The organ of government or official empowered to grant repartimientos and encomiendas was obliged to issue titles, or cedulas of encomienda, to each encomendero. These titles clearly designated the Indians or pueblos which were involved in the grant. The encomendero was required to take formal possession of his repartimiento or encomienda, either in person or by proxy, in the presence of a duly authorized official. The ceremony of possession was semifeudal in nature. After the system was formalized the assignment of encomiendas was not valid until the Crown itself, through the Consejo de Indias in Castile, highest organ of royal colonial government, had approved the grant.

The normal encomienda, that is, the encomienda almost everywhere in the Indies, involved no land tenure by the encomendero. The lands of encomienda Indians and pueblos remained in possession of the Indians themselves, whether as individuals or as a corporate body. This right was carefully safeguarded by the Crown to prevent encroachment by encomenderos on the lands of the Indians. Neither did the grant of a repartimiento or encomienda legally carry with it political authority or jurisdiction over his Indians or pueblos for the encomenderos. Overlordship remained in the Crown alone.

The repartimiento-encomienda was not a perpetual grant, although a carefully regulated line of hereditary succession was established by the Crown. A grant was assigned for one, two, three and sometimes four lives after the institution was formalized, with renewal or confirmation of title by each successor a legal requirement. The Crown or other authorized officials could remove a repartimiento or encomienda from the encomendero at any time, but only for legally stipulated reasons, such as mistreatment of the natives, non-residence in the province in which the grant lay, failure to indoctrinate the Indians in Christianity, or failure to perform military service. Encomenderos throughout the Indies, both as individuals and as a class, persistently sought to have their repartimientos and encomiendas turned into perpetual semifeudal grants, carrying tenure of the land of their Indians and pueblos and political jurisdiction, but the Crown refused to permit this transformation.

In return for the grant of a repartimiento or encomienda the encomendero was legally obliged to protect, and at his own expense, to Christianize, the natives assigned to him, and he was required by law to maintain arms and a horse in readiness to take the field at a moment's notice, whether against Indians, Spaniards who might rise up in rebellion, or European enemies who might attack the colonies. Women and minors who succeeded to encomiendas were obliged to maintain an *escudero,* or man trained to arms, for military service, since they themselves could not perform such duty. In this semifeudal way the repartimiento-encomienda system provided a permanent militia throughout the Indies and was long the basis of the military system on which the overseas possessions of the Crown of Castile rested. Each city and town thus had its garrison, and periodic *alardes,* or musters and reviews, of the encomendero-militia were held. In periods immediately following conquest, when there were many hardened veterans at hand, and on restless frontiers and in other areas where the colonists had to be constantly on the alert, the encomendero-militia had excellent combat value by any standard.

In effect the repartimiento-encomienda might almost be termed a money fief, if a loose feudal parallel is desired. As finally formalized by royal law the repartimiento-encomienda was a right conferred by the Crown to enjoy the tributes of a designated number of Indians, or much more frequently, those of a specifically designated pueblo or pueblos, with obligations on the part of the encomendero: a. to Christianize the natives assigned to him, b. to protect these natives and bring them to a higher state of civilization and welfare, and c. to perform military service.

If the repartimiento-encomienda is thought of as a kind of money fief, or perhaps, in another way, as a pension, it can readily be understood why the institution was of such great importance to the conquistadores and original colonists of any given province. The repartimiento provided the conquistadores and pobladores with food and many articles which they needed for their daily lives, as well as surpluses which they could sell or trade for goods from Spain. Also, until the mid-sixteenth century, the repartimiento-encomienda system legally provided the conquistadores and colonists with labor through which they could create and develop their haciendas, other holdings, and local industries, and also natives for household service. The encomenderos to a great extent maintained themselves and their households through their encomienda Indians. Therefore the winning of repartimiento or encomienda grants was a matter of highest import to all conquistadores and pobladores, and conversely the removal of a repartimiento or encomienda was a matter of gravest financial consequences. Furthermore almost all conquistadores served in conquests at their own cost, incurring great expenditures and indebtedness, hoping to gain compensation and further rewards in the subjugated lands. The repartimiento-encomienda was a principal means of obtaining lasting recompense for arduous military services. It was also a means of providing reward to pobladores for their willingness to undergo the trials of colonization in new areas.

pushed southward into the hinterland. Including the group Xuárez de Avila brought with him, Gonzalo de Alvarado had in all about forty soldiers. Their problems were many. Men and mounts were already worn by their exertions of the past months, and the horses' shoes were almost gone. The company suffered from a shortage of food, despite all the provisions which it had been able to send to San Pedro. The way inland, rough in the best of times, was now made worse by the onset of torrential summer rains. Nowhere were the Indians friendly and the Spaniards had to try to conquer as they went. Supplies were an ever-increasing anxiety.

After three or four months of unending hardship the Spaniards arrived at the pueblo of Lepaera, in the general region where they had expected to find Chávez. There they encamped. Gonzalo de Alvarado had found no trace of Chávez during his march, nor could the Indians tell him anything. He therefore sent his lieutenant, Xuárez de Avila, forward with a detachment to search for Chávez, while he himself moved on to the pueblo of Opoa, about four leagues beyond. After a time Xuárez de Avila returned with the disconcerting news that Chávez had returned to Guatemala with all his men.

Increased pressure from his discontented men had at length made it impossible for Chávez longer to hold his company in Higueras. Much against his will, therefore, he evacuated camp and led his men and Indian auxiliaries back to Santiago de Guatemala, without having established Gracias a Dios or having besieged the peñol. He probably left just about the time Pedro de Alvarado sailed for Castile. Chávez had been unable to accomplish anything lasting. But Alvarado, for jurisdictional purposes, might claim on purely legal grounds that the nominal pacification of the area in which Chávez had temporarily operated had been achieved.

Gonzalo de Alvarado was thus left as the highest-placed Spanish official in the interior of Higueras, and upon him devolved the responsibility that otherwise would have been assumed by Chávez as Pedro de Alvarado's alcalde mayor for Gracias a Dios and its district. Despite the obstacles inherent in his situation Gonzalo de Alvarado steadfastly resolved to carry forward the work of conquest and settlement. His captains and soldiers stood solidly behind him because the apparently heavy population in the area implied an abundance of tribute and services from the Indians and the Spaniards knew that there were precious metals in the region.

Gonzalo de Alvarado resolved to establish Gracias a Dios immediately at Opoa and remain there until the rainy period was over, even though a site believed more advantageous had already been found "two leagues further down," apparently by Xuárez de Avila during his quest for Chávez. This second location was probably considered better because it was thought to lie closer to the center of the Indian population which was expected to serve the new city. Gonzalo de Alvarado then, sometime during the later months of 1536, carried through the long-delayed founding of Gracias a Dios. He named as members of the municipal council those present whom Pedro de Alvarado had designated in the documents of foundation he had drawn up before sailing for Castile and selected others to replace the officers whom Pedro had named but who had departed with Chávez. The Spaniards then began the construction of temporary buildings, aided by natives from the vicinity. Pedro de Alvarado had intended that Gracias a Dios should have about 100 citizens, in accordance with its position as a city and the prospective administrative center of the entire province. As actually founded, Gracias a Dios had about forty citizens. Since Chávez, whom Pedro de Alvarado had designated as his chief lieutenant for Gracias a Dios, was absent, leadership of the new colony temporarily fell to Gonzalo de Alvarado, even though his official rank was only that of an alcalde ordinario. Xuárez de Avila remained his principal subordinate. The Spaniards stayed at Opoa for only a short time, as they had planned, and then transferred Gracias a Dios to the more suitable site.

After the transfer Gonzalo set himself to the task of conquering its district. His forces campaigned widely, even though they numbered but forty, and penetrated to the rich Valley of Comayagua, far to the east. He then placed in effect, as far as possible, the repartimiento drafted by his brother. Gonzalo claimed conquest of "the greater part" of the district of Gracias a Dios but he had far too few men to exercise effective control of any considerable part of it.

Despite all efforts, within a short time after Pedro de Alvarado left for Castile, Honduras-Higueras began to lapse once again into conditions which approximated those existing when he arrived. Restrained by his forceful hand and prestige, few Indians dared to continue to defy the Spaniards while he was present. But with Alvarado gone, many natives passively refused to serve their encomenderos and others openly took up arms. Their hatred of the Spaniards had been stimulated by continued slave raids, the heavy burdens of the encomienda system, and the savage acts of the fierce Achies, or Aches, whom Alvarado had brought from Guatemala as auxiliaries. These Indians attacked, enslaved, and perpetrated all manner of barbarities on the natives of Higueras, who loathed and feared them. Natives deserted their pueblos in large numbers and took refuge in the mountains and dense tropical forests, hoping eventually to find some means to free their land from the invaders. A large part of the district of San Pedro and the entire district of Gracias a Dios, with the exception of a few towns, were soon "at war." The situation of the Spaniards in both places became precarious because of increasing difficulty in obtaining necessary supplies. Discouragement and discontent again became rife.

The situation of Gracias a Dios was more serious than that of San Pedro, although it was bad enough there. Famine threatened the citizens. Even Indians of the pueblos closest at hand finally refused any manner of service. Moreover, the new site of Gracias a Dios was far less advantageous than had first appeared. It was in comparatively low-lying, unhealthful terrain and not amidst the heavy concentrations of native population upon which the Spaniards had intended to rely. Many citizens, already weakened by lack of food, fell ill. A dangerous desire to abandon the region was soon manifest. The authorities of Gracias a Dios appealed to San Pedro for aid, but that town was itself in such straits that it could do nothing. They also appealed to Maldonado in Guatemala for help, but he merely replied that Montejo would soon arrive as governor and bring with him the aid which Higueras again direly needed.

Even though their immediate situation was desperate, most Spaniards of Gracias a Dios undoubtedly saw in their new surroundings much that augured well. It is not too much to suppose that they may have already seen in the region many of the favorable factors which the American diplomat Squier observed in 1855 when he wrote of it as the Department of Gracias, Republic of Honduras. After describing the majestic mountains and numerous streams, the fertile valleys and plains, the varied climate, he says:

The vegetable products, actual and possible exhaust the list of productions of the temperate zones and the tropics. Wheat, rye, barley, the potato etc., grow on the mountains, while sugar-cane, indigo, tobacco, cotton, coffee, cacao, plantains, oranges, etc., flourish in the plains and valleys. Of valuable timber there is also great abundance. Pine . . . covers the hills. There is also much mahogany, cedar, granadillo, Brazil wood, mora, etc., for purposes of dyeing, manufacture, and construction. Copal, balsam, and liquid amber are among the most common gums. . . .

Apart from its agricultural wealth, Gracias is distinguished for its minerals and precious metals. Gold and silver mines are numerous and rich, although but little worked for want of scientific knowledge, intelligence, machinery, and capital. The silver and copper mines of Coloal, in the Mountains of Merendon, are very valuable. The copper ores yielding 58% of copper, besides 98 ounces of silver to the ton. The silver ores of Sacramento yield 8674 ounces of silver to the ton. . . .

Asbestos, cinnabar, and platina are also found in this department. Opals are obtained at various localities, and have been exported to a considerable extent. The most and best have been found near the mountain town of Erandique.[27]

[27] Squier, 1855, pp. 135–36.

II

Francisco de Montejo
and the
Conquest of Higueras
1537–39

5

The Final Conquest of Higueras

MONTEJO ASSUMES THE GOVERNORSHIP OF
HONDURAS-HIGUERAS

WHILE Pedro de Alvarado was rescuing and strengthening Higueras, Francisco de Montejo, having accepted the governorship of Honduras-Higueras, was making extensive preparations in the City of Mexico for a difficult mission. Already heavily in debt, he borrowed 8000 castellanos more to finance the expedition. He gave as security his holdings and other sources of revenue in New Spain, his haciendas, silver mines, buildings, slaves, service Indians, and revenues from his encomiendas, especially the large town of Atzcapotzalco, close by the City of Mexico. He valued these assets at 25,000 castellanos. Also he sold outright part of his hacienda holdings and livestock. The Licenciado Ceynos, an oidor of the Audiencia of New Spain, seems to have helped him make these financial arrangements, and the treasurer of New Spain became his principal creditor. Some of the equipment he purchased had been the property of Pedro de Alvarado, who had extensive holdings in Mexico.[1]

Montejo announced the expedition in the City of Mexico and in Santiago de Guatemala. With the funds raised, he succeeded in recruiting and equipping a considerable number of soldiers, to some of whom he gave monetary grants, or *ayudas de costa*. He also purchased seagoing ships at Vera Cruz, probably through the agency of Juan de Lerma, a friend and financial collaborator who had been appointed a royal treasury official of Yucatan. In everything, Montejo took pains to organize an expedition which would really

[1] Montejo *v.* Fiscal over removal from office in Yucatan, 1552, AGI, Escribanía de Cámara 1006A; Montejo to the Crown, Gracias a Dios, June 1, 1539, DII, 24:250 ff.; Montejo to the Crown, Gracias a Dios, November 4, 1539, AGI, Guatemala 9; Residencia of Montejo for Honduras-Higueras, 1544, AGI, Justicia 300. In connection with financial matters in general it should be noted that under monetary legislation of 1475 and 1497 values of Spanish coinage were as follows: Silver Real, 67 maravedises (the maravedí was the basic unit); Gold Ducado (Gold Ducat) 375 maravedises and containing 4155 grams of gold; Gold Castellano, equivalent to a Peso de Oro; Silver Marco (Silver Mark); containing half a pound of silver; Gold Marco (Gold Mark) 65.333 Gold Ducados and 59 Pesos de Oro or Gold Castellanos and containing 230.045 grams of gold. In the sixteenth century value of Spanish coins came to be as follows (from Diffie, 1945, p. 106, n. 7): Castellano, 480 to 490 maravedises (4.4433 grams of gold of 23¾ carats fineness); Ducat remained 375 maravedises (3.1485 grams of gold of 23¾ carats fineness); Real of silver 34 maravedises (67/72 carats fineness); the Gold Mark continued to contain 230 grams of gold; the Peso de Minas valued 450 maravedises (4.18 grams of gold of 22 carats fineness); Peso de Oro de Tepuzque was worth 272 maravedises; the Peso de Oro Corriente valued 300 maravedises; the Peso de Oro con 3 quilatos anadido was worth 360 maravedises; the Peso de Oro de ley Perfecta was worth 450 maravedises; the Peso de Oro de Minas valued at 450 maravedises; the silver real was worth 34 maravedises (67/72 carats fineness); the silver Peso Fuerte valued 272 maravedises, or 8 reales, and contained 25.563 grams of silver; a silver Mark was worth 5 pesos de oro or 450 maravedises.

accomplish his mission, the establishment of permanent order in Honduras-Higueras.[2]

Montejo wanted to go to his new province as soon as possible, for he had undoubtedly heard from Maldonado in Guatemala that all was not well in Higueras after Alvarado's departure and justly feared that the colony would lapse into anarchy before his arrival. Since his own departure depended on the full organization of the expedition, which necessarily took time, Montejo appointed Alonso de Cáceres, a very capable officer who had served under him in Yucatan, his lieutenant governor and captain-general for Honduras-Higueras. Cáceres was sent ahead with a small party and was given instructions to go to Honduras-Higueras overland, by way of Santiago de Guatemala, where he was to recruit additional soldiers. Montejo expected Maldonado to help and had probably already made such arrangements.[3]

On reaching Santiago de Guatemala, with the aid of Maldonado and other officials, Cáceres raised some twenty more horsemen and procured additional materials of war. He then proceeded to Higueras and arrived at Gracias a Dios in late November or early December 1536, soon after Gonzalo de Alvarado had established the city.[4] Montejo's lieutenant found Gracias a Dios already "the most deplorable thing in the world." The soldiers, arms, and supplies which he brought, however, gave temporary relief, and the assurance that Montejo would soon arrive with a large expedition gave promise for the future.[5]

Politically, though, the appearance of Cáceres led to immediate dissension. Alvarado's partisans did not wish to receive him as chief magistrate or to recognize Montejo as governor. Authorities and colonists alike were almost unanimous in their desire to have Alvarado's governorship continued and their province and Guatemala united. They feared that another governor would both jeopardize the existence of the province and adversely affect their own personal interests.[6] Therefore when Cáceres appeared before the cabildo of Gracias a Dios to receive acknowledgment of his and Montejo's duly appointed positions, the municipal officials, under the control of Gonzalo de Alvarado, refused to recognize Cáceres' authority. The cabildo, however, was very careful not to take a stand that could be construed as disobedience of a

[2] Ibid.
[3] Residencia of Montejo for Honduras-Higueras, 1544, AGI, Justicia 300; Montejo to the Crown, Gracias a Dios, June 1, 1539, DII, 24:250 ff.; Alonso de Cáceres to the Crown, Gracias a Dios, September 4, 1539, AGI, Guatemala 43.
[4] Ibid.
[5] Ibid.; Cabildo of Gracias a Dios to the Crown, December 21, 1536, AGI, Guatemala 44.
[6] Residencia of Montejo for Honduras-Higueras, 1544, AGI, Guatemala 300; Cabildo of Gracias a Dios to the Crown, December 21, 1536, AGI, Guatemala 43; Gerónimo de San Martín to the Crown, San Pedro, April 24, 1537, AGI, Guatemala 49. Fiscal v. Diego García de Celís, 1537, AGI, Justicia 1035-3-1; Pedraza to the Crown, Gracias a Dios, May 18, 1539, AGI, Guatemala 9.

royal cedula or rejection of Montejo as governor by royal appointment. Rather, it based its action on the highly legalistic grounds that the cedula designating Montejo governor made no specific provision for recognition of any lieutenant whom Montejo might appoint in his absence, and included no definitely stated alternative to acknowledgment of Montejo in person. The municipal council seized on these omissions and interpreted Montejo's cedula of appointment to mean that he would have to present himself personally to be acknowledged governor and that the cabildo could not accept any lieutenant designated by him before his arrival. Some members of the cabildo held further that, since Gracias a Dios had been founded under Pedro de Alvarado's authority, it would be impossible to receive the representative of any other official whatso-ever before Montejo himself appeared with his royal appointment, unless in the interim the Crown should specifically order otherwise. Furthermore, the cabildo maintained that Montejo's cedula of appointment had not authorized the presentation of a copy of the original document and that the original alone was valid.[7]

At the same time, the municipal council declared itself fully prepared to receive Montejo as governor when he should finally appear in person. Fur-thermore, they suggested a compromise by which they and their colleagues of San Pedro might elect Cáceres captain and justicia mayor of the province to carry forward the conquest until Montejo arrived. Thus Cáceres' authority would derive from the local cabildos rather than from Montejo. Cáceres forthrightly demanded that he be received solely on the basis of Montejo's authority over the province, but the cabildo remained adamant.[8] With only some twenty men at his command, Cáceres was for the moment helpless before Alvarado's numerous followers. Nevertheless, he did not yield one iota. Ra-ther, he decided to bide his time and plan for the future, meanwhile requesting and receiving permission to remain in Gracias a Dios until Montejo came.[9]

A period of intrigue now began. The cabildo, without authority and quite contrary to its legalistic stand against Cáceres, secretly despatched letters to Maldonado, as acting governor of Guatemala. They requested him, as an interim measure, to send a lieutenant to Gracias a Dios to govern the city and its district as captain-general and justicia mayor. The regidor Xuárez de Avila was the only member of the council who dissented. This move, of course, was designed to keep Honduras-Higueras administratively joined with Guatemala, with Pedro de Alvarado as governor. But it went much further than that, for the cabildo maintained that the area of Gracias a Dios was

---

[7] Residencia of Montejo for Honduras-Higueras, 1544, AGI, Justicia 300.
[8] Ibid.
[9] Ibid.

geographically part of Guatemala and suggested that it be detached from Honduras-Higueras and made Guatemalan territory. At the same time, to safeguard its legal position, the cabildo requested Maldonado to impress upon Montejo the need for personally assuming the governorship of Honduras-Higueras as soon as possible and also forwarded a despatch for Montejo himself, urging haste. Maldonado declined to act on either point because such matters did not pertain to his jurisdiction, which indeed was true. He informed the cabildo, further, that Montejo had already set out for Honduras-Higueras.[10] Besides the despatches to Maldonado and Montejo, the cabildo sent letters to the Crown, recommending that Pedro de Alvarado be authorized to remain governor of Honduras-Higueras and advocating the union of that province and Guatemala.[11]

On December 30, 1536, the cabildo, again on dubious legal premises, elected Juan López de Gamboa, one of the regidores, justicia mayor of the district of Gracias a Dios. Gonzalo de Alvarado and a number of colonists disapproved of this new measure for reasons which are not entirely clear. After the voting of January 1, 1537, López de Gamboa renounced his post, declaring that he had taken it only to supervise the annual election and installation of municipal officers. There can be no doubt that this move was designed to assure control of the cabildo by strong partisans of Pedro de Alvarado and by staunch advocates of the union of Honduras-Higueras and Guatemala, and to set up a counterpoise to Cáceres and Montejo and their possible following.[12]

Even though Gonzalo de Alvarado was founder of Gracias a Dios, brother of the great conquistador, and virtual head of the colony, he was not elected to superior office January 1, 1537. He was, however, chosen to be a regidor. The failure to elevate Gonzalo seems to have rested on a deeper cause than the principle of rotation of office, customarily observed. Besides his disapproval of the political ruse involving López de Gamboa, he appears to have fallen at cross-purposes with certain of his fellow officials and therefore to have been fully prepared to step down as titular leader of the colony.[13]

Meanwhile, Cáceres, who considered himself the legitimate administrative and military head of Honduras-Higueras until Montejo's arrival, was by no means a passive observer. Primarily a man of action, he was carefully and quietly preparing a coup. He withdrew his forces to a native pueblo a short distance from Gracias a Dios, whence he maintained contact with friends and potential supporters in the city itself and kept abreast of developments. He

10 *Ibid.;* Gerónimo de San Martín to the Crown, San Pedro, April 24, 1537, AGI, Guatemala 49.
11 Cabildo of Gracias a Dios to the Crown, December 21, 1536, AGI, Guatemala 44.
12 Residencia of Montejo for Honduras-Higueras, 1544, AGI, Justicia 300.
13 *Ibid.*

conducted a constant campaign to win adherents and succeeded with the influential Xuárez de Avila, who had come to look upon the cabildo's maneuvers against Cáceres and Montejo with disfavor and had withdrawn from the cabildo. Xuárez de Avila now collaborated with Cáceres and actively sought to gain partisans for him, or at least to assure passivity among enough citizens to facilitate Cáceres' plans. Working together, they made progress little by little. Both counted on disorientation among the citizens in face of Montejo's forthcoming arrival and the general insecurity of the province to work in their favor, and they were not mistaken.[14] Cáceres deemed the time ripe for action early in 1537. Moving at night with his twenty well-armed men, he came down suddenly on Gracias a Dios at daybreak, seized the members of the cabildo, including Gonzalo de Alvarado, and threw them into the city's jail. He met no real opposition from the citizens, and was soon in undisputed possession.[15]

Cáceres then declared inoperative the authority of the cabildo, designated himself lieutenant governor and captain-general of Honduras-Higueras in the name of Montejo, and proclaimed the royal cedula naming Montejo governor of the province. To replace the hostile cabildo now overthrown, he appointed officials who were certain to recognize his and Montejo's authority, among them Xuárez de Avila. Cáceres' audacity thus thoroughly intimidated Pedro de Alvarado's partisans, and gave him undisputed mastery in Gracias a Dios. And so it was by violence that Montejo's authority was first made effective in Honduras-Higueras, quite in keeping with the past history of the province.[16]

It is not clear whether the authorities of San Pedro immediately acknowledged Cáceres and, through him, Montejo, but it seems likely that they did, even though in sentiment strongly opposed to Montejo as governor. Alvaro de Sandoval, an alcalde of that town, sent a report of developments to Pedro de Alvarado, protesting Cáceres' high-handed procedure and requested Alvarado to petition the Crown for a judge to take remedial action.[17]

Finally established as lieutenant governor, Cáceres found many serious problems. The Spaniards of San Pedro and Gracias a Dios still effectively controlled only small areas about their towns, basic shortage of supplies continued, and discouragement prevailed. The dissension at Gracias a Dios, which had

[14] Ibid.
[15] Ibid.; Fiscal v. Alvarado, 1537, AGI, Justicia 1035-2-2; Alonso de Cáceres to the Crown, Gracias a Dios, September 5, 1539, AGI, Guatemala 43; Pedraza to the Crown, Gracias a Dios, May 18, 1539, AGI, Guatemala 9; Gerónimo de San Martín to the Crown, San Pedro, April 24, 1537, AGI, Guatemala 49.
[16] Ibid.
[17] Fiscal v. Alvarado, 1537, AGI, Justicia 1035-2-2.

culminated in Cáceres' forcible seizure of the government, had not escaped notice by the Indians and further encouraged their defiance.[18]

Increasing hostility among the natives called for vigorous military action. Not deterred by the small numbers of soldiers available, Cáceres decided on a series of campaigns. Naming Xuárez de Avila his lieutenant in Gracias a Dios, he led a company to the conquest of a nearby mountainous district known to the Spaniards as the province of Cares, in the area of the Peñol of Cerquin. In spite of stiff resistance and a rugged terrain, he met with some success. He moved on far eastward into the Valley of Comayagua and soon brought an extensive section of that rich district under at least nominal control.[19]

Meanwhile, in the City of Mexico, Montejo had completed his preparations. He went overland, as Cáceres had done, taking with him the majority of his soldiers, supplies, and livestock. A smaller number of his men sailed from Vera Cruz, accompanied by Montejo's wife, Doña Beatriz de Herrera, his young daughter Catalina, and his household, with whom he sent additional equipment and supplies. He led his soldiers and native auxiliaries from his great encomienda of Atzcapotzalco to Santiago de Guatemala, arriving early in 1537. He may have recruited more men at Spanish centers along his route.[20]

In Guatemala, Montejo received full co-operation from Maldonado, from whom he secured a further loan of 1500 castellanos, and from other sources got funds which raised the total to 2000 pesos de oro. With this sum and Maldonado's collaboration, he obtained additional soldiers and more stores and war materials. Among the munitions were crossbows, arquebuses, and powder which he bought from a majordomo of Pedro de Alvarado. He also procured extra oxen, sheep, and swine, both for food and for breeding in Honduras-Higueras. Montejo's company now numbered 80–100 Spaniards, including veterans of his campaigns in Yucatan.[21]

After this satisfactory period of recruiting, Montejo arrived at Gracias a Dios

[18] Residencia of Montejo for Honduras-Higueras, 1544, AGI, Justicia 300; Cabildo of Gracias a Dios to the Crown, December 21, 1536, AGI, Guatemala 44; Fiscal v. Alvarado, 1537, AGI, Justicia 1035-2-2; Gerónimo de San Martín to the Crown, San Pedro, April 24, 1537, AGI, Guatemala 49; Pedraza to the Crown, May 18, 1539, AGI, Guatemala 9; Montejo to the Crown, Gracias a Dios, June 1, 1539, DII, 24:250–97; Alonso de Cáceres to the Crown, Gracias a Dios, September 5, 1539, AGI, Guatemala 43; Pedraza v. Montejo, 1539, AGI, Justicia 129-2; Probanzas of Gonzalo de Alvarado, 1548 and 1555, AGI, Patronato 58-4; Probanzas of Gaspar Xuárez de Avila, 1552 and 1560, AGI, Patronato 63-11.
[19] Ibid.
[20] Montejo to the Crown, Gracias a Dios, June 1, 1539, DII, 24:250 ff.; Montejo to the Crown, Gracias a Dios, November 4 and December 15, 1539, AGI, Guatemala 9; Residencia of Montejo for Honduras-Higueras, 1544, AGI, Justicia 300; Montejo v. Fiscal over removal from office in Yucatan, 1552, AGI, Escribanía de Cámara 1006A.
[21] Montejo to the Crown, June 1, 1539, DII, 24:250–97; Montejo to the Crown, Naco, July 28, 1537, AGI, Guatemala 9; DII, 24:250 ff.; Probanza of Juan Martínez de Larraude, 1571, AGI, Guatemala 173; Probanza of Juan Martínez de Larraude, 1572, AGI, Patronato 72-2; Pedraza to the Crown, Gracias a Dios, May 18, 1539, AGI, Guatemala 9; Residencia of Montejo for Honduras-Higueras, 1544, AGI, Justicia 300.

toward the close of March, bringing sorely needed help for the whole province.[22] Meanwhile Montejo's wife and the smaller company of soldiers had
proceeded by sea. When they were at Vera Cruz, Montejo's financial collaborator, Juan de Lerma, arrived at that port, helped procure further soldiers and
supplies, and may have assumed general direction of the sea phase of Montejo's
expedition. Doña Beatriz and Lerma then apparently changed the original
plan for a direct voyage to Honduras-Higueras and sailed to la Habana where
supplies were transhipped, perhaps to a vessel owned by Lerma. He apparently
remained behind there but was soon to proceed to Honduras-Higueras, for
he had been appointed *factor,* or business manager, of united Yucatan and
Honduras-Higueras by the Crown.[23] Although not clear precisely when, it
seems that shortly after the voyage was resumed, somewhere off western Cuba
Doña Beatriz and her company ran afoul of corsairs, probably French. Everyone aboard was forced to take refuge inland. A considerable part of the stores
and most of Montejo's family property were lost, but there was little or no
loss of life and the ship itself was somehow saved. But it was a costly and
disconcerting experience nonetheless. When danger had passed, Doña Beatriz
resumed the voyage with the salvage and in the spring of 1537 reached Puerto
de Caballos, where Montejo, now recovered from a recent illness, met her and
the reinforcements.[24]

Cáceres was still engaged in the pacification of the Valley of Comayagua
when Montejo reached Gracias a Dios, and Xuárez de Avila was governing
the city with the support of the cabildo which Cáceres had appointed following
his *coup de main.* The considerable force Montejo brought with him, combined with those whom Cáceres had led to the province and the reinforcements accompanying Doña Beatriz, placed Montejo in a strong position, as
military leader and as governor.[25]

On March 24, 1537, Montejo appeared before the cabildo of Gracias a Dios
and the royal treasury officials at that city, presented his royal appointment
as governor, and was installed in office without open challenge. Seeing nothing to fear from the former members of the cabildo whom Cáceres had imprisoned and hoping to conciliate them, Montejo now not only released the
prisoners but actively sought their collaboration. Gonzalo de Alvarado was
among those who accepted Montejo's proffered friendship.[26] Montejo next

[22] Montejo to the Crown, Gracias a Dios, June 1, 1539, DII, 24:250–97; Montejo to the Crown, Naco, July 28, 1537, AGI, Guatemala 9; Residencia of Montejo for Honduras-Higueras, 1544, AGI, Justicia 300.
[23] Montejo to the Crown, Gracias a Dios, June 1, 1539, DII, 24:250–97; Juan de Lerma to the Crown, Puerto de Caballos, June 1, 1537, AGI, Guatemala 52; Montejo *v.* Fiscal over removal from office in Yucatan, 1552, AGI, Escribanía de Cámara 1006A.
[24] Montejo to the Crown, Gracias a Dios, June 1, 1539, DII, 24:250–97.
[25] Residencia of Montejo for Honduras-Higueras, 1544, AGI, Justicia 300; Fiscal *v.* Diego García de Celís, 1537, AGI, Justicia 1035-3-1; Probanza of Gonzalo de Alvarado, 1546, AGI, Guatemala 110.
[26] Residencia of Montejo for Honduras-Higueras, 1544, AGI, Justicia 300.

undertook to complete the conquest and develop the province. There was much to do, even in the immediate area of Gracias a Dios, despite Cáceres' campaigns. Many natives throughout the province remained dangerously restive, others were still dispersed, and the savage Achies continued to terrorize more peaceful groups of Indians everywhere, especially the Chontales of the coastal area of Sula. Shortage of supplies persisted and the encomienda system remained disrupted.[27]

On the one hand, Montejo prepared for war on the Indians wherever necessary while, on the other, he planned to apply policies of moderation and fair treatment to win them over peaceably wherever possible. He also urged his subordinates to conciliate the natives and to avoid ill-treatment, abuses, and violations of law, notably in connection with encomiendas, mining, and labor service. A considerable number of the ruthless Achie auxiliaries were soon sent back to Guatemala to relieve the natives of Higueras from cruelty and depredations.[28] Montejo achieved encouraging initial success in the peaceful phase of his efforts around Gracias a Dios. Natives in considerable numbers came back to their pueblos, resumed their normal pursuits, and accepted Spanish control. The encomienda system now functioned much more effectively than ever before and the hitherto serious problem of supplies was largely solved.[29]

After establishing sufficient stability in the area of Gracias a Dios, Montejo despatched reinforcements to Cáceres in the Valley of Comayagua. With their aid, by the late spring or early summer of 1537, Cáceres completed what was then considered the definite conquest of that rich and fertile region. Then, at a location promising great commercial development about midway between the North and South Seas, he founded a town, which he named Santa María de Comayagua. He next began assignment of the pueblos of the district to the citizens in encomienda.[30]

Not long after his arrival Montejo also took the field to pacify restless districts close to the northern coast, leaving Xuárez de Avila his lieutenant in Gracias a Dios. He first moved to San Pedro, where, on April 16, he officially obtained recognition of his authority by the cabildo and the royal treasury officers who resided in that town. Montejo regarded the coastal area of Higueras as incorporated into his Adelantamiento of Yucatan under his Río de Copilco–Río de Ulua grant. He therefore presented the royal cedula of

---

[27] *Ibid.;* Pedraza *v.* Montejo, 1539, AGI, Justicia 129-2; Montejo to the Crown, Naco, July 28, 1537, AGI, Guatemala 9; Montejo to the Crown, Gracias a Dios, June 1, 1539, DII, 24:250–97; Pedraza to the Crown, May 18, 1539, AGI, Guatemala 9.

[28] *Ibid.*

[29] *Ibid.*

[30] *Ibid.;* Alonso de Cáceres to the Crown, Gracias a Dios, September 5, 1539, AGI, Guatemala 43; Probanza of Alonso de Cáceres (drawn up by Cáceres' widow) 1560, AGI, Patronato 63-22.

December 19, 1533, which conferred that grant, in the convocation of the cabildo and royal treasury officials of San Pedro when appearing before them to be recognized as chief magistrate of the region.[31] He obtained recognition on the basis of this cedula rather than by his appointment as governor of Honduras-Higueras so that his authority in the area of San Pedro, Puerto de Caballos, and the Valley of Naco—the region of the Río de Ulua—would from the first rest on his appointment as governor of the territory between the Copilco and the Ulua. His position in the interior of Higueras, including Gracias a Dios, in contrast, rested on his appointment by the Crown as governor of Honduras-Higueras.[32]

The municipal authorities and royal treasury officials well understood Montejo's motives and knew that if the cedula of December 19, 1533, was made fully effective it would detach San Pedro and its district from Higueras. They considered this district with the mines in the Valley of Naco and the fertile Ulua valley as the most important part of the province and so did not accept Montejo on this basis without deliberation. However, they decided that the cedula of 1533 admitted no valid grounds for refusal and Montejo consequently won his point. Notwithstanding, it was a considerable time before the royal treasury officials of San Pedro consented to pay Montejo an annual *ayuda de costa,* or stipend, of 150,000 maravedises which the governorship of the territory between the Copilco and the Ulua carried with it.[33]

On April 17, the day after the recognition of his authority at San Pedro, Montejo declared null and void the repartimientos which Pedro de Alvarado had established for the districts of Gracias a Dios and San Pedro. Thereupon, with the advice of his subordinates and legal counsel, he began to partition the province anew, giving preference to his own soldiers and followers.

The adelantado next turned to military affairs. Dividing his forces, he sent a trusted captain, Alonso de Reinoso, and about 100 soldiers into the mountainous districts of San Pedro while he himself moved into the Valley of Naco, where Andrés de Cerezeda and Pedro de Alvarado had left large numbers of natives dispersed and hostile and many formerly large pueblos greatly depleted in population.[34] Montejo speedily brought the Valley of Naco under control

[31] Residencia of Montejo for Honduras-Higueras, 1544, AGI, Justicia 300.

[32] *Ibid.;* Montejo to the Crown, Naco, July 28, 1537, AGI, Guatemala 9; Montejo to the Crown, Gracias a Dios, June 1, 1539, DII, 24:250-97; Montejo to the Crown, Gracias a Dios, December 26, 1545, AGI, Patronato 184-25; Gerónimo de San Martín to the Crown, San Pedro, April 24, 1537, AGI, Guatemala 49; Treasury accounts of Diego García de Celís, 1540, AGI, Indiferente General 1206.

[33] *Ibid.*

[34] Montejo to the Crown, Naco, June 28, 1537, AGI, Guatemala 9; Montejo to the Crown, Gracias a Dios, June ,1, 1539, DII, 24:250-97; Juan de Lerma to the Crown, Puerto de Caballos, June 1, 1537, AGI, Guatemala 52; Probanza of Alonso de Reinoso, 1542, AGI, Patronato 56-3-3; Probanzas of Gaspar Xuárez de Avila, 1552 and 1560, AGI, Patronato 63-11; Probanza of Rodrigo Alvarez, 1575, AGI, Mexico 900; Pedraza *v.* Montejo, 1539, AGI, Justicia 129-2; Residencia of Montejo for Honduras-Higueras, 1544, AGI, Justicia 300.

and Reinoso met with equal success. Compelled by force of arms, or as a matter of momentary expediency, many caciques came to Montejo and his captains to give homage, just as they had come to Alvarado shortly before. Even certain Maya rulers from southern Yucatan made their way to Higueras at this time to seek out Montejo, offer him allegiance, and beseech him to safeguard the lucrative trade which had for such a long time existed between Yucatan and the region of the Ulua. Montejo gladly accepted these new allies and promised to accede to their requests regarding commerce. With these developments he considered that a wide region along the coast had at last been effectively pacified.[35]

Montejo applied toward the natives of the coastal area the same conciliatory policies which had brought good results in the region of Gracias a Dios. Again he was successful to a considerable degree. Many dispersed Indians returned and resumed their lives within the framework of the encomienda system.[36]

While Montejo was in the Valley of Naco the Spaniards carried on an intensive search for gold and discovered deposits in addition to those already known.[37]

Montejo now returned to Gracias a Dios and prepared to extend military operations into still restive outlying areas. Shortly thereafter Cáceres returned from the Valley of Comayagua to confer upon administrative and military matters, obtain reinforcements to pursue the conquest in the distant eastern section of the province, and assure the permanence of the town of Santa María de Comayagua. Montejo fully supported Cáceres and urged him to use the same policy toward the Indians which had been successfully applied in the districts of Gracias a Dios and San Pedro.[38] Cáceres returned to Santa María de Comayagua, which with the reinforcements from Montejo now had some thirty citizens. He then pushed eastward and began the conquest of territories lying toward the Valley of Olancho.[39]

By the midsummer or early autumn of 1537 Montejo had achieved what he considered lasting subjugation of the province with a minimum of force and with little loss of life to Spaniards or Indians. So light had been his campaigns and so moderate his policies that he was able to say that not fifty Indians had been killed and not 100 enslaved. Much had also been done to bring hostile and dispersed natives back to their normal lives. Gracias a Dios and San Pedro had been strengthened, and, as Montejo saw it, Higueras had been

[35] *Ibid.*
[36] *Ibid.*
[37] *Ibid.*
[38] Montejo to the Crown, Naco, July 28, 1537, AGI, Guatemala 9; Montejo to the Crown, Gracias a Dios, June 1, 1539, DII, 24:250–97; Pedraza to the Crown, Gracias a Dios, May 18, 1539, AGI, Guatemala 9.
[39] *Ibid.*

stabilized throughout. He thought that elimination of remaining centers of resistance and conquest of distant frontiers would not be difficult, and that the warlike part of his task as governor was virtually completed. Confident and well pleased with his work, he now laid farseeing plans for the economic and political development of Honduras-Higueras.[40]

THE GREAT INDIAN REVOLT, 1537–39

Lempira and the Peñol of Cerquin

In being convinced of the pacification of Higueras, Montejo fell into the same error made by Alvarado when he sailed for Castile in mid-1536. Actually, only in limited areas about San Pedro and Gracias a Dios had Montejo's and Cáceres' military efforts been at all thorough. Liberty-loving and high-spirited, the majority of the Indians of Higueras were determined not to accept Spanish domination without resisting the outsiders to the utmost. Many natives were outstandingly warlike, those of the sierras south of Gracias a Dios supremely so. Even from the first the Spaniards could find few native allies in Higueras of whom they could be certain, quite in contrast to the case in many other provinces. Warfare and all it connoted had aroused bitter hatred among the Indians; the encomienda system was intolerable regardless of Montejo's moderation and conciliatory policies. Alvarado and his captains, too, had left their mark of hatred among the Indians. Under such circumstances a fierce renewal of war was inevitable, especially since the Indians by no means felt themselves conquered.[41]

A rude warning of what could be expected soon came. Three Spaniards who had been with Cáceres were set on and killed while passing through a hitherto tranquil region south of Gracias a Dios, not far from the Peñol of Cerquin. This event shook Montejo as he remembered similar happenings in Yucatan and feared that this bloody act might herald a general rising. He decided not merely to punish the natives involved but to take widespread measures to forestall a possible revolt.[42] With a strong company he hastened to the scene and summoned the caciques of the region before him. All but one of the overawed native rulers came, and after an investigation Montejo dealt out

[40] Montejo to the Crown, Naco, July 28, 1537, AGI, Guatemala 9; Montejo to the Cabildo of Santiago de Guatemala, Gracias a Dios, December 11, 1537, AGG, Papers from the Archivo Municipal, Cartas de Personas Ylustres; Residencia de Montejo for Honduras-Higueras 1544, AGI, Justicia 300.

[41] Montejo to the Crown, Gracias a Dios, June 1, 1539, DII, 24:250–97; Pedraza to the Crown, Gracias a Dios, May 18, 1539, AGI, Guatemala 9; Fiscal v. Alvarado, 1537, AGI, Justicia 1035-3-1; Pedraza v. Montejo, 1539, AGI, Justicia 129-2; Residencia of Montejo for Honduras-Higueras, 1544, AGI, Justicia 300.

[42] Montejo to the Crown, Gracias a Dios, June 1, 1539; DII, 24:252–53; Pedraza to the Crown, Gracias a Dios, May 18, 1539, AGI, Guatemala 9; Agent of Montejo to the Cabildo of Santiago de Guatemala, Asiento de Sula, September 27, 1537, AGG, Papers from the Archivo Municipal, Cartas antiguas de Particulares; Probanzas of Gaspar Xuárez de Avila, 1552 and 1560, AGI, Patronato 63-11.

exemplary punishment to those found most guilty. He followed this summary
action by a conciliatory policy toward the other native lords and their people,
seeking to win them over. The caciques promised loyalty and Montejo permitted them to return to their pueblos. He next moved into the Valley of
Comayagua to further its security and continue the assignment of encomiendas
begun by Cáceres. Then he returned to Gracias a Dios.[43]

Although now on the alert, Montejo did not yet know how fully justified
were his fears of revolt. A powerful Indian coalition had quietly been formed
in the rugged southern sierras of the district of Gracias a Dios, to exterminate
or expel the Spaniards. This alliance had its political center in the town of
Entepica, and its most formidable military stronghold in the Peñol of Cerquin.[44] The leader of the resistance movement was the young, capable, and
courageous cacique whom the Spaniards knew as Lempira, or "Lord of the
Mountain." He had already displayed great political and military ability in
intertribal rivalries, and was chosen leader by many native groups, including
the Cares, whose land was close to the Peñol of Cerquin. Although this tribe
had originally been Lempira's enemies, after he had overcome them they loyally
accepted him as overlord. Political skill and warfare had brought still other
native provinces under his control. His territories expanded over a large part
of southern Higueras and into the region of San Miguel. The Spaniards believed that he had become the overlord of about 200 towns and that he could
marshal a host of 30,000 warriors. His vassals held him to be invincible.[45]

The Spaniards had frequently moved through sections of Lempira's domains
and had, so they erroneously thought, subjugated parts of them, especially
the province of the Cares. When they came to central Higueras determined
to stay, Lempira laid deep plans to drive them out. He exhorted his own
people and Indians everywhere to defend their lands, declaring that it was
"shameful that so many valiant men should be held in bondage by so few."
Claiming invincibility, he organized his territory into a well-knit unit, extended
his alliances with other groups, and prepared for the great test of strength.

Lempira and his allies planned with amazing thoroughness, foresight, and
secrecy. Their first step was to be an uprising restricted to Lempira's domains
close around the stronghold of the Peñol of Cerquin. If this was successful,
Indians throughout Higueras and adjoining areas would rally to destroy or
expel their enemies. Lempira and his chieftains guarded their plans so carefully that the Spaniards, even though quite watchful since the killing of their

[43] *Ibid.*
[44] See Herrera, 1601–15, 6-3-19.
[45] *Ibid.*

three countrymen near Gracias a Dios, were not aware of the well-organized opposition.[46]

Thus, confident in his strength, Lempira contemptuously ignored Montejo's legal requerimientos demanding recognition of Castilian dominion and acceptance of the Faith of Rome. He continuously strengthened the naturally sheer, rugged, and almost inaccessible Peñol of Cerquin with well-engineered fortifications so as to be an impregnable base for offense and defense. Here he concentrated large numbers of warriors, huge stocks of food, and a great arsenal.[47] An adequate supply of water was obviously available. One of Montejo's hardened veterans who had served in the Italian Wars said that, "he had never seen anything so strong in Italy." Licenciado Cristóbal de Pedraza, Protector of the Indians and acting ecclesiastical head of the province, paid even more impressive, although exaggerated, tribute:

. . . the Peñol of the Province of Cerquin, where Juan de Chávez went, and which he could not gain, [is] the strongest thing that had been seen among Christians or in the Algarve, or among the Moors and Turks, as I have been told by persons who were there, and who were in many Christian and Moorish lands.[48]

The Peñol of Cerquin was the military key to Lempira's realm and all southern Higueras, as well as the psychological key to the entire province.

Toward the end of 1537, Lempira sounded the tocsin for the uprising in his domains surrounding the peñol. Men, women, and children deserted their pueblos and swiftly gathered at the rocky fortress, where the warriors prepared for total war. In addition to exhorting his own warriors to defend their soil to the last, Lempira now appealed to Montejo's Guatemalan and Mexican auxiliaries, as racial brothers, to desert the Spaniards and join him in a common war on the European invaders. These warriors, however, remained loyal to their Spanish overlords.[49]

---

[46] *Ibid.*

[47] *Ibid.;* Montejo to the Crown, Gracias a Dios, June 1, 1539, DII, 24:250–97; Pedraza to the Crown, Gracias a Dios, May 18, 1539, AGI, Guatemala 9; Probanzas of Gaspar Xuárez de Avila, 1552 and 1560, AGI, Patronato 63-11; Probanza of Alonso de Cáceres, 1560, AGI, Patronato 63-22; Probanza of Juan Ruíz de la Vega, 1548, AGG, Papers from the Archivo Colonial; Residencia of Montejo for Honduras-Higueras, 1544, AGI, Justicia 300.

[48] Pedraza to the Crown, Gracias a Dios, May 18, 1539, AGI, Guatemala 9.

[49] The account of the siege and final taking of the Peñol of Cerquin, the death of Lempira, and the outbreak and crushing of the great general revolt which broke out shortly after the beginning of the siege of the Peñol of Cerquin is based on the following sources: Montejo to the Crown, Gracias a Dios, June 1, 1539, DII, 24:250–97; Montejo to the Cabildo of Santiago, Gracias a Dios, December 11, 1537, AGG, Papers from the Archivo Municipal, Cartas de Personas Ylustres; Montejo to the Cabildo of Santiago de Guatemala, December 24, 1537, AGG, Papers from the Archivo Municipal, Cartas de Personas Ylustres; Pedraza to the Crown, Gracias a Dios, May 18, 1539, AGI, Guatemala 9; Probanza of Juan Ruíz de la Vega, 1548, AGG, Papers from the Archivo Colonial; Probanzas of Gaspar Xuárez de Avila, 1552 and 1560, AGI, Patronato 63-11; Probanza of Alonso de Cáceres, 1560, AGI, Patronato 53-22; Probanza of Luis del Puerto, 1570, AGI, Guatemala 112; Probanza of Juan Martínez de Larraude, 1571, AGI, Guatemala 173; Probanza of Juan Martínez de Larraude, 1572, AGI, Patronato 72-2; Probanza of Rodrigo Alvarez, 1575, AGI, Mexico 900; Agent of Montejo to the Cabildo of Santiago de Guatemala,

Despite efforts to gain intelligence of any native plans for revolt, it was not until Lempira actually gave the signal for war that Montejo and his officers learned of the threat which the Indian coalition represented. Lempira's revolt, serious as it was, thus far involved only the people around the Peñol of Cerquin. But, as the Spaniards immediately realized, successful defiance by him there held the certain threat of a dreaded mass rising by all Indians of the province, and of territories even beyond, as was Lempira's ultimate objective. To the natives Lempira and his stronghold were a bulwark and a symbol of independence; to the Spaniards both chieftain and fortress were a challenge to their military prestige and a menace to the security and permanent colonization of the entire province.

Thoroughly aroused, the conquistadores, capable and experienced soldiers, decided to attack their enemy directly in his great stronghold. Consequently Montejo quickly sent the capable and trusted Cáceres, who had come back to Gracias a Dios from Santa María de Comayagua, with Juan Ruíz de la vega as his *maestro de campo,* or quartermaster, against the peñol at the head of eighty well-equipped Spaniards and a large number of Mexican and Guatemalan auxiliaries. Always desirous of establishing Spanish control without warfare when he could, in fulfillment of royal law, even on this occasion Montejo instructed Cáceres to reach a peaceful settlement with Lempira if possible and to display moderation toward the Indians. In preparing this most important campaign, Montejo not only marshalled the entire strength of the

---

Asiento de Sula, December 27, 157, AGG, Papers from the Archivo Colonial, Cartas antiguas de Particulares; Probanza of Andrés Francisco, 1559, AGG, Papers from the Archivo Colonial; Probanza of Alonso de Funés, Santa María de Comayagua, 1549, AGG, Al. 29:1548:01723 and Papers from the Archivo de Protocolos Coloniales; Treasury accounts of Diego García de Celís, 1540, AGI, Indiferente General 1206; Residencia of Montejo for Honduras-Higueras, 1544, AGI, Justicia 300; Herrera, 1601–15, 6-3-19.

Of the documentary sources Montejo's detailed letter to the Crown of June 1, 1539, from Gracias a Dios (DII, 24:250–97) and Pedraza's lengthy carta de relación to the Crown from Gracias a Dios on May 18, 1539 (AGI, Guatemala 9) provide basic continuous narratives. The probanzas of Juan Ruíz de la Vega, Gaspar Xuárez de Avila, Alonso de Funés, Luis del Puerto, and Andrés Francisco supply important details and aid in establishing chronology. Herrera (6-3-19) is the source for Lempira, his career, and his death. The letter of the Agent of Montejo to the Cabildo of Santiago de Guatemala of December 27, 1537 (AGG, Papers from the Archivo Municipal, Cartas antiguas de Particulares) helps to fix the beginning of the operations against the Peñol of Cerquin. He wrote: ". . . en esta goveron. de higueras d. dos meses a esta parte se an alçado y rrebelado contra el servio. de su Magt. los ss. y yndios de una provia. q. se dize cerquin porq. sin lo merescer ni darles nadie ocasion a ello mataron tres españoles q. desta trra. yvan a esa cibdad [de Santiago de Guatemala] o a la villa de sant salvor. dsde. la probincia d. comyagua do andava el capitan caceres pacificando la trra. solo por roballes lo q. llevavan y por q. en satisfacion de esta se les hizo cierto castigo despues dello y rrequidos. con la paz se an retrayado y encastillado en un peñol muy fuerte q. el capitan caceres por mandado dl. señor adelantado y govor. don franco. de montejo los tiene cercados."

The time of the outbreak of the great general revolt is closely established by two letters from Montejo to the Cabildo of Santiago de Guatemala. The first of these letters, from Gracias a Dios on December 11, 1537 (AGG, Papers from the Archivo Municipal, Cartas de Personas Ylustres) reflects confidence that the Peñol of Cerquin would soon be taken and that with that event the entire province would be under control. The second of Montejo's letters, from Gracias a Dios on December 24, 1537 (AGG, Papers from the Archivo Municipal, Cartas de Personas Ylustres) displays dismay at the magnitude of the great uprising which had just broken out. This letter was rushed to Santiago de Guatemala with all possible speed and was received by the cabildo on January 12, 1538. For the revolt in San Miguel see Chamberlain, 1947a.

province but also urgently requested support from the authorities of Santiago de Guatemala and San Salvador. Cáceres arrived before the peñol about November 1. Following Montejo's instructions, he first sent emissaries to Lempira to assert Castilian overlordship and offer considerate treatment in return for submission. Lempira's reply was to have Cáceres' envoys put to death and to proclaim proudly that, "he recognized no other lord and knew no other law or custom than those he already acknowledged." This was war to the death. Cáceres then attacked the peñol, but soon found it impregnable to direct assault. No roadway led to its summit, and its steep walls prevented any attempt to scale its heights. The well-constructed works protecting its approaches and the large numbers of defending warriors put any sudden, direct onset out of the question. Horses, which had given the Spaniards victory over overwhelming odds on so many hard-fought fields in the Indies, were useless here.

As Chávez had found some months before, there was no alternative to a laborious siege, by which the Spaniards might cut off further supplies for the peñol and so hope eventually to starve the garrison into submission. Meanwhile they could work their lines forward, waiting for any opportunity to storm the peñol. Its approaches, so restricted for easy defense by the Indians, were by the same token so narrow that the Spaniards, few as they were, were able to establish a close siege. Cáceres therefore began his investment of the native stronghold. In constant attack and counterattack, the Spaniards tried to advance their lines, the Indians to drive them off entirely. Cáceres, who had to guard eight places of access to the peñol, had to make the most careful disposition of his men, posting them in more or less equal detachments before each point. Bodies of auxiliaries were posted with each Spanish squad. Five of Cáceres' company soon lost their lives and a large number sustained wounds, among them Cáceres. The Spanish captain held his siege lines firmly during this ebb and flow of combat but could not advance. Each day made clearer to the Spaniards the magnitude of their task.

In the interim, after starting his campaign against the heart of Lempira's domains, Montejo carried forward security operations in other areas. He sent one column under Xuárez de Avila into the territory close around Gracias a Dios and ordered another, composed of about twenty men and a number of native auxiliaries, far southward into the Valley of Xocorro. Montejo himself led a third company of twenty-three soldiers eastward toward the Valley of Comayagua. At the same time he directed the authorities of Santa María de Comayagua to send reinforcements to Cáceres before the Peñol of Cerquin, and fourteen men set out to join the siege.

The column sent into the Valley of Xocorro soon found its operations frustrated, not by hostile Indians but by Spaniards from San Miguel, who claimed that Montejo's soldiers were moving into territory outside his jurisdiction. A small reconnaissance party sent out by Montejo's lieutenant encountered these Spaniards and was taken prisoner. To avoid friction with San Miguel, Montejo's lieutenant then turned back, giving up his efforts to pacify the region and intending to return to Santa María de Comayagua.

THE OUTBREAK OF THE GENERAL REVOLT IN HIGUERAS

The impregnability of the Peñol of Cerquin inspired confidence in the Indians of all Higueras as well as the natives of San Miguel and San Salvador. Lempira and his allies had therefore succeeded in creating the means and opportunity for beginning their main objective, a mass revolt throughout this territory and even in the region of Trujillo. Not quite two months after Cáceres had begun the siege of the peñol, the general rising so greatly dreaded by the Spaniards burst out in all its fury. The revolt was well co-ordinated over a wide area and well timed, for the Spaniards were now scattered in comparatively small groups everywhere except before the peñol itself. Gracias a Dios and Santa María de Comayagua had been virtually stripped of fighting men. The Indians, who found they could contain before the peñol the heaviest single concentration of enemies, now skillfully turned this dispersal of the remaining Spaniards to advantage. What had been a vitally important, but still limited, war in the district of the peñol now became an unlimited war of life and death for both parties.

The uprising was widespread. Lempira's entire domains south of the peñol revolted as one, joined by Indians of the Valley of Comayagua and the mountains of the district of San Pedro. The natives of both San Miguel and San Salvador struck against the Spaniards there, bringing the most serious trials and dangers. Many Spaniards were killed in outlying areas of San Miguel; the town itself was saved from furious assault and siege only by desperate fighting of its garrison and the opportune arrival of a party of armed travelers from Guatemala. Serious military operations also became necessary in San Salvador. Far to the east, Trujillo was likewise affected, although the revolt there was confined to the hinterland.

Yamala, a pueblo of the district of Gracias a Dios, now became the center of a conspiracy to destroy Montejo's company in the region of the Valley of Comayagua. Fortunately for the Spaniards this plot came to naught. The column which had originally operated in the Valley of Xocorro, and which had turned back toward Santa María de Comayagua after penterating territory claimed by the authorities of San Miguel, was suddenly attacked while passing through the pueblo of Guaxeregui. All sixteen of the Spaniards were killed. A negro who was with the Spaniards, either a slave or a leader of a mining cuadrilla, was the only survivor and he was badly wounded. The fourteen Spaniards who were on the march from Santa María de Comayagua to join Cáceres before the Peñol of Cerquin were attacked in the province of the Cares. This detachment intrepidly cut its way through and, although it suffered heavily, reached the peñol.

Realizing that a mass revolt had broken out and doubly alarmed by the massacre at Guaxeregui, the small group of citizens left in Santa María de Comayagua sent a desperate appeal to Montejo. He despatched six horsemen and six footmen, all he could spare, to the threatened town, and they succeeded in reaching Santa María de Comayagua, even though all its approaches were hostile. After sending this detachment, Montejo was left with only eleven men under his direct command. Gracias a Dios found itself with a very few citizens capable of military service and in danger of destruction. The presence of women and children added anxiety. Similar events soon occurred in the district of San Pedro. The Indians killed isolated Spaniards wherever they found them, and the authorities urgently appealed to Montejo for support. The town itself, however, was not in nearly as great danger of destruction as were Gracias a Dios and Santa María de Comayagua. Meanwhile, fearful for the safety of Gracias a Dios, Montejo marched rapidly toward that city with his eleven men. On their march, he and his small group were continually threatened on all sides.

Despite all the surrounding dangers Montejo was still not entirely helpless, as events proved. Following the methods so successfully employed by Lempira at the Peñol of Cerquin, the natives were fortifying a strong peñol not far from Gracias a Dios itself. They were concentrating in large numbers and gathering into thatched storehouses great quantities of food to withstand prolonged siege if necessary. Montejo resolved at all cost to prevent the creation of such a dangerous enemy base so close to Gracias a Dios. Not being able to hazard a direct assault, he resorted to a strategem. He sent a faithful negro personal servant to set fire to the great storehouses. This wholly unexpected setback so dismayed the natives of the entire district that they forthwith gave up all thought of further resistance and came to Montejo asking peace. Montejo attached great importance to the surrender of this fortress-peñol, which could well have developed into a very dangerous threat.

After this almost providential triumph Montejo and his men returned to Gracias a Dios in safety. Its situation, however, remained desperate. The few

Spaniards in the city were still in constant danger of being massacred, or at least forced to abandon the city. Ceaseless vigil was maintained.

The caciques of the territory close by, led by a ruler called Mota, now conspired to seize their opportunity. Of this Montejo learned, however, and in a daring foray took Mota prisoner. The powerful cacique was held at Gracias a Dios but soon managed to escape and, setting up secret headquarters, resumed preparations to move against the city. Through an Indian, Montejo at length discovered where Mota was, and in another swift and desperate raid captured him again. The cacique was now kept under closest guard in the dwelling of Montejo, who let Mota's people know that their ruler was being held hostage to guarantee their actions, a measure which stayed their hands. Thus the most immediate danger to Gracias a Dios was overcome.

The twelve men whom Montejo had sent to the aid of Santa María de Comayagua upon the outbreak of the general revolt were insufficient help for the depleted garrison in face of overwhelming native forces. The massacre of the detachment returning there from the Valley of Xocorro had been a rude blow for the defenders. For the time being, with their countrymen hard pressed everywhere, the Spaniards of this town were cut off from help from any quarter.

Fully aware of their opponents' weakness, the Indians lost no time in descending on Santa María de Comayagua en masse. The small garrison was forced to evacuate the town and painfully fight its way out, aided by cover of night. The Spaniards then began a perilous march toward Gracias a Dios, desperately hoping to reach that city or to meet some other company of their countrymen. Meanwhile the infuriated Indians burned the abandoned town and even killed all livestock which the Spaniards had brought there for the haciendas they were already beginning to develop. The harassed Spaniards finally reached one of the very few peaceful pueblos within the district. There they rested and then went on to join Montejo at Gracias a Dios.

The general revolt was now in full swing everywhere in Higueras, and the very life of the colony hung in the balance. More than ever, Lempira and the Peñol of Cerquin were watchwords for the natives everywhere; they would remain so as long as the peñol stood, as the Spaniards well knew. The latter were very few to face a mass revolt, and, except for the force which was contained at the peñol, they could operate only in small detachments, having to risk all the dangers that diffusion of forces carried with it. They lacked sufficient supplies, arms, and men either to assure defense or assume a sustained offense. For the moment, they were on the offensive only before the Peñol of Cerquin; everywhere else they were fighting defensively for their lives. Almost overnight they had lost all Higueras except small areas about Gracias a Dios and San Pedro.

After eliminating the threat of Mota's conspiracy and now joined by the former garrison of Santa María de Comayagua, Montejo remained in Gracias a Dios to assume general direction of military affairs. He went about his task vigorously and intelligently. He, his captains, and all the colonists resolved to hold the province at all costs.

The Peñol of Cerquin was, of course, the vital point. There Lempira stood with his chosen forces and his principal stronghold, and there the largest group of Spanish men-at-arms was held by the prolonged siege. Montejo had to decide whether or not to detach men from his beleaguering forces at the peñol and send them elsewhere in small groups to reinforce other companies for piecemeal subjugation of other districts. He made the wise decision to keep Cáceres at greatest possible strength against the key peñol, certain that if Lempira and his main forces were defeated, the conquest of a wide area would follow rapidly. Raising the siege to strengthen or reconquer other districts would have been to acknowledge temporary defeat at the peñol, freeing large numbers of confident warriors for the offensive and giving immeasurable confidence to the Indians everywhere. Montejo and his captains renewed their resolve to press the siege.

Montejo now repeated his appeals to adjacent provinces for men, materials of war, supplies of all kinds, and native auxiliaries, especially the savage Achies from Guatemala, whom he excoriated in times of relative peace but now wanted because of the terror they instilled in many of the Indians of Higueras. These reiterated calls went to the cabildo of Santiago de Guatemala, to Maldonado, who was then in San Salvador on governmental duties, to the authorities of San Miguel, and to Francisco de Marroquín, Bishop of Guatemala. Montejo also thought of beseeching the Crown in distant Castile, even though such a plea could not bring results for a long while.

He sent Gonzalo de Alvarado, founder of Gracias a Dios, and Juan López de Gamboa, now alguacil mayor of Honduras-Higueras, to San Salvador to arrange for support and purchase of war materials. Maldonado and the authorities of San Salvador gave unstinted co-operation, making available to Montejo's emissaries munition of all kinds, powder, arquebuses and balls for them, crossbows and bolts, swords, lances, shields, armor, and iron bars from which to fashion the points of crossbow bolts. They also provided livestock. A captain and 100 native auxiliaries, along with 1000 Indian burden-bearers were also placed at their disposal. The burden-bearers were not only to carry the munitions from San Salvador to Higueras but were to remain to serve the

Spaniards. Cáceres likewise sent a representative to San Miguel for help. Even though that town had been in danger from rebellious natives not long before and large sections of its district were still in arms, the authorities generously sent supplies and auxiliaries.

More populous Guatemala, however, gave little aid. The municipal authorities of Santiago de Guatemala first refused to send the auxiliaries Montejo so urgently requested, falsely claiming that he had badly mistreated the Achies and other allies whom Alvarado had taken to Higueras from Guatemala in 1536. The true reasons for their refusal lay in Montejo's policies to protect the natives of Higueras, his restrictions on the mining activities of Guatemalan colonists in Higueras, and his removal of encomiendas which Alvarado had assigned in Higueras to citizens of Santiago de Guatemala. The Guatemalan officials eventually gave minor support, however.

Financial resources were marshalled from every available source: treasury officials of Honduras-Higueras, at Montejo's request, released funds from the *caja real,* the royal coffers of the province; the *diezmos,* or tithes, of the Church were employed; Montejo and others used their personal funds.

THE DEATH OF LEMPIRA AND THE TURN OF THE TIDE

Meanwhile the siege of Lempira's stronghold dragged on month after month, with constant fighting. At times the initiative was with the Spaniards, who, with the reinforcements Montejo had sent them, numbered perhaps just under 100; at other times it was with the Indians. The natives, with their great numbers, could replace their dead and wounded with fresh warriors, but the Spaniards could not.

The Spaniards for a long while suffered acute food shortages, despite what was sent them and what they themselves could gather. There were no supplies close at hand, for the natives of the region had stripped their lands to stock the stronghold. The Spaniards were so short-handed that for a long time they lacked burden-bearers to bring in distant supplies and could spare neither warriors nor auxiliaries from the siege to make up foraging parties.

Thus, for a time the besiegers were reduced to eating the maize they found among the deserted crops close to the peñol, supplemented with herbs and plants. Ironically, the besieged, of course, as yet had no lack of food because they had stored great quantities in preparation. The coming of the season of heavy rains in the spring of 1538 further increased the Spaniards' problems. Fatigued with ceaseless fighting and unbroken vigils by day and night, and weakened by insufficient food, some of the soldiers began to flag; a few even wished to abandon the siege.

Montejo's staunch lieutenant, Cáceres, was fully alive to the military and political implications of the siege and he had a fine sense of loyalty and responsibility. With undiminished zeal, he encouraged his men and held them to their wearisome and dangerous work. When the materials for which the adelantado had arranged in Salvador arrived, and when the help he himself had sent for in San Miguel came, the situation improved. The failing spirits of the soldiers rose.

Through all this, Cáceres had pushed his investing lines slowly closer, but the Spaniards still seemed as far as ever from final triumph. The taking of the peñol and the decisive defeat of Lempira were already too long delayed. Until these two objectives were accomplished the situation of the Spaniards throughout the province would become constantly more critical. Montejo and his captains were poignantly aware of this all-important fact and knew that the elimination of Lempira was increasingly imperative. After six months or more of unavailing blockade, in the spring of 1538 Cáceres finally decided to eliminate Lempira, the heart and soul of resistance, by fair means or foul.

Cáceres knew that not only Lempira but also his followers fanatically regarded him as invincible, a conviction that offered the Spanish captain a way to his own ends. He therefore plotted to invite Lempira to a parley and there assassinate him. At the same time he prepared his men for quick assault on the peñol should Lempira fall into this trap. With perfect faith in his destiny, Lempira accepted Cáceres' invitation. He approached the Spanish lines at the appointed hour, resplendent in a plumed helmet, rich cotton armor, and insignia befitting his rank. A brilliant retinue of officers and vassals accompanied him. If Lempira suspected treachery, he gave no sign of it. Cáceres then sent forward a horseman to admonish the native ruler to give up resistance and accept Castilian dominion. Lempira, after six months of successful defense of his stronghold, disdained peace even more than ever before and replied: "Soldiers do not weary of war, nor do they fear [and] he who was the most capable would gain the victory." [50] Meanwhile Cáceres had carefully placed an arquebusier under cover but within certain range, and had posted all his soldiers for sudden attack on the peñol. While the parley was progressing and Lempira was delivering haughty defiance, the arquebusier took careful aim, fired, and killed the great Indian lord with a ball through his forehead.

The sudden and unworthy death of their inspired leader, whom they had thought unconquerable and impervious to enemy arms, caused instant and utter panic among the defenders of the peñol, who must have been looking down on the parley from their heights. The prepared Spaniards took instant

[50] Herrera, 1601–15, 6-3-19.

advantage of this complete demoralization and, led by a picked assault party, swept forward. In this swift rush they took possession of the peñol without the death of single Spaniard, although some were wounded.[51] Part of the stunned native garrison escaped to nearby mountains, but many warriors gave themselves up without serious attempt at resistance. A large number of older men, women, and children also fell into Spanish hands.

Thus was taken the great fortress which had defied the Spaniards for so many months and which had cost them so much effort, hardship, and peril. Ten Spaniards from a total of about 100 had been killed during the siege and most of the others, including Cáceres, had been wounded at one time or another, some more than once. Neither Cáceres nor any other Spaniard could have been proud of the treachery by which they had destroyed their great adversary, but it was the only means they could devise for the necessary decisive action.

In accordance with Montejo's basic instructions, Cáceres followed the capture of the Peñol of Cerquin with a conciliatory policy toward the vanquished Indians. As a token of his desire for peace he sent textiles and fowls to the caciques of the entire region, after native custom. But to indicate the implacable alternative of war to the end if the Indians were still determined to fight, he also sent lances to the native lords, likewise after the Indian custom. The caciques took counsel among themselves and chose peace and Spanish overlordship, celebrating their decision amidst barbaric ceremonies and festivities. Thus the military heart of Lempira's former domain immediately passed under Spanish control.

Cáceres next freed the captives he had taken at the peñol—warriors, old men, women, and children alike—and sent them home to take up their usual lives. Cáceres' magnanimity following the assassination of Lempira and his overwhelming triumph created a favorable impression among the Indians of the entire region, for they had expected the Spaniards to take ruthless vengeance.

Just as Montejo and Cáceres had anticipated, the death of Lempira and the fall of the Peñol of Cerquin turned the tide and led to rapid pacification of a wide and difficult mountainous region beyond the immediate area. These decisive events had come at an opportune time, for the general revolt was still in full momentum and the Spaniards were on the defensive in an extremely precarious situation. They had held on steadfastly in Higueras for a long while, but it is questionable if they could have continued much longer.

[51] The conquistador Luis del Puerto claimed great personal credit for the taking of the Peñol of Cerquin. In a probanza of 1570 (AGI, Guatemala 112) he said: ". . . yo el dho. luis del puerto me halle con el governador don francisco de montejo en el penon de zerquin en el qual se detuvo todo el exercito mas de zinco meses e no se ganara sino fuera por mi buena industria e diligencia e valor por que yo con quatro compañeros entre estando los yndios descuidados e gane toda la fuerza de que dios e su magd. an sido servidos. . . ."

Montejo had been in danger of losing Higueras in much the same way that he had lost Yucatan in 1534–35. Now the Spaniards could look to the future with renewed confidence, for the soldiers who were concentrated at the peñol could be used elsewhere. Many of the Indians had lost heart; Lempira was dead and his most tried warriors were killed, dispersed, or captured. The Spanish success at the Peñol of Cerquin was of equal moral, military, and political significance. Many hard campaigns and many trials still lay ahead of the Spaniards, but, the great obstacle surmounted, they could at last move to the offensive.

THE CAMPAIGNS IN HIGUERAS AFTER THE FALL OF THE PEÑOL OF CERQUIN

Montejo and his captains immediately exploited their advantage. The Spanish leader sent Xuárez de Avila and Alonso de Reinoso, each with a company, into the Valley of Comayagua and ordered other captains to the rebellious regions of San Pedro. He himself and other subordinates moved against outlying centers of resistance in the district of Gracias a Dios.

Xuárez de Avila and Reinoso began a series of very difficult campaigns.[52] The Indians in the Comayagua area were still determined to resist to the last. The terrain was rugged and well suited to defense. There were many precipitous, mesa-like peñoles, some of which had been artificially strengthened in the manner of the Peñol of Cerquin. Food was scarce under any circumstances and the natives took every possible means to reduce even that. As a result, the Spaniards came near famine, despite supplies and livestock sent by Montejo.

The fighting, too, was hard. Not always content to await attack, the Indians delivered swift thrusts from their strongholds. When on the defensive on their fortified peñoles, they resisted fiercely and added to the effectiveness of their arrows, slings, lances, stone knives, and wooden swords studded with sharp flakes of stone, by rolling boulders and large rocks down on the attackers as they sought to come to grips. For the Spaniards it was a war for their foot soldiers, with their European armament, and such light artillery as they had with them. Their horses were of little use here except for transport. It soon became clear that the subjugation of the Valley of Comayagua would not be easily achieved.

Squier, after giving us a general view of the ruins of some of the former native sites in the Valley of Comayagua, in his description of the great ruins

[52] See Probanzas of Gaspar Xuárez de Avila, 1552 and 1560, AGI, Patronato 63-11; Probanza of Alonso de Reinoso, 1542, AGI, Patronato 56-3-3; Probanza of Alonso de Funés, 1549, AGG, Al. 29:1548:1731 and Papers from the Archivo de Protocolos Coloniales.

of Tenampua conveys the way in which the Indians of Higueras as a whole could fortify their peñoles, including that of Cerquin:

The ruins of Tenampua . . . are situated on the level summit of a high hill . . . elevated about sixteen hundred feet above the plain of Comayagua, of which, in every part, a magnificent view is commanded. The hill is composed of the prevailing soft, white, stratified sandstone of this region, and its sides, except at three points, are either absolutely precipitous, or so steep as to be nearly, if not quite inaccessible. At the accessible point, where narrow ridges connect the hill with the other hills of the group, are heavy artificial walls of rough stones, varying in height from six to fifteen feet. These walls are terraced on the inner side, for convenience of defense. At various points there are towers or buildings designed perhaps for the use of guards or sentinels. The dimensions of the wall correspond to the greater or less abruptness of the slope along which it is carried, and are greatest where the ascent or approach is easiest. Where narrow gullies or natural passes existed, the hollows have been filled with stones, so as to present a vertical outer face, corresponding with the rocky escarpment of the hill. Naturally, I think this place is the strongest position I have ever seen. That it was selected, in part at least, for defense is obvious. . . . The defensive design is made still more apparent by the existence, in the centre of the area of the summit, at a place naturally low and marshy, of two large square excavations, now partially filled up, which were clearly designed for reservoirs.
. . . The level summit of the hill is about one and a half miles long, by half a mile in width. The eastern half of this large area is crowded with ruins. They consist chiefly of terraced mounds of stone, or of earth faced with stone, of rectangular forms, their sides conforming to the cardinal points. Although the stones are uncut, they are laid with great precision. . . .
It is not to be supposed, however, that this was a fortified town, or a place permanently occupied by any considerable population. The summit is rocky, and the soil is thin and poor, affording few of the usual accessories of a large Indian population, viz., abundant water and rich lands. The builders doubtless had their permanent residences in the plain below, and only came here to perform religious rites, or to find safety in times of danger.[53]

When Xuárez de Avila found that he was accomplishing little he joined Reinoso, so that united they could conduct a more effective campaign. Together they succeeded in conquering a number of districts, but even their two companies combined were too small to achieve conclusive results. After Cáceres returned victoriously from the Peñol of Cerquin, Montejo sent him with a considerable force and large quantities of supplies to join Xuárez de Avila and Reinoso and take over superior military and administrative supervision in the general region of the Valley of Comayagua.[54] Cáceres' efforts prolonged

[53] Squier, 1855, pp. 122–29.
[54] Montejo to the Crown, Gracias a Dios, June 1, 1539, DII, 24:250–97.

themselves into the latter months of 1538 without definite issue. Notwith-standing his failure to reconquer the Valley of Comayagua as a whole, he was able to re-establish the town of Santa María de Comayagua.

Meanwhile, Montejo and his captains had encountered no really serious opposition in reducing most of the far-outlying sections of the area of Gracias a Dios which had continued the war after the death of Lempira. Montejo exercised his normal moderation in these military operations and restored Spanish control with a minimum of force. He claimed, in fact, that no Indians were enslaved anywhere during this particular phase. At the same time, the captains Montejo had sent to the north coast succeeded in pacifying the rebellious regions of San Pedro, the Valley of Naco, and the Río de Ulua. On the south side of the province, a column had been sent back into the Valley of Xocorro.

An encouraging measure of order and stability had by this time been imposed over a large part of Higueras. Everywhere Montejo and his captains went they restored the operation of the encomienda system, and all that it meant for the maintenance of the colonists.

The final conquest of the Valley of Comayagua now remained the one great military task. When Cáceres and his subordinates realized that they were making only slow progress there, they appealed for reinforcements to Montejo, who marshalled all available soldiers and, late in 1538, himself moved to the conquest. He designated his brother Juan and the Licenciado Cristóbal de Pedraza, Protector of the Indians and acting spiritual head of the province, as joint administrators in Gracias a Dios during his absence. On his march Montejo raised some 1500 auxiliaries of high fighting quality from among the recently hostile, but now allied, peoples of the district about the Peñol of Cerquin.

In moving eastward, pacifying the regions as he passed, Montejo came before the town of Guaxeregui, where the Spaniards returning from the Valley of Xocorro to Santa María de Comayagua had been massacred at the outset of the general revolt and which still remained a center of desperate resistance. The people of this place, fearing Spanish vengeance, had fortified themselves on a formidable peñol near their town. There they had erected a second town, with strong defensive works, dwellings, temples, shrines, and storehouses, some 200 buildings in all. Within this stronghold were an adequate supply of water and abundant fields for the raising of food. Moreover, they had filled their storehouses with provisions. The warriors seemed entirely prepared for either pitched battle or siege. This fortress was potentially one of the strongest in the entire province, perhaps second only to the Peñol of Cerquin.

Montejo was filled with anxiety on encountering such a strong point and anticipated every kind of difficulty. He first decided on a show of force, however, and must also have had the requerimiento read to the Indians, although he expected no compliance. To his surprise and joy the show of force was sufficient, for so low had the morale of the natives sunk that they forthwith fled from their stronghold without fighting. Montejo had considered the peñol virtually impregnable, and he was "grateful to God" at this surprising outcome. The easy surrender of the peñol must have had considerable influence on neighboring Indians toward submission. Any such incident was welcome evidence to the Spaniards that their prestige was being restored.

Montejo had sent word of his coming to Cáceres, whom he now awaited either at Guaxeregui or at some point farther on, so that together they could carry the conquest forward. Cáceres had continued his campaigns with increased vigor when he learned that Montejo himself was marching to join him. He boldly penetrated a strongly held northwest region of the Valley of Comayagua, where he first besieged and then took by assault a powerful fortress which the natives had set up on another of the peñoles which studded the region, the Peñol of Ojuera.[55] This was probably the outstanding victory of Cáceres' entire Comayagua campaign, and with it caciques on all sides sued for peace. Cáceres then joined Montejo.

After Cáceres came up, Montejo had about 100 men under his command. He was now ready to make a final effort at the conquest of the Valley of Comayagua and to carry the war into adjacent areas. His campaigns moved forward with swift success. The Indians were nowhere strong enough to hold off for long so many well-equipped and experienced Spaniards, and the valley was soon firmly under Spanish control.

Montejo next sent reinforcements, including native auxiliaries now available from many parts of conquered Higueras, to the column operating in the Valley of Xocorro, and then entered that region himself. The area was speedily pacified.

During these operations Montejo's company pushed into the province of San Miguel, and to within sight of the great Bahía de Fonseca, on which the Spaniards looked down from the mountains to the north. Many outlying parts of the province of San Miguel were still at war. It seems, too, that intertribal warfare was raging. The Indians of San Miguel as a whole were in a lamentable state: they were widely scattered, many of their towns lay abandoned or burned, and entire districts had been desolated.[56] Everywhere the

[55] See especially the Probanza of Alonso de Funés, 1549, AGG, Al. 29:1548:01731 and Papers from the Archivo de Protocolos Coloniales, and Probanzas of June Martínez Larraude, 1572, AGI, Patronato 72-2.
[56] Montejo to the Crown, Gracias a Dios, June 1, 1539, DII, 24:250–97. See also Chamberlain, 1947a.

natives complained to Montejo of mistreatment, enslavement, and ruin of their lands, both by Spaniards and other Indians, and besought his protection. Montejo restored peace in some sections, persuading the people to return to their pueblos, and sent the caciques to the authorities of San Miguel to give homage. He also came to an agreement with the authorities of San Miguel under which more considerate treatment was to be accorded Indians there.[57]

These successful campaigns in the Valley of Comayagua and beyond, which were concluded in the first months of 1539, brought the bloody war to an end. In the district of Trujillo risings in the interior, which in the final analysis proved minor, had already been put down without help from Higueras.[58] During the war the Spaniards had many times been on the verge of losing the colony, and also their lives, but finally, through valor and undying determination, had emerged victorious from the crucial test.

Montejo now transferred Santa María de Comayagua to a site which he considered more advantageous than its original location. He appointed a new cabildo and designated thirty-five soldier-colonists as citizens, reapportioning in encomienda the district of the town, now generally called Comayagua.[59] Soon after this move, rich and extensive silver deposits were discovered in the close vicinity, practically "under the houses" as the Spaniards said.[60] In reporting this to the Crown, Montejo enthusiastically declared that these deposits in the newly won territory would prove the richest in all the Indies.

From the Town of Comayagua, Montejo turned his attention to frontier regions to the eastward which had not been directly involved in the great revolt. He moved to within two days' march of the Valley of Olancho, which had never been permanently conquered despite many earlier attempts by captains operating out of Trujillo. Most recent accounts of the valley had been good, and its occupation fitted in well with Montejo's plans. It was said to be heavily peopled, despite the ravages of former campaigns, rich in gold, and fertile; its Indians were reported now willing to receive the Spaniards in peace.[61]

Montejo regarded the Valley of Olancho important not merely for expanded colonization but for strategic value to Honduras-Higueras as a whole. Situated in the hinterland behind Trujillo and east of the Valley of Comayagua,

[57] Ibid.
[58] Cabildo of Trujillo to the Crown, March 12, 1540, AGI, Guatemala 44.
[59] Montejo to the Crown, Gracias a Dios, June 1, 1539, DII, 24:261–62. After its re-establishment following the suppression of the revolt in its region, Santa María de Comayagua seems generally to be referred to as the "Villa de Comayagua." Consequently the name of the municipality will henceforth appear in the text as the "Town of Comayagua" or merely as "Comayagua."
[60] Cabildo of Comayagua to the Crown, September 5, 1539, AGI, Guatemala 43.
[61] Montejo to the Crown, June 1, 1539, DII, 24:250–97; Montejo to the Crown, Gracias a Dios, November 4, 1539, AGI, Guatemala 9; Montejo to the Crown, Gracias a Dios, May 1, 1542, AGI, Patronato 184-25.

the region of Olancho, once occupied, would not only provide greater stability
to the weak city of Trujillo through giving it access to rich, unopened land,
but would also contribute to the security and development of the Town of
Comayagua. Another factor of immediate importance was the need to recompense conquistador-colonists. After the war in Higueras was over the Indians
were too few there to provide encomiendas for all the conquistadores, largely
because of wide dispersal and heavy loss of native life. The population of
the district of the Town of Comayagua, as an example, could not provide
encomiendas to sustain more than the thirty-five or so Spaniards who became
its citizens. The number of Spaniards who could be given the position of
vecinos, or citizen-householders, in the municipalities founded immediately
after conquest was limited by the Indian population of their respective districts and was carefully calculated in each case. It was necessary, therefore, to
look beyond already conquered areas to find encomienda pueblos for those
who had none in the districts of San Pedro, Gracias a Dios, and the Town of
Comayagua. The Valley of Olancho seemed to have the necessary population.[62]

Although Montejo had a sufficient number of men available to occupy the
Valley of Olancho, he considered the undertaking impossible unless his material shortages were made up. He consequently communicated with the
treasurer García de Celís, who had returned from Castile, and the contador
Cerezeda, asking that funds from the war-depleted royal coffers of the province be employed to buy needed supplies. Expecting the officials to acquiesce,
he proceeded with the preliminary organization of his projected campaign
into the Valley of Olancho.[63] But García de Celís and Cerezeda raised the
strongest objections. They declared that no funds were available. Furthermore,
they held that such plans were contrary to current Crown policy, which prohibited officials from undertaking the reduction of new lands without express
authority from the higher agencies of government in the New World and
Castile. Nevertheless they forwarded Montejo's petitions for aid to the authorities of Guatemala to learn if they might be willing to give help, a step which
those officials were not prepared to take.[64]

Taken aback by the refusal of García de Celís and Cerezeda, Montejo sent
a personal representative to persuade them or, if persuasion failed, formally
to "require" that they send necessary aid. He also requested them to use his
own salary to help cover the expenses of his expedition. But García de Celís
and Cerezeda still refused to act. Feeling that he could not successfully occupy
the Valley of Olancho without support, Montejo reluctantly postponed the

[62] *Ibid.*
[63] *Ibid.*
[64] *Ibid.*

expedition.[65] Heavy rains had now begun and so Montejo led his men back to the Town of Comayagua. He nevertheless still hoped, despite García de Celís' and Cerezeda's objections, to find some way of moving into the Valley of Olancho within a short time.

As it turned out, the Crown had already met the technical objections raised by the two treasury officials, but its cedula of January 29, 1538, which would have authorized a move such as Montejo planned, had obviously not yet reached Honduras-Higueras when he was contemplating colonization of the Valley of Olancho. By this decree the governors of Honduras-Higueras and Nicaragua were authorized to establish a town in the uncolonized zone between the two provinces should they consider it expedient.[66] The object was to promote the development and security of the region as a whole by the occupation of this untenanted belt, of which the Crown had received favorable reports.

It is possible that Montejo was already looking beyond the Valley of Olancho to the eventual conquest and settlement of Taguzgalpa, the little known and largely low-lying region stretching east toward the Caribbean.[67]

Montejo was hurriedly summoned to Gracias a Dios in April 1539, by the return of Pedro de Alvarado from Castile. Although Montejo went back to his capital intending to concentrate on the peaceful development of the province, he immediately found himself involved with Alvarado in a controversy over the governorship of Honduras-Higueras. This quarrel was vitally to affect the course of provincial history for the next five years and was to force Montejo to give up the governorship for the time being.

MONTEJO'S LEADERSHIP

Montejo's campaigns in Higueras from the latter months of 1537, when the siege of the Peñol of Cerquin began, to the spring of 1539, when the last embers of the great revolt were extinguished, planted the royal standard of Castile firmly in Higueras for the first time. In all, Montejo had no more than 250 or 300 soldiers at his command during the war, and with them he conquered the province. Time proved that the Indians would not again seriously challenge Spanish supremacy. The shift in importance from the eastern part of Honduras-Higueras to the western, begun by Cerezeda in 1534, was now confirmed. Even though there were areas to the eastward, behind Trujillo, such as the Valley of Olancho, and other parts of the interior of both east and west still to be conquered or colonized, the main work was done and

---

[65] Ibid.
[66] Cedula of January 29, 1538, AGI, Guatemala 402.
[67] Montejo to the Crown, Gracias a Dios, May 1, 1542, AGI, Patronato 184-25.

the Spaniards were now in Honduras-Higueras to remain. With the Indians conquered, San Pedro, Gracias a Dios, and the Town of Comayagua at last on firm foundations, and with Trujillo still in existence in the east, the province as a whole was for the first time in a position to begin its political and economic progress, even though the road was to be long and rough.

The final conquest of Higueras had been accomplished only with the greatest effort and at heavy cost in men and resources. Of the more than 100 men whom Montejo himself had brought to the province, some thirty lost their lives in the war or died as a result of disease and hardship. Expenditures to support the many campaigns took much from the royal coffers of the province, and the colonists themselves had depleted their personal funds and revenues. Many colonists, and officials as well, were left heavily in debt.[68] As leader of the colony Montejo had set the example by personal expenditures for the public service amounting to some 2000 castellanos during the war. The total disbursement from his own incomes after accepting the governorship of Honduras-Higueras was about 12,000 castellanos. Montejo also supplied drugs and medicines for the wounded and ill and distributed wine and other articles from his own personal stocks. He even made his own taxed and officially stamped legal paper available to the notaries of the province so that they could properly prepare public documents.[69]

In addition, Montejo suffered a heavy property loss. While the siege of the Peñol of Cerquin was still in progress and the entire province was in revolt, Montejo's dwelling in Gracias a Dios caught fire during the night. His wife and young daughter were trapped by the flames, and Montejo nearly lost his life in rescuing them. All the household property and Montejo's horses were destroyed. He claimed losses of 10,000 castellanos as a result of this fire, a heavy addition to his already great financial burdens.[70] As partial recompense he took for himself a number of important encomienda towns, some of which Pedro de Alvarado had set aside as his own. Montejo also assigned other towns to members of his family and retainers, so that he could enjoy the incomes of those towns and the services of their Indians. Moreover, he appropriated slaves and mining cuadrillas which Alvarado had left in Higueras, and took Alvarado's haciendas and a certain amount of maize he had stored.[71]

[68] Montejo to the Crown, June 1, 1539, AGI, DII, 24:250 ff.; Pedraza to the Crown, Gracias a Dios, May 18, 1539, AGI, Guatemala 9; Treasury accounts of Diego García de Celís, 1540, AGI, Indiferente General 1206; Residencia of Montejo for Honduras-Higueras, 1544, AGI, Justicia 300; Montejo v. Pedraza, 1539, AGI, Justicia 129-2.
[69] Residencia of Montejo for Honduras-Higueras, 1544, AGI, Justicia 300.
[70] Montejo to the Crown, Gracias a Dios, June 1, 1539, DII, 24:286.
[71] Pedraza v. Montejo, 1539, AGI, Patronato 129-2.

The Spaniards have left little detailed record of the great physical hardship they sustained during the conquest. However, the words of Antonio de Vergara give some idea of what they underwent:

In coming to this land I sacrificed my own personal interests, because my office is that of surgeon. There is no other, nor has there been another, in this land to cure those who were wounded in the war [of 1537–39]. If "Master Antonio" had not been here many persons whom I have cured of serious wounds and sickness would otherwise have died. These persons whom I have healed are alive and sound . . . and I have performed these services without pay or salary from anyone. . . . [72]

Montejo, his able captains, the local officials, and the colonists as a whole, displaying the greatest courage, tenacity, and fortitude, had crushed the great rising with a minimum of help from the outside. The materials of war, food, livestock, burden-bearers, and auxiliaries obtained in San Salvador and San Miguel, and slight help eventually but grudgingly sent from Guatemala, were the sum of aid from other provinces. While this support had come at a critical time, it was definitely limited and not decisive. No Spanish men-at-arms came to the province from elsewhere during the great struggle.

While the war of life and death was running its course, the Spaniards of Higueras labored together in unison and harmony, putting to one side political controversy, personal quarrels, and partisanship. They followed Montejo wholeheartedly as long as the issue was uncertain, giving him their unstinted support. Montejo justified their confidence with his fine leadership, of which they were well aware.

The efforts of Andrés de Cerezeda to conquer and settle Higueras after 1534 would have been as futile as those of the Spaniards who preceded him had not Pedro de Alvarado come to the rescue in 1536. Alvarado had saved the colony from abandonment, and through his campaigns and the founding of San Pedro and Gracias a Dios had contributed to the future stabilization of the province, but his efforts were essentially superficial. What he had done could easily have been swept away. To Montejo is to be assigned credit for the conquest of Higueras and its permanent colonization. Montejo was the true conquistador and founder of the colony. In the words of Licenciado Cristóbal de Pedraza, chief prelate of the province and later Bishop of Honduras: "[Alvarado] laid the foundations; [Montejo] constructed the edifice." [73]

[72] Probanza of Antonio de Vergara, 1543, AGG, Papers from the Archivo Colonial.
[73] Pedraza to the Crown, Gracias a Dios, May 18, 1539, AGI, Guatemala 9.

6

Montejo's Administration in Honduras-Higueras

MONTEJO'S ASPIRATIONS AS GOVERNOR

MONTEJO had by 1539 carried his plans for an expanded adelantamiento to a high point of development and he must have felt considerable confidence of soon being able to realize his personal ambition. The existence of precious metals, the advantageous situation for development of commerce, and the rich fertility of the region led him to regard Honduras-Higueras as the most important province and therefore the eventual center of the territories he hoped to build into his greater adelantamiento.

Montejo fully understood the farseeing wisdom of the broad projects for colonization and economic development which Andrés de Cerezeda had drawn up after moving into Higueras in 1534 and which the adelantado must have discussed at length with Cerezeda, García de Celís, and others. He greatly expanded these projects and made them the basis of his own policies in Honduras-Higueras. He also proposed to develop the region through trade; sound, calculated exploitation of natural resources; and the conservation of the native population as the labor supply. Some of his essential ideas and policies toward any natives under his authority he addressed to the Crown:

> . . . there is no means or advantage [in this land] other than the work of the hands [of the Indians], because . . . there are lacking here [the things] which exist in quantity and surfeit in [other provinces]. Here there is only gold and silver beneath the soil, and, since the citizens have no slaves, and none have been taken here [during my governorship], they are pained to see themselves in want in such a rich land, and without means of making good their opportunities. . . . [The] natives are very few and delicate and to impose harshness on them . . . would be to destroy the land. Rather, they stand in need of care, favor, and support.[1]

The immediate maintenance of the colonists depended on the encomienda system.[2] Its importance as an institution on which the lives of the conquering Spaniards rested in the Indies is well indicated by a phrase often used in connection with it, "dar de comer," or "provide sustenance." Since the number

---

[1] Montejo to the Crown, Gracias a Dios, June 1, 1539, DII, 24:264-65.
[2] See chap. 4, note 26.

of Spanish citizens that could be established in any given municipality in this early period was in direct proportion to the density of the native population available for assignment in encomienda, the satisfactory operation of the system was imperative to the permanence of a colony. Hence, in Montejo's plans, the natives were an essential economic element, to be protected and conserved for utilitarian as well as humanitarian reasons. As wards of the Crown they enjoyed theoretical royal protection.

CONDITIONS IN HONDURAS-HIGUERAS IN 1537

When Montejo assumed the governorship of Honduras-Higueras early in 1537, the political and economic situation of the province had been grave. Both natives and Spaniards were adversely affected. Native society was completely disrupted by the Spanish military campaigns, slaving operations, the havoc wrought by the Achie auxiliaries especially in the coastal area of Higueras, and general ill-treatment.[3] Pueblos were deserted and laid waste, their inhabitants dispersed, and fields left uncultivated. The Indians suffered from shortages of all kinds. Many natives were in open revolt and a number of districts, technically at peace, refused to give service or furnish supplies to the Spaniards. Successive plagues of locusts over a three-year period had destroyed all vegetation throughout a considerable area. Under such circumstances the Spaniards also suffered. Foraging raids, never truly satisfactory anywhere, were worse than useless. The Spaniards of Gracias a Dios are said to have been virtually reduced to eating roots, herbs, and normally nonedible plants for a five- or six-month period; those of San Pedro were in hardly better state. Imports from Castile were almost nonexistent. Even salt was lacking.[4] Over in Trujillo the situation remained as unsatisfactory as ever.[5]

Montejo had to establish some degree of stability among the colonists and restore their morale. He hoped, through exploitation of mines, adjustment of the encomienda system, and development of trade, to afford the settlers adequate recompense in Higueras and thus assure their permanence in the province. In working out these serious problems he could draw on his wide experience in Yucatan between 1527 and 1535.

Success in any effort to return the Indians to their ordinary way of life meant: (1) application of a moderate, understanding policy that would ensure willing service under the encomienda system, without a sense of crushing oppression; (2) elimination of abuses in the encomienda structure; (3) re-

---

[3] Montejo to the Crown, Naco, July 28, 1537, AGI, Guatemala; Pedraza to the Crown, Gracias a Dios, May 18, 1539, AGI, Guatemala 9; Montejo to the Crown, Gracias a Dios, June 1, 1539, DII, 24:250–97; Alonso de Cáceres to the Crown, Gracias a Dios, September 5, 1539, AGI, Guatemala 43.

[4] *Ibid.*

[5] *Ibid.;* Cabildo of Trujillo to the Crown, March 12, 1540, AGI, Guatemala 44.

straint of unlicensed enslavement and the slave trade, and lessening of hardships in forced labor and burden-bearing; and (4) removal of the Achie
auxiliaries.[6]

The Indians of Higueras already needed the most careful nurture. According to the Licenciado Cristóbal de Pedraza, who as Protector of the Indians
was especially charged by the Crown with their welfare, there were by 1539
not more than 15,000 Indians available in the province to reconstitute the
depleted pueblos.[7] Although this figure was given after the suppression of
the great revolt of 1537–39, the decline had seriously set in even before Montejo
arrived.[8] As he had sought to do in Yucatan, Montejo exerted every effort to
bring the natives to obedience by peaceful means, but he was fully prepared
to employ arms if necessary. He wished to avoid the difficulties created by his
predecessors and followed moderate policies until the siege of the Peñol of
Cerquin began.

In carrying out the final conquest of Higueras, Montejo still applied wherever possible temperate measures that would protect all natives who accepted
Spanish dominion, in accordance with the will of the Castilian monarch as
expressed in law. He tried to establish equitable relations between the conquered Indians and the Spaniards and to induce dispersed Indians voluntarily
to return to their towns and quietly resume their ordinary lives. Except in
extraordinary cases, he refrained from inflicting harsh punishment on natives
who had risen in revolt. A certain number of rebellious Indians were enslaved
by Montejo's orders under conditions that had formerly been legal, but those
slaves were not many. The available treasury accounts indicate that only 340
pesos were placed in the royal coffers as the quinto, or royal fifth, of the value
of slaves officially branded in Higueras during the period of revolt.[9]

PROBLEMS OF THE JURISDICTIONAL LIMITS OF
HONDURAS-HIGUERAS

From Honduras-Higueras, Montejo again placed claims for maximum geographical limits for Yucatan and his adelantamiento before the Crown and the
higher agencies of government in the Indies, and sought to extend colonization within his territories. Now realizing more than ever the advantages of
a corridor across Higueras to the South Sea at the Bahía de Fonseca, with
its full port facilities, he claimed this strip and the adjacent province of San

[6] Pedraza to the Crown, Gracias a Dios, May 18, 1539, AGI, Guatemala 9; Montejo to the Crown,
June 1, 1539, DII, 24:250–97.
[7] Pedraza to the Crown, Gracias a Dios, May 18, 1539, AGI, Guatemala 9.
[8] Ibid. and Montejo to the Crown, June 1, 1539, DII, 24:250–97.
[9] Montejo to the Crown, Naco, July 8, 1537, AGI, Guatemala 9; Montejo to the Crown, Gracias a
Dios, June 1, 1539, DII, 24:250–97; Residencias of Montejo for Honduras-Higueras, Chiapas, Tabasco,
and Yucatan, 1544, 1550, AGI, Justicia 244 and 300.

Miguel as part of Higueras and strove to have this territory, as well as the lands between the Río de Copilco and the Río de Ulua, incorporated with his adelantamiento. Occupation of the Valley of Olancho and extension of the conquest into Taguzgalpa were other phases of his large plans. Moreover, although precisely at what time is not clear, he sought control of a district west of the Río de Copilco and within the jurisdiction of the Tehuantepec town of Espíritu Santo. Many of these contentions were important for the development of Honduras-Higueras itself, entirely apart from his personal aspirations.

Montejo's hopes for eventual recognition of his full position were strengthened by the residencia of Alvarado for Guatemala and Maldonado's interim governorship there. At that time it seemed possible that Alvarado might be permanently removed from office in Guatemala, that his influence throughout the region might be finally ended, and that his prestige before the Crown might be irrevocably lost or at least greatly weakened, all to Montejo's advantage.[10]

Montejo's demand for extension of authority over San Miguel was blocked by the old controversy as to whether it was territory of Guatemala or of Honduras-Higueras. Montejo held that the areas of San Miguel and the Río de Lempa, which flowed from southern Higueras into the Pacific northwest of the Bahía de Fonseca, were rightfully part of the jurisdiction of Honduras-Higueras and that authority over those regions had been assumed illegally by the governor of Guatemala. He based this position on a specific royal cedula, which, however, is difficult to identify.[11]

While in the region of San Miguel during the closing campaigns of the conquest of Higueras, Montejo took the opportunity to pursue the question of the jurisdictional status of that town, requesting a conference with the local officials.[12] The captain governing there in name of the superior authorities of Guatemala, Gaspar Avilés de Sotomayor, an alcalde, and two regidores of the town responded and reached a tentative understanding with Montejo as to authority and territorial status.[13] The terms of their agreements are unfortunately obscure, but they appear to have been somewhat prejudicial to Montejo's claims to permanent jurisdiction over the district. Nevertheless, Montejo seems to have been given power to address the Crown in the name of San Miguel, and thus apparently obtained temporary and limited recognition there. The Crown, however, went no further than to declare that

[10] Residencia of Pedro de Alvarado, 1535–37, AGI, Justicia 295–96.

[11] *Ibid.;* Montejo to the Crown, Naco, July 28, 1537, AGI, Guatemala 9; Montejo to the Crown, Gracias a Dios, June 1, 1539, DII, 24:250–97; Pedraza to the Crown, Gracias a Dios, May 18, 1539, AGI, Guatemala 9.

[12] Montejo to the Crown, Gracias a Dios, June 1, 1539, DII, 24:250–97. Pedraza to the Crown, Gracias a Dios, May 18, 1539, AGI, Guatemala 9.

[13] Montejo to the Crown, Gracias a Dios, June 1, 1539, DII, 24:250–97. See also Chamberlain, 1947a.

appropriate action would be taken after due investigation and to urge the governors of Honduras-Higueras and Guatemala to refrain from controversy over territorial limits.[14]

It will be recalled that Montejo's plans for conquest and settlement of the Valley of Olancho immediately following the quelling of the general revolt were nullified by refusal of the treasurer García de Celís and the contador Cerezeda to support him.[15]

Another jurisdictional question involved the western boundaries between Honduras-Higueras and Guatemala. While Montejo was engaged in pacifying the area of San Pedro in 1537 a controversy over these borders arose between him and Alonso Maldonado, judge of residencia and interim governor of Guatemala. Maldonado, accompanied by an armed group, was carrying out a general *visita,* or inspection tour, of Guatemala, and had moved to within a relatively short distance of Gracias a Dios, into territory which Montejo regarded as part of Honduras-Higueras. Montejo considered the district which Maldonado had penetrated as highly suitable for colonization and may himself have been planning to enter it.[16] While at the pueblo of Naco, he and Maldonado established contact with each other, but being unable to come to an agreement, they decided to refer the matter to the Crown. Montejo later followed up these attempts by sending his brother Juan to confer with Maldonado, who had moved on to San Salvador. This further effort failed to solve a typical provincial frontier controversy, and the Crown took no definite action.[17]

In this connection it should be noted that shortly after Montejo arrived in Honduras-Higueras the cabildo of Santiago de Guatemala charged him with having interfered in certain frontier pueblos, which undoubtedly lay in the region under dispute. The cabildo strongly protested his alleged incursions to the Viceroy of New Spain, who in turn communicated with Montejo. The adelantado replied to the cabildo that the pueblos concerned were at war when he came to Higueras, and that Alvarado himself had placed them within the limits of Higueras, assigning them in encomienda to citizens of Gracias a Dios. Montejo persistently maintained jurisdiction of Honduras-Higueras over these and other pueblos along the western and southern frontiers of the province.[18]

14 *Ibid.*
15 Montejo to the Crown, Gracias a Dios, May 1, 1542, AGI, Patronato 184-25.
16 Montejo to the Crown, Naco, July 28, 1537, AGI, Guatemala 9; Cedula of June 26, 1539, AGI, Guatemala 393.
17 *Ibid.*
18 *Ibid.;* Montejo to the Cabildo of Santiago de Guatemala, Gracias a Dios, December 11, 1537, AGG, Papers from the Archivo Municipal, Cartas de Personas Ylustres; Document drawn up by the Cabildo of Guatemala (n.d.), AGG, Papers from the Archivo Municipal, Reales Cédulas, Libro 5.

FIG. 2—EIGHTEENTH-CENTURY ENGLISH MAP OF THE WEST INDIES

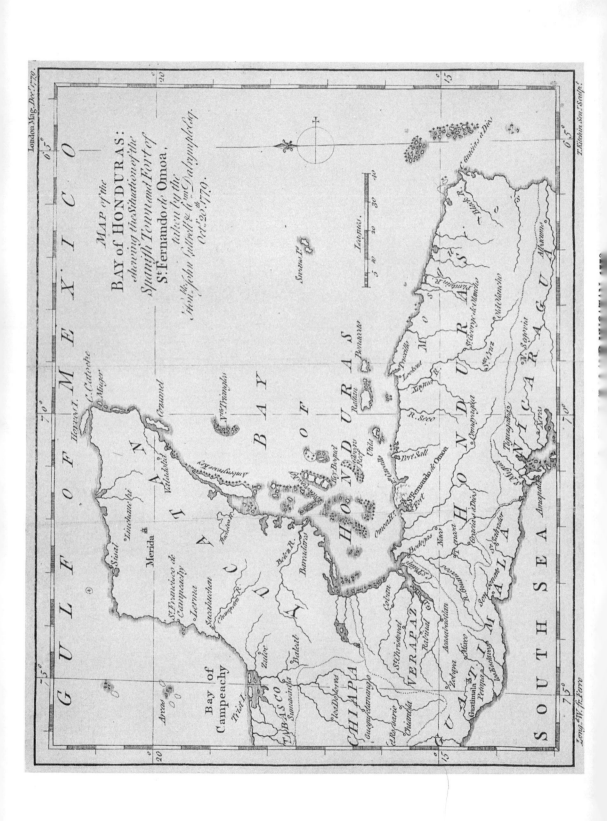

MAP of the
BAY of HONDURAS:
shewing the Situation of the
Spanish Town and Fort of
St. Fernando de Omoa,
taken by the
Honble John Luttrell & Wm Dalrymple Esqr.
Octr 20th 1770.

GULF OF MEXICO

YUCATAN

BAY OF HONDURAS

HONDURAS

NICARAGUA

GUATIMALA

CHIAPA

VERAPAZ

TABASCO

Bay of
Campeachy

SOUTH SEA

MOSQUITO

Leagues

T. Kitchin Sen.r Sculpt.

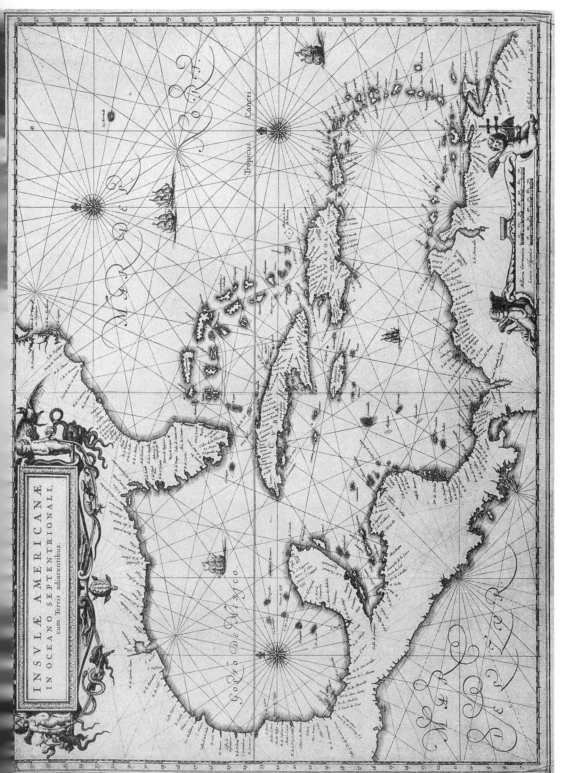

Fig. 4—SEVENTEENTH-CENTURY DUTCH CHART OF THE WEST INDIES

TRUXILLO.

A Promontorium.   D Ecclesia S. Francisci.   G Ecclesia Majora.
B Latus Occidentale.   E Porta.   H Domus in qua pater pictus
C Flumen Quadrarius.   F Fornicibus.   Recaldus.

When he received the royal cedula of 1534 transferring Honduras-Higueras from the jurisdiction of the Audiencia of New Spain to that of Santo Domingo, Montejo remonstrated. He held that it would be more advantageous to the province to remain under New Spain because it was possible to reach the City of Mexico in two months, whereas vessels to and from Santo Domingo were few and the voyage was slow and dangerous. He even asserted that it would be more feasible to appeal directly to the Consejo de Indias in Castile than to the Audiencia of Santo Domingo, since ships could ordinarily reach Europe in fifty or sixty days.[19]

Montejo's private ambition for his adelantamiento is evident here. First, if Honduras-Higueras remained under the Audiencia of Santo Domingo, superior jurisdiction within his territories would be divided between two widely separated tribunals, since the remainder of his provinces were under the Audiencia of New Spain. Complications would inevitably result. Moreover, Montejo was personally acquainted with the higher officials of New Spain, on whose support and favor he counted, but not with those of Santo Domingo. Second, a direct line of appeal to the Consejo de Indias, if he could establish it, would assist his design to erect an adelantamiento depending directly on the Crown and largely independent of superior agencies of government in the Indies. His recommendations and protests to the Crown on these points, however, had no immediate effect.

PLANS FOR COMMERCIAL AND POLITICAL
DEVELOPMENT, 1537–39

The economic and political development of Honduras-Higueras predominated in Montejo's design for a wider adelantamiento. The elements of this idea were first enunciated by Cerezeda and shared by García de Celís, but Montejo showed understanding and foresight in projecting them to their logical conclusion.

A trade route was to be established between the North and South Seas, from the excellent harbor of Puerto de Caballos, where a permanent town was to be founded, through the Valley of Comayagua to the Bahía de Fonseca—a relatively short distance. It was to replace the road across Panama to carry trade between Castile and the West Indies and between Peru and the other South Sea provinces.[20]

[19] Montejo to the Crown, Gracias a Dios, June 1, 1539, DII 24:250–97; Residencia of Montejo for Honduras-Higueras, 1544, AGI, Justicia 300.
[20] Montejo to the Crown, Naco, July 28, 1537, AGI, Guatemala 9; Montejo to the Crown, Gracias a Dios, June 1, 1539, DII, 24:250–97. Montejo to the Crown, Gracias a Dios, May 1, 1542, AGI, Patronato 184-25; Pedraza to the Crown, Gracias a Dios, May 18, 1539, AGI, Guatemala 9; Chamberlain, 1945c.

The plan envisioned the economic evolution of Higueras and the surrounding provinces into an important commercial area. A town was to be founded on the proposed route, midway between the two oceans, as a principal commercial and administrative center for the entire region of Honduras-Higueras, Guatemala, San Salvador, and Nicaragua. San Pedro was to be a point of distribution and transshipment on the north; a new port town or the already existing San Miguel was to serve in like manner on the south. A network of roads to accommodate pack animals and vehicles was to be established between Puerto de Caballos, Trujillo, San Pedro, Gracias a Dios, the Town of Comayagua, San Miguel, the Valley of Olancho, and the Bahía de Fonseca to bind the region together, foster its security, and facilitate trade. These roads were to extend into Guatemala and Nicaragua to bring the widely separated Spanish municipalities of Central America together. The artery of commerce between Puerto de Caballos and the Bahía de Fonseca was to be the axis of this system.[21]

Montejo proposed Comayagua as the metropolis of the Central American provinces.[22] (Cerezeda had thought of establishing a city at the Valley of Comayagua pueblo of Maniani;[23] Alvarado, at Gracias a Dios.[24]) Its central location and excellent geographical surroundings promoted its suitability, and Montejo had pursued the conquest of the Valley of Comayagua with this in mind.

The valley, running roughly north and south, soon proved one of the richest sections of all Higueras, and it indeed offered the most practicable route between the North and South Seas. It was fertile, forested, and well watered; maize and other products abounded; its climate, determined by a moderately high elevation, was temperate and healthful. It was well suited to agriculture and the raising of domestic animals. Rich silver deposits existed, and the native population was at first comparatively dense, although it soon declined.[25] From Puerto de Caballos, streams navigable by canoe led inland to within a few leagues of the Town of Comayagua, where stood a native town at which a trading factory could be erected. A good land route lay from this town to Comayagua, thence to the South Sea.[26]

The authorities and citizens of Comayagua enthusiastically supported Montejo's plans and recommended that, because of its situation, the town should

[21] Ibid.
[22] Montejo to the Crown, Naco, July 28, 1537, AGI, Guatemala 9; Montejo to the Crown, Gracias a Dios, June 1, 1539, DII: 250–97; Pedraza to the Crown, Gracias a Dios, May 18, 1539, AGI, Guatemala 9.
[23] Cerezeda to the Crown, Buena Esperanza, August 31, 1535, AGI, Guatemala 39.
[24] Documents concerning the founding and repartimiento of Gracias a Dios, San Pedro, July 20, 1536, AGI, Patronato 20-4-6.
[25] Cabildo of Comayagua to the Crown, September 5, 1539, AGI, Guatemala 43; Juan de Lerma to the Crown, San Pedro, October 31, 1539, AGI, Guatemala 49.
[26] Cabildo of Comayagua to the Crown, September 5, 1539, AGI, Guatemala 43.

immediately replace Gracias a Dios as capital of the province. They even advocated abandonment of Gracias a Dios and transfer of its citizens to Comayagua. The factor Juan de Lerma also suggested similar action to the Crown. Political developments in the province, however, prevented such a move.[27]

Montejo sought royal sanction for his scheme. The contador Cerezeda, who had first stated the plan, and the treasurer García de Celís, as royal treasury officials of long experience in the province, as well as Pedraza advocated it. The cabildo of Comayagua likewise pressed in most extravagant terms the advantages of the valley as the location for an important city.[28]

While at Court, with Alvarado, Gracía de Celís had already laid before the Crown the project for a route between Puerto de Caballos and the Bahía de Fonseca. He presented the plan in the form it had taken under Cerezeda and Alvarado, and emphasized the importance of founding a town in the interior. Alvarado probably did likewise.

García de Celís (and also undoubtedly Alvarado) discussed the project with Pedraza in Castile. En route to the New World together, Pedraza and García de Celís conferred with the President of the Audiencia of Santo Domingo and Bishop of the island, representing the plan as of great advantage to the Central American provinces as a whole. After arriving and becoming thoroughly familiar with Honduras-Higueras, Pedraza was one of the most vigorous advocates of Montejo's broad plan for economic development.[29] In fact, after Alvarado had in 1539 forced Montejo to exchange the governorship of Honduras-Higueras for that of Chiapas, the factor Lerma suggested to the Crown that the execution of the project be placed in Pedraza's hands.[30]

Furthermore, the Bishop of Guatemala, Francisco de Marroquín, recommended to the Crown that Puerto de Caballos, rather than the New Spain ports of Vera Cruz and Espíritu Santo, should be the point of entry for Guatemala, and also serve as the northern base of a route to replace the way across Panama.[31] Lerma also favored this recommendation.[32]

The Crown approved these projects in principle and strongly endorsed the establishment of a town midway between the North and South Seas and the construction of roads.[33] No action, however, was taken toward supplanting the route across Panama.

[27] *Ibid.;* Juan de Lerma to the Crown, San Pedro, October 31, 1539, AGI, Guatemala 49.
[28] *Ibid.;* Pedraza to the Crown, Gracias a Dios, May 18, 1539, AGI, Guatemala 9.
[29] Pedraza to the Crown, Gracias a Dios, May 18, 1539, AGI, Guatemala 9.
[30] Juan de Lerma to the Crown, San Pedro, October 1, 1539, AGI, Guatemala 49.
[31] See Bishop Francisco de Marroquín to the Crown, San Pedro, January 15, 1543, AGI, Guatemala 156; Marroquín to the Crown, May 10, 1537, Cartas de Indias, 1877, pp. 421–22.
[32] Juan de Lerma to the Crown, San Pedro, October 31, 1539, AGI, Guatemala 49.
[33] Cedula to Montejo of June 7, 1539, AGI, Guatemala 402; Cedulas of March 26, 1546, and November 23, 1547, AGI, Guatemala 393; and October 29, 1540 and December 27, 1532, AGI, Guatemala 402,

Montejo's plans to expand colonization and to develop other aspects of the provincial economy were also well considered. He informed the Crown of his steps to exploit the rich silver mines of the Valley of Comayagua and of his intention to conquer the Valley of Olancho. He proposed to exploit the gold now known to exist in the Valley of Olancho immediately upon its occupation and, as part of a network of communications, to construct roads between Olancho and Trujillo, about forty leagues apart. This would give Trujillo both access to a new region and ready land connections with the remainder of the province, thus ending the isolation imposed by sea communications.[34]

Montejo's proposal to conquer Taguzgalpa was a project of the same type, intended to join Honduras-Higueras more closely with eastern sections of Nicaragua as well as to increase the area of Spanish occupation, the latter supplementing royal authorization to found a town farther west between Higueras and the City of León.

All these projects were part of Montejo's broad program and were intended to weld his several districts into a more compact unit. Even though Cerezeda and García de Celís, through their refusal to provide aid, had prevented Montejo from colonizing the area east of the Valley of Comayagua, he made such preparations as were possible eventually to carry out this eastward expansion.

Montejo considered the location which Gonzalo de Alvarado had chosen for Gracias a Dios too low and unhealthful, too weak militarily, and, contrary to first opinion, too far from centers of Indian population for the service which the city required after peace was established. Doña Beatriz de Herrera, Montejo's wife, and Bachiller Juan Alvarez, his personal chaplain and legal adviser, also advocated its transfer.[35] At length Montejo found an apparently suitable site two leagues away, which upon inspection Pedraza, members of the cabildo, and principal citizens formally approved.[36] When, late in 1538, Montejo went to the aid of Cáceres in completing the conquest of the Valley of Comayagua, he instructed his brother Juan and Pedraza, as coadministrators in Gracias a Dios during his absence, to effect the transfer. This was done early in 1539. The plan of the city had already been traced. As spiritual head of the colony, Pedraza erected a cross on the site of the main plaza, and, after impressive ceremonies, Gracias a Dios began its official life in the new

---

regarding roads; Cedula of January 29, 1538, AGI, Guatemala 402, authorizing the founding of a municipality between Honduras-Higueras and Nicaragua.

[34] Montejo to the Crown, Gracias a Dios, June 1, 1539, DII, 24:250–97; Montejo to the Crown, Gracias a Dios, June 1, 1539, DII, 24:298–310; Montejo to the Crown, Gracias a Dios, November 4, 1539, AGI, Guatemala 9; Montejo to the Crown, Gracias a Dios May 1, 1539, AGI, Patronato 184-25.

[35] Pedraza to the Crown, Gracias a Dios, May 18, 1539, AGI, Guatemala 9; Montejo to the Crown, Gracias a Dios, June 1, 1539, DII, 24:250–97.

[36] Pedraza to the Crown, Gracias a Dios, May 18, 1539, AGI, Guatemala 9.

setting.[37] Thus did Pedraza describe the re-establishment of the city to the Crown:

It is to the best interests of Your Majesty . . . that the Indian pueblos should be close to the city, so that the natives can come to it readily. . . . I gave my [favorable] opinion and vote with regard to the transfer and inspection of the new site, along with the magistrates, regidores and procurador of the city, and along with many other gentlemen who were consulted by the governor. Under the authority the governor gave his brother . . . and me [we transferred the city]. . . . The first step taken was to construct the shrine of the True and Holy Cross at the place where the church was to be built, with the accompanying singing of a hymn. . . . I and all who were there carried the cross on our shoulders and after we set it up we all kneeled and I offered a prayer based on the Gospel of Saint John. In the same manner we constructed an altar at the foot of the cross and hung the bells. These bells are the best there are in all the land. Then I put on my vestments and said the Mass of the Dulcíssimo Nombre de Jesús from the missals of Seville and prayed, . . . for if the city has its foundations laid on holy words it cannot fail to enjoy divine clemency and exist for the benefit of the royal Crown of Your Majesty. . . . Then all the citizens began to build their houses and I began to build mine. I remained in the city until the governor returned and he thanked me profoundly for what I had done and praised God when he saw that the city had been moved and learned that it had been established under such good auspices. . . .

[The new site of Gracias a Dios] is close to all the Indian pueblos of the entire district. This was not the case with the former location, nor was the other place healthful. The other site had no proper entrances and exits, and was situated in a depression where it was in much danger from Indians. . . . The present site is very fine location and is more healthful. It has good means of access and exit and is much better situated with respect to the Indian pueblos. . . . [38]

The site of San Pedro, at first considered favorable, also proved unhealthful and generally unsatisfactory. So Montejo intended to re-establish the town at the point where the routes from the north coast to Comayagua and to the Valley of Naco diverged.[39] He claims to have "reformed" San Pedro and may have moved the town, but it is not clear whether or not the transfer, if actually made, was carried out in full conformance with his original plans.[40]

Montejo also strove to improve the situation of ailing Trujillo. He had confidence in the future progress of this older city, especially since the dis-

[37] *Ibid.*
[38] *Ibid.*
[39] Montejo to the Crown, Gracias a Dios, June 1, 1539, DII, 24:250–97; Montejo *v.* Pedraza, 1539, AGI, Justicia 129-2; Montejo to the Crown, Gracias a Dios, August 25, 1539, AGI, Guatemala 39.
[40] In his letter of August 25, 1539, AGI, Guatemala 39, Montejo speaks of the "reforma" of San Pedro, but does not provide precise details.

covery of additional mines in its district, and considered its development to be intimately linked with his plans for the eventual colonization of Olancho.[41]

As part of his wider economic program, Montejo sought to establish a permanent town at Puerto de Caballos, utilizing its very fine harbor to provide a much-needed port. It was the only harbor of eastern Higueras and could be made to serve that province, Guatemala, and San Salvador. Through the establishment of a permanent town at Puerto de Caballos, Montejo hoped to create a base at the northern end of the proposed trade route and stimulate commerce in general. Although the plan for a town here was not new, Montejo gave it more serious thought than did his immediate predecessors.

Development of Puerto de Caballos had been hampered by numerous factors, including its unhealthful situation. Another was the initial lack of an adequate road to San Pedro, some leagues inland. The citizens of San Pedro went to Puerto de Caballos only when ships arrived from Castile, the West Indies, and New Spain, and remained only long enough to transact business in a miniature fair on the pattern of the great ones which developed at Porto Bello and Vera Cruz. The only buildings were temporary. With no Spanish town in the immediate vicinity, masters of trading vessels and merchants were so reluctant to put in at Puerto de Caballos that development of commerce was seriously handicapped. Few vessels visited the port and none at all arrived during the great revolt, when equipment and merchandise of all kinds were most needed.[42]

Montejo seems to have taken the first steps toward founding a town at Puerto de Caballos soon after assuming the governorship. He gathered natives from nearby pueblos and settled them at the port to serve the prospective town. Then colonists were established there and the place became known as San Juan Puerto de Caballos. The extent of its formal organization is not clear, for it appears to have been placed under the direct jurisdiction of San Pedro. Montejo also intended to construct a much-needed road, passable at all seasons, between San Juan and San Pedro.[43]

Although the permanent existence of San Juan was of measurable importance in his plans, Montejo's effort seems to have been no more successful than earlier ones. The unhealthful climate and the great revolt which demanded concentration of effort elsewhere, made success impossible. By the spring of 1539, San Juan was apparently abandoned. When Alvarado re-

[41] Montejo to the Crown, Gracias a Dios, June 1, 1539, DII, 24:250–97; Montejo to the Crown, Gracias a Dios, June 1, 1539, DII, 24:298–310; Cabildo of Trujillo to the Crown, March 12, 1540, AGI, Guatemala 44.
[42] Montejo to the Crown, Gracias a Dios, June 1, 1539, DII, 24:250–97.
[43] Ibid.

turned from Castile with his armada in April, he had to expend great effort and considerable time to cut a road through to San Pedro.[44]

Under Montejo's administration there was undeniable improvement in communication with Honduras-Higueras and between that province and others, especially Guatemala, even though some of the "roads" could have been little more than trails. He had a road built between the Sula area on the north and Gracias a Dios, improved roads radiating from Gracias a Dios, and seems to have had a short-lived route cut from San Pedro to Puerto de Caballos. Pedraza praised Montejo to the Crown in high terms for these achievements, despite the fact that warfare and unsettled conditions prevented him from really developing his road projects.[45]

MINING IN HONDURAS-HIGUERAS TO 1539

Honduras-Higueras, with its agricultural, commercial, and mining potentialities, was capable of maintaining itself in relative independence from other provinces. Its inability to do so hitherto stemmed from internal dissension, failure really to conquer the Indians, poor administration, and the absence of a true colonial incentive among many of the Spanish settlers, who lacked the foresight to pursue a policy of deliberate and sound economic development.

Deposits of gold and silver proved extensive in Honduras-Higueras. Mines had long been operated in the Trujillo area, and exploitation of precious metals in Higueras had begun shortly after Cerezeda's arrival in 1534, since gold was found in the valleys just back from the north coast. Coincident with the final pacification of the Valley of Comayagua, rich silver lodes were discovered close about Comayagua, just after Montejo had transferred that town to its new site.[46]

This gold and silver promised a great future, and Montejo and the colonists naturally wished to exploit these metals as an immediate source of large revenues. Montejo proposed to develop them moderately and on a long-range basis, whereas the majority of the colonists had no thought but to get as much as they could as quickly as possible. Montejo desired to bring in negro slaves, but opposed the colonists' wish to use large numbers of Indians in forced labor.[47]

[44] *Ibid.;* Alvarado to the Crown, Gracias a Dios, August 4, 1539, DII, 24:311–19.
[45] Pedraza to the Crown, Gracias a Dios, May 18, 1539, AGI, Guatemala 9.
[46] Montejo to the Crown, June 1, 1539, DII, 24:250–97; Montejo to the Crown, Gracias a Dios, August 20, 1539, AGI, Guatemala 39; Montejo to the Crown, Gracias a Dios, May 1, 1542, AGI, Patronato 184-25; Pedraza to the Crown, Gracias a Dios, May 18, 1539, Guatemala 9.
[47] Montejo to the Crown, Naco, July 28, 1537, AGI, Guatemala 9; Montejo to the Crown, Gracias a Dios, June 1, 1539, DII, 24:250–97, 298–310; Pedraza to the Crown, May 18, 1539, AGI, Guatemala 9; Montejo to the Cabildo of Santiago de Guatemala, Gracias a Dios, December 11, 1537, AGG, Papers from the Archivo Municipal, Cartas de Personas Ylustres; Cabildo of San Pedro to the Crown, November 1, 1539, AGI, Guatemala 44.

Mining in Higueras had begun on a large scale with Alvarado and the increased, though temporary, security which his campaigns brought with them. Alvarado, lesser officials of Guatemala, and wealthy colonists of both Guatemala and San Salvador, some of whom had accompanied Alvarado to Higueras, employed specially trained cuadrillas to search for and extract gold and silver wherever Alvarado and his captains penetrated. Officials of Honduras-Higueras also employed such teams.[48]

There were twenty or more of these cuadrillas operating in Higueras during Alvarado's brief period in the province and after he left for Castile. The largest included four, five, or even more Spanish miners, and counted as high as 100 slaves. The average number of slaves for each cuadrilla was probably between fifteen and twenty-five. Alvarado operated several large cuadrillas and Francisco de Castellanos, the treasurer of Guatemala, owned one. Padre Avela, later a cura of Gracias a Dios, and Cerezeda both operated cuadrillas of about fifteen slaves.[49] These mining groups covered a wide area of Higueras, exploring every possibility, and took out precious metals in considerable amounts. A large proportion of gold mining was of the placer type, along the beds of streams, which were diligently followed. Montejo participated in this quest, appropriating the cuadrillas of the absent Alvarado, for his own financial resources were slender at this time.

The colonists of Higueras as a whole owned but few slaves and lacked adequate mining equipment of the kind which the more wealthy colonists of Guatemala and San Salvador possessed. The former were consequently not able to exploit the mineral riches of their province to the extent they desired. Cuadrillas operated by officials and citizens of Guatemala and San Salvador in the year and a half following Alvarado's intervention are said to have mined ore to the value of some 70,000 castellanos, and a single highly successful cuadrilla is said to have found ore to the amount of 7000 castellanos during one *demora,* or period between smeltings. The precious metals extracted by the cuadrillas owned by officials and colonists of Guatemala and San Salvador were taken to those provinces for refining.[50]

The settlers of Honduras-Higueras, notably the royal treasury officials, soon deeply resented the situation. They objected to the personal enrichment of outsiders through the wealth of Honduras-Higueras. They also opposed the removal of their gold and silver to Guatemala and San Salvador for refining,

[48] *Ibid.;* Montejo *v.* Pedraza, 1539, AGI, Justicia 129-2; Cabildo of Santiago de Guatemala for Montejo (n.d.), AGG, Papers from the Archivo Municipal, Ynstrucciones y Cartas; Document drawn up by the Cabildo of Santiago de Guatemala concerning Montejo's restrictions on mining in Higueras (n.d.), AGG, Papers from the Archivo Municipal, Reales Cédulas, Libro 5.
[49] *Ibid.*
[50] *Ibid.*

especially because of the obstacles to their own mining operations. Further-more, the royal treasury of Honduras-Higueras suffered greatly from this practice, since the fifth of precious metals which by law belonged to the Crown from the gold and silver thus taken out of Higueras went into the royal coffers of Guatemala and San Salvador rather than into those of Higueras. In this way the royal treasury of Honduras-Higueras had no use of, and re-ceived no credit for, a great proportion of the precious metals found in the province. Production of wealth and revenues by the provinces of the Indies was closely scrutinized by the higher colonial administration in Castile be-cause of the ceaseless need of the King-Emperor Charles for funds to support his far-flung imperial policies. The importance of any given province was inevitably estimated in terms of the immediate revenues it produced. Also, sufficient incomes were needed in Honduras-Higueras to meet the expenses of provincial administration, as royal colonial fiscal policy, which was based on local financial self-sufficiency, required. Consequently the drain of gold and silver from Honduras-Higueras was both serious and irksome for its colonists from several points of view.[51]

When Montejo took office in Honduras-Higueras the mining situation was brought to his attention at the instance of the citizens of San Pedro. Recog-nizing their plight, he designated an area to which miners of Guatemala and San Salvador were restricted. He also decreed that smelting of precious metals mined in Higueras by cuadrillas operated by colonists of other provinces should be carried out in that province and not in Guatemala, where the ca-bildo of Santiago de Guatemala wished to have it done. Thus Montejo pro-tected the interests of the colonists of Honduras-Higueras and kept the royal quinto on the precious metals of the province for its own royal coffers. Mon-tejo made his views on mining known to the Santiago authorities and strongly protested against mining activities of Guatemalans in Higueras.[52] The colo-nists of Higueras as a group also protested directly to the Crown.[53]

Another factor also played its part in causing Montejo to restrict the activi-ties of the mining cuadrillas. Excessive labor and the unaccustomed climate, as the natives moved alternately through tropical lowland and cooler high-lands, exacted a heavy death toll. Montejo pointed out the high mortality rate and suffering of the Indians to Maldonado and the authorities of Guate-

[51] Ibid.
[52] Montejo to the Crown, July 28, 1537, AGI, Guatemala 9; Document drawn up by the Cabildo of Santiago de Guatemala concerning Montejo's restrictions on mining in Higueras (n.d.), AGG, Papers from the Archivo Municipal, Reales Cédulas, Libro 5.
[53] See Instructions to the procuradores of Honduras-Higueras, Playa de Puerto de Caballos, August 12, 1536, DII, 14; various cedulas issued in benefit of Honduras-Higueras 1537–38, AGI, 402.

mala during the course of his protests regarding the mining activities of Guatcmalans and Salvadorans in Higueras.[54]

The drastic restrictions Montejo imposed made unprofitable continued mining operations by colonists of other provinces, and some cuadrillas were soon withdrawn. Furthermore, apparently influenced by Montejo's protests, Maldonado, as acting governor of Guatemala, later ordered that the rest of the cuadrillas should be returned to Guatemala and San Salvador. It would seem that Maldonado's decree was carefully enforced and that in consequence all outside cuadrillas temporarily left Higueras. As a result, a number of colonists who had gone to Higueras with Alvarado now returned to Guatemala because their greatest source of profits had been eliminated.[55]

The cabildo of Santiago de Guatemala and the treasurer of that province, Francisco de Castellanos, emphatically protested to Montejo and the authorities of New Spain against the enforced withdrawal of the cuadrillas and indicated their intention of carrying the matter to the Crown. They must also have made their opinions known to Maldonado in vigorous fashion. The Viceroy of New Spain, Antonio de Mendoza, was so impressed by these objections that he recommended to Montejo an adjustment.[56]

In their protestations, the Santiago cabildo and Castellanos maintained that serious decreases in royal revenue would result from the absence of large cuadrillas in Higueras, claimed heavy personal losses to colonists of Guatemala, and held that Montejo had no authority whatsoever to restrict the activities of the cuadrillas. They demanded that he reverse his action, threatening to lodge claims against his incomes and holdings, on behalf of the caja real of Guatemala, of 1000 pesos de oro annually for each cuadrilla withdrawn from Higueras and a total lump sum claim of 10,000 pesos de oro should he leave the restrictions in force. These sums were far beyond Montejo's income.[57]

The measures which Montejo decreed undoubtedly caused a reduction in mining in Higueras and a consequent decline in royal revenues for the province during 1537. After that year, war and disturbed political conditions hindered the exploitation of precious metals for some time. Montejo was between two fires, the opposing interests of Guatemala and Honduras-Higueras. Naturally he wished to benefit his own province. In addition, he sought to develop sound mining for the good of Honduras-Higueras as a whole, rather than

[54] Montejo to the Crown, Naco, July 28, 1537, AGI, Guatemala 9; Montejo to the Crown, Gracias a Dios, June 1, 1539, DII, 24:250–97, 298–310.
[55] Ibid.; Cabildo of Santiago to Montejo (n.d.), AGG, Papers from the Achivo Municipal, Ynstrucciones y Cartas; Document drawn up by the Cabildo of Santiago de Guatemala concerning Montejo's restrictions on mining in Higueras (n.d.), AGG, Papers from the Archivo Municipal, Reales Cédulas, Libro 5.
[56] Ibid.
[57] Ibid.

permit unfettered exploitation to strip the region of its most readily accessible riches overnight.

Partly to heed the protests from the authorities of Guatemala and the recommendations from the Viceroy of New Spain and partly again to stimulate mining in Higueras and increase its falling revenues, Montejo finally modified the restrictions to the extent of permitting colonists of Guatemala and San Salvador to mine anywhere within the province, but firmly required that refining should take place only in Higueras.[58] Nevertheless, he had accomplished his main purpose: exploitation of local riches by outsiders had been checked and the quinto had been protected for the royal coffers of Honduras-Higueras itself. The outbreak of the great revolt late in 1537, furthermore, prevented the return of a number of cuadrillas which had left Higueras after Montejo first decreed his restrictions and thus lessened the protests from neighboring provinces.

Unsettled political conditions and warfare were the main hindrances to gold and silver production in Higueras for a time after 1537. Nevertheless, the annual refining of gold in Higueras in 1538 seems to have amounted to 58,770 pesos. In 1539 about 7,800 pesos were refined at Gracias a Dios, where the cabildo, after Alvarado returned from Castile, declared that if the cuadrillas had not been sent home, 150,000 pesos de oro could have been produced in the province. Likewise, the authorities of Santiago de Guatemala held that each of the twenty or more cuadrillas owned by citizens of Guatemala and San Salvador would have produced 5000 to 6000 pesos a year if they had been permitted to operate unhindered.[59]

The Crown directed that the refinement of precious metals for Higueras should be carried out in San Pedro. This measure drew criticism from Montejo, who held that refining should be done in the administrative center, Gracias a Dios, where the principal royal treasury officials resided and which was more centrally located. He maintained that the smelting of ore at Gracias a Dios was important to the welfare of the city, and that refining at San Pedro would cause needless expense and effort to the citizens of Gracias a Dios. Furthermore, absence of any considerable number of citizens would leave Gracias a Dios inadequately garrisoned during the refining period. Montejo consequently requested the Crown to order that refinement of ore for all Higueras be carried out in Gracias a Dios. A *casa de fundición,* or smelter where precious metals were assayed, refined, and officially stamped, was later

[58] Montejo to the Cabildo of Santiago de Guatemala, December 11, 1537, AGG, Papers from the Archivo Municipal, Cartas de Personas Ylustres; Montejo to the Crown, Gracias a Dios, June 1, 1539, DII, 24:250–97, 298–310.
[59] Treasury accounts of Diego García de Celís, 1540, AGI, Indiferente General 1206; accounts of refining of precious metals in Gracias a Dios and Puerto de Caballos, 1539–41, AGI, Patronato 180-74.

erected there.[60] Montejo also recommended to the Crown that adequate mining equipment be made available to the province, since most colonists did not have the funds to import such tools.[61]

In general Montejo did everything he felt reasonable to promote mining in Higueras. It was the first region under his control in which gold and silver existed and he wished to make the most of it in accordance with what he considered the best interests of the province. During his quarrel with the authorities of Guatemala regarding mining, and after he had relaxed his original restrictions, Montejo on December 11, 1537, stated his viewpoint in a letter to the cabildo of Santiago:

Many days before receiving your letter, I provided that gold might be mined anywhere, even though this is to the prejudice of the citizens and settlers of this province, since the land is already at war and all the citizens are engaged in the campaigns of pacification.

The citizens of this province suffered as a result of the harmful practices employed by the cuadrillas and miners of Guatemala in extracting gold. These cuadrillas and miners did not wish to search for gold themselves, but went to each river, gulley and deposit following behind those who really explored for it, accompanied by four or five miners and fifteen or twenty Indians. They did no more than go along the stream beds without ever leaving them and exploited them to the fullest. They left the rivers completely robbed and the land deformed, when there was much gold to be found elsewhere. They took all they could get without having to expend any real effort and avoided labor which might prove difficult. These are not colonists of the province, and the real colonists suffer from their activities.

The miners of Guatemala reap the rewards unfairly.

To the time of my restrictive decree those from the outside had discovered no new deposits and were aware of only those which were originally known. . . . Even after I removed the restrictions these miners made no efforts to discover more gold deposits, and they had no desire to do so. . . .

With regard to smelting, which was touched on by the cabildo, I have ordered that those engaged in mining shall bring in their ore for refining on January 10, [1538], and they sent a petition demanding that the period be extended, that the refining take place at the close of March, and that smelting be carried out at the mines. I have answered saying that I would be satisfied if the miners place the gold in the houses of the royal treasury officials. I have done all that I can to aid those who mine gold and facilitate their work, and shall continue to do so. I desire good feeling and cooperation with the authorities and citizens of Guatemala.[62]

---

[60] Cedula of June 30, 1537, AGI, Guatemala 402; Montejo to the Crown, Naco, July 28, 1537, AGI, Guatemala 9; Montejo to the Crown, Gracias a Dios, June 1, 1539, DII, 24:250–97; Residencia of Montejo for Honduras-Higueras, 1544, AGI, Justicia 300.

[61] *Ibid.*

[62] Montejo to the Cabildo of Santiago de Guatemala, Gracias a Dios, December 11, 1537, AGG, Papers from the Archivo Municipal, Cartas de Personas Ylustres.

GENERAL ADMINISTRATIVE MEASURES, 1537–39

In seeking to spare the Indians, Montejo turned to negro slavery. He requested the Crown to send 100–200 negro slaves to the province for mining, road construction, and other labor. The cost of these additional slaves (there were already a number in Honduras-Higueras) was to be met in the colony itself, mainly by individual colonists. Negroes were believed to have much greater stamina in resisting hardships and the climate, and to be able to do the work of many times their number of natives.[63] The Crown did not respond to this request immediately, but later sent a large number to the province.[64]

Montejo desired additional colonists to strengthen the province. He informed the Crown of the need for more Spaniards, expressing the hope for favorable action.

Montejo also sought promulgation by the Crown of a number of measures for the general economic benefit of the province. They concerned reduction of the royal quinto on precious metals to a *diezmo,* or tenth, for a stipulated period, freedom from the *almojarifazgo,* or import and export duties, and other similar measures which were normally adopted to aid the development of colonies during their early stages. Within the province Montejo sought to encourage the colonists, who were left impoverished and wanting in all the requirements of normal colonial life after final conquest of the province.[65]

In reply to Montejo's despatches, the Crown expressed great interest in the construction of an adequate system of roads and in the stimulation of mining. Royal measures already had been ordained with respect to Montejo's other petitions, in response to the similar requests presented by García de Celís and the procuradores in Castile.[66] Furthermore, in 1539, the Crown directed Maldonado, as interim governor of Guatemala, to give every aid to Montejo and Honduras-Higueras because the province obviously needed support and because Montejo was understood personally to be lacking in resources and heavily in debt.[67]

On the death of the veedor of the province, Francisco de Barrientos, Montejo requested the Crown to appoint his brother Juan to that office, but Diego de Valdés had already been designated for the post by royal appointment. Montejo meanwhile placed his brother as acting veedor until the royal appointee should arrive.[68]

[63] Montejo to the Crown, Gracias a Dios, June 1, 1539, DII, 24:250–97.
[64] See *Asiento* for 300 slaves contracted for by Pedraza, Lisbon, July 9, 1541, AGI, Contractación 3281A. Of these, 200 were to be male and 100 female. The price of each was fifty-five "pesos de buen oro de ley perfecta de quilates de 450 maravedís cada peso."
[65] Montejo to the Crown, Naco, July 28, 1537, AGI, Guatemala 9; Montejo to the Crown, Gracias a Dios, June 1, 1539, DII, 24:250–97.
[66] See various cedulas in benefit of Honduras-Higueras, 1537–45, AGI, Guatemala 393 and 402.
[67] Cedula of June 26, 1539, AGI, Guatemala 393.
[68] Montejo to the Crown, Naco, July 28, 1537, AGI, Guatemala 9.

There are indications that Montejo may have introduced, or at least encouraged, wheat growing in Higueras, especially in the Valley of Comayagua.[69] By the mid-century a considerable amount of wheat was produced in that region.[70]

The Crown also took action to meet the manifest needs of Honduras-Higueras and stabilize conditions there. In 1538 it directed that all colonists should each year employ one-tenth of all income gained within the province to promote its economic development. The Crown wished this tithe to be invested in construction of buildings; acquisition of land for the development of haciendas or for specialized forms of agriculture; purchase of livestock, plants, and trees; and furtherance of mining and local industrial and commercial activities. The provincial authorities were strictly to enforce this royal measure and were each year to register the incomes of all Spaniards within the province and determine if they had actually carried out the royal decree. The findings were to be reported to the Consejo de Indias. The Crown believed that the required investments would have numerous beneficial results. Colonists already there would remain in the province, new ones would be attracted, and temporary residents would take more interest in the province if forced to increase their holdings. The Crown was convinced that such measures could not fail to build up the colony, bring it stability, and place it on the road to progress.[71]

[69] See Residencia of Alonso de Maldonado and the oidores of the Audiencia de los Confines, 1548, AGI, Justicia 299.

[70] Taxation of tributes and services of the pueblos of the district of Audiencia de los Confines, 1549–51, AGI, Guatemala 128.

[71] Cedula of January 29, 1538, AGI, Patronato 20-4-7. The text of this interesting and unusual cedula, which went to the root of the problems which were encountered in a number of provinces, follows: Don Carlos e dona Juana . . . a vos el nro. governador ques. o fuere de la provincia de ygueras y cabo de onduras salud y gra. sepades que por quanto pr. esperincia a parecido que una de las cosas que an estorvado el aumentamiento de la poblacion de los cristianos nuestros subditos e vasallos en las nuestras yndias yslas y tierra firme dl. mar oceano a sido y es que muchos de los conquistadores e pobladores y otra personas que alla se an ydo y van no an tenido ni tienen yntencion de permanecer ni poblar en ellas sino de haver alguna cantidad de oro o plata y otras cosas y volverse con ello a estos reynos y aun fuera dellos e que no solo se a sequido estorvo de su poblacion pero tambien dello a resultado el mal tratamiento de los dhos. yndios y grand desacato en la conversion dellos a nuestra santa fee catolica y uno de los remedios que a parecido que seria provechoso para acrescentar la dha. poblacion y perpetuar los vezinos y moradores en ellas y despues todos ellos an recibido y reciben de nos merced ansi de tierra como de vacios y solares e facultad de sacar oro y plata y otros metales y pescar perlas y tienen otros aprovechamientos en la dha. tierra y otros oficios publicos todo en honra y utilidad de sus personas y bienes que todos ellos asi los que al presente moran en la dha. tierra como adelante fuesen a morar en ella estuviesen de vivienda asi por via de vezindad como por trato de mercaderia o de otro qualquier manera que esten de asiento sean tenudos en cada un año de comprar o gastar en edeficios y labores o en plantas de viñas e arboles que lleven fruto y en ganados y otras cosas que permanezcan en esa tierra la dezena pte. de lo que ovieren e adquerieren en la dha. tierra ansi por via de rescate y mercaderias y tributos que dan los yndias y oro y plata y otros metales que se sacan en ella o de otra qualquier manera que ovieren de provecho en la dha. tierra para que en los que ansi compraren y gastaren sea suyo propio y puedan en qualquier tiempo disponer dello en vida o en muerte como de cosa libre sin ympedimiento ni enbargo alguno y teniendolo se aproveche dl. fruto de la que asi comprare labrare plantare y edificare por que aunque la tal persona salga de las dhas. yndias y traiga consigo todo lo que ouiere avido y ganado en ellas quedarian los dhos. compras plantas y edificios en ornato de la republica y aprovechamiento de otros veccinos dlla [y] sea de usa dellos yran con mejor voluntad a morar en ellas y seria causa dl. aumentamiento de la dha. poblacion y se sequirian otros muchos de que dios nro. señor seria servido lo

THE SPANIARDS AND THE INDIANS, 1537–39

As normally required of governing officials, Montejo visited various districts of Higueras during periods of peace and immediately after pacification of each successive region. His purpose was to supervise and improve administration, see to the welfare of the Indians and establish normal conditions of life among them, and become personally acquainted with conditions everywhere. The extensive campaigns he had conducted, moreover, gave him intimate knowledge of a wide area and insight into governmental needs.[72]

In carrying out his visitas, Montejo required the encomenderos to favor the Indians of their towns and supply them with maize for food and for planting. Montejo himself furnished food to needy Indians, and sought to procure their supplies everywhere. As Montejo declared:

. . . they informed me of ill treatment of the Indians, and I [then] treated the natives very well and made their encomenderos help them with supplies of maize so that they could harvest and sow, for they had remained in need because of the war which they had made on the Spaniards. Afterward, whenever the Indians were in need I have required their encomenderos to provide for them, and I myself furnish them with many supplies. . . .[73]

One of the most important and difficult administrative problems facing Montejo was to persuade, or if necessary to force, the Indians to return to their pueblos and resume their normal lives following wide dispersal during warfare. This was a delicate and complicated task at any time and especially complex and arduous in the many regions involved in the great revolt as they were subjugated one by one. Montejo had found such measures necessary

---

qual todo visto y platicado en nuestro consejo de las yndias fue acordado que deviamos mandar dar esta nuestra carta para vos en la dha. razon por la qual mandamos que de aqui adelante todos los conquistadores y pobladores y mercaderes y tratantes y sus factores y las otras personas que estuvieren en la dha. tierra de qualquier estado y condicion que sean asi los que al presente estan y viven y moran en ella como los que de aqui adelante fuesen a morar y labrar estuvieren por vecindad o en otra manera de asiento sean obligados en cada un año [to comply with the foregoing] sin embargo ni impedimiento alguno o para los susos dhos. se quarde y cumpla enteramente mandamos a vos el dho. nuestro presidente oidores y a los otros juezes y justicias de la dha. trra. e cada uno de vos en vrs. lugares y jurisdicion que como cosa muy importante al servicio de dios nuestro señor e nuestro e a la conservacion e aumento dla. republica desa trra. lo agais asi guardar y complir mandando que en cada ciudad villa o lugar della en cada un año o en principio del vos los dhos. justicias con los regidores agais asentar en un libro por antl. escrivano dl. consejo de . . . tal ciudad villa o lugar los vezinos y moradores y las otras personas de suso nombradas que a la dha. saçon morasen o vivieren en ellos para que en fin dl. dho. año con juramento declaren lo que ansi an ganado y adquerido en el dho. año para que de aquello se sepa la dezima conforme a esta nuestra carta y no lo haviendo comprado vos los dhos. justicias los compelais por todo rigor de dro. por manera que aya afeto y se cumpla lo por nos de suso hordenado y embiareis en fin de cada uno de los dhos. años ante los dl. dho. nuestro consejo el sumario dl. conplimiento dello aprecibiendos que si en ello fueredes negligente cometeremos el complimiento dello a persona q. a vra. costa lo aga y por que venga a noticia de todo y ninguno dello pretende ygnorancia mandamos questa dha. carta sea apregonada en los lugares desa dha. provincia que estoviesen poblados . . . Villa de Valladolid, 29 de enero del año . . . de 1539 Yo la Reina. . . .

[72] Residencia of Montejo for Honduras-Higueras, 1544, AGI, Justicia 300.

[73] *Ibid.*

when he first arrived as result of Cerezeda's and Alvarado's campaigns and had met with considerable initial succcss, notably in some parts of the districts of Gracias a Dios and San Pedro. But after the suppression of the revolt this policy received a much greater test. The best interests of both Spaniards and Indians required re-establishment of the latter in their pueblos so that they could cultivate the soil and serve under the encomienda system. Montejo, aided by the provincial officials, especially Pedraza, municipal authorities, and the encomenderos themselves, personally supervised the task of repopulating the Indian towns. Besides striving to draw the natives back to their pueblos, he transferred some towns to new sites he considered more advantageous for both Indians and Spaniards.[74]

After the war Montejo found it virtually impossible to reconstitute many towns with more than a fraction of their original population. As extreme examples, the pueblo of Talva, which numbered some 400 households when Alvarado arrived, was re-established with 35; Careano, originally of 500, with 20; Yopoa, of 270, with 30; Araxuagua, of 200, with 40; and Lepaera, of 400, with 78. By the summer of 1539, this work had been completed as far as circumstances permitted.[75] The effect on the encomienda system, and therefore on the colony, of this decrease of population in many pueblos was naturally weighty. Nevertheless, the quelling of the great revolt meant security for the Spaniards, and the situation became more stabilized. The Spaniards had something on which they could count with some degree of certainty. With the final establishment of undisputed Castilian supremacy, therefore, even though with fewer Indians at hand, the encomienda system could at least be expected to function in a more orderly manner than before, with the attendant solution of the major problem of supply.[76]

The practice of unrestrainedly enslaving Indians in large number had been carried on, or permitted, in Honduras-Higueras by the governors who preceded Montejo. Not only had natives taken in war been enslaved under law, but illegal slave raids were made against peaceful towns. Many Indians, first from Trujillo, and after 1534 from Higueras, were carried to the West Indies to be sold. Some were branded according to royal ordinances governing enslavement, but the majority seem to have been taken with but little pretense to legality. Before Montejo came a large proportion of the colonists appear to

---

[74] Montejo to the Crown, Naco, July 28, 1539, AGI, Guatemala 9; Montejo to the Crown, Gracias a Dios, June 1, 1539, DII, 24:250–97; Pedraza to the Crown, Gracias a Dios, May 18, 1539, AGI, Guatemala 9; Montejo to the Crown, Gracias a Dios, November 4, 1539, AGI, Guatemala 9.

[75] Montejo to the Crown, Gracias a Dios, June 1, 1539, DII, 24:250 ff; Pedraza to the Crown, Gracias a Dios, May 18, 1539, AGI, Guatemala 9.

[76] Ibid.; Montejo to the Crown, November 4, 1539, AGI, Guatemala 9.

have been engaged in slaving operations in one form or another.[77] They had kept comparatively few Indian slaves, despite the numbers taken under earlier governors, including Cerezeda and Alvarado, since it seems to have been much more lucrative to sell them outside the province. As their situation became more permanent, and as mining developed and needs for labor in general increased, the Spaniards became convinced that large numbers of Indian slaves were necessary for the economic development of the province.[78]

The effects of slaving policies before the arrival of Montejo contributed to the decrease in native population and greatly disorganized native society. To establish tranquillity and confidence among the Indians, Montejo resolved to terminate practices which were so flagrantly in violation of royal policy and which, moreover, went contrary to his own beliefs and the true welfare of the colony. He informed the Crown of the evil consequences of the slaving activities of his predecessors and, ignoring the feeling among the colonists, introduced strong measures to curb indiscriminate enslavement.[79]

Notwithstanding his fundamental principles, Montejo believed that some Indian slaves were needed for labor and therefore permitted the taking of natives in war in accordance with royal law. He also requested specific authorization from the Crown to enslave Indians under the conditions stipulated by royal ordinances and for permission to carry on a controlled trade in *esclavos de rescate,* or Indians enslaved by other natives under their own customs. Thus, he asked for license to carry on carefully controlled enslavement and a regulated slave traffic, even though only a very few natives were enslaved and branded during the campaigns of pacification conducted by him before the outbreak of the great revolt. Most of these few slaves were soon set free by Montejo's order.[80]

Montejo's policy displeased the colonists, accustomed to laxity in the enforcement of royal regulations designed to protect the natives and used to following their own inclinations with regard to the taking of slaves. About the time the great general revolt broke out, the colonists demanded of Montejo that for a period of six months he permit enslavement of Indians above the age of fifteen under conditions until then permitted by law. They told Montejo that this measure was necessary to prevent the abandonment of the

[77] *Ibid.;* Montejo to the Crown, Naco, July 28, 1537, AGI, Guatemala 9; Cedulas of January 29 and January 30, 1538, AGI, Guatemala 402; Memorial of Pedraza to the Consejo de Indias (n.d.), AGI, Indiferente General 1380; Pedraza to the Crown, Gracias a Dios, May 18, 1539, AGI, Guatemala 9.

[78] *Ibid.*

[79] Montejo to the Crown, Naco, July 28, 1537, AGI, Guatemala 9; Montejo to the Crown, Gracias a Dios, June 1, 1539, DII, 24:250–97, 298–310.

[80] *Ibid.;* Montejo to the Crown, Gracias a Dios, November 4, 1539, AGI, Guatemala 9; Residencia of Montejo for Honduras-Higueras, 1544, AGI, Justicia 300; Pedraza to the Crown, May 18, 1539, AGI, Guatemala 9.

province, since they could not maintain themselves without a sufficient number of slaves.[81] Under this pressure, Montejo yielded somewhat and, against
his will, sanctioned their petition, prescribing, however, that royal laws should
be observed with the utmost care. He was aware that it would be difficult to
enforce the pertinent laws, but, under the circumstances, felt it necessary to
meet the colonists' demands temporarily. He wrote to the Crown, requesting
approval of the measure, and meanwhile placed it in effect. However, not
many slaves seem to have been taken during the six months' period involved.[82]

Crown policy concerning enslavement of Indians was in transition at this
time, and earlier ordinances permitting slavery were under question. There
were growing trends which were to culminate in the celebrated New Laws
of 1542-43, trends which under the influence of Francisco de Vitoria, Bartolomé de las Casas, and others of their high-minded school, were designed
to prohibit enslavement entirely. The Crown therefore issued a cedula directly to Montejo forbidding the export of slaves from Honduras-Higueras.
This cedula, which arrived after the general uprising had been suppressed,
strengthened Montejo's hand in breaking indiscriminate enslavement and
preventing extensive commerce in slaves.[83]

Even before these developments the Crown had taken specific action against
illicit enslavement of Indians in Honduras-Higueras and their sale in the West
Indies under sanction of earlier governors. In 1537 the Audiencia of Santo
Domingo was directed to investigate reports of violation of royal ordinances
concerning slavery by the authorities of the province, enforce all pertinent
laws, liberate natives illegally enslaved, and punish all offenders. The audiencia committed the enforcement of these instructions to a Dr. Blázquez, whom
that tribunal was sending to Nicaragua to take the residencia of the governor.
Blázquez was to go to Honduras-Higueras after the completion of his mission in Nicaragua. Nothing is known, however, of any investigation Blázquez might have carried out in Honduras-Higueras. It is to be assumed that
he did not go there, perhaps because the outbreak of the general revolt made
an investigation impossible or because the prohibition of unrestricted slaving
operations by Montejo led the audiencia to hold its investigation in abeyance.[84]

The colonists of Honduras-Higueras held that Indians from outside who
served as auxiliaries in war could later be colonized among the natives as
allies of the Spaniards. Alvarado, Gracía de Celís, and Montejo all subscribed

[81] Ibid.
[82] Ibid.
[83] Cedula to Montejo of June 7, 1539, AGI, Guatemala 402; Cedula of January 29, 1539, AGI,
Guatemala 402.
[84] Audiencia of Santo Domingo to the Crown, May 30, 1537, and December 31, 1538, AGI, Santo
Domingo 49.

to the view that such colonization was desirable. Indeed, this theory was common throughout the Indies. Montejo himself had brought in foreign auxiliaries, some of whom were Nahuas from his Valley of Anahuac encomienda of Atzcapotzalco.[85] Those who accompanied him, however, could not have been numerous enough to exert permanent influence, and they were kept closely controlled.

On the other hand, the 1000–2000 Achies whom Alvarado brought from Guatemala were a large enough group to affect gravely the natives of Honduras. Little is known of these fierce, warlike, and pitiless Indians, who are said to have practiced cannibalism and human sacrifice. They may have been a Mexican Nahua island among the Maya and other peoples of Guatemala. Carrying death, destruction, and terror wherever they went, the Achies also conducted ruthless slave raids. They were particularly a scourge to the people of the north coast of Higueras. According to Licenciado Cristóbal de Pedraza, they carried off 6000 men, women, and children, of whom, under their own customs, they enslaved 3000. Many of the natives who fled in abject terror when the Achies approached refused to return home as long as these fierce aliens remained near. Such circumstances added to the desperation of the natives of Higueras, and Montejo and others claimed that the savagery of the Achies was one of the factors that drove them into revolt. To repeat Montejo's words, the Achies were truly "fire for the land." [86] A large number of Achies formed a part of Juan de Chávez' expedition into the hinterland, and this group fortunately returned to Guatemala with him. Montejo, who recognized the evil consequences of their presence, sent a great part of the remainder of these Achies back to their homeland.[87]

During the great revolt, however, when he needed all the auxiliaries he could find, Montejo had requested the authorities of Guatemala to send him more Achies because of the terror they produced.[88] The cabildo of Santiago refused, claiming that the Indians who had accompanied Alvarado had been retained in Higueras too long and that large numbers had died in war and as a result of a strange climate. They further charged that the auxiliaries had been so ill-treated and neglected in Higueras that to provide more for Montejo "would be to send them to the slaughter-house according to exper-

[85] See Cedula of January 28, 1550, regarding the taking by Montejo of Indians from his encomienda of Atzcapotzalco, AGI, Mexico 1689.

[86] Montejo to the Crown, Naco, July 28, 1537, AGI, Guatemala 9; Pedraza to the Crown, May 18, 1539, AGI, Guatemala 9; Montejo to the Crown, Gracias a Dios, June 1, 1539, DII, 24:250–97. The quotation is from Montejo to the Crown, Naco, July 28, 1537.

[87] Ibid.

[88] Montejo to the Cabildo of Santiago de Guatemala, December 24, 1537, AGG, Papers from the Archivo Municipal, Cartas de Personas Ylustres.

ience that has been had of the matter. . . ."[89] After the suppression of the revolt, little is heard of the Achies.

Forced labor by free Indians was another cause of dissension between Montejo and the colonists. In accordance with royal ordinances, Montejo opposed forced labor in mining, burden-bearing, and other excessively hard work, which in many cases quickly led to gross mistreatment, illness, and death. He insisted on the employment of only such legally enslaved Indians as were available and natives who might, with promise of recompense, voluntarily consent to participate in the more arduous activities fostered by the Spaniards. Also, as already indicated, he wished to employ negro slaves to the extent permitted. The colonists especially wished to employ their unpaid encomienda Indians as laborers. While interim governor, Maldonado had prohibited such forced labor in Guatemala, and Montejo adopted parallel measures in Honduras-Higueras. Pedraza, as Protector of the Indians of Honduras-Higueras, took a similar strong stand after his arrival in 1538.[90]

Absence of adequate communications made it necessary to employ natives to carry supplies, merchandise, encomienda tributes, and many other things to all parts of the province. Many natives were needed for this transport service and the weights they carried were frequently very heavy. Burden-bearers were especially necessary during the annual rains, when roads and trails were virtually impassable to animals, let alone vehicles. Burden-bearing worked special harm on the Indians, since those of the highlands had to go to the hot, tropical coast, and those of the coast had to go to the higher, cooler, mountainous interior, just as occurred in connection with mining. Many deaths and much illness resulted from the hard labor and climatic conditions.[91] This transport service was inescapably a type of forced labor, even though the law required that all free natives so employed should be fairly paid, and despite the beneficent intentions of officials such as Montejo and Pedraza. In practice, the obligation to pay was often ignored.

There were other abuses as well. Encomenderos hired out their Indians to merchants and others in return for agreed sums. The Indians thus contracted for were frequently placed under overseers who had no regard whatsoever for their welfare and who neglected and mistreated them in every way.[92]

Construction of roads over which pack animals and carts could freely move

---

[89] Undated documents drawn up by the Cabildo of Santiago de Guatemala, AGG, Papers from the Archivo Municipal, Instrucciones y Cartas and Consultas.

[90] Montejo to the Crown, Naco, July 28, 1537, AGI, Guatemala 9; Pedraza to the Crown, Gracias a Dios, May 18, 1539, AGI, Guatemala 9; Montejo to the Crown, Gracias a Dios, June 1, 1539, DII, 24:250–97, 298–310; Residencia of Montejo for Honduras-Higueras, 1544, AGI, Justicia 300.

[91] *Ibid.,* Residencia of Alonso Maldonado and the oidores of the Audiencia de los Confines, 1548, AGI, Justicia 299.

[92] *Ibid.*

was the only alternative to transport service by the Indians. The evils of the system of burden-bearing were admitted by all who were familiar with it, and the need to alleviate the burdens of the Indians played its part in Montejo's plans for the building of adequate roads. Until such roads were constructed, however, Montejo had no choice but to permit burden-bearing in order to meet the colony's requirements. It was not until some time after Montejo's first period as governor of Honduras-Higueras, which came to a close in mid-1539, that burden-bearing was formalized and brought more closely under official regulation as the system of *tamemes*.

In conducting the repartimiento of Higueras, Montejo diligently sought to give conquistadores and pobladores as adequate a recompense for their services as the numbers and resources of the native population permitted. There were some areas, however, notably the Valley of Comayagua, which had too few Indians to permit assignment of encomiendas to all conquistadores. Indeed, Alvarado had found this true in the district of San Pedro after he had founded that town. Following the suppression of the great revolt the situation was everywhere more critical. There were now few large encomiendas for anyone. Montejo's plans to extend the conquest into new areas had as one of their objectives the furnishing of recompense in the form of encomiendas to conquistadores for whom there were no pueblos in already subjugated territory.

Repartimientos always called for extreme care everywhere in the Indies. Distribution of encomiendas to the satisfaction of the conquistador-colonists was an important, although very difficult, matter, since discontent with the pueblos assigned to them on the part of any considerable proportion of colonists could readily cause difficulties for the governing officials, and in extreme cases could even jeopardize permanent occupation. The least of the adverse results to which such discontent could lead was to jealous bickering and endless litigation.[93]

The scarcity of Indians and pueblos quite understandably caused dissatisfaction among the conquistadores of Higueras for whom there were no encomiendas and among many others who considered that the towns they received did not give them adequate reward for their services. Montejo could do nothing more than express regret that there were not enough pueblos for all and appeal to those who did not have encomiendas to await the occupation of the supposedly well populated Valley of Olancho, where he promised that pueblos would be available. These assurances, of course, failed to allay dis-

[93] Montejo to the Crown, June 1, 1539, DII, 24:250 ff.; Montejo to the Crown, August 20, 1539, AGI, Guatemala 39; Montejo to the Crown, Gracias a Dios, November 4, 1539, AGI, Guatemala 9; Montejo to the Crown, December 15, 1539, AGI, Guatemala 9; Montejo v. Pedraza, 1539, AGI, Justicia 129-2.

content and it is said that fourteen or fifteen colonists, impatient of further delay, soon left Higueras. The problem was serious and there was no solution open to Montejo other than to continue his efforts to bring back dispersed Indians and plan for the conquest of new territory.[94]

The vicious practice of selling encomiendas as though they were personal property existed in Honduras-Higueras, contrary to all royal law. Encomiendas might be called semifeudal royal grants in usufruct, with title in the Crown. They were not the property of the encomendero. Encomenderos throughout the Indies during the first period of colonization, and before the legal form of the encomienda was finally fixed by royal legislation, wished to turn their towns into permanent holdings, with title in themselves and their descendants. Encomiendas were also exchanged among colonists without due process. *Naborias,* or Indian household servants, were likewise exchanged, and sometimes sold, entirely contrary to law. Montejo overlooked certain of these illegal practices and indeed may himself have sold encomiendas by subterfuge, as did many governors.[95] In a cedula to the governor of Honduras-Higueras, issued at the request of Pedraza, the Crown in 1539 prohibited any further sale of encomiendas and naborias.[96]

The conquistador-colonists had expended great efforts and had run many dangers in occupying the province and, in the main, they were greatly dissatisfied with Montejo's moderate policies toward the Indians, which curbed the fullest immediate exploitation of the region and its native inhabitants. The Spaniards considered what they themselves held to be adequate compensation for their services as their just due, and they felt that such compensation could be obtained only through precious metals and the untrammeled exploitation of the Indians.

Montejo realized that his efforts to defend the Indians would in time arouse serious opposition. Nevertheless, he set his long-range plans for sound development, against the desires of the colonists for rapid and ruinous exploitation of both natural and human resources, and persevered in his efforts. Defending these policies to the Crown against the protests of both lesser officials and colonists, and inferentially appealing for royal support, he declared:

Your Majesty may well believe that if I should not have acted [in defense of the Indians], this province [of Higueras] would be in the same situation as Honduras and the Valley of Guynaco, where already there are no people or towns. . . . Should another who would not have taken the care I have shown in protecting the Indians have been sent here, [this province] would

[94] *Ibid.*
[95] Residencia of Montejo for Honduras-Higueras, 1544, AGI, Justicia 300.
[96] Cedulas of January 29, 1538, AGI, Guatemala 402.

not have been settled, nor would it have reached its present [good] state. And if anyone should do less, the results will be such as I have described. . . . [97]

PEDRAZA, ECCLESIASTIC, PROTECTOR OF THE INDIANS, AND ROYAL JUDGE

The monarchs of Castile worked closely with the Church of Rome, since they firmly held—and applied—the medieval concept of co-operation between the secular and spiritual arms as the representatives of the two aspects of God's power on earth. They went even further and, with authority from the Pope, made the Church of their overseas possessions in effect a part of the State. Consequently the Church in the New World always received careful attention, so that it would be strongly organized and powerful and so that it could fully minister to the Spaniards and at the same time bring the natives under its sheltering mantle. Conversion of the Indians to the Faith of Rome was one of the principal obligations of the Castilian monarchs under their papal dispensation to conquer and hold the New World.

The Crown wished to bring the Church to its full organization in its provinces of the Indies as soon as possible after colonization was achieved. It was not long, therefore, before an independent see of Honduras was proposed.[98] Meanwhile, after 1538, the Bishop of Guatemala, Francisco de Marroquín, exercised superior oversight of the ecclesiastical affairs of the province.[99]

In the mid-1530's the Crown had appointed a bishop for Honduras-Higueras, Fray Alonzo de Guzmán, a Jeronomite, and because of the urgent need for a royal provincial governor at that time intended that he should be chief magistrate as well. Guzmán did not accept his dual appointment, however, and the Crown then named Montejo governor, but for the time being did not designate a new bishop. There was also no Protector of the Indians in Honduras-Higueras, and in view of reports of mistreatment of the local natives the Crown wished to place such a royal officer there. The office of Protector of the Indians was a civil one, but its duties were such that it was closely allied to religious matters, and members of the clergy were therefore most appropriate as appointees.[100]

In 1537–38 the churchman Cristóbal de Pedraza was chosen as a royal officer to protect the Indians and guide the spiritual affairs of Honduras-Higueras until an independent bishopric was finally established. Pedraza was to play an extremely important part, both civil and spiritual. Later he became Bishop

[97] Montejo to the Crown, June 1, 1539, DII, 24:250 ff.
[98] See Cedula appointing Montejo Governor of Honduras-Higueras, March 1, 1535, AGI, Guatemala 402.
[99] Cedula to Bishop Francisco de Marroquín, February 12, 1538, AGI, Guatemala 393.
[100] Cedula appointing Montejo Governor of Honduras-Higueras, March 1, 1535, AGI, Guatemala 402; Cedula to Bishop Francisco de Marroquín, February 12, 1538, AGI, Guatemala 393.

of Honduras, but at first his role in civil affairs, for which his legal training had prepared him, outweighed his place in the spiritual life of the colony.

Pedraza was at Court when his appointment in Honduras-Higueras came, but he already knew the Indies from having served in New Spain. He went there in 1533, first serving as a *chantre* of the Cathedral of the City of Mexico, and then as a Protector of the Indians in the western province of Nueva Galicia.[101] If his own account is correct, Pedraza was very active in Nueva Galicia. Among other things he established a school for Indian children, especially sons of caciques, where they were taught the rudiments of civil education and religion. Pedraza claimed to have founded this school on his own initiative and despite opposition from lay Spaniards. It had been a great success, and many Indian children had attended. He also declared that he had mediated a violent quarrel between Cortés and Nuño de Guzmán, first President of the Audiencia of New Spain and conqueror of Nueva Galicia. While it is not clear just when he returned to Castile, this occurred sometime in the middle 1530's.[102]

In New Spain, particularly in frontier Nueva Galicia, Pedraza fought against gross ill-treatment of the Indians. He protested these abuses to the Crown and, with sincere zeal, resolved to do everything possible to better the lot of the natives through protecting them, obtaining justice for them, and winning them to the Faith. He was strongly influenced by the las Casas school of thought and held advanced theories with respect to the conversion and "peaceful reduction" of Indians everywhere. Pedraza hoped to win the natives for the Crown and the Church through preaching, considerate treatment, assuring words, and good example, and he placed his ideas before the Crown, which heard them with sympathy.[103] Pedraza was apparently young, enthusiastic, idealistic, and sincere. He was also firm, even stubborn, when he felt a stand was necessary, and had a high sense of duty. In every respect he was an excellent instrument through which to advance the religious phases of royal policy.

On the basis of what must have been highly creditable service in New Spain and the obvious sincerity of his ideals, the Crown in November 1537 appointed Pedraza *Protector y Defensor de los Indios* of Honduras-Higueras. As such, he was empowered, on his own responsibility, to take whatever steps he might deem necessary to advance the welfare of the natives. He could conduct investigations into conditions among the Indians and, on the basis of

[101] Memorial of Pedraza to the Consejo de Indias (n.d.), AGI, Indiferente General 1380; Chamberlain, 1945a.
[102] *Ibid.*
[103] *Ibid.*

his findings, proceed against anyone found guilty of offenses against them, whether governor or private citizen. He could also take the initiative in sending officers anywhere within the province to look into and report on Indian affairs. Although such investigating officers were actually appointed by the governor, their designation was based on the protector's recommendation. As Protector of the Indians, Pedraza was also to inquire into the employment and acts of the *calpisques,* or major-domos, whom the encomenderos placed in their encomienda towns as administrators. These calpisques were usually Spaniards but sometimes Negroes, or even people considered to be *moriscos*—converted Moors. The use of calpisques throughout the Indies had given rise to many abuses, and the practice of appointing them came under criticism from many quarters. Pedraza was to report on this problem as it concerned Honduras-Higueras and was to see that henceforth only Spanish Christians of good character were to be employed as calpisques by the encomenderos.[104]

Pedraza was likewise to investigate the whole problem of enslavement in view of the charges which had reached the Crown during the period before Montejo assumed office. The charges, as already outlined, maintained that the governors of Honduras carried on, or at least permitted, the illegal enslavment of Indians, the taking of many slaves without official branding, and the carrying of large numbers of natives to other provinces for sale. Pedraza was to assure the return to Honduras-Higueras of all Indians who had been carried elsewhere contrary to law and was to liberate all natives illegally enslaved. It was also apparently at Pedraza's request that the Crown issued the already mentioned cedulas forbidding sale of encomiendas and naborias in Honduras-Higueras.

Pedraza was to make the findings from his investigations known either to the Audiencia of Santo Domingo or directly to the Consejo de Indias, accompanied by an opinion from the governor, for final determination and the enforcement of punishment against those guilty of breaking laws and maltreating the Indians. Any charges against lieutenants appointed by the governor were to be placed before the latter; any against the governor, Pedraza could handle by virtue of his own authority. In such a case the governor had the right of appeal to the Audiencia of Santo Domingo or the Consejo de Indias. In assigning such powers to the protector, however, the Crown made clear that it was not intended that he should enjoy authority superior to that

<hr>

[104] The cedulas appointing Pedraza Protector of the Indians and acting prelate of Honduras-Higueras, and those concerning measures he was to carry out in connection with those offices, were issued on January 29, 1538, with the exception of that regarding calpisques, which was issued on April 8, 1538. All these cedulas are found in AGI, Guatemala 402.

of the governor or exercise jurisdiction in civil affairs except as it concerned the welfare of the natives. The protector was assigned no jurisdiction in criminal cases between Indians, since all such matters were under the governor and lesser officials. In purely civil cases regarding Indians, the protector was given limited jurisdiction, and could assess fines up to 50 pesos, regardless of appeal.

The Crown wished to correlate the efforts of clergy already in Honduras-Higueras, pending the establishment of a separate diocese, thus to make more effective their dual task of ministering to the Spaniards and converting the Indians. Therefore, early in 1538, Pedraza was given ad interim charge of all spiritual and ecclesiastical matters in the province. His duties within Honduras-Higueras were to be those normally performed by a bishop, but he was placed under the broader authority of Bishop Marroquín, to whom he was to look for guidance. Thus the Bishop of Guatemala was in effect to act in the capacity of an archbishop with relation to Pedraza and Honduras-Higueras until the full ecclesiastical organization of the province had been completed.

Pedraza was specifically instructed, as acting spiritual head of the colony, to minister to and indoctrinate the Indians and to administer the payment of the diezmos, or tithes, of the Church. Collection of the diezmos, which were almost always given in kind, had hitherto been handicapped in Honduras-Higueras by unstable conditions and lack of adequate transportation. Furthermore, at Pedraza's petition, the Crown provided that an Indian pueblo should be set aside to afford revenues, through tributes, for the establishment and support of a school such as he had founded in Nueva Galicia.

Since the Crown had been informed that there was no official taxation of the tributes and services which the natives of Honduras-Higueras were to give to their encomenderos and that some encomenderos imposed excessive requirements on their pueblos, Montejo and Pedraza were directed to remedy the situation. They were to make a careful survey to determine the types and amounts of tribute and service which the Indians had given to their native lords before the Spaniards came, and were to find precisely what went to their encomenderos after the conquest. On the basis of their conclusions Montejo and Pedraza were jointly to establish a just and equitable schedule of tributes and services for each encomienda town, in accordance with the population, resources, and agricultural and handicraft activities of each.

The Crown intended that Montejo as governor, and Pedraza, as acting ecclesiastical head of the province and Protector of the Indians, should work harmoniously in all things. Thus the temporal and spiritual leaders of the province were to co-operate in accordance with the theory on which the Castilian monarchy rested.

Pedraza was at Court at the same time as Alvarado, the treasurer García de Celís, and the two procuradores of Honduras-Higueras, Nicolas López de Yrarraga and Francisco Cava. He conferred extensively with them and thereby became well versed in matters of the province. Indeed it is quite possible that the presence of these officials may have turned his interest toward Honduras-Higueras, and that they, especially Alvarado, may have been of influence in obtaining his appointment.

Pedaraza was also designated royal judge to mediate between Montejo and Alvarado in the controversy now pending between them over the governorship of Honduras-Higueras. It was this position which was to give Pedraza such an important role in Honduras-Higueras on his first arrival.

On his return to the New World in the spring of 1538, Pedraza was accompanied by the treasurer García de Celís. They halted at Santo Domingo, where Pedraza conferred at length with the bishop and the president of the audiencia about his own duties and the affairs of Honduras-Higueras, which fell within the jurisdiction of the audiencia. Pedraza and García de Celís on October 6 reached Puerto de Caballos, whence Pedraza went to San Pedro for two weeks before going on to Gracias a Dios to meet Montejo, who was directing the war against the rebellious Indians. Montejo, other officials, and prominent citizens of Gracias a Dios gave Pedraza a hearty welcome, as befitted the spiritual head of the colony.[105] Montejo especially looked upon Pedraza as a valuable and honored collaborator, and "rejoiced" at his arrival, greeting him as "a brother." He had a dwelling erected for Pedraza, and assigned him in encomienda a desirable town close to Gracias a Dios.[106]

Montejo immediately sought to establish true collaboration between himself and Pedraza in governmental, ecclesiastical, and Indian affairs, and made him a principal counselor on all administrative matters. When he went to complete the pacification of the Valley of Comayagua toward the close of the war with the Indians, Montejo appointed his brother Juan and Pedraza coadministrators in Gracias a Dios, to govern until he returned. Montejo shared Pedraza's views toward the natives, and held that Pedraza's help was "greatly needed to foster the good treatment of the Indians." He therefore accepted Pedraza wholeheartedly, both as the highest representative of the Church in the province and as Protector of the Indians. With the war against the Indians still raging and the great task of rehabilitation impending, the need for full

[105] Pedraza to the Crown, Gracias a Dios, May 18, 1539, AGI, Guatemala 9.
[106] Montejo to the Crown, Gracias a Dios, June 1, 1539, DII, 24:250 ff.

co-operation was more than manifest. Montejo knew vaguely of Pedraza's appointment as mediator between himself and Alvarado and, somewhat anxious about Pedraza's powers in that regard, was the more desirous of having Pedraza's friendship.[107]

Having absorbed Alvarado's point of view at Court, Pedraza was somewhat aloof from Montejo at first; but as he became familiar with problems of Honduras-Higueras at first hand, watched Montejo's policies in operation, learned his aims, and observed him direct the war against the Indians, he conceived a high regard for the older man, both as an individual and as a high official, and willingly labored with him.[108] Among the specific matters which Montejo and Pedraza soon took up were an official schedule of tributes and services for the Indians ordered by the Crown, a generalized system for collection of the diezmos of the Church, and the establishment of a school for Indian children. Settlement of the first two were necessarily held in abeyance until the revolt had everywhere been crushed.[109] Pedraza apparently agreed to continued use of such tithes as could be collected to support the war. The tithes of the Church had produced the equivalent of 180 pesos in Buena Esperanza in Cerezeda's time, slightly less than 860 pesos de oro in San Pedro during 1537 and 1538, and but 163 pesos in Gracias a Dios in 1538. Because of the war and unsettled conditions none were collected in Gracias a Dios during 1539. Most of the tithes for 1537 and 1538 were employed by Montejo and his subordinates to help finance the war.[110]

The proposed school, however, was soon set up at Gracias a Dios, with Montejo's full support, and the revenues of the pueblo of Talva set aside to maintain it. Sons of caciques and other native children of the area about Gracias a Dios were given religious training and rudimentary lay education under Pedraza's guidance, as had been planned. This institution, the first of its kind in the province, met with immediate success.[111]

Anxious to promote full harmony, Pedraza composed the old quarrel between the treasurer García de Celís and the contador Andrés de Cerezeda which had developed at Buena Esperanza before Pedro de Alvarado's rescue of the colony.

Pedraza wished to place his theories of peaceful reduction to the test of the

[107] *Ibid.*
[108] *Ibid.;* Pedraza to the Crown, Gracias a Dios, May 18, 1539, AGI, Guatemala 9; Montejo *v.* Pedraza, 1539, AGI, Justicia 129-2.
[109] Cedula of January 9, 1538, AGI, Guatemala 402; Pedraza to the Crown, Gracias a Dios, May 18, 1539, AGI, Guatemala 9; Montejo to the Crown, Gracias a Dios, June 1, 1539, DII, 24:250–97; Montejo *v.* Pedraza, 1539, AGI, Justicia 129-2.
[110] Treasury accounts of Diego García de Celís, 1540, AGI, Indiferente General 1206.
[111] Montejo to the Crown, Gracias a Dios, June 1, 1539, DII, 24:250 ff.; Pedraza to the Crown, Gracias a Dios, May 18, 1539, AGI, Guatemala 9; Montejo *v.* Pedraza, 1539, AGI, Justicia 129-2.

war that was still going on. He was aware, of course, that matters had gone too far to permit any attempt at extensive application of such idealistic plans, for extreme bitterness and hatred foredoomed large-scale success. Nevertheless he proposed to enter still unconquered districts with a protective guard of only six horsemen to try to win the natives back to allegiance through moral suasion, preaching, and good works. He petitioned the Crown for direct royal approval, apparently desiring protection against possible interference by military or civil authorities. Although Montejo undoubtedly would have permitted Pedraza to proceed, even though most others must have viewed his plan with scepticism and disapproval, the protector, as far as is known, never actually tried to carry it out.[112]

Pedraza conscientiously strove to convert the Indians wherever the opportunity arose and did everything possible to help them, with Montejo's full support. Like the latter, Pedraza issued decrees prohibiting indiscriminate employment of Indians for labor in the mines, especially free natives,[113] inevitably arousing opposition. The authorities of San Pedro eventually went so far as to protest to the Crown.[114] Pedraza soon found, as had Montejo, that any measures to help the Indians which ran counter to the immediate desires of the colonists would arouse the harshest condemnation and criticism.

When Pedraza arrived no churches of permanent construction had yet been completed. Other public or private buildings, or temporary structures, were used for divine services. In Gracias a Dios mass was said in Montejo's own dwelling. Pedraza began to conduct services in the newly constructed casa de fundicíon, or smelter.[115]

There had been five members of the secular clergy in Honduras-Higueras before Pedraza came, including Montejo's chaplain, Bachiller Juan Alvarez. These clerics served as *curas,* or curates, of the several municipalities, none of which was without at least one member of the clergy. Juan Avela, who had been in the province for some time, and Juan Alvarez served in Gracias a Dios, Luis Díaz in San Pedro, Francisco Guerra in Comayagua, and Francisco Pinedo in Trujillo.[116]

To further the work of the Church and hasten the conversion of the Indians, the Crown about 1537 proposed to send three Dominican and three Franciscan friars from Santo Domingo, apparently at the request of the procuradores

[112] Pedraza to the Crown, Gracias a Dios, May 18, 1539, AGI, Guatemala 9; Chamberlain, 1947c.
[113] Probanza of Pedraza, 1539, AGI, Indiferente General 1206. The important captain and official, Alonso de Cáceres, declared that Pedraza showed great zeal in converting the natives and in striving to benefit them (Cáceres to the Crown, Gracias a Dios, September 5, 1539, AGI, Guatemala 43).
[114] Cabildo of San Pedro to the Crown, November 1, 1539, AGI, Guatemala 44.
[115] Pedraza to the Crown, Gracias a Dios, May 18, 1539, AGI, Guatemala 9.
[116] See Montejo *v.* Pedraza, 1539, AGI, Justicia 129-2; Montejo to the Crown, June 1, 1539, DII, 24:250-97; Pedraza to the Crown, Gracias a Dios, May 18, 1539, AGI, Guatemala 9.

of Honduras-Higueras in Castile. For some reason, however, it was a considerable time before members of the regular orders actually appeared.[117]

SUMMARY OF MONTEJO'S POLICIES AND PROJECTS

Montejo's farseeing projects for the commercial and economic development of Honduras-Higueras were unfortunately vitiated by the outbreak of the great Indian revolt in 1537 shortly after being started. He had no sooner re-established peace and again devoted himself to his program when Alvarado returned from Castile in the spring of 1539, and the consequent controversy over the governorship, releasing pent-up opposition to Montejo among Alvarado's partisans, not only frustrated his further efforts for the time being, but finally forced him temporarily to leave the province.[118]

The unhealthful climate and the revolt thwarted Montejo's attempt to establish a permanent town at Puerto de Caballos. By the spring of 1539, it had been abandoned, and the route which Montejo had cut there from San Pedro had disappeared.[119]

The measures which the adelantado took to benefit Trujillo accomplished no permanent results in that part of the province, except possibly with respect to mining. The authorities and citizens of Trujillo continued to fear that they might have to abandon the place. Revolts of Indians in outlying areas of their district, even though easily suppressed, certainly did not add to their feeling of security. In a despatch to the Crown in 1540 they complained that the governors of Honduras-Higueras either adopted measures that prevented the real exploitation of precious metals in their region, or conducted a slave trade that destroyed the native population. Thus, they claimed, the development of the district was made impossible, and the colonists suffered thereby. They declared that there were only fourteen or fifteen citizens left in Trujillo and that most of these were old, ill, or infirm. All were poverty stricken. It was claimed that only 150 Indians remained to serve the citizens in encomienda, a number that could not possibly meet their needs.[120] The factor Juan de Lerma reported, too, that conditions in Trujillo remained abject and that its situation was very precarious.[121]

In 1539 there were from thirty to thirty-five citizens in Gracias a Dios and approximately the same number in Comayagua and in San Pedro. There were about thirty-five encomiendas in the area of Gracias a Dios, thirty-five or forty in that of Comayagua, and sixteen or seventeen in the district of

---

[117] Cedulas of October 5, 1537, AGI, Guatemala 402.
[118] See Montejo v. Pedraza, 1539, AGI, Justicia 129-2.
[119] See Alvarado to the Crown, San Pedro, August 4, 1539, DII, 24.
[120] Cabildo of Trujillo to the Crown, March 12, 1540, AGI, Guatemala 44.
[121] Juan de Lerma to the Crown, San Pedro, October 31, 1539, AGI, Guatemala 49.

Trujillo. Even the largest of these encomiendas had but very few Indians by the standards of New Spain or Peru. Trujillo and Gracias a Dios were of *ciudad,* or city, status; Comayagua and San Pedro were of *villa,* or town, rank. San Pedro in the first part of 1539, had but twelve private dwellings of permanent construction.[122]

The cabildo and citizens of Comayagua, convinced of the advantages of its location and believing that their town should become the administrative and commercial center of the province as Montejo planned, recommended to the Crown that the Spaniards of Gracias a Dios be transferred there. They said that, "one large town is of more advantage than a number of smaller ones which are of no significance," and that the governors of the province, "were accustomed to found many towns, so that they may, in their own interests, claim that they had founded 'so many' towns and places, towns which actually became only sepulchres for the dead. . . ."[123] Lerma also suggested to the Crown that the citizens of Gracias a Dios be transferred eastward to form a single important and unquestionably stable community in that rich section of the province.[124]

Also, it is within the bounds of possibility that Montejo, in whose political and economic plans Comayagua had such a large place, may have contemplated an eventual transfer of the citizens of Gracias a Dios to the more eastern town. Lerma, and even Pedraza, now adversely criticized the final location which Montejo had selected for Gracias a Dios, and to which Pedraza and Juan de Montejo had moved the city in the first part of 1539. Pedraza, and undoubtedly Lerma also, had originally enthusiastically approved the site, but reversed their opinions after it had been occupied for some time.[125] Lerma further held that the location of San Pedro was unhealthful and advised that the town be transferred to Puerto de Caballos, where, on the coast, it would serve as a port of entry for both Higueras and Guatemala. Such a measure would, of course, have moved San Pedro to a location which experience thus far had shown was more open to disease than the one where it already was. Lerma also recommended that a town be re-established at Buena Esperanza, which was indeed a good site. Lerma considered this location of Cerezeda's former town one of the best in the entire province.[126] No immediate action was taken on these various proposals, however.

[122] *Ibid.;* Montejo to the Crown, Gracias a Dios, November 4, 1539, AGI, Guatemala 9; Cabildo of Trujillo to the Crown, March 12, 1540, AGI, Guatemala 44; Cabildo of Comayagua to the Crown, September 5, 1539, AGI, Guatemala 43.

[123] Cabildo of Comayagua to the Crown, September 5, 1539, AGI, Guatemala 43.

[124] Juan de Lerma to the Crown, San Pedro, October 31, 1539, AGI, Guatemala 49.

[125] *Ibid.;* Montejo *v.* Pedraza, 1539, AGI, Justicia 129-2; Pedraza to the Crown, Seville, June 28, 1544, AGI, Guatemala 164.

[126] Juan de Lerma to the Crown, San Pedro, October 31, 1539, AGI, Guatemala 49.

Roads in Honduras-Higueras remained inadequate despite Montejo's efforts and plans, although for a while, before the revolt interrupted the development of his broad projects, conditions had temporarily improved. The roads which existed became almost wholly impassable during the rainy season, which lasted from about May to December. Bridges were infrequent and many streams could not be crossed when swollen by rains. Thus, Montejo's well laid plan of establishing a system of roads to facilitate supply and transport, develop trade, to bind the province together politically, commercially, and militarily, and to connect it with other regions, was far from realized.

The design for developing a trade route from the North to the South Sea to replace the avenue across Panama came to nought, although it was revived later in the century and afterward. Neither did commerce with the outside improve greatly for a long while. But few ships arrived from Castile or the West Indies during Montejo's administration; none at all came during the year and a half of the great revolt. Goods and animals from Spain were extremely scarce and everything was expensive. A hog came to be valued at six pesos, a chicken at one, and an *arroba* of vinegar eleven castellanos. Little is said of clothing, but there must have been great shortage, with attendant exorbitant costs. It is not known what horses, so necessary to military operations, cost at this particular time, but to judge from prices under somewhat similar circumstances elsewhere a good mount must have been valued at 200–300 gold pesos. Arms were proportionately expensive.[127]

Mining was continued with over-all profit under Montejo's governorship, despite its interruption by the great revolt and Montejo's restrictive policies. Because of the war and Montejo's measures designed to protect the Indians and prevent undue exploitation, however, the general incomes were not so great as before he came. Even then, though production of gold and silver decreased somewhat, new deposits were discovered.[128]

Contemporaneous reports and recommendations to the Crown regarding Honduras-Higueras as it was in the first part of 1539, after the great revolt had been crushed, make interesting reading and afford evaluations of Montejo's work and plans. Pedraza gave a glowing account of the province and its possibilities and bestowed lavish praise on Montejo:

[The geographical situation of the province of Higueras] . . . is the most important thing for the service of Your Majesty in all these parts, for New Spain as for all other regions. . . . I say that [this province] is the most

---

[127] Montejo to the Crown, Gracias a Dios, June 1, 1539, DII, 24:250–97; Residencia of Montejo for Honduras-Higueras, 1544, AGI, Justicia 300.

[128] See Treasury accounts of Diego García de Celís, 1540, AGI, Indiferente General 1206.

important thing because it lies between the one sea and the other. . . . From the one sea to the other and from the several cities and places to the others everything is [now] secure and no person who goes between these places runs risk, which is a matter of great importance to Your Majesty in these parts, and one which is of the greatest advantage for the increase of Your Royal Estate. For that reason such conditions should be held in esteem and be counted as much. Infinite thanks should be given to God that in Your [Majesty's] days all these lands should have been pacified, that these roads should have been discovered, and that they are traveled from one part to another, all of which is for the glory of God. . . .

Your Majesty will learn from another letter which I hope to write at greater length in which I shall relate as in this, how truly the governor [Montejo] has rendered very great services to Your Majesty, because one of the things I had in mind to recommend to him to do in name of Your Majesty [when I came] was that he should found a town in the middle of this route from sea to sea, [as he has done]. And thus one day we discussed such a plan, the Very Reverend Bishop of Santo Domingo and I, while speaking of the affairs of this land. [The bishop] is a person who is very expert and resolute in all these matters.

If I remember correctly the treasurer of this province, Diego García de Celís, presented a memorial on this plan to the Royal Council of Your Majesty. While I was still in Spain he told me that the founding of a town between the two seas was a very important matter and that I should work for its accomplishment as soon as I arrived in these parts. He also declared that military campaigns should be made in connection with carrying out the project, since its completion would be a very great thing for the increase of Your Majesty because the two seas are here close to each other. . . . With the founding of a town between the two seas a road would be built between them and would be traveled, and everything which comes from Peru would be able to pass over it in the least possible time and without danger. This land would flourish greatly as a result.

Before I arrived here Our Lord was pleased to enlighten the governor [Montejo] to such an extent that he had already founded such a town, [the Town of Comayagua]. It is peopled and established in the most appropriate part of all the land, and in the best location within the entire province. . . . It has on all sides the best and richest mines of gold and silver that there are in all this land. These mines are almost inside the houses. And this silver especially is in very great quantity. The town is situated in the most beautiful and fruitful valley of all this land, a region where everything that grows here is raised and where will be made to grow all the things of Castile, [including] wheat and the vine in abundance, and where livestock, especially sheep, can be bred in great numbers. The valley is watered by three rivers, which is a glorious thing to see. [The governor] realized that in truth the principal city should be founded [in this valley] and that everything which is most important for all this land should be developed there, even though there are [now] few

Indians in the region. All the benefit which will come to the province [will come] through trade between the two seas. I have given my opinions on this subject to the governor and he understands their importance. He also realizes that Your Majesty should favor us through giving us authority over the town of San Miguel, which has been placed in the province of Guatemala through usurpation of jurisdiction. San Miguel is without any doubt a part of this province [of Higueras]. . . . If San Miguel is joined to this province Your Majesty will have [in Higueras] a territory which possesses coasts on both seas. . . .

[In connection with the return of Alvarado and his antagonism toward Montejo] it is of great importance that Your Majesty should have one *alcaide,* [or commandant], to command a single fortress rather than two pages, so that the stronghold can better be guarded and defended, because one house ruled by two lords cannot be well governed, especially if they are powerful lords, as are the governors of these parts. . . . Your Majesty will very well understand and will do that which is most expedient to Your Royal Service in this connection, since the governor Don Francisco de Montejo is worthy of being given honors by Your Majesty. He will certainly receive these honors [at Your Majesty's hands], because I trust in Our Lord that Your Majesty will be Lord of the World, which in truth Your Majesty already is, and in consequence everything is given into Your Majesty's hands [to act as is just].

The roads here are good so that people can come and go over them everywhere in these parts. And so that Your Majesty may praise God even more and give Him thanks, may Your Majesty know that I have seen [people] come from the City of León and from Guatemala to embark in this Puerto de Caballos, all by land, and from Tabasco, which is close to Yucatan, and almost on the border of Vera Cruz. . . . They come here each day by land, through country where in times past, when a certain Cerezeda governed, no one dared go two leagues outside a town, [Buena Esperanza, which Cerezeda founded] and where he remained for nearly the entire time he governed. . . .

As I have said, everything has changed [as compared with earlier times]. . . . At the time I write this letter there are people in the town of San Pedro who have come from Peru, from León, from the province of Nicaragua, and from Guatemala, to await passage for Spain all of which is for the glory of God. . . .

. . . All other [governors] who have come after [Cortés], until [the time of the arrival of] Montejo, have been stepfathers [to the province], according to what seems so manifest in the ruin of past times, because, from then until now, as a result of the destruction [of the province] and the [evil course] which events took, neither the land nor its Indians have ever [before] been so pacific, so tranquil, so secure, and so inclined to remain in their homes and work their fields as they are today. All the Spaniards declare that since they have been in the land no governor, nor his captains, have ever achieved the peace which exists today nor have they ever before seen such a thing. . . .[129]

[129] Pedraza to the Crown, Gracias a Dios, May 18, 1539, AGI, Guatemala 9.

The treasurer Diego García de Celís, who wished to see Alvarado replace Montejo as governor of Honduras-Higueras and who could therefore scarcely be expected to praise Montejo without real cause, declared after his return from Castile in 1538 that

he had never expected to find the land in such [fine] condition, nor in all the days of his life did he think that the natives [of this province] could be so quiet, or so peaceful, nor that they would serve their masters as they do today, nor that they would sow their crops, nor that they would have sufficient to eat. . . .[130]

The cabildo of Comayagua also wrote enthusiastically to the Crown about plans for the economic development of Higueras, for the establishment of a trade route across the province, and for the future of the town itself:

In order that Your Majesty should be informed of everything [concerning this province] and may consequently provide that which appears most fitting, Your Majesty should know that this town [of Comayagua] is located mid-way on the road between the North Sea and the South Sea, 26 leagues from the South Sea and its harbor, [the Bahía de Fonseca], and almost the same number of leagues from the North Sea. . . . And there is a river which comes from Puerto de Caballos to within 12 leagues of the town, over which canoes can come. . . . There is an Indian town [at a convenient place on this river] where a trading factory can be established in name of Your Majesty. All merchandise which comes from [Puerto de Caballos] could be taken to this trading factory by canoe very safely. . . .

Because of all the factors which have been mentioned the Town [of Comayagua] is the most important thing that Your Majesty has in all these parts of the Indies. Everything from Peru can come through this town, as can likewise everything from Castile pass through it on the way to Peru. This commerce would move through this valley from one sea to the other over a very level road and would reach the ports of this province after shorter navigation [from Castile]. Trade would flow across the province more securely than by way of Panama and people would be in less danger of falling ill, since this land is very healthful and very well provided with all kinds of supplies.

It has seemed good to us, pending the final judgment of Your Majesty and the officials of Your very high Council, to recommend to Your Majesty that this Town [of Comayagua] rather than Gracias a Dios should be made the principal city of this province. Gracias a Dios is situated in a less important location than this town and there is no reason why, since it has only about thirty citizens, it should call itself a city. [Comayagua] could readily have a citizen body of about sixty. This town has great potentialities because of

---

[130] Quoted by Pedraza in his letter to the Crown of May 18, 1539, AGI, Guatemala 9.

the trade which it is hoped will develop in view of its proximity to both seas. [Comayagua] aspires to be a greater city than Guatemala, or any other except the City of Mexico. A city established here, since it would be located in the center of all the land . . . would contribute much to the security of the entire country. Your Majesty should therefore direct that in all these regions there be but one strong town in the best section of all, so that the land can be protected and conserved, rather than that there should be so many places of little conse- quence of the kind which the governors are accustomed to establish. . . .[131]

It is not surprising that Montejo himself, who confidently hoped to reap the full rewards of many years of ceaseless labor in the Indies, should give an overoptimistic picture of Honduras-Higueras following the final pacification of the province. Montejo told his sovereign that

the land [now] rests in such tranquility that I give thanks to God for it. Everyone [among the Spaniards] has begun to work and concern himself with his holdings. Many mines of gold and silver have been discovered in various parts. The City of Trujillo, which was the most ruined thing in the world, where even in times of its prosperity, gold was never extracted, has become the best thing in the land since my arrival, and everyone mines gold. . . . The land is so tranquil and so in repose, and the Indians are so quiet, that whoever sees it marvels, because it seemed impossible that the prov- ince should ever come to be in the [good] state in which it is. . . .[132]

The factor Juan de Lerma, however, drew a contrastingly dismal picture of the state of the province. In the autumn of 1539, after Alvarado had forced Montejo to relinquish the governorship of Honduras-Higueras to him, Lerma informed the Crown that Honduras-Higueras was again in urgent need of support so that the colonists would be encouraged to remain permanently. He declared that the Indians were few and poor and that they gave little tribute and service. As a result of earlier slaving operations, war, and disease, he said, the entire province had fewer Indians than a single moderate-sized encomienda in New Spain. He pointed out that the natives themselves pro- vided no gold or silver in tribute and that the tributes which they gave from the products of their agriculture and simple industry—maize, beans, peppers, cotton, turkeys, eggs, cloth, *petates* (rush mats), pots, jars, and the like—were scanty as compared with those in many other parts of the Indies. He held that the Spaniards would have to supply the natives with the seeds necessary for the planting of sufficient fields to sustain themselves and the colonists.

---

[131] Cabildo of Comayagua to the Crown, September 5, 1539, AGI, Guatemala 43.
[132] Montejo to the Crown, Gracias a Dios, August 25, 1539, AGI, Guatemala 39.

The Spaniards found it very difficult to maintain themselves under existing conditions, he concluded.[133]

Lerma was a friend and collaborator of Montejo's of long standing, and his report was undoubtedly directed against Alvarado, as Montejo's bitter enemy. It was designed, at least in part, to call Alvarado's right to the governorship into question, and therefore to aid Montejo to regain royal favor. Consequently, although many of Lerma's statements were basically correct, his report cannot be taken entirely at its face value.

By the spring of 1539, Montejo was firmly and justly convinced that the perpetuation of Honduras-Higueras was the result of his efforts and that the achievements of Alvarado in the province in 1536, though valuable, were in the ultimate analysis only superficial and ephemeral. Although Higueras had been torn asunder by warfare, the province was now conquered beyond any doubt and a considerable measure of stability had finally been attained. The foundations on which slow and orderly progress might rest had been laid.

Overoptimism, desire for recognition, and exaggeration in the highly favorable accounts of Montejo, Pedraza, and García de Celís must be discounted, just as antagonism against Alvarado in Lerma's report must likewise be evaluated. Taking everything into consideration, however, we can have no doubt that, despite harrowing war, Higueras in the late spring of 1539 was in a better position to progress than ever before. The relative tranquility which existed after the suppression of the great revolt was Montejo's work in both the civil and military fields.

Montejo's experience in Honduras-Higueras and his comprehension of the province's political and economic potentialities had aroused his abiding interest. Over and above that, he could rightly feel that he was the conquistador of Higueras, whereas in contrast his efforts to conquer and colonize Yucatan had thus far failed. He had now determined to make Honduras-Higueras, rather than Yucatan, the center of the wider adelantamiento he so much desired to create. Honduras-Higueras had greater agricultural and commercial possibilities than Yucatan. The province also had gold and silver, which his northern territories entirely lacked. Montejo's plans for the development of Honduras-Higueras clearly show the primary place which the province had assumed in his thoughts. While wishing, of course, to incorporate Honduras-Higueras into his adelantamiento, still if that plan failed Montejo desired to retain the province for its own sake, even at the expense of Yucatan. In Honduras-Higueras Montejo had enjoyed his first real opportunity to demonstrate fully his qualities as a military leader and had been vouchsafed a better chance than at any other

---

[133] Juan de Lerma to the Crown, San Pedro, October 31, 1539, AGI, Guatemala 49.

time in his career to put into play his great talents as an administrator. He had measured up to high standards as both a military and a civil leader in Honduras-Higueras, and his knowledge of that fact endeared the province to him. In Honduras-Higueras Montejo had displayed all the characteristics of a true builder of colonies. He would indeed have been in a position to move forward to the uninterrupted development of Honduras-Higueras had not Pedro de Alvarado come back from Castile determined to take the governorship of the province for himself. Alvarado's return immediately plunged Honduras-Higueras once again into turmoil and administrative chaos, which further impeded its progress and development, for Montejo was just as determined to retain the governorship of the region as Alvarado was to wrest that high office from him.

III

Honduras and Higueras
From the Conquest of Higueras to the
Installation of the Audiencia de Los Confines
1539-44

7

The Quarrel Between Alvarado and Montejo
Over the Governorship

THE CAUSES OF CONTROVERSY

THE FINAL conquest of Higueras by Montejo was followed by five years
of jurisdictional and administrative controversy, which, however, did not
lead to bloodshed among the Spaniards, even though armed conflict was but
narrowly avoided on several occasions. During this period the development
of the province, so carefully planned by Montejo, was seriously impeded and
little from his great economic projects was left standing. Nevertheless, conquest and settlement were advanced in outlying regions, new and rich mines
were discovered and exploited, and in the end governmental stability was
achieved when the Audiencia de los Confines was installed at Gracias a Dios
in the first half of 1544.

The five years of governmental strife began with the return of Pedro de
Alvarado from Castile in the spring of 1539. He arrived in Honduras-Higueras just as Montejo had completed the subjugation of the Valley of Comayagua, bringing the conquest of Higueras to a triumphant close. Confirmed
in the governorship of Guatemala by the Crown, Alvarado came back to the
New World determined to take Honduras-Higueras for himself and unite
it with Guatemala, for which he still desired Puerto de Caballos as a port
on the North Sea. Because of his rescuing the Spaniards of Higueras in
1536, his selection as chief magistrate by Cerezeda and the citizens of Buena
Esperanza, his campaigns of conquest, and his founding of San Pedro, Alvarado was convinced of his rightful claim to authority over Honduras-Higueras.
He also wanted control over its rich gold and silver mines. Furthermore, he
was still enraged with Montejo for what he considered the latter's perfidy in
finally accepting the governorship after expressing willingness to relinquish
authority in exchange for Alvarado's territory of Chiapas. The fact that Montejo had eventually gone to Honduras-Higueras under peremptory orders from
the Crown and the Viceroy of New Spain did not alter Alvarado's attitude
in the slightest.[1]

[1] For the aims, attitude and plans of Alvarado and his followers see: Diego García de Celís to the
Crown, Isla Terceira, February 3, 1537, AGI, Contratación 5103; Diego García de Celís to the Crown,
Isla Terceira, March 5 and April 30, 1537, AGI, Santo Domingo 168; Fiscal v. Diego García de Celís,
1537, AGI, Justicia 1035-3-1; Fiscal v. Alvarado, 1537, AGI, Justicia 1035-2-2; Gerónimo de San Martín
to the Crown, San Pedro, April 24, 1538, AGI, Guatemala 49; Alvarado to the Crown, Gracias a Dios,
August 4, 1539, DII, 24:311–19; Montejo v. Pedraza, 1539, AGI, Justicia 129-2; Montejo v. Alvarado,
1541, AGI, Justicia 134-3; Residencia of Montejo for Honduras-Higueras, 1544, AGI, Justicia 300.

On his part, Montejo was just as determined to keep authority over Honduras-Higueras. With its commercial potentialities and mines, that province had retained central place in his plans to construct a great adelantamiento, and he had no intention of yielding to anyone except under direct instructions from the Crown. The fact that his original province, Yucatan, was still unoccupied by Spaniards following his heart-breaking failures between 1527 and 1535 intensified Montejo's resolve to retain control over Honduras-Higueras. Moreover, he maintained more firmly than ever that the Crown had already declared territory of Higueras as far eastward as the Río de Ulua as a part of his adelantamiento. In view of the bloody war of 1537–39 he denied that Alvarado had accomplished anything of value with respect to the conquest of Higueras and held that but for his own success in subjugating the Indians the province would have been lost.

The odds were wholly in Alvarado's favor in his quarrel with Montejo. During his long stay at the Castilian Court Alvarado had not only overcome all adverse criticism, but had won the highest favor with the Crown, partly because of his own great talents and his achievements in the Indies and partly because of the influence of the Duque de Albuquerque, a relative of his deceased first wife, Francisca de la Cueva, and therefore of his recent bride, Beatriz, her sister. The Crown listened with entire approval to Alvarado's claims, which were vigorously supported by the treasurer Diego García de Celís and the procuradores Francisco Cava and Nicolás López de Yrarraga while at Court with Alvarado, and also by officials and colonists of both Honduras-Higueras and Guatemala, who wrote from the New World. Even the contador and former acting governor Andrés de Cerezeda, a friend of Montejo, had at first doubted the latter's ability to keep order in Honduras-Higueras and had so informed the Crown. There was a widespread conviction that the vigorous Alvarado was the better governor for Honduras-Higueras and that it was to the advantage of that province to have it united with Guatemala.

Over and above these views, a number of Montejo's policies, such as his concern for the Indians, turned the majority of the colonists of Honduras-Higueras against him. More important, nullification by Montejo of the repartimientos of Higueras which Alvarado had made before he sailed for Castile in 1536 and Montejo's reassignment of encomiendas to the soldiers who accompanied him to the province aroused bitter antagonism among the original encomenderos. Although such reallocation of encomiendas to their own followers by new governors was common in the Indies, it was always sure to arouse hostility among the dispossessed. Through the tributes and services which their Indians gave to their encomenderos, encomienda pueblos were the most constant and permanent reward for their services to which conquistador-colonists could look.[2]

In nullifying Alvarado's assignments of encomiendas, Montejo rightly claimed that Alvarado's repartimientos were based on wholly inadequate information about geography and of the numbers and status of the native population of Higueras. Montejo also held, again with justice, that Alvarado had assigned encomiendas in regions still unconquered. The former therefore maintained that it was impossible to place Alvarado's repartimientos in effect. He even went further, declaring that Alvarado had no legal right to assign encomiendas in Honduras-Higueras because the Crown had not given him specific authority to do so. The enraged encomenderos whom Montejo had dispossessed naturally sent the strongest protests both to Alvarado at Court and to the Crown, requesting that Montejo be compelled to restore their holdings.

Montejo, unwisely and with little pretense to legality, also appropriated the encomiendas which Alvarado had set aside for himself in Honduras-Higueras and confiscated Alvarado's landholdings, houses, mining cuadrillas, and other property in the province. Alvarado, thus further incensed, petitioned for full restitution.

Additional complaints against Montejo and his mining policies arrived at Court from Guatemala, declaring that Montejo's measures to safeguard the gold and silver of Higueras for its own colonists and provincial coffers constituted unjust discrimination. Such action, they claimed, was extremely detrimental to the revenues of Guatemala.

In this way Montejo and Alvarado fell into irreconcilable controversy on both broad and narrow issues. Their contentions are best set forth by contemporary statements. Alvarado and his partisans declared:

Because the province of Higueras was falling into ruin and the Spaniards who were in it were about to be lost . . . the Contador Andrés de Cerezeda sent the Treasurer Diego García de Celís to call Pedro de Alvarado to the rescue of the province. At the instance and request of the Contador Andrés de Cerezeda, acting governor, and of the colonists of the land, because of the pleas which the Treasurer Diego García de Celís made to him in name of Your Majesty, since the matter concerned the royal service of Your Majesty, and so that the land would not be entirely lost [Alvarado] went to the province of Higueras with many Spaniards and Indian auxiliaries, taking a great amount of supplies, other materials, and money with him. At the cost of more than 20,000 ducats in all [Alvarado thus went to the rescue of Higueras], moved by zeal for the royal service and with the previous consent of the

[2] See chap. 4, note 26.

Adelantado Montejo and the Viceroy of New Spain, and even at their request and petition, for it was clear that neither they nor anyone else [except Alvarado] could remedy the situation of the land of Honduras, since [Alvarado] was then closest at hand [and alone was in a position to act]. Furthermore, Montejo did not wish to go to Honduras and had relinquished office [as governor of that province]. Even though [Alvarado] was at the time engaged in his own affairs and had not only begun, but had almost carried to completion, the organization of an armada [for the South Sea] he nevertheless went to the help of Higueras.

[After his arrival in Higueras, Alvarado] pacified the land and overcame the fortifications where the Indians had their greatest strength, which had hitherto caused a great deal of harm to the Spaniards. He also founded two towns and placed citizens and dwellers in them and assigned the Indians of the province to the citizens in encomienda. The colonists then became contented with the province, remained satisfied, and gave up any thought of leaving the region. [Before Alvarado came] the colonists had already begun to leave the province. The colonists also began to set up haciendas after don Pedro de Alvarado arrived. [Alvarado] was then elected captain general [of Honduras-Higueras].

When the Adelantado Montejo learned how the land [of Higueras] had been saved and that the Indians had been pacified, and when he was informed of the soldiers and Indian auxiliaries which [Alvarado] had taken to Higueras, he decided to go to the province without soldiers or resources, so that he might profit from everything which [Alvarado] had accomplished, even though Montejo now had no authority to go to Higueras because [Alvarado] had already conquered the province under authority and powers from Your Majesty and had governed it in conformance with those powers and also with the consent of the colonists. Without the slightest thought of serving Your Majesty, and with even less thought of bringing permanent benefits to the land [of Higueras], Montejo, along with one of his captains, then entered into the province and did so much to harm the natives . . . that they were goaded into making war once again, . . . [Alvarado] had left the Indians in peace.

[Montejo] also reassigned [the encomiendas of Higueras], taking away from the original colonists, who had aided in conquering the land, all the repartimientos which [Alvarado] had granted to them, reassigning them to whomsoever he wished, including those who came to the province with him, although they had not served [in the conquest] and did not merit the encomiendas. Not content with this action, and wishing to enrich himself through the labors and financial resources of [Alvarado], the Adelantado Montejo took and appropriated for himself the pueblos and Indians which [Alvarado] possessed in the province, and which [Alvarado] had justly merited and earned through his conquest [of Higueras]. Even worse, [Montejo] took for himself [Alvarado's] haciendas and other property. . . . [3]

[3] Montejo v. Pedraza, 1539, AGI, Justicia 129-2.

Montejo opposed that:

if this province [of Honduras-Higueras] is joined to Guatemala, within two years not an Indian will remain, because up to now the colonists of Guatemala have been under such lax control with respect to the Indians that no sentence has been given against anyone [who mistreated them]. This [ill-treatment of the natives] has become the custom [among the colonists of Guatemala] and has been permitted because that land is so productive and its natives are numerous. In contrast, this land is not so productive and the Indians are few and delicate, and if they are dealt with as have been those of Guatemala, as I have already said, there will be none left within two years. Even the colonists of this province in past times have not been of different practices [than those of Guatemala]. . . . [Because of my policies directed toward protection of the Indians] the colonists are in opposition to me. I certify to Your Majesty that if another who did not take the care which I have taken in protecting the Indians were here [the province] would not now be colonized, nor would it have risen to the [good] state in which it now is, and if there is no one to do as I have done, the result will be that which I have described. . . .

With respect to what [Alvarado] tells Your Majesty with regard to the City of Gracias a Dios, which it is said is to be joined to Guatemala, he did not conquer or pacify any part of its district, nor did any of his captains. In this province there is no other thing of value except the district of that city, because everything that Cerezeda formerly had under his authority [and the Valley of Comayagua] had been allocated to its jurisdiction. I, my captains, and the soldiers I brought with me, who are more than one hundred, are the ones who actually conquered and pacified all this area. Many of my soldiers died in the war [with the Indians], and all the rest are in debt and are worn by their efforts. Well may Your Majesty understand how these men have labored and suffered, and I with them, and therefore well may Your Majesty judge whether or not it is just that those who [came with Alvarado] and then went away to their homes to enjoy themselves in Guatemala and San Salvador, where they have many good repartimientos, and those who went away to Castile and left all the land at war, should profit by the fruits of what [I and my captains and men] have accomplished here in the past three years through our conquests and labors, at the cost of many dead and wounded and after suffering so many trials and disappointments. This city [of Gracias a Dios and its area] are the entire province, and without them there is nothing. . . . [4]

I declare that when I came to this province and land I found nearly all of it at war and without a governor nor a lieutenant governor. A lieutenant governor [Juan de Chávez], whom it is said had been left in the province by the Adelantado don Pedro de Alvarado, had gone away to Guatemala, abandoning the land because of the many demands to leave the province which it is said were presented to him by citizens of Guatemala and San

[4] Montejo to the Crown, Gracias a Dios, June 1, 1539, DII, 24:274–75, 279–80.

Salvador [who were with him]. These citizens . . . said to the lieutenant governor that he should go away [from Higueras] because [Higueras] was a separate province and was one which was very difficult and dangerous to conquer, and that it also was a region in which little profit was to be found. As a result this lieutenant went away and abandoned the land without leaving in it a lieutenant governor or captain to conquer it. I and my captains and the men I brought with me conquered all the land with the help of those who were already here, and pacified and peopled it, as is well known. I "reformed" the City of Gracias a Dios and the town of San Pedro, conquering most all of the pueblos within their respective limits and districts. I also prepared to people a town in the Valley of Comayagua, and I conquered and pacified all the pueblos of the district of the town of [Comayagua], in which some Christians and horses were killed and where [the Spaniards] suffered many labors and hardships. I pacified all these districts with the least possible harm to the natives. Since the natives of this province are few and since the land is very important, it is hoped that its pacification will serve God Our Lord well and that His Majesty will be benefited, since all the region is very rich in gold and silver mines and is fertile. The province has many good, secure parts, and a way can be established across it [from the North Sea] to the South Sea.

After having conquered, pacified and peopled the land I divided it [in repartimiento] among those who participated in the conquest and those who were already in the land, according to what God and my conscience gave me to see, and in accordance with what His Majesty has ordered. I also conducted the repartimiento in conformance with the possibilities of the land [with respect to resources and population].

When the Adelantado don Pedro de Alvarado [first] came it is said that he partitioned all the land in repartimiento without truly having conquered and colonized it, and even without having really seen it. Because of the brief time he was in the province [Alvarado] could not have gained [adequate] information concerning its pueblos. He therefore issued many cedulas of repartimientos and encomiendas which were contrary to each other. He granted pueblos under three or four different names and gave the names of rivers, peñoles, and mountains as those of pueblos, assigning them in encomienda. In this manner he assigned one hundred or more repartimientos in the district of this City of Gracias a Dios [alone], whereas there are now no more than thirty-five repartimientos. Many encomiendas are so small that they can scarcely afford sustenance [to their encomenderos]. In the same manner [Alvarado] assigned some individuals [entire] provinces, declaring that certain towns and all their subject pueblos were granted to these individuals, and then turned about and assigned all the various pueblos of these provinces to other encomenderos. He also granted pueblos within the district of one [Spanish] town to citizens of another. Then [Alvarado] went off [to Castile] without legally placing the citizens in possession of their encomiendas and without even leaving in his stead a lieutenant who could place the encomenderos in possession of their pueblos, for at the time when don Pedro de Alvarado embarked for Castile his lieutenant Juan de Chávez had already abandoned the land. . . .

I saw that the repartimiento made by [Alvarado] could not be placed in effect or complied with, or even adjusted satisfactorily . . . , and I realized that many lawsuits over possession of encomiendas would result if any attempt were made to place [Alvarado's] repartimiento into effect, with attendant disquietude and dissatisfaction among the colonists. Such disquietude and dissatisfaction could well lead to the depopulation and loss of the province.

Furthermore, the Adelantado don Pedro de Alvarado did not have, and never had, authority from His Majesty to divide the province in repartimiento. . . . Even then [Alvarado] revoked and nullified the repartimiento [of Higueras] which Andrés de Cerezeda, governor for His Majesty, had already made [before Alvarado arrived].

I partitioned the province, and in doing so I took some pueblos for my own maintenance and removed pueblos from some persons who were already in the land and who possessed no titles, although I took this action with the least possible prejudice to conquistadores and original colonists. If any of the persons from whom I removed encomiendas held titles for such encomiendas I have never seen them, nor have any such titles been presented to me by the Adelantado don Pedro de Alvarado or any other person. . . .

If don Pedro de Alvarado states that I have taken his pueblos from him, I reply that I do not possess such pueblos and further I declare that I do not consider that any such pueblos were ever legally held by don Pedro de Alvarado. I have never seen any titles to any pueblos which [Alvarado] might possess. . . .[5]

[5] Montejo v. Pedraza, 1539, AGI, Justicia 129-2. It was customary for the Spaniards to consider that a native "province," or district, had accepted Castilian dominion if the ruler or his designated representatives gave homage, either upon being conquered, in answer to the requerimiento, or voluntarily. When caciques, or their representatives, from territory never entered by the Spaniards came before Spanish captains to make submission, such a place could thereupon technically be considered "pacified" and under Castilian dominion. As Alvarado and his followers stated this principle: ". . . viniendo uno o dos yndios en nombre de su pueblo se entiende de aver venido y rescibido el tal pueblo o cabecera de paz e sus subjetos" (Montejo v. Pedraza, 1539, AGI, Justicia 129-2). Diego García de Celís declared that these general principles of "pacification" and the establishment of Castilian dominion were recognized as valid in the New World by the Consejo de Indias "porque asi se hizo en el Reyno de Granada y que ansi se havia determinado" (Montejo to the Crown, Gracias a Dios, June 1, 1539: DII, 24:266–68). In this way García de Celís held that such a principle was established during the reconquest of Granada by the sovereigns of Castile.

Montejo pointed out that many native rulers came insincerely, whether with outward willingness or through coercion, and that in most cases they were ready to take up arms against the Spaniards at the first opportunity. In his letter to the Crown of May 18, 1539, Pedraza set forth the following views to the Crown (AGI, Guatemala 9): "It cannot be said that the land is at peace, or remains at peace, if a lord or two of the natives, or an Indian or two, or three, should come to see the governor or his captain, or captains when they first come to conquer the natives, declaring that they wish to come to peace, for all the Indians act in this way when they see an army or group of Christians, come to their pueblos or into their vicinity when they are at war, as has happened and has been observed. . . . They come under guise of peace only to see who the men-at-arms are, how many there are, and how many are horsemen and how many are foot soldiers . . . , so that they can make war more effectively. Even though they are told about Your Majesty, they still try to find out who these Spaniards are and what they wish, and they say to them that they and the other natives of their pueblos [want to do what the Spaniards wish] only to satisfy the Spaniards and to reassure them. They then go away and never again return, except with their bows in their hands. They go up into the mountains, and from there they send back to the Spaniards whatever message happens to occur to them, and then they laugh at the Spaniards. Such a manner of procedure does not bring the land to peace. . . ."

DECISION BY THE CROWN IN SUPPORT OF ALVARADO

The Crown reviewed the entire situation carefully and came to the conclusion that Alvarado, with his great prestige and strong hand was indeed in a far better position than Montejo to bring to Honduras-Higueras the permanent security and order which it had so long needed. Montejo's prestige at Court had suffered greatly from his failure in Yucatan. In addition, the outbreak of the great Indian revolt which threatened the existence of Honduras-Higueras only a few months after he had taken office did nothing to improve his situation, since it was not known in Castile for a considerable time that through the campaigns of pacification which he initiated, he was in the process of achieving a military triumph of a high order.

Therefore the Crown turned back to the original bases on which Montejo, Alvarado, and the Viceroy of New Spain, Antonio de Mendoza, had earlier negotiated for an exchange of the governorships of Honduras-Higueras and Chiapas. The Crown confirmed its authorization for such an exchange, declaring that Montejo had already signified his willingness to accept it. The Crown wished that any agreement between the two governors should be voluntary, at least nominally, but it is nevertheless clear that the Crown now intended that Alvarado should possess himself of Honduras-Higueras and unite the province with Guatemala. The former union of Yucatan and Honduras-Higueras was tacitly to go by the board.

In return Montejo was to receive authority over Chiapas, which he had claimed as part of Yucatan for some years, along with any other compensation upon which he and Alvarado might agree. Mendoza was confirmed as arbiter and mediator and was empowered to approve their arrangements as long as their compact served the best interests of the Crown.[6]

The Crown also took full cognizance of the protests against Montejo's

---

[6] Cedula of May 25, 1538, AGI, Guatemala 393: "Don Antonio de Mendoza, our Viceroy and Governor of New Spain and President of our Royal Audiencia and Chancellory which resides in New Spain. Don Pedro de Alvarado, our Adelantado, Governor and Captain General of the Province of Guatemala has informed me that he conquered and peopled Puerto de Caballos, which is in the Province of Higueras and the Cape of Honduras, the government of which, as you know, we have entrusted to the Adelantado don Francisco de Montejo, and has informed me that they [Alvarado and Montejo] have discussed the exchange of Puerto de Caballos for the City of Ciudad Real de los Llanos de Chiapa, and that they also discussed the exchange of other things of their respective jurisdictions, as they may determine. The Adelantado don Pedro de Alvarado has requested that any such exchange be confirmed and approved, or that I should make disposition as I deem expedient.

"This proposal was discussed by the members of our Council of the Indies, and after approval by the Emperor, My Lord, it was agreed that this my cedula should be issued to you [Mendoza], and I assented. In consequence I order that in case the Adelantados don Pedro de Alvarado and don Francisco de Montejo agree between themselves to exchange any pueblo or pueblos, or anything else within their respective jurisdictions, you [Mendoza] shall give them license and faculty to come to an agreement and to make an exchange, if it seems to you that such an agreement is for the good of both the provinces [of Honduras-Higueras and of Chiapas], and if both governors [Alvarado and Montejo] are in conformance with each other. Under such circumstances you [Mendoza] shall issue whatever legal documents are necessary to confirm [the agreement]. . . . Valladolid, May 25, 1538. I the Queen."

revocation of Alvarado's encomienda assignments in Higueras and of Alvarado's complaints against Montejo's appropriation of his personal holdings and property. In a peremptorily worded cedula the Crown ordered Montejo to restore pueblos to all encomenderos to whom Alvarado had assigned them throughout all territory which Alvarado had actually or nominally subjugated. The drastic penalty of removal from office in Honduras-Higueras and forfeiture of property to the royal treasury was to be imposed on Montejo should he fail fully to comply with this royal decree.[7] At Alvarado's specific

[7] Cedula of April 30, 1538, AGI, Guatemala 402: "To the Adelantado don Francisco de Montejo, Our Governor of the Provinces of Higueras and the Cape of Honduras and of Yucatan and Cozumel. On behalf of certain conquistadores of that province of Honduras it has been related to me that those conquistadores went to that province with the Adelantado don Pedro de Alvarado, Our Governor and Captain General of the Province of Guatemala and aided in the conquest of the province [of Honduras-Higueras], for which service [Alvarado] assigned them certain pueblos of Indians in encomienda. [I am now also informed] that you have . . . removed these encomiendas from these conquistadores, as a result of which they have sustained grievance. These conquistadores have therefore requested me to order you to return and restore their encomiendas to them, or to make provision as I consider most expedient.

"The members of Our Council discussed this matter and drew up a memorandum, which contains two articles, the tenor of which is as follows:

"That there should be issued to the Adelantado Montejo a decree, providing for grave penalties and declaring that the persons to whom the Adelantado [Alvarado] granted encomiendas of Indians shall possess them, and that if certain encomiendas have been removed from such persons to their prejudice, they shall be returned to them . . . along with the revenues which they have produced. If the Adelantado don Pedro de Alvarado has granted certain encomiendas to persons who hold Indians in encomienda in another province [beside Honduras-Higueras], such persons are to be ordered to select the [one] repartimiento they wish and are to relinquish the other within twenty days, so that it can be reassigned in encomienda. This latter provision does not apply to . . . Alvarado [himself].

"If don Pedro de Alvarado has assigned certain Indians in encomienda without actually having conquered such Indians, and if afterward the Adelantado Montejo effectively pacified such Indians, the repartimiento which the Adelantado Montejo made of such Indians is to be considered valid.

"If [Alvarado] assigned certain Indians in encomienda to persons who are not in the [Province of Honduras-Higueras] and who did not participate in the conquest [of that province] and who have not gone there to take possession [of their encomiendas] or to dwell in the province, and if the Adelantado Montejo has reassigned such encomiendas, . . . such persons [as now hold them] should rather be permitted to retain them.

"If any citizen of Trujillo has had his encomienda Indians removed from him by any of the governors [of Honduras-Higueras], such Indians are to be returned.

"These measures are to be applied and complied with until such a time as other provisions are decided upon, and for that reason I order you [Montejo] to take cognizance of the above incorporated provisions [of the Council of the Indies] and to apply them and comply with them, and cause them to be applied and complied with to the letter. . . . you are to return and restore to don Pedro de Alvarado and to the persons whom he took with him to the conquest of that Province of Honduras-Higueras all encomiendas which [Alvarado] granted to such persons if the encomienda Indians concerned have actually served the Adelantado [Alvarado] and the persons to whom he assigned them in encomienda. In case Indians of certain pueblos which are subject to principal native towns have not actually served the Adelantado don Pedro de Alvarado or the persons [to whom he assigned them], it is sufficient that such natives should have served the principal native towns concerned to establish the validity of the encomienda grants, unless the principal native towns involved later rebelled and rose in arms and you [Montejo] then finally conquered them.

"If you [Montejo] have removed and revoked the assignment of certain encomiendas of the category just described in prejudice to those who first held them, you are to restore them, along with all the incomes and revenues which they have produced from the time of their removal to the time of their restitution to their original grantees, except such funds as persons to whom you reassigned the encomiendas shall have expended and distributed from the revenues of the pueblos for the good of the pueblos themselves, and such amounts as you verify have been expended by the persons who held them in encomienda by your assignment for the indoctrination of the Indians of the pueblos in Our Holy Catholic Faith.

"I order you [Montejo] to execute and comply with this cedula under penalty of loss of offices and forfeiture of goods to our royal treasury. You are further warned that if you do not act in accordance with this cedula and comply with its provisions we shall send an official from our Court at your expense to carry out and enforce the provisions of this cedula. You [Montejo] will likewise provide that the

request, the Crown appointed Licenciado Cristóbal de Pedraza, already designated Protector of the Indians and acting spiritual head of Honduras-Higueras,
as royal judge to enforce it.[8] This cedula became the turning point when
the issues between Alvarado and Montejo were finally joined in Honduras-
Higueras itself. It was the legal vehicle through which Montejo was finally
forced to relinquish the governorship to Alvarado.[9]

---

pueblos which you return to the original encomenderos under the provisions of this cedula shall have
in them a person who will administer them well and will indoctrinate the Indians in the matters of Our
Holy Catholic Faith. You will also see that the Indians of these pueblos will be maintained in order, a
matter for which you will be principally responsible. . . .

"If the Adelantado don Pedro de Alvarado has assigned certain encomiendas to a person who holds
encomienda Indians in another province you, [Montejo], are to order such a person to select the one
repartimiento which he wishes to retain and to give up the other so that the one relinquished may be
reassigned in encomienda. This provision does not apply to the Adelantado don Pedro de Alvarado
[himself].

"If [Alvarado] has assigned certain Indians in encomienda to persons who are not in that province of
Honduras-Higueras and who did not take part in the conquest of the province, and who did not come
there and have not resided in the province, and if you, [Montejo], have reassigned such Indians, you
are to provide that these Indians are to continue to serve those who at present hold them in encomienda
and you are not to remove them.

"If you, [Montejo], or the Adelantado don Pedro de Alvarado have removed encomienda Indians from
certain citizens of Trujillo, such Indians are to be returned to them.

"I order these provisions to be executed and complied with until such a time as other measures are
provided for, and I endow the Licenciado Cristóbal de Pedraza, Chantre of the Cathedral Church of
Mexico and Protector of the Indians of that Province [of Honduras-Higueras] with powers to investigate
this matter of encomiendas and to make a report to us as to how the foregoing provisions of this cedula
are executed and complied with. I order that this cedula be fulfilled in the manner which best con-
forms with Our service and the good of the Province of (Honduras-Higueras). Valladolid, April 30,
1538. I the Queen."

[8] Cedula of May 13, 1538, AGI, Guatemala, 402: "Licenciado Cristóbal de Pedraza, Chantre of Mexico
and Protector of the Indians of the Province of Higueras and Cabo de Honduras. Know that I ordered a
cedula to be issued to the Adelantado don Francisco de Montejo, Our Governor of the Province [of
Honduras-Higueras], to the effect . . . [that he should readjust the assignment of encomiendas in that
province].

"Now, the Adelantado don Pedro de Alvarado has petitioned me to order you [Pedraza] to compel
. . . compliance with that cedula . . . should the Adelantado don Francisco de Montejo appeal from
its provisions, or should he not wish to comply with them, for in that case [Alvarado] would receive
grievance.

"After discussion of the matter by the members of Our Council of the Indies, they decided to recommend that we order this present cedula to be issued to you [Pedraza], and I approved the recommendation. Consequently I order you [Pedraza] to take cognizance of the cedula [regarding readjustment of
encomienda assignments in Honduras-Higueras] and if the Adelantado don Francisco de Montejo does
not observe and comply with that cedula you are to compel him to observe its provisions and to comply
with them. You are not to permit any obstacles or impediments whatsoever to stand in the way of
fulfillment of the cedula, and you are to send a report of the manner in which its provisions are complied with. . . . Valladolid, May 13, 1538. I the Queen."

[9] An earlier cedula forbidding Montejo to remove encomiendas from those to whom Alvarado had
assigned them, issued on June 30, 1537 (AGI, Guatemala 402) read:

"The Adelantado don Francisco de Montejo, Our Governor of Higueras and Cabo de Honduras.
Francisco Cava, in name of that province, has stated to me that We were already aware of the great
trials and the great labors which the conquistadores [of that province] have suffered, and that when
they were at the point of being lost, and the province was being abandoned, . . . the colonists, all in
agreement, sent word to Guatemala to 'require' the Adelantado don Pedro de Alvarado in our name to
come to their support so that the province [of Honduras-Higueras] would not be lost, and that the
Adelantado [Alvarado], realizing the straits in which the colonists found themselves when he was 'required' in Our name, went to their help in person, with all the Spaniards, horsemen and footmen, whom
he could gather. . . . Displaying great diligence [Alvarado] arrived at the mountains of Gracias a
Dios and began to conquer and colonize [the province]. He also went to the Valley of Naco and conquered all the land and brought the greater part of it to peace. When the land was conquered and
colonized Andrés de Cerezeda, our Contador of that province [of Honduras-Higueras], who at that
time was acting as governor, required [Alvarado] to assume the administration of justice and [also]
assume the government in all things in both peace and war, since such action would be expedient for
our service, for there was no other who could perform such a service. [Cerezeda] then relinquished the

The Crown also ordered Montejo to return to Alvarado all encomiendas and property which Alvarado had possessed in Honduras-Higueras and which Montejo had appropriated for himself. Furthermore, Montejo was to give Alvarado full compensation for any monetary losses which he might have sustained through failure to enjoy the current revenues from such holdings and property, notably incomes which his mining cuadrillas would have produced for Alvarado had they remained in his service.[10] These losses of current income were set by Alvarado between 16,000 and 20,000 pesos de oro, a great sum.[11] Pedraza was designated royal judge between the two governors in

office of governor to [Alvarado], who, to serve us, accepted the charge and then passed forward against a great native lord . . . in that land named Ciçumba, the native ruler who had done all the harm to the Christians who had come to the land. [Alvarado] besieged this lord and took him prisoner, along with all the principal persons of that land. These native lords then became Christians of their own volition and agreed to serve the Spaniards in peace. As a result of these events all the remainder of that province gave obedience. When the Indians were brought to peace [Alvarado] then divided the land in repartimiento, in conformance with the merits of the conquistadores and pobladores, so that they all remained reassured and satisfied.

". . . You [Montejo] have gone to the province [of Honduras-Higueras] with Our provisions of office and have assumed the government. It might so happen that you should wish to take away and remove the repartimientos of Indians which the governors Andrés de Cerezeda and don Pedro de Alvarado have assigned . . . and therefore [Francisco Cava] has requested and petitioned Me as a royally granted favor, to order you [Montejo] not to take away and remove such repartimientos. . . .

"This matter was discussed by the members of Our Council of the Indies and they recommended that this my cedula should be issued to you [Montejo]. In consequence I order you that, until the repartimientos of the Indians of that province [of Honduras-Higueras] carried out by don Pedro de Alvarado and Andrés de Cerezeda shall have been reviewed by us and We shall have provided that which is expedient for Our royal service, you [Montejo] shall not remove or take away from the conquistadores and pobladores the Indians whom don Pedro de Alvarado and Andrés de Cerezeda assigned them in encomienda. If you have already dispossessed any conquistadores and pobladores of encomiendas assigned by don Pedro de Alvarado and Andrés de Cerezeda you are to restore and return the encomiendas to them . . . , so that they may hold them in conformance with the grants which were made to them, and you are to do nothing contrary to the provisions of this cedula. . . . Valladolid, June 30, 1537. I the King."

[10] Cedula of January 30, 1538, AGI, Guatemala 402: "The Adelantado don Pedro de Alvarado, Our Governor and Captain General of the Province of Guatemala, has informed us how, to serve us, he conquered, pacified and peopled the Province of Honduras and how, to help to develop the province, he built a house in the town of San Pedro and helped to construct the houses of its citizens [through employing his own slaves], so that the Indians of [Higueras itself] would not have to be employed in labor other than for the development of agricultural holdings.

"It has now come to the attention of [Alvarado] that you [Montejo] have entered into the province [of Honduras-Higueras] and have appropriated the building and agricultural holdings which he had in the district of the Río de Balaliama and in the pueblo of Naco and in the region of Cansema. [Alvarado] states that he assigned the town [of San Pedro] these holdings and lands, as well as assigning *caballerías* to the citizens. He also declares that he was granted land for grazing livestock between the town of San Pedro and Teapa and that these lands were likewise taken from him, and that a large amount of maize and other things were also taken. The confiscated maize was for the use of slaves who were searching for gold. [Alvarado] states that he has suffered serious grievances as a result of these acts and that he has received damages to the extent of more than 15,000 ducats, and he has petitioned me to order that all confiscated holdings and property shall be returned to him, along with compensation for all losses and damages . . . or to provide for such measures as I might see fit.

"After the members of Our Council of the Indies had deliberated on the matter they recommended that I should issue this my cedula to you [Montejo], and I have accepted their recommendation. Therefore I order you [Montejo] to return and restore to the Adelantado don Pedro de Alvarado, or whosoever may have his power of attorney, his buildings, lands, slaves, maize, and agricultural holdings as soon as this cedula is officially presented to you.

"You [Montejo] are to comply with this cedula in full, and if you do not do so we commit its execution to the Licenciado Cristóbal de Pedraza, Our Protector of the Indians of that province [of Honduras-Higueras], whom We order to act as mediator and whom We command to enforce the fulfillment of and compliance with this cedula, for which purpose We endow [Pedraza] with complete authority. . . . Valladolid, January 30, 1538. I the Queen."

[11] See Montejo *v.* Pedraza, 1539, AGI, Justicia 129-2.

this matter also.[12] This decree regarding Alvarado's personal holdings and
property was worded entirely in his favor. As judge of this phase of the
quarrel, Pedraza was empowered to proceed against Montejo rather than to
act as a mediator of claims and counterclaims. Pedraza thus became a royal
official of high rank and great influence.

In this manner the stage for an intense struggle for power between Montejo
and Alvarado was early set both in Castile and in the Indies, and when
Alvarado returned to Honduras-Higueras in the spring of 1539 he was ready
to act. Not only did he have the will of the Crown and instruments of law
at his back, but he also brought to the Indies an armada of three ships, which
carried some 250 well equipped men-at-arms, including arquebusiers and pikemen, and large stores of munitions and supplies destined for his long-delayed
South Sea expedition. If necessary, these men could be added to Alvarado's
partisans within Honduras-Higueras, who already outnumbered Montejo's followers. Montejo soon declared, "it appears to me that [Alvarado's] armada
was intended for action in this province rather than for use elsewhere. . . ,
[for] according to indications he has his expedition [here] for no other
purpose than to direct it against me. . . ." [13]

RETURN OF ALVARADO FROM SPAIN

On arrival at Puerto de Caballos, Alvarado spent some days unloading supplies and munitions and cutting a way through to San Pedro. It required
200 men to clear this path, since whatever road Montejo had earlier constructed
between those points had by now been overgrown. More time was consumed
in carrying the cargo to San Pedro, partly by canoes sent upstream and partly
overland. At this period Montejo sent no word to Alvarado, much less offer
help for the difficult transport. Only after it was too late to be of service did
Montejo send instructions to his lieutenant in San Pedro to extend aid and

[12] Cedula of January 30, 1538, AGI Guatemala 402: "Licenciado Cristóbal de Pedraza, Chantre of
the Cathedral Church of the City of Mexico, Protector of the Indians of the Province of Higueras and
the Cabo de Honduras. Don Pedro de Alvarado, Our Governor of the Province of Guatemala, has made
known to Me that through another cedula, as We are well aware, We have ordered the Adelantado don
Francisco de Montejo, Our governor of the Province [of Honduras-Higueras] to return and restore all
the buildings and slaves and maize and lands and all other things whatsoever that he took from [Alva-
rado] after [the latter] departed from the province . . . for through such confiscations [Alvarado]
has suffered heavy damages.
"[Alvarado] has now requested me that I order you [Pedraza] to cause him to be compensated for
all . . . which he has suffered as a result [of the confiscation of his property and holdings by Montejo].
He has also requested me to order that all the incomes and profits which have been produced by all the
holdings which Francisco de Montejo may have taken from him be returned, dating from the day on
which they were confiscated. . . .
"After discussion by the members of Our Council of the Indies it was determined that this cedula
should be issued to you [Pedraza], and I have approved. Consequently, I order you to investigate the
circumstances dealt with above. After having heard the cases of the parties concerned, you are to take
such action and adopt such measures with respect to the matter as you find appropriate, executing complete and speedy justice. . . . Valladolid, January 30, 1538. I the Queen."
[13] Montejo to the Crown, Gracias a Dios, August 25, 1539, AGI, Guatemala 39.

comfort to Alvarado. Alvarado took this lapse of formal Castilian courtesy as a gratuitous insult, especially as his new bride, the young and aristocratic Doña Beatriz de la Cueva, had returned with him. He even accused Montejo of refusing help in the hope that he and his men would fall victims of fever on the hot, pestilential coast. Although this accusation was baseless, Montejo did in fact permit himself the hope that Alvarado and his men would move on to Guatemala without halting in Higueras for any length of time, and he certainly did not wish to facilitate Alvarado's entry into the province.[14]

The entire coastal region of Honduras-Higueras passed under Alvarado's control from the very moment that he and his men established themselves in San Pedro. The citizens and authorities of that town were his followers almost to a man and received him joyfully. Montejo and his officials were henceforth unable to exert the slightest influence in the northern districts of the province. Alvarado's partisans in Gracias a Dios and elsewhere likewise disregarded Montejo and his officials. Although the colonists had loyally united under Montejo to suppress the great revolt between 1537 and 1539, now that the danger from the Indians was over and Alvarado had returned, all those who were partisans of Alvarado or who for any reason opposed Montejo's policies turned against him. Montejo's prestige thus rapidly disappeared everywhere except in the Town of Comayagua, whose citizenry was made up almost entirely of his own men. Even though Montejo clung tenuously to control of the cabildo of Gracias a Dios for some weeks, that of itself did not improve his position in his own capital city.[15]

Alvarado's mere presence was sufficient to reduce Montejo to impotence, but Alvarado went further. He openly displayed the utmost contempt for Montejo, acting as though his rival was even not present, much less royal governor. Actually Alvarado immediately "began to administer as a governor." He cryptically implied that he was already chief magistrate of the province and that, with royal approval, he could readily "send Montejo off to Castile in chains." He said that, "Montejo had done him evil in his absence and that now, being present, he would render Montejo worse." Some of Alvarado's more violent followers, one of them a captain, declared that Montejo and his whole household "should be killed" out of hand. Without informing Montejo or even consulting Pedraza, Alvarado forthwith took over all the encomiendas, holdings, and property in the coastal area of which he claimed Montejo had despoiled him.

14 Alvarado to the Crown, Gracias a Dios, August 4, 1539, DII, 24:311–19.
15 See Montejo to the Crown, Gracias a Dios, June 1, 1539, DII, 24:250–97; Montejo to the Crown, Gracias a Dios, June 1, 1539, DII, 24:298–310; Montejo to the Crown, August 25, 1539, AGI, Guatemala 39; Montejo v. Pedraza, 1539, AGI, Justicia 129-2.

On one occasion Alvarado refused to recognize the authority of a bailiff whom Montejo had sent to the Valley of Naco to apprehend a Spaniard who had escaped from prison in Gracias a Dios, where he was about to be tried for clubbing five Indian *principales* to death and stealing a large amount of maize which had belonged to them. Alvarado had gone to the pueblo of Naco for a time to repossess his holdings in its district, and as the bailiff was conducting his prisoner through the pueblo on his return to Gracias a Dios the malefactor called out to Alvarado's followers for help. They set on the bailiff and freed the prisoner, whom Alvarado then actively protected in flout of Montejo's protests.[16]

With his authority over the coast lost and his jurisdiction in Gracias a Dios unheeded by Alvarado's partisans, Montejo's position each day became worse. Going beyond merely setting him at naught, Alvarado's followers in Gracias a Dios presently became so menacing that Montejo feared for the safety of his wife and family. Disorders and crimes occurred with impunity. Montejo, at first stunned by the course which matters were taking, at length tried to rally his followers to oppose Alvarado by force if necessary and to re-establish at least a semblance of control over Gracias a Dios. His efforts fell far short.

I swear before Your Majesty [he despairingly wrote to the Crown] that there is a conflagration in this city and province, and such unrest among [both] Spaniards and Indians that if God does not bring us remedy I do not know where it will end.[17]

For a long while Montejo remained wholly ignorant of Alvarado's true powers and the royal will regarding his own and Alvarado's positions, since the cedulas which the Crown had issued in connection with their rival claims were kept from him. He realized, however, that he must have almost completely lost royal favor, since otherwise Alvarado would not have acted as he did. Sensing that the Crown wished Alvarado to replace him in the governorship of Honduras-Higueras, he greatly despaired, especially since the Crown had earlier held him in such high regard.

Among all the things which weigh upon me [he wrote to his King], that which grieves me most is the knowledge that I have so lost credit with Your Majesty, and with the members of Your Majesty's very high Royal Council, that I am no longer believed, even though nothing but the truth was found in me all the while I was at the Court of Your Majesty [in years past] and since I left there. Perhaps my communications have not been seen [at Court], since everything that has been ordained [by Your Majesty] is contrary to the

16 *Ibid.*
17 Montejo to the Crown, Gracias a Dios, June 1, 1539, DII, 24:303.

information which I have provided and has been so to the prejudice of this land that it now seems to lie beneath the influence of some malign planet which does not permit it tranquility.[18]

PEDRAZA AS MEDIATOR

Pedraza had arrived in Honduras-Higueras in the autumn of 1538 thoroughly imbued with the viewpoint of Alvarado and his partisans, but he soon came to recognize Montejo's great military achievements, the merit of his farseeing policies, and his worth as an administrator. As royal judge he now began to take an active part in the quarrel which was throwing the province into such administrative disorder. He had great sympathy for Montejo, "this poor old man of a governor," but also knew it was the royal will that Alvarado should assume the governorship of Honduras-Higueras.[19]

Conscientious, judicious, zealous, a man of integrity, and resolved to use his powers wisely and for the good of the province and the royal service, Pedraza considered his role as that of a true mediator between Alvarado and Montejo as well as an officer appointed to enforce royal decrees. He was gravely concerned with the deleterious effects which the quarrel between the two governors could bring down upon newly conquered Higueras and also with the administrative chaos which existed everywhere except in the littoral, where Alvarado was already personally in control. It was far from impossible, Pedraza felt, that Alvarado's followers would indeed resort to overt action against Montejo, for "other governors had been killed for less cause" than that which Montejo had given his more powerful opponent. He also feared that Montejo, driven by desperation, might resort to reckless but hopeless military action. Moreover, Pedraza and other thoughtful lesser officials and colonists believed that the Indians, who observed dissension among the Spaniards, might take advantage of the quarrel once again to rise in revolt. In fact

when the Indians saw that [Alvarado] had disembarked with so many men, arquebusiers, pikemen and others with other arms, and likewise saw that the Adelantado Montejo . . . made ready to resist, or at least defend himself against [Alvarado], there was such a great tumult among them that they all wished to leave their homes and go to the mountains, which would have led to the depopulation of the entire province.[20]

Pedraza therefore resolved to negotiate a personal agreement between Alvarado and Montejo. Under this agreement Alvarado was quietly to take over

[18] Montejo to the Crown, Gracias a Dios, June 1, 1539, DII, 24:275.
[19] Pedraza to the Crown, Gracias a Dios, May 18, 1539, AGI, Guatemala 9; Montejo v. Pedraza, 1539, AGI, Justicia 129-2.
[20] Pedraza to the Crown, Seville, December 26, 1544, AGI, Guatemala 164.

the governorship of Honduras-Higueras and unite the province administratively with Guatemala, while Montejo was to assume authority over Chiapas
without further stimulating the quarrel through prolonged legal procedure
which would inevitably be required if a settlement was made solely on the
basis of the cedulas which the Crown had empowered him to enforce against
Montejo. Under his plan Pedraza proposed to have all encomiendas which
Montejo had removed from Alvarado's followers revert to them automatically
once Alvarado assumed the governorship. In the same manner Montejo was
to permit Alvarado to take over all holdings and property confiscated while
Alvarado was in Castile. The new governor was to forego all purely monetary
claims for losses through Montejo's confiscation of his property, since Montejo
was so heavily in debt that he could not possibly satisfy them. Pedraza had
pride and confidence in his ability as a conciliator, especially in view of his
claims that he had adjusted a quarrel between Cortés and Nuño de Guzmán.[21]

As Pedraza was in Gracias a Dios when Alvarado arrived in the province,
he personally counseled moderation to Montejo and, by correspondence, recommended conciliation to Alvarado and his partisans. He planned to go to
San Pedro to interview Alvarado, but the situation in Gracias a Dios was so
tense that his continued presence there seemed necessary. His pleas that both
parties stay their hands were effective for a while and allayed the mob spirit
of Alvarado's most extreme followers in Gracias a Dios—a tribute to his
persuasiveness—but nevertheless the situation remained explosive.

Although Pedraza deferred his interview, he probably was instrumental in
persuading Montejo to send his brother Juan to confer with Alvarado. Montejo, who hitherto had refused any direct communication with his opponent,
now sent his brother to Alvarado to ascertain his desires and intentions. Juan
de Montejo returned from San Pedro with nothing but a strong confirmation
of Alvarado's determination to take the governorship of the province for
himself.[22]

Montejo was now poignantly aware that his cause was utterly lost unless
there was a rapid and unforeseen reversal. His only hope was a change in
Crown attitude or a legal decision in his favor. On June 1, he drew up the
first of a series of documents for the Crown, stating his achievements and
defending his policies in Honduras-Higueras, pleading his long years in the
royal service, appealing for confirmation as governor of Honduras-Higueras,

---

[21] *Ibid.*
[22] Montejo to the Crown, Gracias a Dios, June 1, 1539, DII, 24:298–310; Montejo to the Crown,
Gracias a Dios, August 25, 1539, AGI, Guatemala 39; Montejo to the Crown, Gracias a Dios, November 4
and December 15, 1539, AGI, Guatemala 9; Montejo *v.* Pedraza, 1539, AGI, Justicia 129-2; Montejo *v.*
Alvarado, 1541, AGI, Justicia 134-3; Alvarado to the Crown, Gracias a Dios, August 5, 1539, DII,
24:311–19.

accusing Alvarado of attempted usurpation, and charging Alvarado and his partisans with lawless acts. Montejo well knew that the rate of communication between the Indies and Castile could not bring speedy answers to his urgent pleas, but he hoped meanwhile to gain time through prolonged litigation with Alvarado in the province itself. Only such a plan held the slightest promise of a favorable outcome.

All this while Alvarado, impatient for direct action, finally decided on a quick solution. Sometime in June he moved out from San Pedro at the head of a powerful company, "all armed and prepared for war," to march on Gracias a Dios and bend Montejo to his will by force of arms. Montejo, panic-stricken, made frantic efforts to organize his own outnumbered partisans.[23]

Pedraza was gravely concerned by the threatening crisis, for he wished at all costs to avoid having the province torn apart by civil war. Leaping into the breach as royal judge, he must first have dissuaded Montejo from trying to resist Alvarado by armed action and promised that he would do everything possible to persuade Alvarado not to employ force. Further, it is obvious that he discussed with Montejo the specific terms on which the latter must now come to an agreement with Alvarado, both for a transfer of the governorship to Alvarado and for a settlement of Alvarado's personal claims. Pedraza, accompanied by officials and foremost citizens, thereupon hastened to parley with Alvarado. His major hope was to settle the entire controversy then and there along the lines of the proposed personal agreement.

Alvarado took a stubborn position at first, for he saw no need to negotiate with the powerless Montejo. He openly proclaimed his intention of humbling and punishing his rival by force of arms. Pedraza's arguments prevailed, nevertheless, and Alvarado at length renounced his martial purpose, accepting Pedraza's bases for peaceful negotiation. Pedraza then seems to have returned to Gracias a Dios to inform Montejo of his success and to insure that Alvarado's entry into the city would be orderly and quiet. He also persuaded Montejo personally to receive Alvarado and Doña Beatriz in courteous fashion. Montejo was gratified at this unexpected opportunity to negotiate, and Alvarado's entry into Gracias a Dios was thus peaceful, owing entirely to the efforts of Pedraza, whose words on this subject bear repeating.

It was necessary for me to rise up from my sickbed [he wrote] and go out twelve leagues to receive the Adelantado Alvarado to try to establish friendship between him and the Adelantado Montejo. As a result of my efforts I caused [Alvarado] to remove his forces from a war footing and to renounce the evil purpose which he gave me to understand he had entertained against

[23] *Ibid.*

[Montejo]. I caused [them] to become friends and brought [Alvarado] and his wife Doña Beatriz de la Cueva . . . to the City of Gracias a Dios and had the Adelantado Montejo and all the citizens . . . receive them nearly half a league from the city, where [the two adelantados] met each other with great cordiality. . . .[24]

Alvarado and Montejo now established formally correct relations with each other, as befitted Castilian noblemen. If the relations were but formal, however, their wives found a mutual bond of sympathy and formed a friendship that did much to bring Alvarado and Montejo temporarily closer together.[25] Pedraza patiently and skillfully guided these rapprochements, and when the time was ripe he pressed for final agreement. Terms were readily arranged, for there had of course not been time for the Crown's reply to Montejo's appeals, and his basic position was still as weak as ever, although not as dangerous.

Under the agreement now reached, Montejo was to relinquish the governorship of Honduras-Higueras to Alvarado in return for Alvarado's territory of Chiapas, just as the Crown had authorized. Since Honduras-Higueras was a much more important province than Chiapas, Montejo was also to receive Alvarado's great encomienda of Xochimilco, just south of the City of Mexico, which was almost a province in itself and which, with its large native population, produced rich tributes. Alvarado was to have back all the holdings and property which Montejo had confiscated from him, but he gave up his heavy personal claims for monetary losses incurred through Montejo's usurpation. This generous renunciation on Alvarado's part arose from his wife's friendship with Montejo's wife, as much as from Pedraza's efforts to obtain a just settlement, for Montejo's manifest indebtedness made it clear that insistence on payment would work the greatest hardship on Montejo and his family. Encomiendas which Alvarado had assigned to colonists before he went to Castile in 1536 and which Montejo had removed from them and reallotted to his own followers were unobtrusively to revert to the former grantees. Thus both Alvarado and Montejo finally accepted the bases of agreement, of which a report was sent to the Viceroy Antonio de Mendoza as royally designated arbiter concerning any exchange of territory.[26]

Montejo at first gladly accepted the surprisingly moderate terms of this agreement but soon began to shift his ground. This change of attitude began

---

[24] Pedraza to the Crown, Seville, December 26, 1544, AGI, Guatemala 164.

[25] Ibid.; Montejo to the Crown, Gracias a Dios, June 1, 1539, DII, 24:298–310; Montejo to the Crown, Gracias a Dios, August 25, 1539, AGI, Guatemala 39; Montejo to the Crown, Gracias a Dios, November 4 and December 15, 1539, AGI, Guatemala 9; Montejo v. Pedraza, 1539, Justicia 129-2; Montejo v. Alvarado, 1541, AGI, Justicia 134-3; Alvarado to the Crown, Gracias a Dios, August 4, 1539, DII, 24:311–19.

[26] Ibid.

when he finally learned about the actual texts of the royal decrees under which both Alvarado and Pedraza were empowered to act. These cedulas had been withheld from him until negotiations were actually in progress. Believing that he saw escape clauses which might enable him to save his situation through involved legal procedure, or at least permit him to delay matters until the Crown had replied to his despatches, he now attempted to nullify the agreement. He protested that it had been entered into wholly against his will and because both Alvarado and Pedraza had misrepresented their own powers as well as the royal will. He claimed that there was no real reason for him to give up the governorship of Honduras-Higueras. To delay matters further he held that, in any case, the compact just concluded was not valid until Mendoza should give formal approval. Alvarado and Pedraza insisted that the pact be placed in effect immediately.

Furthermore, Montejo took no real steps toward readjusting the assignments of encomiendas. He sent another despatch to the Crown telling of the agreement and of his decision to abrogate it, giving his reasons, and made it clear that he expected the Crown to permit him to remain as governor of Honduras-Higueras in view of his military and administrative achievements. He even mentioned resuming his plan for the conquest of the Valley of Olancho "when the season of rains was over," and wrote of projects to improve the situation of Trujillo, construct more roads, and exploit the rich silver lodes of the Valley of Comayagua after Alvarado should have departed from Honduras-Higueras.[27] Thus Montejo turned suddenly from complete dejection to unreasoning and ill-founded confidence. Pedraza was dismayed by Montejo's abrogation of the agreement he had so carefully nurtured; Alvarado, with whom Montejo broke off all contact, was infuriated.

PLANS FOR LEGAL ACTION AGAINST MONTEJO

Montejo now turned on Pedraza, who, he claimed, had tricked him into believing that no course was open but to relinquish the governorship of Honduras-Higueras when such was not the case at all. He even accused Pedraza of treacherously acting as Alvarado's agent in the matter. Such an accusation was, of course, utterly without foundation. Montejo not only refused to heed Pedraza's counsels but denounced him as a bitter, sinister enemy.

Having rejected Pedraza as a counselor, Montejo turned exclusively to his legally trained chaplain, the Bachiller Juan Alvarez, for advice. With Alvarez' guidance he hoped to be able to set aside the cedulas through recourse to legal technicalities. Alvarez consequently assumed an extremely impor-

[27] *Ibid.*

tant position, attested by the violent antagonism he aroused in Pedraza and Alvarado and the latter's partisans, who held him largely responsible for Montejo's course.[28]

Although Montejo had originally brought Alvarez to Honduras-Higueras as chaplain and legal counselor in administrative affairs, he seems also to have given him minor governmental posts, even though Alvarez was trained only in canon law. Montejo's opponents openly protested that Alvarez had been assigned offices which carried with them civil and criminal jurisdiction. Alvarez had earlier advised Montejo that it would be legally valid for him to nullify Alvarado's repartimientos and carry out his own as he saw fit. From the first he had advised Montejo that he was under no obligation to obey the royal cedulas regarding repartimientos, Alvarado's holdings, or even an exchange of jurisdiction, since the Crown had acted in all three matters without adequate information. Alvarez invariably encouraged Montejo to assume an aggressive attitude toward both Alvarado and Pedraza and undoubtedly was instrumental in turning Montejo against Pedraza. He certainly advised Montejo to attempt to retain the governorship, renounce his agreement with Alvarado, and refuse to comply with the cedulas which required restitution of encomiendas, as well as those which ordered restoration of Alvarado's appropriated holdings.[29]

Further, as Montejo's representative, Alvarez sought in every manner to gain wider support for him among the colonists and to arouse opposition against Alvarado, even though these were hopeless tasks. In addition to his official and quasi-official duties, Alvarez seems for some time to have acted as a personal agent to keep Montejo and Doña Beatriz de Herrera informed of the opinions of the colonists so that Montejo could single out and deal with principal local enemies. Such employment as an informer added to the number of Alvarez' enemies. It was even alleged by his enemies that Alvarez had expressed the extreme papal doctrine that the province belonged to the Pope rather than the King, to whom the Pope had donated the New World, and that therefore Montejo was not obligated to observe royal decrees.[30]

Moreover, Alvarez was criticized as a roistering, brawling, gaming type of person, who belied his ecclesiastical status and who entirely failed to fulfill his spiritual duties. He was accused of frequenting taverns, playing with false cards, and housing men of evil life who openly kept Indian concubines. It was said that on one occasion Alvarez even struck Montejo himself during a dispute over cards. At one time, when he was the only cura resident in

[28] Residencia of Montejo for Honduras-Higueras, 1544, and for Chiapas, 1546, AGI, Justicia 300.
[29] *Ibid.*
[30] *Ibid.*

Gracias a Dios, many colonists refused the sacrament at his hands, nor would they confess to him. Pedraza soon began an investigation of his official and personal conduct. This action intensified the animosity between the two clerics and later led to important repercussions when both were in Castile. Although Alvarez was resourceful, he was obviously the worst possible counselor for Montejo when sound, careful, and measured advice was needed above all else.[31]

Since his patient mediation had utterly failed and Montejo had turned from him to Alvarez, Pedraza now was forced to see that Alvarado was placed in the governorship of Honduras-Higueras as soon as possible. He was like-wise obliged to carry out his duties as judge to enforce in full legal form the cedulas which required an adjustment of the encomienda assignments in Honduras-Higueras and the restoration of Alvarado's personal holdings. The impatient Alvarado must have wished to take shorter and more direct methods, to which his great superiority in armed strength lent itself, but Pedraza pre-vailed on him to move entirely within the framework of law. As a result the controversy between the two governors now passed into a legal phase in which Pedraza took up his duties as a royal judge against Montejo in the most com-plete sense, with Alvarado standing behind him with his armed men, ready and willing to intervene at any time to force the issue and to support Pedraza's legal decisions.

Consulting with Alvarado, whose impetuosity he had constantly to hold in check, Pedraza carefully plotted his legal course. Under Pedraza's new plans Alvarado himself was to initiate action against Montejo. On June 30 Alvarado began litigation through his brother-in-law, Francisco de la Cueva, who served as his legal representative. Brusquely demanding compliance to the letter, de la Cueva presented to Montejo the royal cedulas requiring him to restore to the original encomenderos all pueblos which he had removed from them and directing that he return Alvarado's confiscated possessions. It will be recalled that the royal decree which ordered this restitution carried as penalty for failure to comply, removal from office and forfeiture of goods to the Crown.[32]

Montejo haughtily delayed several days in giving his reply, which was a round rejection of Alvarado's demands on the ground that the royal cedulas concerned were based on false premises, since the Crown was not informed of the situation in the province. Montejo denied that he had taken anything from Alvarado unjustly. However, he conceded that he was prepared to return to Alvarado any encomiendas for which the latter could present legal title. In

[31] *Ibid.*
[32] The entire section on the legal aspects of the quarrel between Alvarado and Montejo is based on Montejo *v.* Pedraza, 1539, AGI, Justicia 129-2. Only where other materials are employed will references be cited.

conclusion Montejo referred the entire matter to Pedraza, hoping to create delays.

Alvarado then had de la Cueva request Pedraza to proceed to the enforcement of the pertinent decrees. De la Cueva asked for vigorous action against Montejo as "a powerful person because he is governor of the land." Pedraza replied that he was prepared to proceed "in accordance with justice" and forthwith began a series of secret and thorough investigations concerning all points at issue, calling before him the royal treasury officials of the province, municipal authorities, and colonists. When Montejo learned of the investigations he wished to introduce carefully selected witnesses on his own behalf; this Pedraza not only refused to permit but went so far as to forbid any notary to draw up legal documents for Montejo.

Pedraza concluded his closed investigations rapidly and made his first move against Montejo on July 7. Through a notary, accompanied by men-at-arms, he informed Montejo, who was then in his own home, of Alvarado's demands for immediate enforcement of the cedulas. Montejo flew into such a rage that the notary, fearing personal harm, fled to the street and the protection of his armed guards. In giving testimony against Montejo, the notary later described this incident:

[Montejo] invited me into a room saying that he wished to speak to me. Since I did not wish him forcibly to take away from me the documents which I held in my hand, I requested that "His Grace should pardon me for not accepting his invitation, and that if he wished to say something of importance to me he should say it before witnesses. . . ," since I was wary of entering into the room as he wished. He then ordered the alguacil mayor of this city to seize me and throw me into stocks. When I realized that such was his purpose I went back to the dwelling of the Señor Judge of Enforcement to tell him what had transpired so that he could render justice in the matter.

Despite his anger, Montejo was impressed by Pedraza's action. On that same day, July 7, he had the royal cedula which required him to restore encomiendas to the original recipients proclaimed "twice in the public plaza, once before the dwelling of the governor and the other time before the lodgings of the Adelantado Alvarado and the Licenciado Pedraza, Protector of the Indians, ..." and announced that he was ready to return encomiendas to all colonists who could produce legal title, or cedulas of encomienda, which had been issued by Alvarado. Pedraza followed Montejo's proclamation by issuing one of his own, stating that all encomenderos who had been dispossessed of their pueblos by Montejo should present their titles to the latter at once.

On the other side of the ledger, Montejo sent a representative to Pedraza to demand the presentation of final proof of his authority to act as an arbitrary judge in the controversy. Montejo declared that he himself was the highest representative of royal authority in the province and that neither Pedraza nor Alvarado could hold jurisdiction over him in any manner. He flatly took the position that Pedraza "was not a judge." Pedraza's reply was equally intransigeant; he would not swerve from his fixed course as long as Montejo displayed such stubbornness. He was no longer acting as a mediator and forthrightly declared that he was not "a judge to determine the merits of Montejo's case, but rather was one who was to enforce and carry out that which His Majesty specifically ordered."

Montejo considered that his mere promulgation of the cedula requiring restoration of pueblos and his examination of encomienda titles placed before him during the following few days had met the legal demands of the situation. Therefore he took no action to return pueblos to their first encomenderos. Neither did Montejo take the legal steps to restore Alvarado's holdings and property which the situation demanded. He consequently played into Alvarado's hands and gave Pedraza a sound juridical basis for further procedure.

Pedraza now repeatedly demanded that Montejo restore to Alvarado all his confiscated holdings and that Montejo comply with the cedula requiring readjustment of encomienda assignments, under penalty of removal from office as stipulated by the Crown. Each time such demands were presented Montejo vigorously restated his position, declaring that he "did not hold Pedraza to be a judge" and that Pedraza was "usurping jurisdiction." The notaries whom Pedraza sent to notify Montejo of his demands were invariably accompanied by armed guards, for on each occasion Montejo's reaction was an angry one. Montejo finally ordered, although without the slightest effect, that no local officials or citizens should acknowledge Pedraza's authority and demanded that Pedraza permit him to appeal the entire controversy to the Crown, which Pedraza refused.

Meanwhile, held in restraint by Pedraza while legal action was developing, Alvarado sat back, certain of the outcome but impatient of delay. Notwithstanding, he gave Pedraza a free hand, for soldier though he was, he realized that it was best in the long run to rest his position on unassailable legal foundations.

Just past the middle of July, Pedraza was ready for final action. He had completed legal groundwork for the removal of Montejo from office and for his complete personal discomfiture. Nevertheless, although his position was reinforced by law and by Alvarado's armed strength, Pedraza decided to

give Montejo one more chance gracefully to reaffirm the agreement he had so
rashly repudiated. The proposal which Pedraza now advanced is a high tribute
to him and might have led to a reasonable settlement of all points at issue had
Montejo not exceeded himself in obstinacy. Montejo was motivated by fierce
pride, renewed determination to preserve Honduras-Higueras for his jurisdiction if possible, and realization that, with Yucatan still unconquered, he
would be reduced to minor status as governor of Chiapas. Pedraza proposed
a commission consisting of Gonzalo Ronquillo, Veedor of Guatemala; Alonso
de Cáceres, Montejo's trusted captain; Gaspar Xuárez de Avila, now a regidor
of Gracias a Dios, who had served with Gonzalo de Alvarado and then became one of Montejo's earliest important partisans in Honduras-Higueras;
and Diego Díaz de Herrera, a citizen of Guatemala. This group was to attempt mediation. By another reading to Montejo of the royal decrees, word
for word, it was to be made clear to him that the only alternative to full
compliance with the royal will was immediate and irrevocable removal from
office in Honduras-Higueras. Pedraza wrote:

I [myself] . . . , Gonzalo de Ronquillo, captain Alonso de Cáceres, Gaspar
Xuárez de Avila, a regidor of this city, and Diego Díaz de Herrera went about
trying to establish concord and peace and to mediate between the Adelantado
Montejo and the Adelantado Alvarado to determine whether, without strife,
they could act within proper reason and thereby reach a concert in their
[controversy], as I requested and begged. [I sought to] have them meet as
friends, in all good feeling to adjust [their differences]. Montejo was informed to the letter, and sentence by sentence, of all the decrees which Alvarado carried [regarding their quarrel].

Pedraza's impartial gesture unfortunately broke down completely. Montejo
refused to meet Alvarado, remained as obdurate as ever, and would have
nothing to do with Pedraza's effort at a reasonable settlement.

Pedraza next called together in his own dwelling the contador Andrés de
Cerezeda, the treasurer Diego García de Celís, the veedor Alonso de Valdés,
the factor Juan de Lerma, the alguacil mayor Juan López de Gamboa, and
the regidores Hernando de Almao and Martín de Alaráz, as an extraordinary
cabildo, or junta, representing the opinions of most citizens of Gracias a Dios,
and of the province as a whole for that matter. Cerezeda, García de Celís,
Valdés, and Lerma were treasury officials by royal appointment; Almao was
a municipal councilman by election. They conferred at length, especially over
Montejo's refusal to acknowledge Pedraza's authority as judge and to carry
out the royal decrees regarding encomiendas and Alvarado's personal claims,
and discussed the best means of enforcing these decrees.

Pedraza besought the members of the junta, of whom Lerma was loyal to Montejo and Cerezeda was certainly not hostile, to plead with Montejo for compliance and to make him realize that if he refused this last chance he would be deprived of office. They found Montejo in company with the alcalde Gonzalo de Alvarado, who had a sincere regard for Montejo even though he wished to see his brother back in the governorship, and informed him in detail of Pedraza's demands and intentions. Montejo replied as before: that he had already complied with the cedulas ordering restitution of encomiendas and Alvarado's holdings, that he in no way recognized Pedraza "to be a judge over him" in any matter concerning encomiendas or his controversy with Alvarado, and that Pedraza possessed no authority whatsoever to question his acts as governor. Montejo looked upon the convocation of a cabildo by Pedraza only as another usurpation of authority, and since Alvarado's followers were again showing signs of restlessness, he once more feared for his life.

The Licenciado Pedraza [he declared] called together a cabildo in his house, and there by his own order he convened the officials of justice and the municipal councilmen of this city. This junta was concerned with the question as to whether the governorship should be taken away from the Adelantado Montejo, and it met many and diverse times in Pedraza's house. Pedraza and the others in this junta then decided to take the governorship away from the Adelantado [Montejo] with the support of the municipal officers of justice and the councilmen, and to provide new governors, and ordered that the Adelantado [Montejo] should not be obeyed in any manner, because he was no longer governor. . . .
Each day they came to me with many armed followers of the Adelantado don Pedro de Alvarado to notify me of their demands, and the affair reached such a point that they placed their hands on their swords against me while I was seated in my own house. They offered me other insults and threats, even though I was governor in name of Your Majesty, and displayed great effrontery and haughtiness. They acted thus because I still would not come to an agreement with [Alvarado], to exchange the governorship [of Honduras-Higueras for that of Chiapas]. Don Pedro de Alvarado threatened me with the soldiers of his armada and employed as his messengers the tesorero [García de Celís], the factor [Lerma], and an alcalde named Gonzalo de Alvarado. . . . Many others also came to inform me that they were planning to kill me and Juan de Montejo, my brother.[33]

Since all effort to persuade Montejo to be reasonable had thus failed, Pedraza quickly set in motion the now well-prepared machinery to remove him from office and to force an agreement with Alvarado. Pedraza once more convoked

---

[33] Montejo to the Crown, Gracias a Dios, December 15, 1539, AGI, Guatemala 9. See also Montejo to the Crown, Gracias a Dios, August 25, 1539, AGI, Guatemala 39.

the junta and reviewed the entire course of the controversy, declaring repeatedly that while still at Court he had been ordered to send Montejo, if failing in obedience, "to Castile in irons." He also emphasized that, despite the severity of Court attitude, he himself had been extremely patient and moderate toward Montejo.

Conforming with Castilian constitutional practice, Pedraza next arranged for the appointment of interim administrators to assume control of the province until Alvarado and Montejo should have concluded their agreement, whereupon Alvarado would take over the government. With the help of the junta as an advisory council he chose the contador, Andrés de Cerezeda, twice acting governor of the province in earlier years, and the treasurer, Diego García de Celís, as coadministrators. As members of the junta, both men must have had the approval of the group.

MONTEJO REMOVED FROM OFFICE

At eight o'clock in the morning of July 21 Pedraza summoned

His Lordship, don Francisco de Montejo, Governor, to appear before me, either in person or through a legal representative, since I have sentenced you in name of His Majesty, in accordance with the penalties stipulated in his royal decrees. . . . You are to appear before me within the next three hours, even though I am not obliged to grant you any time whatsoever. . . .

One hour later Montejo announced his refusal to appear before Pedraza and again replied in his former vein. He declared that

he does not hold the [Licenciado Pedraza] to be a judge . . . , and he appeals . . . to His Majesty and to those of his very high Council [of the Indies, and that] if the Licenciado Pedraza [nevertheless] insists that he is judge over me . . . he should have care in what he does. . . .

Pedraza's final sentence swiftly followed:

Having noted the reply of the Adelantado [Montejo], which is in rebellion and contumacy, and having noted the slight respect which he displays for the royal decrees of His Majesty and that he has not been inclined to obey anything which His Majesty . . . and I, in his royal name, have ordered, . . . and since [Montejo] has given it to be understood to all persons in this province that they shall neither acknowledge nor obey me as a judge, . . . seeing that [long since] I could have . . . condemned him in name of His Majesty . . . [but nevertheless] have been patient, [I now pronounce the following sentence]:

. . . In name of His Majesty I condemn him in the penalties contained in the [pertinent] royal decrees, namely deprivation of offices and forfeiture of goods to the treasury and coffers of His Majesty. . . . I order that the officials of the royal treasury of this province of Honduras and Higueras place his goods at the disposal of the royal treasury and that these goods shall not be returned to him until it is provided otherwise by those of His [Majesty's] very high Council [of the Indies]. . . . In condemning [Montejo] to deprivation of the offices and charges which he enjoys as governor for His Majesty in this province of Honduras and Higueras, I order the officials of justice, regidores, and loyal subjects of this province that henceforth they shall not acknowledge nor obey him as governor, and that they shall not admit him in their cabildos nor courts. . . .

Pedraza now proceeded to designate Cerezeda and García de Celís as interim coadministrators of the province.

Until His Majesty provides . . . that which is most expedient for his service [he declared] in name of His Majesty, I order that their lordships Andrés de Cerezeda, Contador of His Majesty, and Diego García de Celís, His [Majesty's] Treasurer, shall take charge of the government until His Majesty provides otherwise, . . . notwithstanding any reasons . . . which they may advance to the contrary [and I declare that if they do not accept their offices] the responsibility for any difficulties, public scandals, dissension, disorders, and deaths which may result from their refusal will be theirs alone. . . .

At four in the afternoon of the same day, July 21, Pedraza lay his sentence before Montejo, privately but with full observance of legal form. Fearing a violent outburst or rash action from Montejo, he sent twenty well-armed men to guard the notary who was to serve notice of the sentence. This time Montejo's reaction was dangerously quiet, for as the inevitable blow fell he was desperately planning an armed move. His only reply was another refusal to recognize Pedraza's jurisdiction and an indication that he would continue the legal procedure of placing the entire matter directly before the Crown.

Pedraza delayed several days before proclaiming the sentence publicly. In his resolve to be scrupulously fair he may still have sent representatives, especially persons close to Montejo, in another attempt at persuasion. Alvarado and his partisans simultaneously threatened coercion. Montejo remained defiant.

On July 24 Pedraza publicly proclaimed sentence, including the designation of Cerezeda and García de Celís as coadministrators, and this was accepted by the cabildo of Gracias a Dios. Montejo took the most ill-timed and ill-advised action of which he could possibly have conceived under the circumstances. He first called the cabildo of Gracias a Dios together in his residence and announced his intention of proclaiming once more his royal appointment as governor as a counter-measure to Pedraza's sentence. Then, setting Pedraza at naught and defying Alvarado and his soldiers, Montejo attempted to protect his position as governor by armed force. He urgently

sent summons to all the citizens [of Gracias a Dios] . . . to come to his residence with their arms and horses. . . . A page of the Adelantado [Montejo] . . . went about to summon the citizens and many of them answered, some with their horses and swords while others went on foot. . . .

He may have intended to arrest Pedraza through a sudden stroke, or even have dared to hope that he might seize Alvarado unaware. But Montejo vacillated at the crucial moment. Instead of taking an aggressive stand before the citizens who responded to his call—the outnumbered hard core of his own followers—he gave them neither leadership nor clear instructions. They consequently did nothing but mill about aimlessly in the main plaza before his home.

Pedraza and Alvarado had anticipated a possible overt move by Montejo. Alvarado had 100 arquebusiers standing ready under command of Francisco Cava, who intensely hated Montejo and had earlier declared that Montejo and his household should be done away with summarily. Fifty of these arquebusiers were stationed under cover in Pedraza's dwelling, which was close to Montejo's on the public plaza; the other fifty were posted in the house of Gonzalo de Alvarado. Pedro de Alvarado's horsemen were undoubtedly also under alert. Pedraza and Alvarado were thus so completely masters of the situation that they were annoyed rather than alarmed by Montejo's feeble attempt to employ force. Pedraza merely ordered all citizens who had heeded Montejo's call to arms to return to their homes, threatening heavy penalties if they did not disperse at once; they forthwith ceased their useless "rioting and creation of disorder" and quietly drifted away. Meanwhile all but a few of the members of the cabildo who had responded to Montejo's convocation had left his dwelling. Montejo's fiasco sealed his fate more certainly than ever.

Montejo's own version of this incident is interesting. He wrote to the Crown:

After the sentence had been delivered against me depriving me of office, another decree was issued forbidding anyone from obeying me as governor. When this decree was proclaimed I called together the alcaldes, regidores, royal treasury officials, and certain honored persons from among the citizens, and when some of them had answered my summons I told them that they well knew that I was governor and that the Protector [of the Indians, Pedraza] had no authority to do that which he had done and that I was going to publish my provisions of office [anew]. They informed the Protector [of my intention] and he requested the Adelantado [Alvarado] to send him men-at-arms. . . . [Alvarado then] sent the Protector one of his captains named Francisco Cava at the head of one hundred musketeers all armed, and with their arquebuses loaded and their matches lighted. . . . When those who were with me learned of these moves, and also because the Protector issued a decree ordering that they leave my dwelling under pain of death and loss of their property, they all went away and left me there alone.[34]

With even more frantic urgency than before, Montejo now tried to rush his protests against Alvarado to the Crown. He fiercely repeated his attacks on Pedraza as treacherous, deceitful, lacking in integrity, and merely an agent of Alvarado. He charged that Pedraza was the worst possible designate for the office of Protector of the Indians, maintaining, without the slightest vestige of truth, that "there is no man more brutal toward the Indians or who ill-treats them to such an extent as he: so that wherever he is there can be no tranquility." He further accused Pedraza of usurping authority in removing him from office and that in doing so Pedraza had not only acted in violation of law but had unjustly used legal procedures to serve Alvarado's personal interests. Montejo well knew that no results could come from these charges in time to alter his position, because the controversy would be settled in Alvarado's favor even before his letters could leave the shores of the New World, but he nevertheless counted on them to work to his future benefit.

After Pedraza notified him of his sentence on July 21, Montejo secretly and hastily despatched his chaplain and legal adviser, Juan Alvarez, to give his version of developments to the viceroy and the Audiencia of New Spain, and to protest the acts of Pedraza and Alvarado. Alvarez carried documents setting forth Montejo's views and was to begin suit against Pedraza and Alvarado before the audiencia. Through this move Montejo hoped to find means of retaining the governorship of Honduras-Higueras and of preventing the viceroy from approving the final agreement for an exchange of Honduras-Higueras for Chiapas with Alvarado, which he now realized was otherwise inevitable. Should his efforts in the City of Mexico not speedily promise favorable results, Alvarez was to go on to Castile to place Montejo's case directly before the Crown.

With the public proclamation of the sentence removing Montejo from office on July 24, the time had come for Cerezeda and García de Celís to take office as coadministrators, but both advanced objections. García de Celís now pro-

[34] *Ibid.*

posed the constitution of a junta composed of Pedraza, the royal treasury officials, including García de Celís himself, and the municipal representatives of each city and town of the province to choose a temporary chief magistrate to serve until Alvarado could take over the government in due legal form. It will be seen that, while at Court with Alvarado, García de Celís had placed a proposal providing for action of this nature before the Council of the Indies in an effort to establish permanent constitutional procedure for the selection of an interim chief magistrate in Honduras-Higueras in the vacancy of the governorship. Pedraza's urgings, however, persuaded Cerezeda and García de Celís to accept the joint administration, and they assumed their duties.

MONTEJO COMES TO TERMS

Completely broken and again fearful for his own and his family's safety, Montejo now indicated to Alvarado and Pedraza his wish to come to terms. It is not surprising that Alvarado should now be hardly eager for an agreement, especially since he had won a complete triumph. Pedraza had therefore to undertake further delicate mediation, which he carried out with skillful impartiality, despite the drastic action he had taken against Montejo. Supported by the treasury officials and the cabildo of Gracias a Dios, he pleaded with Alvarado to accept the terms of the original compact, urging him for "the service of God and His Majesty and for the general good of the land which would result from his acquiescence." Alvarado listened to these pleas and in the end indicated his willingness, proving less haughty and obdurate, and much more reasonable, than Montejo had been.

A formal agreement was signed by the two adelantados on August 1. By this time Alvarado had generously moderated his attitude and Montejo had been softened by circumstances so that the two rivals could regard each other with mutual tolerance, if nothing more. The compact, which because of Pedraza's mediation was liberal beyond anything asked of Alvarado to satisfy the Crown's requirements of mere justice, included eight major articles, the principal of which were part of the earlier agreement whereas others dealt with recent matters:

1. Alvarado was to relinquish to Montejo the chief magistracy of Ciudad Real de los Llanos de Chiapa, that is, the governorship of the province of Chiapas, in return for that of Honduras-Higueras;

2. Alvarado was to set to one side claims which he had finally fixed at 17,000 pesos de oro for losses resulting from confiscation of his property and holdings by Montejo;

3. Alvarado was to place in Montejo's possession his great encomienda of

Xochimilco, south of the City of Mexico, with all rights pertaining to and revenues originating from that town, in compensation for the difference in political and economic importance between Honduras-Higueras and Chiapas;

4. As additional compensation for the difference in importance between the two provinces Alvarado was to pay Montejo an additional 2000 pesos de oro within six months;

5. In accordance with his powers as royally designated arbiter between Montejo and Alvarado in any exchange of territory which they might effect under the authorization which the Crown had given for such an exchange, the Viceroy of New Spain, Antonio de Mendoza, was to approve the agreement within five months to render the compact valid;

6. Montejo's chaplain and legal adviser, the Bachiller Juan Alvarez, and any other representatives whom Montejo might have sent to New Spain or Castile to present his side of the controversy to higher authority, were to be called back by Montejo, and in return Alvarado was to recall all despatches which he had sent to Castile and New Spain during the course of the quarrel;

7. Alonso de Cáceres, Montejo's former lieutenant, was designated *juéz executor,* or executive, to assure compliance with the agreement by both parties;

8. The two adelantados were to swear to a *pleito homenaje,* or solemn engagement as Castilian noblemen, guaranteeing that they would carry out the agreement in all sincerity.

The pleito homanje to which Montejo and Alvarado were to subscribe was drawn up immediately after the basic agreement was signed. The parties also concurred in naming Mendoza as judge of any disagreements which might arise after he had signified his approval of the compact and it had thereby officially gone into effect. Under this pledge Montejo gave his word not to take any action whatsoever to regain the governorship of Honduras-Higueras or to initiate legal procedure of any nature that might embarrass Alvarado in his administration.

Pedraza presided over the conclusion of the agreement and the drawing up of the pleito homenaje. His difficult task as royal judge had been completed faithfully and well. He had achieved the end the Crown desired—the replacement of Montejo by Alvarado in the governorship of Honduras-Higueras and the provision of adequate compensation for Montejo elsewhere. That Alvarado should have permitted Montejo such surprisingly good terms after complete victory was Pedraza's work alone. So ably and conscientiously had he performed his mission that Juan de Lerma, Montejo's old friend and financial collaborator during his campaigns in Yucatan and now Factor of Honduras-Higueras, could write to the Crown that Pedraza had been a judge "so good that he has very justly and impartially given to each his own." [35]

[35] Juan de Lerma to the Crown, San Pedro, October 31, 1539, AGI, Guatemala 49.

Following their agreement, Alvarado and Montejo sent a joint report to the Crown telling of their compact, declaring—not with entire truth, however —that each party had reached agreement by his own free will, and requesting the Crown specifically to confirm the terms of the compact, notwithstanding the fact that full royal authorization to give final approval had been accorded the viceroy Mendoza.[36] They likewise sent a copy of the agreement to the viceroy requesting immediate approval.[37] In another despatch Alvarado petitioned the Crown to confirm the integral union of Honduras-Higueras with Guatemala so that the two provinces could permanently receive mutual benefits from such unity. Alvarado declared that otherwise Honduras-Higueras would fall into irreparable decay, since that region "without the other [province] was of no value."[38] This statement coincided perfectly with the current sentiments of the majority of the local authorities and was couched in almost the exact words in which Montejo and his lieutenant Alonso Dávila had earlier advocated the now inoperative union between Yucatan and Honduras-Higueras. Mendoza approved the agreement at once, and the Crown gave its supreme sanction when the joint report reached Castile.

Immediately upon the conclusion of the agreement Cerezeda and García de Celís stepped aside and Alvarado was duly installed as governor of Honduras-Higueras by the cabildo of Gracias a Dios. As the distressed Montejo witnessed the installation, "The officials of justice who had received their staffs of office from my hands entered into the cabildo to receive the Adelantado don Pedro de Alvarado [as governor]."[39] The union of Honduras-Higueras with Alvarado's central province of Guatemala thus became a practical reality, with royal approval. Alvarado soon moved on to Guatemala to prepare for the South Sea enterprise which had long been his objective; Montejo remained in Gracias a Dios for a few more months.

The loss of Honduras-Higueras was a grievous blow to Montejo's great plans to build a wider adelantamiento, for he continued to look upon Honduras-Higueras as the core of the regions that he wished to weld together. Yucatan, his first province, was still unoccupied. Despite his agreement with Alvarado he hoped somehow to regain control over Honduras-Higueras. He not only failed to recall Alvarez from the City of Mexico and to call back despatches already forwarded to the Crown attacking Alvarado and Pedraza, but he also sent additional letters to Castile claiming the governorship of Honduras-Higueras as rightfully his and leveling further bitter accusations

[36] Alvarado and Montejo to the Crown, Gracias a Dios, August 10, 1539, AGI, Guatemala 9.
[37] See Montejo v. Alvarado, 1541, AGI, Justicia 134-3.
[38] Alvarado to the Crown, Gracias a Dios, August 4, 1539, DII, 24:318.
[39] Montejo to the Crown, Gracias a Dios, December 15, 1539, AGI, Guatemala 9.

against Alvarado, Pedraza, and others whom he considered his enemies. He now violently charged that Alvarado had forced him to relinquish the governorship of Honduras-Higueras against his will and literally at sword's point, and he besought redress. Of his agreement with Alvarado and conditions during the period preceding his removal from office Montejo said, "Seeing myself lost and in order not to lose my life, I declared that I wished to come to an agreement, and the terms which were reached were exactly those which the Adelantado [Alvarado] wished. . . ." [40]

Pedraza tried to prevent Montejo's despatches from leaving the province, but Montejo evaded the censorship, on one occasion secretly placing letters in the hands of a Spaniard from Peru who was passing through Honduras-Higueras on his way to Castile. Furthermore, Alvarez, who had hastened to the City of Mexico, had immediately begun legal action before the audiencia on Montejo's behalf, although this litigation did nothing whatsoever to delay the viceroy's approval of the compact between Montejo and Alvarado. Mendoza wanted nothing more to do with the controversy once the agreement had been placed before him and he had approved it at once.

When it became clear that he could not hope for the slightest support from Mendoza at this time, and since any action by the Crown would necessarily be long delayed, Montejo and his household, their embargoed property finally released, set out for Chiapas late in 1539 or very early in 1540, moving overland by way of Santiago de Guatemala. He assumed the governorship of Chiapas early in 1540. Two years later Montejo was to return to Honduras-Higueras under the most unexpected circumstances.

[40] *Ibid.*

8

Jurisdictional Problems, 1539–44

HONDURAS-HIGUERAS AS A PROVINCE SUBORDINATE
TO GUATEMALA

AFTER Alvarado had compelled Montejo to relinquish the governorship of Honduras-Higueras to him in exchange for Chiapas through their agreement of August 1, 1539, the new governor remained in Honduras-Higueras only long enough to consolidate his position and bring order to provincial administration. Among measures to this end was the readjustment of encomienda grants to satisfy his partisans. Then, after securing his authority over the province and uniting it with Guatemala, he hastened to Santiago de Guatemala to prepare for his long-projected South Sea enterprises. Alvarado arrived in mid-September and, under royal cedula, once more assumed the governorship of Guatemala. The acting governor, Alonso Maldonado, then returned to the City of Mexico, to resume his duties as an oidor of the Audiencia of New Spain.

On leaving Honduras-Higueras, Alvarado appointed Montejo's former subordinate, the able and experienced Alonso de Cáceres, as his lieutenant governor and captain-general, endowing him with full civil and military authority, and a seat of government at the Town of Comayagua. This transfer from Gracias a Dios was based on the universally recognized merits of Montejo's idea to develop Comayagua into the principal municipality of the province.[1] Alvarado had been impressed by Cáceres' military and administrative talents and had finally won him to his service, for when Montejo had withdrawn, Cáceres had at first wished to go elsewhere. Even though he had served Montejo since 1526, he no longer considered him to have any but "slight possibilities."

Once back in Guatemala, Alvarado speedily organized his South Sea armada. Shortly before embarking on his enterprise, he designated his young and aristocratic brother-in-law, Licenciado Francisco de la Cueva, as his lieutenant governor and captain-general for Guatemala during his absence. Since before leaving Castile Alvarado had obtained a royal decree empowering him so to appoint de la Cueva for all provinces of his jurisdiction, the young man thus enjoyed superior authority over Honduras-Higueras. Thither de la Cueva sent

---

[1] See Alonso de Cáceres to the Crown, Comayagua, September 5, 1539, AGI, Guatemala 43; Cabildo of Comayagua to the Crown, September 5, 1539, AGI, Guatemala 43.

his credentials and was recognized as governor in Alvarado's name by all Alvarado's lieutenants, the royal treasury officials, and the cabildos of the province. Cáceres remained as lieutenant governor and captain-general.[2]

In furtherance of its policy to unite Honduras-Higueras with Guatemala the Crown in 1541, while the acting prelate Cristóbal de Pedraza was in Castile, confirmed the assignment to Francisco de Marroquín, Bishop of Guatemala, of ecclesiastical jurisdiction over Honduras-Higueras until a bishop should be named for that province, even though Pedraza's final designation as Bishop of Honduras was then pending.

In this way, just as the majority of the colonists had wished, Honduras-Higueras was joined to Guatemala in both administrative and ecclesiastical matters.

Meanwhile Alvarado had taken his South Sea armada to the west coast of Mexico. There, late in 1540, he came to an agreement with the Viceroy of New Spain, Antonio de Mendoza, for collaborative South Sea enterprise. Montejo was also on the west coast seeking a meeting with Mendoza at this time, in connection with complications arising from his compact with Alvarado over Honduras-Higueras. Before Alvarado and Mendoza could put their new plans in effect, however, the great Mixton War broke out in Nueva Galicia in 1541. The colonists of that province were hard pressed by the Indians, and Alvarado, always restless, hastened to their aid. In June he met an untimely death from injuries received before the native stronghold of the Peñol de Nochistlan, and Castile thus suddenly lost one of her great conquistadores.[3]

The viceroy sent news of Alvarado's death to de la Cueva, the cabildo of Santiago de Guatemala, and the Bishop of Guatemala. As highest authority of New Spain, Mendoza confirmed de la Cueva as lieutenant governor of Guatemala and its related provinces and authorized him to remain interim governor until the Crown should appoint a successor to Alvarado. Mendoza emphatically directed all concerned to recognize de la Cueva's authority. Nevertheless the cabildo of Santiago de Guatemala, on September 9, adopted the unprecedented measure of naming Alvarado's widow, Doña Beatriz de la Cueva (La Sin Ventura or Unfortunate One, as she called herself after her husband's death), *gobernadora* of Guatemala. She accepted the office, but designated her brother, Francisco de la Cueva, her lieutenant and gave him full powers to act in all matters of government except the assignment of

[2] For general governmental developments in Guatemala from 1539 to 1542 see Remesal, 1619; Bancroft, 1883–87; Milla and Gómez Carillo, 1879–97. The appointment of Alonso Maldonado by the Viceroy and Audiencia of New Spain to replace the interim governors in Guatemala who were locally elected in Guatemala following Alvarado's death and Maldonado's appointment of Juan de Chávez as his lieutenant governor in Honduras-Higueras are found in AGI, Guatemala 965.
[3] See Kelly, 1936, for a biography of Pedro de Alvarado.

encomiendas. The cabildo of Santiago de Guatemala then approved the gobernadora's appointment of her brother as the official who was actually to
govern. The unfortunate widow, however, perished in a great flood from
the slopes of the nearby Volcán de Agua, which destroyed the Santiago de
Guatemala on the night of September 10–11, 1541. With the sudden death
of the gobernadora, Guatemala was again left, at least technically, without
an administrative head.

The concejo of Santiago de Guatemala, that is, the cabildo and citizen body
together, now met on September 14 and began deliberating on the selection
of new governing authorities and on either reconstruction or transfer of the
city. The cabildo decided that de la Cueva's powers, whether derived from
Alvarado or Doña Beatriz, were no longer valid and that consequently new
elections were necessary. Doctor Blas Cota, a jurist of Portuguese nationality
who had served in high administrative capacity in the Azores and who came
to the New World with Alvarado when he returned from Castile in 1539, was
also consulted and gave the opinion that de la Cueva could no longer act
under his existing appointments. At the request of the cabildo, de la Cueva
stepped down.

The cabildo itself then elected de la Cueva and the Bishop of Guatemala as
joint interim governors of Guatemala to serve until the Crown designated a
new chief magistrate. De la Cueva accepted office at once, but Marroquín,
believing that temporal duties would interfere with spiritual obligations, needed
more persuasion. The cogovernors were finally installed, however, and the
viceroy and Audiencia of New Spain signified approval.

It is interesting to note that the name of Montejo, now governor of nearby
Chiapas as well as Adelantado of Yucatan, came up during the balloting for
the interim governorship. Also, Juan de Chávez, whom Alvarado had selected
to conquer the interior of Higueras and found Gracias a Dios in 1536, but
whose discontented soldiers had forced him back to Guatemala before he
could accomplish his mission, was recommended by Marroquín, who considered Chávez to be a soldier, administrator, and nobleman of the highest
type.[4]

The independence of this election by the cabildo of Santiago de Guatemala
was of constitutional significance, because in thus choosing governors for its
own province it was by the same action choosing governors for the subordinate
districts of Honduras-Higueras, San Salvador, and San Miguel. In arrogating
to itself such prerogatives, the cabildo of Santiago de Guatemala acted without
any real consultation with the cabildos of the towns and cities of the attached

[4] Marroquín to the Crown, Santiago de Guatemala, October 6, 1541, AGI, Guatemala 156.

provinces, an action soon to produce important effects in Honduras-Higueras. Likewise, in selecting its own chief magistrates for Guatemala and the attached provinces, the cabildo of Santiago de Guatemala ignored the confirmation which the Viceroy of New Spain had given to Alvarado's original appointment of de la Cueva. They had so jealously sought to reserve the right to designate their own interim governors that they overlooked the possibility that subordinate provinces might not wish to accept their appointments.

Despite original enthusiasm for union with Guatemala, the Spaniards of Honduras-Higueras now began to feel that such a union fell far short of their anticipations. Control of the province from a distance proved distasteful and caused ever-mounting dissatisfaction, a feeling which, in fact, had developed even before Alvarado's death, for he naturally gave preference to Guatemala, the province from which his authority stemmed. Looking upon Honduras-Higueras as a subordinate and less important area, he had governed accordingly, as the colonists of Honduras-Higueras should have foreseen. They thus came to feel discriminated against and neglected.[5]

A revival of the old question of exploiting the precious metals of Honduras-Higueras by colonists of Guatemala was part of this picture. When the two provinces were joined under Alvarado's jurisdiction there were no longer any restraints such as those imposed by Montejo. Colonists of Guatemala, with authority from Alvarado and later from de la Cueva, came back to Honduras-Higueras untrammeled and exploited gold and silver deposits everywhere. Gold was again carried off to Guatemala for refinement. Continued lack of resources prevented the colonists of Honduras-Higueras from operating large mining cuadrillas, whereas colonists of Guatemala could afford to do so. In this manner much of the gold and silver of Honduras-Higueras was once more removed to Guatemala, and Honduras-Higueras itself was denied the full benefits, both for its colonists and for the enrichment of the royal treasury of the province. The Spanish settlers still considered gold and silver their only immediate means of wealth, largely ignoring the other economic potentialities of the province, and they deeply resented the renewed intrusion from Guatemala. Thus, even under Alvarado, union with Guate-

[5] The changed sentiment in Honduras-Higueras toward union with Guatemala, and the reasons for this change, are shown by the following documents: Royal Treasury officials of Honduras-Higueras to the Crown, Puerto de Caballos, July 30, 1540, AGI, Guatemala 49; Juan de Lerma to the Crown, Gracias a Dios, November 30, 1541, AGI, Guatemala 49; Diego García de Celís to the Crown, San Pedro, March 14, 1542, AGI, Guatemala 49; Juan López de Gamboa to the Crown, Gracias a Dios, April 27, 1542, AGI, Guatemala 52; Montejo to the Crown, Gracias a Dios, May 1, 1542, AGI, Patronato 184-25; Royal Treasury Officials of Honduras-Higueras to the Crown, San Pedro, May 15, 1542, AGI, Guatemala 965; Royal Treasury Officials of Honduras-Higueras to the Crown, Gracias a Dios, July 21, 1542, Guatemala 49; Montejo to the Crown, San Pedro, April 1, 1543, AGI, Patronato 184-25; Documents concerning the election of García de Celís and López de Gamboa as interim coadministrators of Honduras-Higueras, October 21, 1541, AGI, Guatemala 965; Residencia of Montejo for Honduras-Higueras, 1544, and for Chiapas, 1546, AGI, Justicia 300.

mala failed to please them. The royal treasury officials of Honduras-Higueras declared to the Crown in 1540 that the gold and silver mines of the province were the only real source of wealth and protested the draining of precious metals to Guatemala. An added source of dissatisfaction lay in the assignment of some of the richer encomiendas of Honduras-Higueras to citizens of Guatemala.

The colonists who had supported Alvarado against Montejo had expected to have a free hand in exploiting native labor, as well as deposits of precious metals, under Alvarado's governorship. Montejo's refusal to permit unregulated use of Indian labor was an important cause of his unpopularity. The colonists of Honduras-Higueras, however, now found that Cristóbal de Pedraza, as ecclesiastical head of the colony and Protector of the Indians, imposed the same restrictions in defense of the Indians that Montejo had established. Only in the period immediately after Alvarado arrived was license possible, and this Pedraza soon ended, dashing the colonists' expectations under Alvarado's laxity in such matters.

After the union of Honduras-Higueras and Guatemala, Alvarado and his successors in Santiago de Guatemala exercised judicial as well as administrative authority over Honduras-Higueras. Higher judicial questions and appeals had to be referred first to the Guatemalan lieutenants in Honduras-Higueras and then to the officials in Guatemala itself. Santiago de Guatemala was distant and difficult to reach. Expenses of travel there were high and lengthy delays in the administration of justice were unavoidable. Many settlers of Honduras-Higueras consequently became convinced that union with Guatemala gravely impaired the proper administration of justice for their own province.

There also grew up strong sentiment against subordination to Guatemala on the basis of provincial pride alone. Many Spaniards soon came to dislike government from another province once it had become a reality, especially after years of independence. The union with Yucatan had never had any practical application because of Montejo's withdrawal from that province in the mid-1530's. Those who had in the past advocated union with other provinces for strength, soon lost enthusiasm when they found it meant complete subordination, disregard of their own interests, and neglect of their province.

THE DISSOLUTION OF THE UNION WITH GUATEMALA AND THE ADMINISTRATION OF GARCÍA DE CELÍS AND LÓPEZ DE GAMBOA

Though not popular, de la Cueva had been accepted in Honduras-Higueras as Alvarado's lieutenant as long as that great conquistador lived. De la Cueva was new and inexperienced, not "a man of the Indies," and was considered haughty and arrogant. With Alvarado's death, Honduras-Higueras saw no further reason to hold de la Cueva in any regard whatsoever, although he and Marroquín had sent their new powers of cogovernorship before the cabildos of Honduras-Higueras, along with the decree by which the Viceroy of New Spain had recognized de la Cueva's authority as acting governor of Guatemala.

Discontent and resentment in Honduras-Higueras had progressed so far by this time that the cabildos no longer had the slightest intention of remaining subordinate to Guatemala. Upon making formal scrutiny of the documents which de la Cueva and Marroquín sent to them, the cabildos readily found technical grounds for rejecting their authority. On the basis of Mendoza's decree, which was couched in general terms and failed to specify Honduras-Higueras as territory attached to Guatemala, they refused to recognize the authority of either de la Cueva or Marroquín.[6] Although Marroquín, unlike de la Cueva, was held in high esteem, the bishop also represented subordination to Guatemala and therefore had to be rejected.

De la Cueva speedily created the opportunity to break free which the colonists of Honduras-Higueras sought. He was adamant regarding his authority over that province and persisted in despatching administrative decrees there and in demanding that superior matters of justice be sent before him in Santiago de Guatemala. He continued Alvarado's policies on mining, ordering that the refining of gold mined in Honduras-Higueras by colonists of Guatemala should be carried out in Guatemala. In contrast, Marroquín does not seem to have concerned himself over-much, leaving civil administration entirely to de la Cueva.

Their general resentment thus stimulated by de la Cueva, the local authorities defied his continued efforts to govern their province. They declared that if he would come to Honduras-Higueras to reside they would recognize his authority, but that they would under no circumstances longer tolerate subordination to Guatemala. They well knew that de la Cueva could not, and would not, transfer the seat of government to Honduras-Higueras. De la Cueva was sufficiently familiar with the ways of Honduras-Higueras through his stay there with Alvarado in 1539 to know enough not to press his claims further. The tie with Guatemala was thus actually cut, and Honduras-Higueras was in an advantageous position to move from *de facto* to *de jure* separation.

Meanwhile Alonso de Cáceres, who had remained in Honduras-Higueras as the lieutenant first of Alvarado and then of de la Cueva and Marroquín,

[6] See the above references, especially documents concerning the election of García de Celís and López de Gamboa as interim coadministrators of Honduras, October 21, 1541, AGI, Guatemala 965.

had already lost all practical authority except by such influence as he could personally wield in Comayagua, his seat of government. He had lost ground not only because the colonists were against him, but also because while governmental changes were taking place in Guatemala, he was absent trying to conquer the Valley of Olancho, where he had founded the town of San Jorge and discovered rich gold deposits. Even though he hastened back at Alvarado's death expressly to assert the jurisdiction of his Guatemalan superiors, he could accomplish nothing. Having cast aside the authority both of the governors of Guatemala and of their lieutenant, Honduras-Higueras was for the time being without centralized executive authority of any kind.

Rejection of external authority was one thing, but maintenance of internal order was quite another. A grave administrative problem now arose. In accordance with normal constitutional procedure, government temporarily lapsed into the hands of the several municipal cabildos, each of which sought to exercise control within its district, at the same time maintaining contact with the other cabildos for general co-ordination. The inveterate factionalism soon produced its effects. Disturbances and disorders developed and created anew the fear that the natives might take advantage of such conditions to rise up in arms. The complete anarchy with which the province had been cursed so many times before seemed about to repeat itself, and there was imperative need for the creation of an interim central government which could promise firm control, as the more responsible citizens fully realized.

In their capacity as direct appointees of the Crown, the royal treasury officials stepped into the breach. Headed by García de Celís, they proceeded to elect administrators until the Crown or a high agency of government in the New World should designate a new chief magistrate. García de Celís justified such a move on the basis of petitions which he had presented to the Consejo de Indias when he was in Castile with Alvarado.[7]

The experience of García de Celís in Honduras-Higueras before Alvarado's rescue of Higueras in 1536 had convinced him of the need to provide fixed, legal procedure within the province itself for establishing responsible authority upon vacancy of the governorship for whatever cause. (In the case of Andrés de Cerezeda, the dying royal governor, Diego Alvítez, had himself named Cerezeda as interim governor.) Lack of fixed machinery for selecting acting chief magistrates and incompetent administration by interim authorities had heavily contributed to the disorder which had so retarded the development of the province. For example, Cerezeda's total inadequacy and failure to

---

[7] Documents concerning the election of García de Celís and López de Gamboa as interim coadministrators of Honduras-Higueras, 1541, AGI, Guatemala 965; Diego García de Celís to the Crown, San Pedro, March 14, 1542, AGI, Guatemala 49.

command even a minimum of respect wrought great detriment to the originally promising colony of Buena Esperanza.

García de Celís proposed as broad a base as possible for the selection of acting chief magistrates, so that the officials chosen might function with the fullest possible support of all concerned until the Crown appointed a new royal governor. Choice of acting governors was consequently to be made by representatives of all groups and all types of interests. To this end García de Celís petitioned the Crown to authorize the nomination of interim chief magistrates, or administrators, by a provincial junta composed of royal treasury officers, higher ecclesiastical officials—notably the spiritual head of the province—and procuradores of the several cabildos, who would speak for the colonists. In this manner all factions were represented.

The Consejo de Indias studied this farseeing petition carefully. The secretary of that high body added a *capítulo* on the margin recommending that in the vacancy of the governorship, the royal treasury officials, the ranking prelate or the Protector of the Indians, and the alcaldes and a regidor of each municipality should convene as a junta and elect an interim chief magistrate to serve until the Crown itself named a governor. The whole proposal was not formally acted upon by the consejo, so no cedula was issued to place it in effect. Nevertheless, in view of the recommendation by the secretary of the consejo, García de Celís and other officials of Honduras-Higueras considered that the supreme tribunal for overseas affairs had given its tacit approval. They therefore took the position that they had valid grounds for action within the province whenever occasion required.

It was this *capítulo del Consejo* to which García de Celís now, in the autumn of 1541, appealed as an instrument through which to provide Honduras-Higueras with interim central authority.[8] He persuaded the cabildos of Gracias a Dios, San Pedro, and Comayagua to take action under it. These municipal councils then elected representatives for the junta, which, as finally constituted, was composed of Gonzalo de Alvarado, now again an alcalde, and Francisco de Mexía, the procurador, for Gracias a Dios; Francisco del Barco, an alcalde, and Juan de Cabrera, a regidor, for Comayagua; Nicolás López de Yrarraga, an alcalde, for San Pedro; the churchman Martín de Toribio, as representative of the Protector of the Indians, Pedraza, who had already sailed for Castile; and García de Celís himself. The junta met in Gracias a Dios on October 21, 1541, and with a minimum of discussion elected the prime mover of the action, García de Celís, and the alguacil mayor of the province, Juan López de Gamboa, as "administrators of government and higher justice and captains-general"

---

[8] *Ibid.*

until the Crown should appoint a governor or take other appropriate action. These two, by will of the majority, were thus assigned plenary civil and military authority over Honduras-Higueras, and were immediately sworn into office by Gonzalo de Alvarado. Although both officials were nominally to share their all-inclusive powers, it was clearly understood that, because of his warlike experience, López de Gamboa should have charge of military affairs while García de Celís handled civil matters. Certain members of the junta had wished to win the capable Cáceres away from loyalty to Guatemala and make him captain-general under the two administrators, but this proposal was not adopted. The election was proclaimed in Gracias a Dios and all subordinate officials and colonists throughout the province were ordered to obey.[9] This method of selecting interim governors from a broad representation had its roots in the highly developed democracy of medieval Castile, of which there were still traces despite the advance of royal absolutism.

The junta, of course, had not met without hostile manifestations from dissident minorities, so it directed García de Celís and López de Gamboa to take vigorous action against any rioters. But the anticipated disturbances did not materialize and the coadministrators entered upon their duties tranquilly as far as Gracias a Dios was concerned.[10]

On October 24 the veedor Alonso de Valdés and the factor Juan de Lerma, as officers of the royal treasury and "perpetual municipal councilmen" of the province by royal appointment, approved of the election. The cabildos of Gracias a Dios, San Pedro, and Comayagua also duly confirmed it; the cabildo of Trujillo, which had not sent representatives, gave tacit recognition, although in practice that older city was soon to follow an almost autonomous course. Report of the election was sent to the Crown, and probably also to the Viceroy and Audiencia of New Spain. Thus separation from Guatemala was formally consummated, and Honduras-Higueras once again had its own chief magistrates, by its own independent choice. With the action of the junta Gracias a Dios once again became the governmental seat of Honduras-Higueras.

All this evoked strong protest in Santiago de Guatemala, where the union was naturally popular. Although the Viceroy of New Spain was urged to re-establish the administrative union, he did not act immediately but eventually adopted collateral measures of vital influence.[11]

Neither did Cáceres, back in Comayagua from the Valley of Olancho, readily accept the junta's action. Still nominally lieutenant governor of Honduras-

[9] Ibid.
[10] Ibid.
[11] Residencia of Montejo for Honduras-Higueras, 1544, AGI, Justicia 300.

Higueras in the name of the Guatemalan authorities, he was at first prepared to attempt the preservation of their jurisdiction, even by force of arms. He gathered a company of Spanish followers and native auxiliaries and prepared to act, but López de Gamboa marched on Comayagua with a strong force, which likewise included Indian warriors. The usual civil strife would have ensued had not the treasurer of Guatemala, Francisco de Castellanos, hastened from San Miguel, where he was carrying out an official inspection, to offer mediation, which both Cáceres and López de Gamboa accepted just as their forces were about to join battle. Cáceres now gave up any further thought of restoring Guatemalan jurisdiction, and García de Celís and López de Gamboa thus removed the only remaining challenge to their authority.

Castellanos gives an account of this near recurrence of civil strife:

When news of the death of . . . Alvarado in Jalisco reached this city [of Santiago de Guatemala] a captain named Juan López de Gamboa rose in rebellion and called himself Administrator of Justice [in Honduras-Higueras]. He gathered men to move to Comayagua against Captain Alonso de Cáceres, who governed there with powers from the Adelantado don Pedro de Alvarado, to force Cáceres to accept his authority. . . . Cáceres thereupon likewise raised a large number of Spanish soldiers in the town of Comayagua, to defend himself from Juan López de Gamboa.

When these developments were taking place, the Treasurer [Castellanos] was in the town of San Miguel, which is thirty leagues from Comayagua. . . . He left immediately, like a good servant of His Majesty, and went to the town of Comayagua in a day and a half, whereas by post six days are necessary, to work for peace between the two captains so that they would not break with each other and so that no deaths would result, as was then expected.

Having arrived at the town of Comayagua the Treasurer [first] consulted with . . . Cáceres as to the manner in which hostilities might be prevented, and [then] in that very hour, about midnight, he set out in haste and arrived at the camp of Captain Juan López de Gamboa, which was about five leagues from the town of Comayagua, and where Captain Juan López de Gamboa was preparing his men to march forward. When Captain Juan López de Gamboa saw the Treasurer he made legal demands upon him that he take up arms and march with him against . . . Cáceres, but the Treasurer responded that he had come only to serve God and His Majesty and to establish peace between the two opposing captains, so that they would not break with each other, and to prevent killing [of Spaniards]. Then the Treasurer discussed with Captain Juan López de Gamboa terms upon which he might come to an agreement with . . . Cáceres so that they would not fight among themselves. On the basis of what was agreed upon in this discussion the Treasurer then returned as quickly as possible to the town of Comayagua to inform . . . Cáceres of the results of his interview with Juan López de Gamboa. After that he went back and forth between the two captains five or six times, covering twenty-five or thirty leagues in these journeys. Meanwhile Juan López de Gamboa was continuing his march on Comayagua and Alonso de Cáceres had moved out against him. Finally the two captains and their men came within crossbow range of each other.

It was then about nightfall and the two companies were about to attack each other, with their lances and swords in their hands, their crossbows with the quarrels in them, and the matches for their arquebuses lighted. Then, by his good diligence and through the many warnings he gave to both parties the Treasurer caused the two captains to come to an agreement with each other and to become friends, and influenced everyone else to be satisfied.

If it had not been for the very great diligence, solicitude and labor which the Treasurer displayed in giving attention to this misunderstanding it is certain that the two captains would have engaged in armed conflict. Through his efforts the Treasurer served God Our Lord and His Majesty well, since otherwise that province would have suffered risk of being ruined, because if some Spaniards had been killed and wounded in an encounter those who still remained unhurt and those who were wounded could have been very easily killed by the Indians who went in their company [as auxiliaries] and the other [natives] who were in the land. If this happened the Spaniards would not have had the strength to mine gold in the Río de Guayape, which had been discovered a very short time before. . . . [12]

Even though Honduras-Higueras was now a separate province, its political problems were still far from solved, for no other province of all the Indies was less fitted to attempt dual government. Dissension and jealousy arose between García de Celís and López de Gamboa, who encroached upon each other's respective civil and military duties. They functioned with an utter lack of co-ordination. García de Celís was by nature irascible and domineering, and chronic ill-health further shortened his temper. He acted on important matters without consulting his colleague, who strongly resented such usurpation. Both accepted contrary and, at times, ill-conceived advice from opposing quarters. As they fell increasingly at cross-purposes, contending factions formed behind them. In short, García de Celís and López de Gamboa were of "different estate and character," and "that which one mastered the other sought to dispose of." With this complete lack of harmony, administration, which needed a firm hand, lapsed into all too familiar chaos.[13]

Other factors also were involved. When Cáceres returned from the Valley

[12] Probanza of Francisco de Castellanos, Santiago de Guatemala, 1560, AGG, Papers from the Archivo Colonial, Section of Guatemala, leg. 264, exped. 1.

[13] Juan de Lerma to the Crown, San Pedro, November 30, 1541, AGI, Guatemala 40; Diego García de Celís to the Crown, San Pedro, March 14, 1542, AGI, Guatemala 49; Royal Treasury Officials of Honduras-Higueras to the Crown, Gracias a Dios, July 21, 1542, AGI, Guatemala 49; Residencia of Montejo for Honduras-Higueras, 1544, AGI, Justicia 300.

of Olancho after founding San Jorge de Olancho, matters went badly there; only a mere outpost remained to hold the westward fringe of the region. Furthermore, there was anxiety in Honduras-Higueras that the authorities of San Miguel might encroach northward on territory of Gracias a Dios and Comayagua and take for themselves encomienda pueblos there. Also, as always when Spaniards showed division among themselves, fear of an Indian revolt persisted.[14]

Meanwhile, Trujillo, oldest city of the province, had by now moved toward virtual autonomy. The citizens had remained deeply resentful of Cerezeda's transfer westward of the center of gravity in Honduras-Higueras in 1534, and of the confirmation of that shift by Alvarado and Montejo. They felt that their interests had not in any way been properly served, even by Montejo, who had made definite plans to strengthen the position of their city.[15] With Higueras now falling into chaos under the ineffectual administration of García de Celís and López de Gamboa, Trujillo set its independent course and elected Juan García de Lemos interim alcalde mayor of the city and its district, that is, of Honduras proper. Thus the local authorities acted on the constitutional premise that jurisdiction reverted to the cabildos of the province in the absence of a governor named by the Crown or by the highest agencies of government in the New World. Henceforth, until well into 1542 Trujillo had little contact with the authorities of Higueras, who were too weak and confused to make good their jurisdiction in the Honduras section of the province.[16]

As though internal difficulties were not enough, the authorities of Guatemala sent a representative, Alvaro de Paz, in another attempt to recover Honduras-Higueras. García de Celís, López de Gamboa, and the cabildos roundly and successfully rejected such a move, but at the same time the coadministrators appointed Paz their *visitador general* of Honduras-Higueras.[17]

The situation within the province became more and more dangerous as the weeks passed. By the close of 1541, governmental anarchy, failure to improve the foothold in the Valley of Olancho despite several efforts, pressure from Guatemala, threats of disorders among the unruly colonists, and the lurking peril of an Indian uprising caused everyone, including García de Celís and

[14] *Ibid.*
[15] Fiscal *v.* Juan Pérez de Cabrera, 1556, AGI, Justicia 296-4-1; Juan de Lerma to the Crown, Gracias a Dios, November 30, 1541, AGI, Guatemala 49; Juan López de Gamboa to the Crown, Gracias a Dios, April 27, 1542, AGI, Guatemala 52; Royal Treasury Officials of Honduras-Higueras to the Crown, Gracias a Dios, May 1, 1542, AGI, Guatemala 49; Montejo to the Crown, San Pedro, April 11, 1543, AGI, Patronato 184-25; Cedula of August 23, 1543, AGI, Guatemala 393; Residencias of Montejo for Honduras-Higueras, 1544, and for Chiapas, 1546, AGI, Justicia 300; Residencia of Juan Pérez de Cabrera, 1544, AGI, Justicia 63.
[16] *Ibid.*
[17] Probanza of Alvaro de Paz, Santiago de Guatemala, 1559, AGI, Patronato 62-13.

López de Gamboa themselves, to feel that their essay in dual government was a miserable failure. The need for strong control by a single individual was once more apparent. García de Celís now tried to push López de Gamboa to one side and become sole governor, but it was quickly made clear that no one would tolerate him and he sent an appeal to the Audiencia of Santo Domingo to appoint a chief magistrate for the province without delay. Certain colonists, apparently acting through representatives, also despatched similar petitions to the audiencia.

It will be recalled that in 1534 the Crown had transferred Honduras-Higueras from the jurisdiction of the Audiencia of New Spain back to that of the Audiencia of Santo Domingo. It was only because Guatemala, to which Honduras-Higueras was administratively united in 1539, was under the jurisdiction of the Audiencia of New Spain that the Mexican tribunal, of which Mendoza was president, could seek to claim authority in Honduras-Higueras. Since Honduras-Higueras had cast off union with Guatemala, García de Celís and the citizens who appealed for the appointment of a new governor carefully and deliberately moved through the Audiencia of Santo Domingo, thus adhering to and reinforcing their position on the jurisdictional status of the province.

There were decisive moves in Honduras-Higueras for the selection of a governor, nevertheless, before the Audiencia of Santo Domingo could act on the requests for the gubernatorial appointment, since the state into which the province had fallen demanded a rapid solution to prevent irreparable disaster. The initiative for such speedy action soon came from many quarters within Honduras-Higueras, although López de Gamboa probably took the lead. About the turn of the year 1541–42 the representatives of the municipal cabildos met with him in Gracias a Dios to elect a sole governor, acting under the same capítulo de consejo through which García de Celís and López de Gamboa had been elected coadministrators. This time García de Celís, ill, discouraged, and rejected, was not present in the junta.[18]

After careful deliberation the junta unanimously decided to recall Montejo. They voted for him because, in retrospect, they tardily realized the true worth of his military achievements in Honduras-Higueras and the farseeing wisdom of his administrative policies. On the purely legal side they acted on the premises that the Crown had never revoked Montejo's appointment as governor and that, in view of Alvarado's death, the agreement by which Montejo

[18] Residencia of Montejo for Honduras-Higueras, 1544, and for Chiapas, 1546, AGI, Justicia 300; Royal Treasury Officials of Honduras-Higueras to the Crown, Gracias a Dios, July 21, 1542, AGI, Guatemala 49; Juan López de Gamboa to the Crown, Gracias a Dios, April 27, 1542, AGI, Guatemala 52; Audiencia of Santo Domingo to the Crown, March 10, 1543, AGI, Santo Domingo 49.

relinquished authority over the province was no longer valid. They also took cognizance of the fact that, although they had been joined with Guatemala for a time, the Crown had never officially dissolved the earlier union with Yucatan. Meanwhile, the situation in Yucatan had been fundamentally altered. Under Montejo's authority, his natural son and his nephew, both of whom bore his name, were, with lesser captains, rapidly advancing the conquest of that province. Hence the union of Yucatan and Honduras-Higueras, which had not been practicable before and which the Crown had tacitly but not officially abandoned, was now quite possible. The junta therefore resolved to recall Montejo to Honduras-Higueras, as "a just and pacific nobleman who is zealous of the royal service, [and who would govern] for the good of the land." Montejo was to hold authority over the province "in the same manner which he had formerly, and until the Crown should provide otherwise." [19]

As a matter of form the junta requested López de Gamboa to relinquish his *vara,* or staff of office, whereupon they made him temporary administrator of the province until Montejo should arrive. All niceties of law and constitutional practice were carefully observed. The re-election of López de Gamboa for temporary service pushed aside the resentful and unpopular García de Celís, whose death lay not many months ahead.[20] The junta sent an emissary, Pedro Dolano, posthaste to Chiapas to give Montejo the documents recalling him to the governorship and to urge, even demand, that he accept for the best interests of the province and the royal service.[21]

THE RETURN OF MONTEJO AS GOVERNOR

In order to understand the circumstances which brought Montejo back to Honduras-Higueras, we must turn again to the period before Alvarado's death in 1541.

After installation as governor of Chiapas early in 1540 Montejo had been very active on a number of counts. He had not relinquished hope of eventually regaining authority over Honduras-Higueras, nor had he by any means given up determination to build the wider adelantamiento for which he still regarded Honduras-Higueras as the most advantageous center. Since that province was lost to him for the time being, he turned his attention once again to his original province, Yucatan. He commissioned his natural son, likewise a man of great military and administrative talents, to undertake the conquest of Yucatan soon after he arrived in Chiapas. Montejo the Younger was at

[19] *Ibid.*
[20] *Ibid.*
[21] *Ibid.*

this time lieutenant governor in nearby Tabasco, which had come under his father's direct authority through assignment of the governorship of the territory between the Río de Copilco and the Río de Ulua in 1533. The adelantado also actively recruited captains, soldiers, and colonists as well as marshaling his personal resources. Montejo the Younger began what proved to be the final conquest of Yucatan late in 1540 or early in 1541, and with the aid of the adelantado's nephew and other lieutenants had assured its subjugation and settlement by 1545.[22]

Upon assuming the governorship of Chiapas, Montejo had first found it necessary to establish firm control, for there were unruly Spaniards in that frontier province as well as in Honduras-Higueras. Then, toward the close of 1540, he went to New Spain to advance litigation with Alvarado in connection with their quarrel over Honduras-Higueras. His representative, Bachiller Juan Alvarez, had begun suit before the Audiencia of New Spain shortly after the signing of the agreement of August 1, 1539, between him and Alvarado and had then gone on to Castile to continue litigation at Court.[23]

When Montejo arrived in the City of Mexico, the viceroy was far to the northwest, drawn by interest in the elusive Seven Cities of Cibola, which were even then attracting Francisco Vázquez de Coronado to amazing deeds of exploration. Montejo's continuation of his suit against Alvarado before the audiencia soon led him against a blank wall. He learned that the viceroy was returning to the west coast of New Spain to meet Alvarado, who was now sailing up from Guatemala in the first stage of his South Sea expedition; Mendoza was interested in enterprise in the vast Pacific Ocean and wished to come to an understanding with Alvarado in that connection. Montejo decided to meet the viceroy and take up his quarrel directly with him and with Alvarado. He found them at Puerto Nuevo de la Navidad at the end of 1540 or the first of 1541.

Formal legal action as presented to the viceroy brought no immediate results, but Montejo and Alvarado reached temporary reconciliation through Mendoza's efforts. Alvarado had by this time turned all interest to his new adventure and displayed little concern with Honduras-Higueras. While the three principals and other notables were seated around a table in Mendoza's lodging, Montejo declared that

he wished no quarrel with Alvarado, and that he would be glad to permit Alvarado free choice as to whether he would [either] place [the encomienda

[22] See Chamberlain, 1947b.
[23] Montejo v. Pedraza, 1539, AGI, Justicia 129-2; Montejo v. Alvarado, 1541, AGI, Justicia 134-3; Residencias of Montejo for Chiapas, Tabasco, and Yucatan, 1546–50, AGI, Justicia 244 and 300.

of] Xochimilco [which Alvarado had agreed to turn over to him in partial recompense for loss of the governorship of Honduras-Higueras] in his possession or return the governorship of Honduras-Higueras to him, and that thereafter he would remain content, whatever Alvarado's decision would be.

Alvarado just as graciously responded that

since Montejo was so good as to give him free choice, he would prefer to retain Xochimilco and would restore to Montejo the governorship of Honduras-Higueras whenever Montejo might desire.[24]

This conciliatory exchange failed to bring about a permanent solution, however, and when Mendoza returned to the City of Mexico Montejo also went there to continue formal litigation against Alvarado. The viceroy, impatient with this persistence, cut Montejo short by abruptly telling him to appeal directly to the Crown, should he so wish. Mendoza had long since regarded the matter closed and wanted nothing more to do with it.[25]

Having failed either to regain Honduras-Higueras or acquire the rich encomienda of Xochimilco, and having advanced his recruiting and financing for the conquest of Yucatan in the City of Mexico, Montejo returned to Ciudad Real de Chiapas in mid-July 1541. Meanwhile, as we have seen, Alvarado received his mortal injury before the Peñol of Nochistlan. His death closed the personal account between the two great conquistadores, although, of course, it heightened Montejo's hopes for reinstatement in Honduras-Higueras. Such a possibility probably prevented him from going to Yucatan personally to lead the conquest of the peninsula.

Back in Chiapas, Montejo devoted himself to affairs of that province. In conjunction with the Bishop of Guatemala, to whom the Crown had assigned temporary spiritual jurisdiction over this province as well as over Honduras-Higueras, he conducted a visita general and established a fixed taxation of tributes and services from the Indians. He also made plans for the economic development of the region, sent an expedition to pacify stubbornly rebellious Indians on the rough frontier with Tabasco, and took measures to better the lot of all peaceful natives of the province. He was still engaged in carrying out his visita general when, early in 1542, Pedro Dolano arrived with word from the cabildos of Honduras-Higueras recalling him to the governorship.[26]

[24] Montejo v. Alvarado, 1541, AGI, Justicia 134-3.
[25] Ibid.
[26] All following sections which treat of Montejo's return to Honduras-Higueras and of the jurisdictional controversy which developed between Montejo, Juan Pérez de Cabrera, and Alonso Maldonado as rival claimants for authority over Honduras-Higueras and of the conflicting claims of the Viceroy and Audiencia of New Spain, on the one hand, and the Audiencia of Santo Domingo, on the other, are based on the following interlocking and almost all-inclusive sources: Residencia of Montejo for Honduras-Higueras, 1544, and for Chiapas, 1546, AGI, Justicia 300; Residencia of Juan Pérez de Cabrera, 1544,

Wishing to remove all legal obstructions for such a return, he told Dolano that he would inform the authorities of New Spain of the request and abide by their decision. The viceroy and audiencia were slow in answering. But the authorities of Honduras-Higueras, upon receiving Montejo's reply, refused to accept delays. They sent to him a second representative, Lorenzo Duque de Colmenares, further demanding his immediate return. They told of the antagonism between García de Celís and López de Gamboa and declared that if Montejo did not come at once, disorders and revolts could be expected. Avowing that his refusal to heed summons "would be to send the province to total destruction, to the great disservice of His Majesty," they charged Montejo's conscience in the matter.

The extreme urgency of this second appeal brought Montejo's acceptance without further hesitation. Informing the Viceroy and Audiencia of New Spain of the circumstances, he set out for Gracias a Dios with a small retinue, without further delay, and left a lieutenant governor in charge of Chiapas. His wife and daughter were to follow with the remainder of his household.

Montejo appeared before the cabildo of Gracias a Dios on April 7, 1542. López de Gamboa was present as interim chief magistrate. In the name of the cabildo and citizens Alonso Polo, procurador of the city, formally requested that Montejo again be received as governor of Honduras-Higueras,

since he had conquered and pacified the land and has governed in benevolent and benign fashion, and is not haughty or vainglorious, for he has governed like a father, visiting our houses and persons, being concerned with our welfare and prosperity, sorrowing at our trials, aiding our churches, and helping the poor. . . . [27]

Polo then went on to say that Montejo had unjustly been driven from the province by Pedraza, and pointed out that the Crown had neither revoked the cedula of 1535 by which Montejo had first been appointed governor nor designated any other official following Alvarado's death. Montejo then presented the cedula of 1535, López de Gamboa formally relinquished office, and Montejo was sworn to the governorship "to serve until His Majesty should provide otherwise." It is significant that two of Montejo's most violent enemies of 1539, Hernan Sánchez de Alvarado, a relative of Pedro de Alvarado, and Francisco Cava, who had advocated killing Montejo out of hand, were mem-

AGI, Justicia 63; Fiscal v. Juan Pérez de Cabrera, 1556, AGI, Justicia 286-4-1, Informacion hecha a peticion de Juan Licenciado Maldonado sucesor del Adelantado D. Pedro de Alvarado en la Gobernacion de Guatemala (1542), AGI, Guatemala 965. Citations will therefore be given only when other materials are concerned, or for major quotations within the mentioned sources.
[27] Residencia of Montejo for Honduras-Higueras, 1544, AGI, Justicia 300.

bers of the cabildo which unanimously restored him to authority over the province.

The cabildo of Comayagua, to which Montejo sent the cedula of 1535, accepted him on April 24; the cabildo of San Pedro received his lieutenant, his former enemy Cava. Montejo still based his authority over San Pedro on the cedula of 1533 granting him the governorship of the territory between the Río de Copilco and the Río de Ulua, and technically held that the town and its district were recognized by the Crown as a definite part of his adelantamiento of Yucatan. In Trujillo, with its self-proclaimed semi-autonomy, the locally elected alcalde mayor, Juan García de Lemos, continued to govern for a while longer but was replaced after Montejo established himself firmly in Higueras.

Montejo, López de Gamboa, the royal treasury officials, and cabildos notified the Crown of Montejo's renewed assumption of authority over Honduras-Higueras, and not only requested royal approval of their actions but also a new cedula specifically confirming Montejo as governor. In these communications it was emphasized that, although Montejo was aged and wearied by long service, he had nevertheless responded to the needs of Honduras-Higueras, thereby serving the best interests of the Crown and the province. With emphasis on the fact that it was Montejo who had conquered the province and had governed well between 1537 and 1539, it was petitioned that, since he was once more chief magistrate, no change be made in the governorship as constant new appointments bred confusion. Montejo and the local authorities also wrote to the Audiencia of Santo Domingo requesting confirmation.

Montejo's hopes for a great adelantamiento now reached their highest point. He was at one and the same time—but under different appointments and dispensations—adelantado, governor and captain-general of Yucatan, governor and captain-general of Honduras-Higueras, governor and captain-general of Chiapas, and royal governor of all the wide lands between the Río de Copilco and the Río de Ulua, including all of Tabasco. Now more than ever he was bent on bringing to royally approved actuality his cherished dream.

When Montejo returned to Honduras-Higueras he of course found the province "all upset, harassed by many scandals," and even on the verge of more civil strife. With his very coming, as he declared, the tense situation was eased and political "peace and concord" took its place. Nevertheless the basic situation remained extremely grave and, since the province was "in such a state that he felt deep sorrow," the most arduous kind of labor lay ahead. He was convinced that unless effective measures were speedily taken, the province was in danger of being "totally ruined within two [more] years." There was again a shortage of supplies from the outside. Forced labor in the mines, burden-bearing, which had been systematized to some degree by García de Celís, and harsh mistreatment in all respects after 1539, had further reduced the Indian inhabitants and disrupted native life. The population of some districts is said to have decreased two-thirds from what it had been even after the revolt in 1539. The Indians were again famine-ridden. Thus the individual encomiendas shrank in size and value, to the great dissatisfaction of the encomenderos, who were alarmed at seeing so few Indians "to provide them sustenance."

Montejo resolved to repair these deplorable conditions as best he could. The first step was to guarantee political stability by gathering power firmly into his own hands. Tactfully but inexorably he established rigid control over the municipal cabildos and appointed only vigorous and trusted lieutenants in the several districts. His plans for the economic development of Honduras-Higueras and his broad policies remained those of his first governorship but their achievement was now even more difficult because of the general deterioration.

In order to provide the colonists with more encomienda Indians and more gold, Montejo once more looked eastward to the Valley of Olancho, where renewed efforts at conquest and settlement after 1539 had thus far failed to guarantee permanent results. On the side of long-range policy, occupation of the Valley of Olancho was, as before, designed to foster the military security of the colony and provide Trujillo with an area which that city could exploit. Montejo also planned to move beyond the Valley of Olancho proper to the Río de Guayape, where rich placer gold had already been found, and eventually farther eastward into the still little known region of Taguzgalpa. He also revived the plan to establish a town on the route southward to the City of León to foster better communications between Honduras-Higueras and Nicaragua. Improvement of existing roads and construction of new ones between the municipalities of Honduras-Higueras and from them to neighboring provinces was again one of his projects. Neither had he abandoned his master plan of eventually establishing a route of commerce across Higueras from Puerto de Caballos to the Bahía de Fonseca.

Montejo had scarcely begun his heavy task when new complications unexpectedly arose. His right to the governorship of Honduras was disputed by two other claimants: Alonso Maldonado, again appointed interim governor of Guatemala by the Viceroy and Audiencia of New Spain, and Juan Pérez de Cabrera, designated governor of Honduras-Higueras by the Audiencia of Santo Domingo.

PÉREZ DE CABRERA, GOVERNOR OF HONDURAS-HIGUERAS IN THE NAME OF THE AUDIENCIA OF SANTO DOMINGO

Juan Pérez de Cabrera was a member of the Castilian nobility who possessed holdings in the region of Cuenca. He was attracted to the New World by reports of riches in Nueva Granada, where Gonzalo Ximénez de Quesada had recently overthrown the powerful Chibcha Empire. He took service with his relative, Alonso Luis de Lugo, Adelantado of the Canaries, and governor of Santa Marta, on the north coast of South America, on the latter's departure for the New World. At his own expense and with his brother, Rodrigo de Anaya, as chief lieutenant, Pérez de Cabrera organized a well-equipped armada of about 380 men in Castile, for which he provided the necessary ships for transport. He was made maestre de campo by Lugo and expected financial recompense and at least some additional measure of authority and initiative in Lugo's territories in the Indies. As the expedition was raised not only for military purposes but also for permanent colonization, Pérez de Cabrera included a number of married men and women of quality in his company.

When Pérez de Cabrera reached Santo Domingo with Lugo, however, his plans changed. Whether convinced that his opportunities lay elsewhere than in northern South America, or at odds with Lugo, who no longer trusted him, or—most likely—persuaded to turn toward Honduras-Higueras by the Audiencia of Santo Domingo, he and his men remained behind when Lugo sailed on for Nueva Granada in April 1542. The disconcerting reports from Honduras-Higueras and direct appeals for the appointment of a new governor in the months following Alvarado's death had made the audiencia keenly aware of the need for a chief magistrate who could rule with a strong hand. Pérez de Cabrera, with a large and excellently organized armada, seemed in an admirable position to fill the requirements. Since the mines of the province were rich, the audiencia had a persuasive argument to back up any appeal to Pérez de Cabrera's sense of duty to the Crown in bringing order to a turbulent and unstable province.

In any case, the Audiencia of Santo Domingo, which had not yet learned of Montejo's return to Honduras-Higueras, on June 12, 1542, appointed Pérez de Cabrera governor of the Province of the Cabo de Honduras. It stipulated that he should enjoy authority equal in all ways to that which Alvarado had wielded and endowed him with plenary civil and military powers. The audiencia issued detailed instructions, under which Pérez de Cabrera was to work for the expansion of royal revenues, the increase of the Spanish population, the welfare of the natives, the extension of the Faith, and the permanence of the province. It emphasized that he should act in every manner possible to bring peace and order to the province. He was to strive for the well-being of the Indians in co-operation with the chief prelate and the Protector of the Indians. Mining activity was to be stimulated, and local governmental offices were to be given only to principal citizens of the colony itself. The audiencia, determined to maintain control over Honduras-Higueras, ordered Pérez de Cabrera carefully to obey and enforce all decrees it might issue.

The most important article of these instructions, from the point of view both of Montejo and of the political situation in Honduras-Higueras, was that which declared that Pérez de Cabrera's appointment had been made with the provision that if upon his arrival in Honduras-Higueras "there should be in the province another governor, named by the Crown, or by another royal audiencia, a governor already received in the province," he should not attempt to exercise authority. In such circumstances Pérez de Cabrera's appointment would become null and void, and if he still sought to take office he did so under "the penalties incurred by those who exercise jurisdiction without authority." Further, it was specifically stipulated that he should not remove encomiendas from those who already possessed them. Regarding Pérez de Cabrera as a replacement for Alvarado, the audiencia reported his appointment as governor of Honduras-Higueras to the Crown, which was even further behind events than the island tribunal and gave its assent.

Meanwhile, the Viceroy and Audiencia of New Spain had in March 1542 taken steps to assert jurisdiction over Honduras-Higueras and revive the union of that province with Guatemala. These moves were rejected by Montejo and the cabildos of Honduras-Higueras at the very time the Audiencia of Santo Domingo was designating Pérez de Cabrera governor of the province.

Pérez de Cabrera arrived at Puerto de Caballos in July, with one of the largest expeditions ever to come to Honduras-Higueras. On the 18th he presented his credentials before the cabildo of San Pedro, which accepted them without demur, since they came from the high tribunal of Santo Domingo. Francisco Cava, Montejo's lieutenant in San Pedro, seeing no alternative, gave up authority, whereupon Pérez de Cabrera was inducted into office as governor of the town and its district. Since legal points were always important, the cabildo of San Pedro rested its acceptance of Pérez de Cabrera on the technical ground that, upon his return to Honduras-Higueras, Montejo had not appeared personally before the cabildo to be received as governor, but had attained recognition through a lieutenant. On his part Pérez de Cabrera held that his appointment by the Audiencia of Santo Domingo superseded the designation of Montejo as governor by the authorities and colonists of Honduras-Higueras and that Montejo's royal appointment of 1535 was no longer operative because he had relinquished the governorship to Alvarado in 1539. Pérez de Cabrera therefore maintained that under existing circumstances he was not bound by the instruction from the audiencia making his own appointment invalid if another governor was already ruling in Honduras-Higueras.

Once accepted and established in San Pedro, Pérez de Cabrera rapidly and firmly consolidated his authority. He appointed new alcaldes and regidores, whom he henceforth closely controlled, and removed and reassigned encomiendas as he saw fit, despite instructions to the contrary from the Audiencia of Santo Domingo. Wielding a kind of censorship, he also confiscated all despatches which contained complaints against any of his acts.

The arrival of Pérez de Cabrera with powers from the Audiencia of Santo Domingo and his recognition by the cabildo of San Pedro inescapably created confusion in the seat of the provincial government, Gracias a Dios. Montejo was greatly taken aback, especially since Honduras-Higueras had already been separated from Guatemala with accompanying denial of the authority of the Audiencia of New Spain, and Montejo and the local authorities had but recently turned to the Audiencia of Santo Domingo for his confirmation as governor. Since the Viceroy and Audiencia of New Spain had already taken steps to make good their authority over Honduras-Higueras on the basis of the former union of that province and Guatemala, it was clear to the local authorities that a serious conflict of jurisdiction between the Audiencia of Santo Domingo and the Viceroy and Audiencia of New Spain was inevitably in the making. They were consequently at first perplexed as to the course which they should take.

Not only were the authorities in Gracias a Dios in a quandary, the conflict of jurisdiction and the multiplicity of appointments to the chief magistracy also caused disquietude among the easily aroused colonists, portending a state of chaos and anarchy. The colonists, who in any case felt themselves all too poorly repaid for their trials, dangers, and expenses, now saw what little they possessed jeopardized even further and decided to send a representative to the Crown to petition a definite clarification of the governmental status of the province.

The royal treasury officials of the province were likewise greatly disoriented and in a letter to the Crown of July 21, 1542, they also pleaded for immediate action to resolve the jurisdictional conflict. At the same time they expressed strong opposition to any possible reincorporation of Honduras-Higueras with Guatemala. The attitude of the royal treasury officials toward Pérez de Cabrera is perhaps the most accurate gauge of opinion among the authorities and colonists of Gracias a Dios regarding the legality of his position. As trusted guardians of the province's royal coffers, they were fearful of any possible misdirection of funds and refused to pay Pérez de Cabrera the salary which the Audiencia of Santo Domingo assigned to him, on the ground that he had not been appointed directly by the Crown. Pérez de Cabrera demanded payment and even threatened to appropriate the equivalent of the funds assigned to him from the royal coffers of San Pedro, but he did not carry out his threat, realizing that such action would place him in serious difficulties. His salary was withheld throughout his entire stay in the province, and he and his heirs later had to bring suit before the Crown.

Despite the confused jurisdictional status, Montejo was determined to defend his authority over Honduras-Higueras against Pérez de Cabrera to the last, whether by legal means or by force of arms. He lost no time in aligning the authorities and citizens of Gracias a Dios and Comayagua to block any efforts by Pérez de Cabrera to extend his authority into the interior. Meanwhile he studied means of restoring his own control over San Pedro. In Gracias a Dios, Montejo personally spoke with the citizens to assure himself of their support, declaring that "he wished to know who were his friends." He also obtained an official statement from the cabildo which unequivocally supported him and rejected *a priori* any claims from Pérez de Cabrera. However, Montejo had to use abusive language against one of the alcaldes, Gonzalo de Cartagena, who at first had some legal doubts in the matter. Montejo went far beyond these measures, however. He called together the citizens of Gracias a Dios as a body, exhorted them to resist Pérez de Cabrera by armed force should he demand recognition in the city, and organized them for military action. A group of armed followers was lodged in his residence as a kind of permanent guard and large stores of munitions were placed in the homes of two citizens, one of them a regidor, ready for issue to Montejo's partisans. Montejo considered that such preparations were especially necessary in face of Pérez de Cabrera's numerous and well-equipped company. He did not know to what lengths Pérez de Cabrera might go and, recalling his discomfiture at the hands of Alvarado several years before, was determined to be fully prepared.

Just as Montejo had anticipated, Pérez de Cabrera did not wait long before seeking to extend his authority over Gracias a Dios. Knowing of Montejo's resistance, however, and now wishing to avoid conflict and establish his jurisdiction by purely legal means if possible, he moved from San Pedro toward Gracias a Dios with only a small party. Montejo nevertheless decided to marshal his armed followers and ordered the alguacil mayor of the province, Lorenzo Duque de Colmenares, to place all citizens under arms to resist Pérez de Cabrera should he display hostility. He made no effort to prevent Pérez de Cabrera from entering the city, however.

Montejo, who had carefully prepared the cabildo for the rejection of his rival's claims, and who was fully assured of the unwavering armed support of the citizens, now permitted Pérez de Cabrera to appear before the municipal council to present his provisions of office. The cabildo had met in the church of Gracias a Dios for the occasion, with Montejo present. Pérez de Cabrera then presented his document of appointment. Montejo thereupon countered by declaring that the cedula of 1535 through which the Crown had appointed him governor of Honduras-Higueras had never been revoked and that, by virtue of the continued validity of that cedula and his recall by the authorities and colonists, he was lawful governor of Honduras-Higueras in accordance with the will of the Crown. Especially since he was still governor on the fundamental basis of his cedula of 1535, Montejo maintained that the instructions of the audiencia which forbade Pérez de Cabrera to claim jurisdiction if another governor were present applied to the conditions which existed and that Pérez de Cabrera consequently had no grounds whatsoever upon which to claim authority. Furthermore, even though it was apparent that the Audiencia of Santo Domingo intended that Pérez de Cabrera should govern Honduras-Higueras as a whole, his actual appointment mentioned only the Cabo de Honduras. Montejo contended that the absence of specific mention of Higueras in his appointment prevented Pérez de Cabrera from having any basis for claiming jurisdiction there. The cabildo of Gracias a Dios followed Montejo to the letter, of course, and flatly refused to acknowledge Pérez de Cabrera as governor until the Crown should have been informed of the circumstances and had made known its will.

It is interesting to note that Montejo and the cabildo of Gracias a Dios had learned of the audiencia's detailed instructions to Pérez de Cabrera not from the latter but indirectly through Montejo's former lieutenant in San Pedro and the cabildo of that town. Aware of their content, Montejo and the cabildo demanded that Pérez de Cabrera produce them in due legal procedure, but he refused on the excuse that the document had been lost. Montejo and the cabildo then seized upon this refusal as additional legal grounds upon which to reject his claims to the governorship.

In this way Pérez de Cabrera was legally blocked in every direction in Gracias a Dios. His party was greatly outnumbered by Montejo's armed followers, and he would have to return to San Pedro to marshal his men and march on Gracias a Dios in full military fashion if he chose resort to force. Meanwhile Montejo, whose mastery of the situation was complete, restrained his own followers. After Pérez de Cabrera's rejection as governor, the personal relationship between the two rivals became outwardly cordial, and Montejo displayed great hospitality toward his opponent.

Pérez de Cabrera nevertheless had no idea of relinquishing jurisdiction over the coast or of permanently foregoing his claims over the interior. He soon returned to San Pedro and it was believed that he intended to return to Gracias a Dios at the head of all his men to seek an armed decision. He seems fundamentally to have had a high sense of duty and responsibility, however, for when he was once again in San Pedro, he decided against any move which would turn Spaniard against Spaniard. Neither did Montejo threaten to move against San Pedro with armed force.

After reaching San Pedro, Pérez de Cabrera devoted himself to further consolidation of his authority there and to the achievement of recognition in territory elsewhere than Gracias a Dios, which had proved a stronghold of Montejo's authority. He sent his credentials to the cabildos of Trujillo and Comayagua, and began to look toward the Valley of Olancho and the gold-bearing Río de Guayape. In both of these latter areas the Spanish foothold was still weak, for despite his plans Montejo had as yet found no opportunity to assure Spanish control over those regions. The authorities of Trujillo welcomed Pérez de Cabrera as governor and he went there toward the first of November 1542 to be received personally, leaving his brother Rodrigo de Anaya as his lieutenant in San Pedro. The cabildo of Comayagua, however, remained loyal to Montejo and summarily rejected Pérez de Cabrera's claims.

While Pérez de Cabrera was in Trujillo, the natives of both the Valley of Olancho and the region of the Río de Guayape rose in revolt. Making the most of this opportunity, he sent his brother to suppress the revolt and at the same time extend his authority into the eastern interior. Anaya not only crushed the revolt, but greatly strengthened the position of the Spaniards in the Valley of Olancho and the Río de Guayape and brought the general area, with its town of San Jorge de Olancho and rich gold deposits, firmly under his brother's dominion. Anaya's campaigns, in fact, at last made enduring Spanish occupation of the Valley of Olancho and guaranteed the permanence of San Jorge. By the first months of 1543, therefore, Pérez de Cabrera held authority over San Pedro, Trujillo, and San Jorge de Olancho and their districts, as well as the area of the Río de Guayape; Montejo remained in control of Gracias a Dios and Comayagua and their districts.

Authority in Honduras-Higueras was once more divided, with Pérez de Cabrera firmly holding the coast of both Honduras and Higueras and a part of the hinterland of Honduras, and with Montejo just as firmly seated in the interior of Higueras. Fortunately this was a clear-cut cleavage of authority. Even though the province as a whole was administratively divided, each governor had complete control over his respective territory and the support of its colonists. Consequently, with an armed clash between Montejo and Pérez de Cabrera no longer threatening, there was considerable confusion but no universal anarchy. Nevertheless, the usual menace of a mass native uprising under such conditions caused concern to both Montejo and his opponent.

Since he opposed any military action against Pérez de Cabrera and his coastal territories, Montejo now sought a legal solution of the administrative dilemma through further urgent appeals to the Audiencia of Santo Domingo for sole recognition. He, the municipal authorities of Gracias a Dios and Comayagua, and the royal treasury officials sent to the audiencia a full account of the developments which followed Pérez de Cabrera's arrival. They pointed out the dangers of divided administration and requested that Montejo be confirmed as sole governor. One of the principal points which Montejo made in his representations was that Pérez de Cabrera had assumed power in violation of the audiencia's instructions not to claim authority if another duly recognized governor was present in the province when he arrived. Montejo clearly stated his argument that, in view of his royal appointment as governor and his recall by the local authorities and colonists, legality of his position as chief magistrate was unquestionable. These claims were placed before the audiencia by despatches and representatives.

In addition to the action taken by Montejo and his followers, there was another factor which influenced the situation. Pérez de Cabrera had continued to remove and reassign encomiendas in the district of San Pedro; and when Trujillo came under his control he did likewise. This caused the dispossessed encomenderos personally to send to the Audiencia of Santo Domingo vigorous protests, which reached Santo Domingo despite Pérez de Cabrera's censorship and which inevitably helped Montejo.

By the turn of the year 1542–43 Montejo was thus engaged in decisive legal action before the Audiencia of Santo Domingo aimed at assuring his position as governor, a fight which was to bring him ultimate success, although meanwhile he was forced to confront a renewed challenge from New Spain and Guatemala.

MALDONADO AS CHIEF MAGISTRATE OF HONDURAS-HIGUERAS BY APPOINTMENT OF THE VICEROY AND AUDIENCIA OF NEW SPAIN

While Montejo and Pérez de Cabrera were contending for jurisdiction over Honduras-Higueras, the Viceroy and Audiencia of New Spain were taking measures of great consequence. When, early in 1542, the viceroy had received Montejo's information of the situation in Honduras-Higueras and of his return as governor at the request of the colonists, he refused approval. Neither he nor the audiencia had recognized the independent action of Honduras-Higueras in separating itself from Guatemala, and so they still claimed superior jurisdiction over both provinces. According to their view, Honduras-Higueras had no right to set up its own administrators or to recall Montejo as governor. Further, they held that the union of the two provinces inaugurated under Alvarado's governorship, with royal approval, not only still stood but superseded the royal cedula of 1534 which had placed Honduras under the jurisdiction of the Audiencia of Santo Domingo. Added strength was given to their contention by the fact that the Crown had in 1533 assigned to Montejo, as Adelantado and Governor of Yucatan, authority over the territory between the Río de Ulua and the Río de Copilco, all of which except parts of Higueras, were clearly under the jurisdiction of the Audiencia of New Spain. On the basis of continued union, the viceroy and audiencia also considered it in the best interests of the royal service to appoint their own governor for Guatemala (and therefore for Honduras-Higueras) to replace the coadministrators, Francisco de la Cueva and Bishop Francisco de Marroquín.

Therefore, on March 12, 1542, they appointed the experienced and legally trained Alonso Maldonado, formerly acting governor of Guatemala and still an oidor of the audiencia, as chief magistrate of the combined provinces. This meant the removal of Montejo from authority in Honduras-Higueras and the effective renewal of its union with Guatemala. The Crown was so informed. On May 17, 1542, Maldonado reached Santiago de Guatemala, where he immediately took office and made his seat of government. A few days later the new governor appointed Juan de Chávez, who had served in Higueras under Alvarado in 1536 and to whom Alvarado had originally committed the founding of Gracias a Dios, as his lieutenant for Honduras-Higueras, with plenary powers.

On July 10 Chávez presented his credentials to the cabildo of Gracias a Dios. Both the city, which not only wished to keep Montejo as governor but greatly resented the attempt to subordinate Honduras-Higueras to Guatemala once again, and Montejo, who had no more intention of yielding to Maldonado and Chávez than to Pérez de Cabrera, refused to accept Chávez. He was formally told that Montejo was now back in the governorship by the will of the cabildos of Honduras-Higueras and that, because of the cedula of 1534 by which the Crown had transferred the province from the jurisdiction of New Spain to that of Santo Domingo, the Audiencia of New Spain no longer had any authority whatsoever over Honduras-Higueras. The municipal council of Comayagua likewise refused to recognize Chávez' jurisdiction. Thus Montejo and the cabildos called on the Audiencia of Santo Domingo to support their position against the Viceroy and Audiencia of New Spain.

Chávez returned to Guatemala. Maldonado reported to New Spain the rejection of his authority over Honduras-Higueras and requested drastic action. Meanwhile he went on government business to San Salvador, where he received news of the arrival of Pérez de Cabrera at San Pedro, carrying his appointment as governor of Honduras by the Audiencia of Santo Domingo. As governor of the united provinces under the dispensation of New Spain, Maldonado was bound to oppose any encroachment from the Audiencia of Santo Domingo. Furthermore, in the interests of the Crown, he wished to forestall disorder in Honduras-Higueras and prevent any possible armed conflict between Montejo and Pérez de Cabrera. Maldonado heard with concern of Pérez de Cabrera's acceptance in San Pedro and rejection in Gracias a Dios, where he was reported set on a solution by force.[28] All these new developments were of course retailed to the Viceroy and Audiencia of New Spain.

Maldonado was thus ready to intervene in Honduras-Higueras at the proper moment. When the situation reached a point which he considered imminently dangerous, he hastened to Gracias a Dios, where he found that Pérez de Cabrera had returned to the coast and that danger of armed conflict had disappeared. He also realized that Montejo was in a stronger position than ever in the interior of Higueras. Seeing that the time was not yet ripe for assertion of his own claims and that his mediation was not needed, he then went south to San Miguel, which by now was almost universally recognized as territory under jurisdiction of Guatemala. At no time during this period did Maldonado challenge Pérez de Cabrera's authority on the north coast of Honduras-Higueras.

In the meantime, the authorities of New Spain had taken further measures to impose their authority on Honduras-Higueras, now directed against the Audiencia of Santo Domingo and Pérez de Cabrera as well as Montejo. In a decree of September 22, addressed to Montejo as "Adelantado and governor of the Provinces of Yucatan and Cozumel and of the City of Ciudad Real of the Province of Chiapas," the viceroy and audiencia peremptorily ordered all cabildos throughout Honduras-Higueras, together with all other provincial authorities and loyal citizens, to recognize Maldonado's jurisdiction over the entire province and to accept immediately any lieutenants whom he might appoint. Montejo, threatened with deprivation of offices and forfeiture to the

---

[28] See Maldonado to the Cabildo of Santiago de Guatemala, San Salvador, September 5, 1542, AGG, Papers from the Archivo Municipal, Cartas de Personas Ylustres.

Crown of property and encomiendas for failure to obey, was ordered to leave Honduras-Higueras at once and proceed either to Chiapas or to Yucatan, where his son and his nephew had by now conquered a wide area. The authorities and colonists were threatened with loss of offices, confiscation of property, and even death for refusal to recognize Maldonado's authority.

Although the viceroy and audiencia were determined to retain control over Honduras-Higueras in administrative and political matters because of their contention that the province was still united with Guatemala, they nevertheless made concessions to the Audiencia of Santo Domingo in purely judicial affairs in view of the cedula of 1534 through which the Crown had placed Honduras-Higueras under that body. Averring that they had no intention of interfering in legal matters, they directed Maldonado and any lieutenants to allow such appeals to the Audiencia of Santo Domingo.

These decisions gave Maldonado his desired mandate and he set out at once for Gracias a Dios. Arriving toward the close of 1542, he presented to the cabildo the implementing decrees, to which Montejo and the cabildo of Gracias a Dios could now find no effective reply. Montejo therefore relinquished office and Maldonado became governor. Nevertheless, Montejo and the cabildo officially recorded that Maldonado and reunion with Guatemala had been accepted against their will, and that in the legal sense they were "aggrieved" because they had no other alternative.

Montejo was thus forced from the governorship of Honduras-Higueras a second time, but he remained in Gracias a Dios, "hoping and convinced that the Crown would confirm him as governor of [Honduras-Higueras] as the man who had conquered and pacified the land." He trusted that not only the Crown but also the nearer Audiencia of Santo Domingo would heed his petitions. Surprisingly enough, Montejo's hopes were not vain, for he was to have one more period of office before losing out forever.

Following Maldonado's assumption of the governorship, his relations with Montejo and Doña Beatriz, never personally inimical, became cordial. Maldonado came from one of the most powerful families of Salamanca of Castile, Montejo's birthplace, where their families had long known each other. With this basis for friendship, the relationship soon grew into a family alliance, for within a short time Maldonado married Montejo's daughter Catalina.

After installation at Gracias a Dios, Maldonado sent lieutenants to present his credentials to all the municipalities of Honduras-Higueras. He was recognized by the cabildo of Comayagua at once; later by San Jorge de Olancho and the Spaniards of the area of the Río de Guayape, who renounced Pérez de Cabrera. The cabildo of San Pedro, still loyal to Pérez de Cabrera, had recognized him because of appointment by the Audiencia of Santo Domingo and would neither acknowledge the authority of New Spain nor admit reunion with Guatemala. A town apparently re-established at Puerto de Caballos, where Montejo's efforts to found a settlement between 1537 and 1539 had failed, likewise refused to acknowledge Maldonado, as did Trujillo. Pérez de Cabrera, however, would not renounce his claims over San Jorge de Olancho, the Valley of Olancho, and the region of the Río de Guayape, where occupation had been made permanent through his brother's campaigns and where a number of his men had remained as colonists. Consequently, even though officially recognized in those eastern regions, Pérez de Cabrera's stand created difficulties for Maldonado.

Early in 1543, during the course of an administrative visita of his territory, Maldonado went to San Pedro in the hope of persuading the authorities to recognize him. He was accompanied by Bishop Marroquín. Pérez de Cabrera was in Trujillo at the time and so was unable to counter Maldonado's weighty arguments. The cabildo was on the point of receiving Maldonado as governor when the aroused Pérez de Cabrera appeared at the last moment and quashed the idea.[29] Maldonado now held direct conference. Stressing his own appointment from the authorities of New Spain and reminding Pérez de Cabrera of the Santo Domingo instructions not to assume jurisdiction if a governor was already in the province, Maldonado tried to persuade his opponent to renounce all claims to the governorship. This Pérez de Cabrera refused, even though Maldonado's appointment actually antedated his and Maldonado had sent Juan de Chávez to Honduras-Higueras as his lieutenant before Pérez de Cabrera arrived. As Maldonado could not press his case further at this time and did not wish to cause more political dissension, he contented himself with officially presenting his commission and stating his demands so that the juridical record could be kept straight. Pérez de Cabrera made no objections to these legal moves since they had no immediate practical importance. Neither does he seem to have pressed any counterclaims for recognition in Gracias a Dios or Comayagua.

On the basis of their discussions, the two rivals at length agreed, in the best interests of the colony as a whole, not to interfere further in each other's zones of clear-cut influence. This did not apply to the Valley of Olancho and the region of the Río de Guayape, however, over which Pérez de Cabrera claimed title by right of permanent conquest, even though the local authorities had now recognized Maldonado. Another phase of this compact, one which

[29] See Maldonado to the Cabildo of Santiago de Guatemala, San Pedro, January 4, 1543, AGG, papers from the Archivo Municipal, Cartas de Personas Ylustres; Marroquín to the Crown, San Pedro, January 15, 1543, AGI, Guatemala 156 and Maldonado to the Crown, 1545, DII, 24:346.

does great credit to Pérez de Cabrera, provided for the withdrawal of the majority of his soldiers from the mainland to the Bay Islands of Utila and Guanaja (the latter was Columbus' first landfall off the coast of Honduras in 1502). By this it was hoped to eliminate any chance of an armed clash between Pérez de Cabrera's men and other Spaniards. It is clear that neither Maldonado nor Pérez de Cabrera had any desire to plunge the province into violence. Both displayed forbearance, understanding, and statesmanship of a nature which Honduras-Higueras had long needed at such times. Bishop Marroquín, who had accompanied Maldonado to San Pedro, had anxiously watched these moves, ready with his high position and prestige to mediate if necessary, and he may well have had a hand in consummating this agreement.

Pérez de Cabrera now made Trujillo his capital. His residence there must have given great satisfaction to its citizens, for they had never ceased to resent the shift of the province's center westward after 1534, nor the neglect into which they felt the governors had since permitted their city to fall. Until Pérez de Cabrera's arrival no governor had resided in Trujillo for the better part of a decade, or had even honored the citizens with a visit.

Jurisdiction over Honduras-Higueras, of course, remained divided, just as while Montejo was in authority. In fact, Maldonado had inherited all Montejo's problems, and the practical solution he had found within the province was much the same as Montejo's. This time, however, the governors directly represented New Spain on the one hand and Santo Domingo on the other, thus pitting their superior authorities against each other. Such a clash of jurisdiction was bound to produce acute disturbances. While Montejo was governor, both he and Pérez de Cabrera could refer their important problems to a single agency of government, the Audiencia of Santo Domingo; now there were two to consider. Confusion abounded, despite the zones of influence upon which Maldonado and Pérez de Cabrera had agreed, and there was even more danger that the situation would degenerate into complete disorder. The Spanish settlers feared that their province would become permanently split between the two audiencias. The royal treasury officials reported to the Crown widespread apprehension of renewed anarchy, deploring the continuous rivalry for governorship and the consequent disorientation among both local authorities and colonists. They spoke of disconcerting "novelties," of what "one claimant did the other undid," and of inevitable ruin for all vassals of the Crown, whether Spaniards or Indians. They pleaded that "for the service of God, the good of the natives, and the general welfare [of the province]" it was essential that Honduras-Higueras should have a single royally appointed governor and a single tribunal of appeal. They then petitioned the Crown to designate Montejo, now more universally respected than ever, as sole governor,

since it appears to us that two results would follow such an appointment: first that as the man who more than any other has conquered and settled this province, and who therefore knows its needs, [he will best promote its welfare], and second [in being appointed governor] he will receive reward for all that which he had accomplished and labored for, as well as recompense for having been despoiled of the government of this province without direct orders from Your Majesty.[30]

Despite confusion and foreboding, violence and complete anarchy did not materialize. Montejo was eventually returned to the governorship for a third and final period. When he was again replaced, it was by a new audiencia for the Central American provinces which was at length to end the internal and jurisdictional disorder from which Honduras-Higueras had suffered so many years.

MONTEJO'S THIRD AND FINAL PERIOD AS GOVERNOR OF HONDURAS-HIGUERAS

During this period the Audiencia of Santo Domingo followed the troubled course of events in Honduras-Higueras with deep and anxious attention. The tribunal was now kept well aware of developments through despatches and documents which constantly arrived from Montejo, Pérez de Cabrera, the cabildos, and even private citizens, as well as through representatives of the several factions. The purpose of the audiencia in appointing Pérez de Cabrera had been to bring about order and stability in Honduras-Higueras, not more confusion. The controversy between Montejo and Pérez de Cabrera was serious enough of itself; when Maldonado appeared as a third claimant to the governorship by appointment of the Viceroy and Audiencia of New Spain, a solution was even more urgent. The Audiencia of Santo Domingo therefore sought means not only to rectify the situation as it concerned Montejo and Pérez de Cabrera, but also to defend its jurisdiction over Honduras-Higueras against what it considered to be encroachment by New Spain.

After careful deliberation, the island tribunal decided that Montejo had justly held the governorship when Pérez de Cabrera arrived and that therefore the latter had violated at least the spirit of his instructions. Furthermore, the protests from colonists of the territory controlled by Pérez de Cabrera

---

[30] Royal Treasury Officials of Honduras to the Crown, San Pedro, February 20, 1543, AGI, Guatemala 49.

against his reassignment of encomiendas, contrary to orders, had considerable influence. More important, the audiencia wished to solve the controversy speedily to avoid the danger of chaos.

Having finally decided in favor of Montejo, the audiencia, on February 23, 1543, decreed that Pérez de Cabrera should immediately renounce authority in Honduras-Higueras and stand residencia, to be conducted by the veedor, Alonso de Valdés. It was further decreed that "the Adelantado Montejo should administer the province and govern as before [Pérez de Cabrera's arrival], until the Crown should provide otherwise," Montejo being directed to detain Pérez de Cabrera, if necessary, to assure that he stood residencia.

Montejo was also to restore all encomiendas to those from whom Pérez de Cabrera had removed them and to assume jurisdiction in any subsequent litigation. Lest Montejo punish those who had renounced his authority in favor of Pérez de Cabrera, he was further ordered to be lenient to officials and citizens of San Pedro and Trujillo.

The audiencia now appointed the comendador, Diego de Buyca, as treasurer of Honduras-Higueras to replace the deceased García de Celís, and had him convey the documents removing Pérez de Cabrera from office and reinstating Montejo. Buyca, who had come from Castile with Pérez de Cabrera and had served with him in Honduras-Higueras before returning to Santo Domingo, arrived at Puerto de Caballos on March 8, 1543. Two days later he placed the audiencia's decree before the cabildo of San Pedro and Pérez de Cabrera's lieutenant, who perforce accepted the new dispensation.

Upon learning of the audiencia's action, Montejo hastened to San Pedro from Gracias a Dios, where he had been living as a private citizen, and was formally received as governor in that district. He soon appointed Buyca as his lieutenant. On April 9 the decree confirming Montejo as governor was presented, by a representative whom he designated, to the cabildo of Trujillo, which now acknowledged Montejo but with no great enthusiasm. Pérez de Cabrera could not attend this meeting of the municipal council and he had to abide by the decision of the audiencia, to which he sent unavailing protests. He also objected directly to the Crown, for he had an able representative at Court in the person of his brother, whom he had sent to Castile early in 1543 to protect his long-range interests. All protests were unavailing, even though his residencia was not begun until September 13, 1544. Pérez de Cabrera emerged from this judicial review with a remarkably clear record and returned to Castile, apparently with most of his men, although some remained as colonists, especially in San Jorge de Olancho and the region of the Río de Guayape which his brother had conquered.

Thus did Montejo once more become governor of San Pedro and Trujillo and their districts. Nevertheless, there still remained the regions where Maldonado's authority had been recognized. In replacing Pérez de Cabrera in the coastal districts, Montejo automatically ran counter to Maldonado, and the province for the time being remained just as divided as before. There are no details available, but upon Pérez de Cabrera's removal it can be assumed that confusion was unallayed in San Jorge de Olancho and the region of the Río de Guayape, where Maldonado had been acknowledged governor but where Pérez de Cabrera had never renounced authority and still had a strong following.

Many citizens of San Pedro and Trujillo were greatly displeased with Pérez de Cabrera's removal, despite his reassignment of encomiendas. His government throughout his nine months' tenure had been firm and in the main just. He seems to have had an instinctive understanding of the problems of Honduras-Higueras and to have displayed marked administrative talents. So highly was he regarded by some colonists that a minority of the citizens of San Pedro, supported by certain local authorities, strongly protested Montejo's confirmation and vainly sought to have the Audiencia of Santo Domingo return Pérez de Cabrera to authority.[31] The completion of the conquest and settlement of the Valley of Olancho and the strengthening of the Spanish hold on the rich gold-bearing region of the Río de Guayape by his brother Rodrigo de Anaya were important and long-desired contributions to the expansion of Spanish control over the province. The earliest attempts at conquest and colonization had led to no permanent results, and the efforts by Cáceres, López de Gamboa, and García de Celís from 1540 until the arrival of Pérez de Cabrera had by no means assured continued occupation. Furthermore, since he had restored to resentful Trujillo some of its former prestige by making it his capital, the Spaniards there naturally regretted his departure and their subsequent decline.

Once reinstated in San Pedro and Trujillo, Montejo was of course resolved to use the Santo Domingo decree to extend his jurisdiction over all Honduras-Higueras. Maldonado had by this time returned to Guatemala, leaving a lieutenant over the sections of the province under his control. When the Audiencia of Santo Domingo issued its decree in February, it was still unaware that Maldonado had shortly before forced Montejo from office by virtue of his authority from the authorities of New Spain. Therefore, it assumed that, upon the removal of Pérez de Cabrera, Montejo would take control of all Honduras-Higueras. But Montejo did not act immediately. First, he wanted

[31] See Alvarado de Paz *v*. Alvaro and Lorenzo Dorrego, 1547, AGI, Justicia 281-2.

to prevent further disorder and, second, he wanted from the Audiencia of Santo Domingo unassailable guarantees before he confronted Maldonado and the powerful authority of New Spain. He also hoped that meanwhile the Crown would act on his earlier petitions for vindication and that royal cedulas backing his position would soon be at hand.

Montejo therefore continued to advise the Audiencia of Santo Domingo of the general situation, appealing for further support so that he might successfully oppose Maldonado and the high authorities of New Spain. He now employed Bachiller Juan Alvarez, his chaplain and legal adviser, to state his position to the Audiencia of Santo Domingo. It will be recalled that Montejo had sent Alvarez first to the City of Mexico and then on to Castile, in an attempt to obtain a favorable resolution of his quarrel with Alvarado in 1539. Although Alvarez had failed, he nevertheless had so ably presented Montejo's cause in Castile that he temporarily improved his client's position before the Crown. Alvarez then returned to the New World and began action before the Audiencia of Santo Domingo on June 15, 1543. He emphasized the fact that royal action in 1534 had placed Honduras-Higueras under the jurisdiction of that tribunal. He protested against the intervention of New Spain and pointed out that continued interference would certainly cause increasing administrative confusion. Alvarez then requested the audiencia to defend its rightful jurisdiction over Honduras-Higueras and to enable Montejo to make good his authority over the whole province.

The Audiencia of Santo Domingo, itself most desirous of such action, on June 19 issued a decree to just this effect, ordering Maldonado to permit Montejo untrammeled jurisdiction over the entire province. Other general instruments required that Montejo's authority should be acknowledged everywhere in Honduras-Higueras, regardless of the action taken by the Viceroy and Audiencia of New Spain.

Montejo was now in a stronger legal position than at any time since his recall early in 1542. On July 18 he placed the new instruments from the audiencia before Maldonado's lieutenant in Gracias a Dios and the local cabildo, which, on the following day, accepted him as governor. Maldonado's lieutenant had to relinquish office. The authorities of Comayagua, the cabildo of San Jorge de Olancho, and the Spaniards of the Río de Guayape also forthwith definitively acknowledged Montejo.

Maldonado, who was still in Guatemala, was speedily informed by the Audiencia of Santo Domingo of this assertion of its authority and of Montejo's return to the governorship of the whole of Honduras-Higueras. He thereupon accepted the full situation and was soon followed by the high authorities of New Spain. Montejo now had a clear field: Honduras-Higueras had once more been separated from Guatemala, and the Crown confirmed the action of the Audiencia of Santo Domingo as soon as reports reached Court.

Although some colonists of San Pedro and many in Trujillo had regretted the removal of Pérez de Cabrera, the citizens of Gracias a Dios, which remained Montejo's administrative capital, and of Comayagua hailed his return, as did the royal treasury officials. As Montejo's old friend the Factor Juan de Lerma wrote to the Crown:

> I am certain that the Audiencia [of Santo Domingo confirmed Montejo as governor] . . . because the natives respect him . . . and because the conquistadores and colonists have desired and have requested to have him as their chief magistrate, since they have known him for a long while and he knows them, for he has been with [the Spaniards] in the conquest and pacification of this land. He is familiar with everything that it is necessary to do in this province because of his long residence here. I know also that he has a desire to protect and favor the natives. . . . [32]

Montejo's final period as governor was characterized by order and relative stability. The great majority of Spaniards were behind him. The only dissenting note came from those whom he had deprived of encomiendas and from the elements in San Pedro and Trujillo still loyal to Pérez de Cabrera. Their opposition and factionalism, however, was not of a dangerous nature. Montejo did everything possible to promote unity and to lead the province toward the political and economic progress which he had so long planned. Although he lacked time to carry his projects very far before yielding to the new Audiencia de los Confines, his administration in the main gave promise for the future.

That such an intricate, provocative, and potentially strife-laden situation as that which had existed in Honduras-Higueras from Montejo's recall early in 1542 until his final emergence, over a year later, as sole governor should not have led to insubordination, assassination, and utter disaster was remarkable in light of earlier years. Such good fortune can be explained only by the facts that (1) the rival governors involved in the controversies of 1542 and 1543 were fundamentally men of a high sense of responsibility and (2) the implacable influence of evolving royal, absolute colonial government was making itself felt in the form of the Viceroy of New Spain and the Audiencias of New Spain and Santo Domingo. Had these elements of stability not existed, Honduras-Higueras would undoubtedly have been torn apart by the distur-

[32] Juan de Lerma to the Crown, San Pedro, March 10, 1543, AGI, Guatemala 49.

bances similar to those of former days. After many years filled with strife and uncertainty, the colony was at last progressing, even though painfully, toward political maturity.

THE COMING OF ROYAL ABSOLUTE GOVERNMENT WITH THE CREATION OF THE AUDIENCIA DE LOS CONFINES

While the triangular controversy over the governorship of Honduras-Higueras and the jurisdictional contest between New Spain and Santo Domingo were going on, policies of the greatest significance were being formulated in Castile for the better government of the entire Indies and for the protection of the natives. These policies were expressed in the celebrated New Laws of 1542–43. The Crown had become increasingly concerned by the disturbed state of government in Honduras-Higueras, its economic backwardness for which there was no excuse in view of its potential resources, its lack of religious development, and the decrease of native population. Since these matters had been continuously reported from all quarters for many years, with suggested remedies, the Crown resolved on definitive action as a part of general reforms and wide-sweeping administrative measures for the Indies.

It will be remembered that before 1530 the Crown had sought to better conditions in Honduras-Higueras through the direct appointment of royal governors, but that because of unfortunate circumstances in the province—"the influence of some malign planet," as Montejo had put it—this solution had been ineffectual. By the time of the New Laws, consequently, the Crown had decided to create an audiencia similar to that of Santo Domingo to govern not only Honduras-Higueras but all provinces of Central America. The former treasurer, Diego García de Celís, had suggested that the Crown appoint two oidores to govern Honduras-Higueras,[33] and Bishop Marroquín had advocated the establishment of a full-fledged audiencia there.[34] Montejo's own ideas were naturally the reverse. He urged the Crown to make the province independent of both existing audiencias in judicial as well as political matters, and to put all authority in the governor, with appeals in legal matters going to the Consejo de Indias alone. Montejo also petitioned that, to prevent governmental confusion, the Crown designate an organ of government within the province upon which authority would automatically devolve temporarily whenever the governorship became vacant.

The creation of an audiencia to govern the Central American provinces was not designed solely for the purpose of solving administrative problems, whether

---

[33] Diego García de Celís to the Crown, Gracias a Dios, November 30, 1541, AGI, Guatemala 49.
[34] Marroquín to the Crown, San Pedro, January 15, 1543, AGI, Guatemala 156.

recent or long standing. It was also a deliberate extension of the inexorable process through which the Crown was bringing the forms of royal absolutism it most desired to all regions of the New World where Spaniards were firmly established. The audiencia as a governmental institution was in effect a commission made up of a president, judges, a Crown attorney, and lesser officers, who exercised combined and frequently not clearly differentiated executive, administrative, military, and judicial powers, which were all summed up in the excellent political concept that "the proper administration of justice" was the foundation of good government. As a governmental body the audiencia, composed largely of jurists steeped in Roman law, was peculiarly amenable to the royal will. The Crown deemed the time now ripe for this type of institution in Central America. An audiencia was ordained for great and wealthy Peru at the same time, but there the vast importance of the province led to the appointment of a viceroy, who was also the president of the audiencia. The provinces of Central America, however, were to remain under the nominal superior political authority of the Viceroy of New Spain. In practice the new audiencia referred political matters directly to the Crown except under the most unusual circumstances, and in judicial matters it was self-sufficient, with line of appeal directly to the Crown and the Consejo de Indias.

The specific ordinances for the new audiencia were issued on September 13, 1543.[35] Beside the president, there were to be four judges. Recommended by the "Apostle of the Indies," Bartolomé de las Casas, Alonso Maldonado was designated president because of his experience in administration and his satisfactory service as an oidor of the Audiencia of New Spain. The audiencia was to have jurisdiction over Honduras-Higueras, Guatemala, San Salvador, Nicaragua, Costa Rica, Panama, Chiapas, Tabasco, and Yucatan. Each was to retain its former territorial integrity within the wider district of the audiencia. The new audiencia was to have complete control in all respects, except in Yucatan, where Montejo held authority as adelantado by special royal patent, but even here the audiencia had legal jurisdiction.[36] The Crown indicated Comayagua, now known also as Nueva Valladolid, as its first choice as the seat of the audiencia, a clear recognition of the plans to develop that town into the administrative and commercial center of Central America which had been advanced by Montejo, Pedraza, and others.

Since the audiencia for Central America was to replace royal governors, with Yucatan an exception, it was ordered that, upon installation of the tribu-

---

[35] See various royal cedulas issued on September 13, 1543 in AGI, Guatemala 402.

[36] Chiapas, Tabasco, and Yucatan had hitherto been answerable to the Audiencia of New Spain in superior judicial affairs. Tabasco and Yucatan were later removed from the jurisdiction of the Audiencia de los Confines, which came to be known as the Audiencia of Guatemala, and returned to the former tribunal.

nal, like other Central American governors, Montejo and his lieutenants in Honduras-Higueras and Chiapas were immediately to relinquish jurisdiction over those provinces to the new agency. Montejo was then to undergo residencia for Honduras-Higueras and Chiapas, where his period of government was closed, and also for Tabasco and Yucatan, despite the fact that he still governed the latter.[37]

Some months necessarily elapsed between issuance of the ordinances for the new audiencia and its actual installation in the New World. The members of the audiencia finally gathered at Gracias a Dios in the spring of 1544, and since they considered that site better than Comayagua as their capital, the tribunal was installed there early in May. It was first known as the Audiencia de los Confines de Guatemala. The audiencia called upon Montejo to relinquish authority over both Honduras-Higueras and Chiapas to it on May 16, and he complied, thus ending his governorship in those two provinces.

[37] Cedulas of September 13, 1543, AGI, Guatemala 402. One of the originals of the cedula requiring Montejo to relinquish office is found in the Archivo General del Gobierno, Guatemala, among the papers which were formerly in the collection of the Archivo de Protocolos Coloniales. This original may be the very one which Montejo "took in his hands, kissed, and placed upon his head, declaring that he obeyed . . . the orders of His Majesty," in the formal ceremony of obedience required under such circumstances. This cedula has the annotations of the notary who recorded the act.

9

Military, Administrative, and Economic Developments in Honduras-Higueras, 1539–50

EXTENSION OF THE CONQUEST

MONTEJO had achieved the final conquest of Honduras-Higueras during his first governorship between 1537 and 1539. Thenceforth the task remaining to the Spaniards was to extend dominion into outlying regions. Despite all the jurisdictional controversies which plagued the province, this expansion continued from mid-1539 to the time of the establishment of the Audiencia de los Confines.

As governor after mid-1539, Alvarado had directed his lieutenant Cáceres to extend Spanish occupation eastward from Comayagua into the Valley of Olancho, which was quite populous and believed to be rich in gold. The natives of the area had recovered from early attempts at conquest and since all previous efforts at its colonization had ultimately failed, the region had remained outside the Spanish orbit.[1] It will be recalled that Montejo had intended to move into the Valley of Olancho in the spring of 1539 but had been prevented bv lack of personal resources and by refusal of the royal treasury officials to make funds available. Even during his controversy with Alvarado, Montejo had not abandoned his plans to occupy the Valley of Olancho, for he had hoped to emerge from the quarrel still wielding authority over the province.

Since Cáceres had been fully conversant with these plans and had played an important part in the conquest of the Valley of Comayagua, he was particularly well prepared to carry Spanish colonization to the adjoining district. He gathered a considerable company of Spaniards, including Juan de Chávez, with Indian auxiliaries and left for the Valley of Olancho sometime in 1540. In high hope of gold, mining cuadrillas made up of Indian and negro slaves

---

[1] Probanza concerning the services of Alonso de Cáceres, 1560, AGI, Patronato 63-22; Probanza concerning the services of Pedro de Alvarado, 1556, AGI, Patronato 60-5-3; Probanza of Alonso Hernández, 1560, AGI, Patronato 60-3-3; Relación of Bishop Cristóbal de Pedraza, DIU, 13:405; Probanza of Alonso de Funés, 1549, AGG, Al.29:1548:61723; Probanza of Pedro Gómez de Rueda, 1553, AGG, Papers from the Archivo Colonial; Probanza of Alonso Hernández, 1553, AGG, Papers from the Archivo Colonial; Probanza of Francisco de Castellanos, 1560, AGG, Papers from the Archivo Colonial; Documents concerning the election of Diego García de Celís and Juan López de Gamboa as interim coadministrators of Honduras-Higueras, October 21, 1541, AGI, Guatemala, 965. See also Alonso de Cáceres to the Crown, Comayagua, September 5, 1539, AGI, Guatemala 43.

and headed by Spanish miners were taken along.[2] Cáceres first established a camp, or *real,* in the district of Guarabuqui, and from this base carried out a series of campaigns. Although meeting with heavy opposition, he brought a considerable area under nominal control. Then he founded San Jorge de Olancho and assigned the pueblos of the region in encomienda to his soldiers, whom he intended to be citizens of the new municipality.[3] In gratifying confirmation of their hopes the Spaniards soon found that "all that land is very rich in gold," which they began to mine in large quantities, using their slaves and employing great numbers of "free" Indians of the Valley of Olancho, despite the fact that such employment was illegal.

Although Cáceres had achieved measurable initial success, the Indians soon became restive. They resented the demands of tributes and services, especially the hard labor. Some resorted to passive resistance, refusing to furnish supplies, which of itself was serious because San Jorge was distant from other Spanish centers. Many others took up arms again, and still more fled from their pueblos to escape the onerous tasks. Displacement of population and deaths in the mines soon led to a serious decrease in the population of the Valley of Olancho, which in turn further complicated the problem of supply, impaired the workings of the encomienda system, and hampered full exploitation of the mines.[4] Cáceres nevertheless sent out armed exploration parties and mining cuadrillas. After a time a cuadrilla came upon rich placer gold along the course of the Río de Guayape, back of Trujillo. Many other cuadrillas rushed to the region to exploit this great new find.[5]

Despite all the obstacles set up by native hostility Cáceres, a capable and persevering leader, might well have made permanent the Spanish occupation of the Valley of Olancho and the Guayape region, had not news of Alvarado's death in Nueva Galicia arrived. As the highest official of Honduras-Higueras by Alvarado's appointment, he considered that he owed obedience to the superior authorities elected in Santiago de Guatemala to replace Alvarado. Cáceres therefore felt that he was needed in either Comayagua or Gracias a Dios to maintain the authority of his Guatemalan superiors. He was opposed to the choice of García de Celís and López de Gamboa as coadministrators of Honduras-Higueras and the consequent separation of that province from Guatemala, and was prepared to defend his position by force of arms. The very difficulties he had encountered in occupying the Valley of Olancho in some measure influenced the Spaniards, who wished to see the conquest hast-

---

[2] *Ibid.*
[3] *Ibid.*
[4] *Ibid.*
[5] *Ibid.,* especially Probanza of Francisco de Castellanos, Santiago de Guatemala, 1560, AGG, Papers from the Archivo Colonial.

ened to a conclusion, in electing the coadministrators. Since López de Gamboa was given charge of the military affairs of Honduras-Higueras, including superior command over operations in the Olancho area, Cáceres' position was just as anomalous in the military sense as in the political.[6]

Therefore Cáceres reluctantly left Olancho toward the end of 1541 and went to Comayagua, his capital, with most of his soldiers. He must have found it particularly difficult to leave the gold so recently discovered. Only eleven resolute men remained at the base at Guarabuqui—technically to ensure the existence of San Jorge until he or another captain could return to complete the occupation.[7] Since Cáceres was entirely unsuccessful in upholding Guatemalan authority, he ceased to figure in military affairs as well as in the political sphere.

The little band left to hold the Olancho territory maintained itself only at the greatest sacrifice, for they were threatened on all sides by hostile Indians and suffered greatly from illness and want of food. Repeated pleas for supplies and reinforcements over many months were in vain. The determination and high spirit of the group carried them through, however, until help finally came after about a year and a half. One of this number, Alonso de Funés, has left a record of these uncertain days:

The . . . conquistadores had constantly to maintain a double guard so that the Indians would not kill them, for they came to try to massacre them on various occasions.

Some of the Spaniards at times wanted to abandon the land because of the great hunger and illnesses and the many other hardships which they suffered without receiving aid from anywhere. Alonso de Funés pleaded with the other Spaniards not to leave the land because if [they remained and] the land was finally conquered they would be able to command a greater reward than others. He also pointed out to them that they had sent for supplies for their camp and for support, [which they should await]. Because of his pleadings the Spaniards maintained themselves until aid arrived.[8]

The little band was at length reinforced by López de Gamboa late in 1541, after Cáceres had been set to one side. Even though they had earlier refused

---

[6] *Ibid.*

[7] *Ibid.* The Treasurer of Guatemala fixes the approximate time of the discovery of gold along the Río de Guayape. Writing of his intermediation to prevent armed strife between Alonso de Cáceres, as lieutenant governor of Honduras-Higueras in name of the authorities of Guatemala, and Juan López de Gamboa, as a coadministrator of Honduras-Higueras by election of the cabildos and colonists of that province after the death of Pedro de Alvarado, Castellanos said that at that time "oro enl. rrio de guayape . . . se avia descubierto muy pocos dias avia . . ." and that "se coje y se a cojido hasta oy [1560] gran cantidad de pos. de oro de que a llevado su mgt. de sus rreales quitos pasados de trezientos y cincuenta myll. pos. de oro . . ." (Probanza of Francisco de Castellanos, 1560, AGG, Papers from the Archivo Colonial).

[8] Probanza of Alonso de Funés, 1549, AGG, Al.29:1548:01723.

similar help to Montejo, the treasury officials assigned 200 pesos from the
royal coffers to support López de Gamboa's company, composed of Spaniards
from Gracias a Dios and allied Indian warriors.[9] The campaign seems to have
run into serious resistance from the Indians from the first and a shortage of
supplies soon added to the difficulties. García de Celís therefore came to the
aid of López de Gamboa. Through united efforts they nominally re-established Spanish control over most of the Valley of Olancho and gave the town
of San Jorge a more tangible existence. There were now about fifty Spaniards
in the region, including citizens of San Jorge and soldiers engaged in conquest.[10]

Mining was quickly resumed in the valley, and armed Spaniards and cuadrillas hastened back to the region of the Río de Guayape, where conquest
and feverish exploitation of placer gold advanced simultaneously. More negro
slaves were brought in for mining, and numerous Indians enslaved in warfare and "free" Indians were employed. The area of the Río de Guayape seems
soon to have proved more abundant in gold than any other part of Honduras-
Higueras. These placer deposits, along with gold already found in the valleys
of Naco and Olancho and the heavy silver lodes of the Valley of Comayagua,
raised Honduras-Higueras momentarily to the rank of a "rich" province. It
was to be some time, however, before Spanish occupation of this region was
to be assured beyond question. The intolerable burdens imposed by the Spaniards caused increasing hostility among the natives and many outraged districts rose in arms. Shortages of supplies among the Spaniards, characteristic
under such circumstances, became acute. They even lacked adequate stocks
of arms. Displacement of the Indians continued, whether through transfer
from their homes to the mines, or through flight from their pueblos to outlying
areas beyond reach of their taskmasters, from which they could better make
war. This displacement, combined with deaths in war and from overwork
in the mines, soon led to such a dwindling of native population that the
Spaniards were gravely concerned. Many encomenderos of San Jorge became
dissatisfied with their revenues, which diminished as the population dropped.
Despite the gold in the area, it was constant return from their encomiendas
in the form of tributes and services to which these citizens looked as their
long-range income.[11]

Hostility and local revolts among the Indians of the Valley of Olancho and

[9] Juan de Lerma to the Crown, Gracias a Dios, November 30, 1541, AGI, Guatemala 49; Diego
García de Celís to the Crown, San Pedro, March 14, 1542, AGI, Guatemala 49. See also Documents concerning the election of Diego García de Celís and Juan López de Gamboa as interim coadministrators of
Honduras-Higueras, October 21, 1541, AGI, Guatemala 965; Juan López de Gamboa to the Crown, Gracias
a Dios, April 27, 1542, AGI, Guatemala 52; Royal Treasury Officials of Honduras-Higueras to the Crown,
Gracias a Dios, May 1, 1542, AGI, Guatemala 49.
[10] Ibid.
[11] See Montejo to the Crown, San Pedro, May 1, 1542, AGI, Patronato 184-25.

around the Guayape finally built up into a dangerous, full-fledged rebellion in the latter part of 1542. Discontented negro slaves in the mines, now perhaps as many as 1000, joined the rebellious Indians, resulting in a true servile revolt. Everywhere hard pressed, the Spaniards were driven from their placer mines in the Río de Guayape and even from San Jorge.[12]

By this time the quarrelsome coadministration of García de Celís and López de Gamboa had, of course, long since been replaced. One point at issue between the two men was the conduct of the conquest of the valley. Despite the fact that the more experienced López de Gamboa was to have had sole charge of the military affairs of the colony, García de Celís insisted that the authorities of San Pedro had authorized him to conquer that region. López de Gamboa and the cabildos had pushed García de Celís to one side, it will be recalled, and had summoned Montejo back from Chiapas to take over the governorship early in 1542. But Montejo became so deeply concerned with administration and his jurisdictional controversies with Pérez de Cabrera and Maldonado that he was unable to give attention to the Valley of Olancho and the Guayape, despite his great interest in both areas and his realization of their importance to the whole province.

Pérez de Cabrera, in control of the coast under his appointment by the Audiencia of Santo Domingo, saw in the revolt an unparalleled opportunity not only to perform valuable services as a governor, but to extend his own authority as opposed to Montejo's and Maldonado's claims. With numerous soldiery spoiling for action, especially in a region so rich in gold, Pérez de Cabrera alone was in a position to mount an extended campaign. He was in Trujillo attending to governmental matters when news arrived of the widespread revolt, so he empowered his brother and captain-general, Rodrigo de Anaya, whom he had left in San Pedro as lieutenant governor, to suppress the rising and restore Spanish control over the entire region. Anaya awaited the arrival of thirty horses purchased in Cuba in anticipation of just such a campaign and then marched out from San Pedro at the head of a strong company, perhaps as many as 250 or 300 men.[13]

The fighting which followed was fierce. The negro slaves matched the natives in stubborn resistance. Many of Anaya's soldiers perished and his entire force suffered greatly from the hardships of a rough country. But Anaya was an able soldier and early in 1543 crushed the revolt. He then re-established San Jorge some "seventy leagues from Gracias a Dios" to the eastward, restoring some encomiendas to the original grantees and assigning other pueblos

12 Información hecha a petición de Juan Pérez de Cabrera, Trujillo, 1543, AGI, Guatemala 110; Residencia of Juan Pérez de Cabrera, 1544, AGI, Justicia 63; Fiscal v. Juan Pérez de Cabrera, 1556, AGI, Justicia 286-4-1.
13 Ibid.

to his own men. Spaniards and their cuadrillas hurried back into the Río de Guayape area to continue exploitation of its gold.[14]

His difficult task well completed, Anaya then returned to San Pedro, leaving in the Valley of Olancho a heavy garrison, probably intended as permanent colonists. He had meant to push even farther eastward than the Guayape after his success there, but in the end he found that warfare and hardships had exacted such a heavy toll from his men that this was impossible.[15] This well-conducted, although costly, campaign at length secured Spanish occupation of the Valley of Olancho and assured the permanence of the hitherto precarious town of San Jorge. Exploitation of the riches of the area was also assured. There would be minor risings in the region later, but Anaya had struck the major blow and in doing so had made a very important contribution to the conquest and colonization of Honduras-Higueras as a whole, for he at long last confirmed occupation of a wide and rich area of the hitherto unsettled interior to the east of the Valley of Comayagua and behind Trujillo.

After being confirmed as governor for the third time, Montejo finally found an opportunity to return to his long-delayed plans for eastward expansion. In 1544 he sought to found a town in the general region of the Guayape, a municipality intended to advance Spanish colonization beyond San Jorge.[16] He sent one of his most faithful captains, Alonso de Reinoso, eastward

to the conquest and pacification of a land which lies between Olancho and Trujillo, and which extends from the stream which is [believed to be] . . . the outlet from the Lake of León to the North Sea . . . , [a] land said to be rich.

This expedition was made up in part of soldiers recruited in now firmly established San Jorge. Reinoso had served Montejo ably in the conquest of Higueras between 1537 and 1539 and then campaigned with Montejo the Younger during the final conquest of western Yucatan between 1540 and 1542, after which he returned to Honduras-Higueras to be with the adelantado.[17]

Reinoso conquered part of this eastern region but only after overcoming stiff opposition (although the Indians of the area seem to have been few), and only after surmounting many other difficulties of terrain and climate. He then founded a town named Nueva Salamanca "twenty leagues beyond San

[14] *Ibid.*
[15] *Ibid.*
[16] Residencia of Montejo for Honduras-Higueras, 1544, and for Chiapas, 1546, AGI, Justicia 300; Audiencia de los Confines to the Crown, December 30, 1545, DII, 24:438; Probanza of Miguel de Casanos, 1548, AGG, Papers from the Archivo Colonial, Section of Honduras, leg. 62, exped. 1; Probanza of Luis de Aguilar, 1550, AGG, Papers from the Archivo Colonial, Section of Honduras, leg. 57, exped. 1.
[17] Probanza of Alonso de Reinoso, 1542, AGI, Patronato 56-2-3.

Jorge," and divided the subjugated territory among his soldiers in encomienda. By the time the Audiencia de los Confines took office in the spring of 1544, Montejo had another captain, Francisco del Barco, operating in this newly won eastern territory, probably in conjunction with Reinoso.[18] The fact that the town which Reinoso founded was named after Montejo's birthplace, Salamanca of Castile, is testimony to the importance which eastward expansion held in Montejo's plans.[19]

Conquest and colonization to the east were temporarily halted after the installation of the Audiencia de los Confines, through a royal cedula, issued in July 1546, which directed that newly undertaken conquests should not be pushed forward.[20] Meanwhile, Nueva Salamanca, which at first did not have a formal cabildo, seems to have attained considerable, if only ephemeral, importance, for it organized a formal council and appears to have taken on city status. In 1548 Miguel de Casanos, "one of the first conquistadores" of the municipality, drew up a probanza of merits and services "in the city of Salamanca" before "Rodrigo Alvarez, alcalde"; [21] and in 1550 Captain Luis de Aguilar, " one of the first pobladores," who was also alguacil mayor of the town, drew up a similar document in the "City of Nueva Salamanca of the gobernación [or province] of Honduras and Higueras." Carlos de Segura and Juan de Villa Sante were now alcaldes ordinarios of the municipality

[18] Residencia of Montejo for Honduras-Higueras, 1544, and for Chiapas, 1546, AGI, Justicia 300; Pedro Ramírez de Quiñones to the Crown, Gracias a Dios, July 25, 1545, DII, 24:394; Probanza of Miguel Casanos, 1548, AGG, Papers from the Archivo Colonial, Section of Honduras, leg. 62, exped. 1; Probanza of Luis de Aguilar, 1550, AGG, Papers from the Archivo Colonial, Section of Honduras, leg. 57, exped. 1; Probanza of Andrés Francisco, 1559, AGG, Papers from the Archivo Colonial. The Probanza of Miguel de Casanos (Nueva Salamanca, 1548, AGG, Papers from the Archivo Colonial, Section of Honduras, leg. 62, exped. 1) includes the following statements concerning the founding of Nueva Salamanca: ". . . soy uno de los primeros conquistadores e pobladores desta cibdad de salamanca ques. de quando nuevamente vyno a ella el capitan al de reynoso . . ." (statement of Miguel de Casanos himself), and "este testigo y el dho. miguel casanos an andado en conpañia con el capitan alo. de reynoso que fue el que poblo esta cibdad . . ." (testimony of Juan de Villasante). Casanos had also served as an alcalde and a regidor of Nueva Salamanca.

With respect to encomiendas Casanos declared that he was assigned the pueblos of Xagua and Tanguara, each of which had "veynte yndios." In his probanza Luis de Aguilar declared that he had served in the "poblacion y conquista de esta cibdad de seys años a esta parte" and ". . . al typo. ql. capitan alonso de reynoso vino con ciertos españoles a poblar e pacificar esta provincia e poblar en la dha. cibdad de salamanca vine yo el dho. luys de aguilar en su compañia q. puede aver seys años poco mas o menos. . . ." (Nueva Salamanca, 1550, AGG, Papers from the Archivo Colonial, Section of Honduras, leg. 57, exped. 1).

With respect to Francisco del Barco's campaigns Andrés Francisco declared:

"After the greater part of these provinces was pacified the Adelantado sent [Captain Francisco del Barco] to conquer and pacify the Valley of Olancho, and when Captain Francisco del Barco went out Andres Francisco sent a man named Juan Yres to the conquest, with arms which Andrés Francisco supplied at his own cost, and [also] thirty or forty friendly Indians. Andrés Francisco at the time was in the City of Comayagua as an alcalde. In this post he had a great amount of work watching over the city and supplying the Valley of Olancho with the things it needed, since there was not a second alcalde at that time . . ." (Probanza of Andrés Francisco, Valladolid de Comayagua, 1559, AGG, Papers from the Archivo Colonial).

[19] Ibid.

[20] Cedula of July 9, 1546, AGI, Guatemala 402.

[21] Probanza of Miguel de Casanos, 1548, AGG, Papers from the Archivo Colonial, Section of Honduras, leg. 62, exped. 1.

and Pedro Gómez de Rueda was one of the regidores.[22] There seem to have been very few Indians left in the district of Nueva Salamanca by 1550, for Aguilar declared that "when Captain Alonso de Reinoso divided this land in repartimiento he gave and assigned to me in encomienda, in name of His Majesty, the pueblos of Xoanya and Paragri, which between them [now] have only four or five Indians."[23] In 1548 Casanos declared that the pueblos of Xagua and Tanguara, which Reinoso had assigned to him in encomienda, had but twenty Indians each. The history of this new "City of Nueva Salamanca" after 1550 is obscured.[24]

The eastern hinterland—the Valley of Olancho and the region of the Guayape—retained its importance as a gold-producing area for a long while. Even though production in the mines of Olancho, where there were eventually about 1500 negro slaves,[25] fell off somewhat within a few years,[26] "each slave [still] takes out half a peso or a ducat each day."[27] Gold production along the Guayape remained heavy for several years.

Permanent Spanish occupation of Honduras-Higueras had been ensured by Montejo's campaigns from 1537 to 1539. Nevertheless, there were indomitable Indians who still hoped to expel the invaders. A revolt which involved "a great part of the Indians of the town of Comayagua, the town of Olancho, another town which is called Nueva Segovia, and [also] Indians of the City of San Pedro," broke out sometime in 1544.[28] The movement seems to have been co-ordinated, and may have been an attempt by the Indians to repeat their inspired achievements of 1537–39. If so, the rebels fell far short of their objective, for this time there was no genius like Lempira to lead them. The natives killed a few Spaniards and some of their negro slaves who were working in the mines, and even forced the Spaniards temporarily to abandon a few mines.[29] Nevertheless, the uprising was easily crushed, for the Spaniards were now too numerous, too experienced, too firmly organized, and too determined to remain, to permit the Indians to become truly dangerous anywhere except along the fringes of the province.

Indians of the Valley of Olancho also again attempted to free themselves of their masters two years after the more widespread movement of 1544 had

[22] Probanza of Luis de Aguilar, 1550, AGG, Papers from the Archivo Colonial, Section of Honduras, leg. 57, exped. 1.
[23] Ibid.
[24] Probanza of Miguel de Casanos, 1548, Papers from the Archivo Colonial, Section of Honduras, leg. 62, exped. 1.
[25] Maldonado to the Crown, San Pedro, January 15, 1543, DII, 24:351.
[26] Ibid.
[27] Ibid.
[28] Alonso García to the Crown, Gracias a Dios, February 8, 1546, AGI, Guatemala 9.
[29] Ibid.

been crushed. They covertly planned to rise suddenly and massacre the citizens of San Jorge. A Spaniard named Benito Carrasco reports:

In the year 1546 the natives of this town of San Jorge rose up and rebelled and came against the town on Holy Wednesday to kill the Spaniards of the town, who were off guard and felt secure, since they had no warning of the revolt. I was coming to the town and arrived at the pueblo of Celicia, which lies three leagues from it, when night was falling. I learned from the Indians of that pueblo that the entire land had risen up and that the Indians were going to attack this town on the next morning to burn it and kill the Spaniards. I, Benito Carrasco, to prevent the evil and harm which would result from such an event came to the town by night as speedily as I could and warned the authorities of the plot. They made due preparations so that when the Indians came close to the town they saw what had taken place and went away without doing any harm or damage.[30]

Besides warfare with the natives, there is somewhat elusive evidence that sometime during Montejo's final period in office the Habsburg-Valois wars extended as far as Honduras-Higueras. There is a vague reference that French "corsairs," who were active in the Caribbean, appeared off the north coast, where they made an unsuccessful attack which led to their capture.[31] The Crown most certainly had ordered that a fortress be built at the key harbor of Puerto Caballos to ward off just such attacks.

With the thorough occupation of areas east of Comayagua and back of Trujillo, initial colonization of the most important parts of Honduras-Higueras had been completed by the time the Audiencia de los Confines was installed in 1544. Henceforth the settling of these already controlled territories by

[30] Probanza of Benito Carrasco, 1554, AGG, Papers from the Archivo Colonial, Section of Honduras, leg. 27, exped. 1.

Durón (1927, p. 48) states that San Jorge de Olancho was later destroyed by volcanic eruptions: "se perdío por haber hecho erupción dos volcanes en cuyas faldas estaba la ciudad. La mayor parte de los habitantes, atravesando las montañas, se dirigieron al Occidente y fundaron Olanchito. Del resto, unos se establecieron en el sitio llamado Ciudad Vieja y otros se fueron a Nueva Segovia. Se refiere que los vecinos de Olancho eran tan ricos que ponían a sus caballos herraduras de oro." Moñsenor Federico Lunardi (1946b, p. 37), who had made an extensive study of the early municipalities of Honduras and Higueras, has this to say regarding the location of San Jorge de Olancho: Yo visité las ruinas de San Jorge de Olancho el 29 de mayo de 1943, frente al Boquerón ví los cimientos de la pequeña iglesia; se encuentran todavía ladrillos gruesos cuadrados de los españoles . . . Cuando el 25 de abril de 1944 estuve en Olanchito, y después el día 26 visité la CIUDAD VIEJA de Olanchito que esta a unos 4 kilometros al SE., en la margen derecha del Río Aguan, supe que la tradición que se conserva allí, es que en aquel sitio fundaron la ciudad los españoles al venir del Boquerón, donde estaba la ciudad vieja de San Jorge de Olancho, pero que al ver que se morían mucho, la trasladaron al lugar actual, aun cuando el agua era escasa."

[31] See Audiencia of Santo Domingo to the Crown, 1545, AGI, Santo Domingo 49: ". . . por esta real audia, se hiço relacion a V. Mt. de los daños y robos q. por aca hizieron el año pasado ciertos navios de corsarios de francia q. pasaron a estas mares y despues de nosotros venidos tenemos nueva q. . . . se apartaron los dhos. corsarios y el un parte de los qu. llevava con veynte dos frances fue apartar a honduras donde fue tomada y los tienen presos y otra nao q. hazia mucha agua fue a reparar a la ysla de cuba de cabo al puerto q. dizen de matanza de donde salio tomo una nao q. venia de la nueva españa y les robo lo q. traya. . . ."

expanding colonization, rather than further conquest, was to follow a natural course. The inhospitable extreme east of the province, toward Cabo Gracias a Dios (that is, a large part of the general area then known as Taguzgalpa) was to prove permanently unattractive, and for that reason was long ignored. Later in the century the foundations of what was to become the City of Tegucigalpa, south of Comayagua and deep in the center of the province, were laid.

ADMINISTRATIVE MEASURES DESIGNED TO PROMOTE DEVELOPMENT

The Crown, after 1537, in answer to petitions from Honduras-Higueras, issued a number of decrees which concerned the political and economic status of the province. Those growing out of Montejo's requests between 1537 and 1539 have already been noted. Others, originating under Alvarado's auspices, either while Alvarado, García de Celís, López de Yrarraga, and Cava were at Court in 1537 and 1538 or afterward, were also of importance to the colony, and their influence reached beyond the period of Montejo's first governorship.[32]

The procuradores, Nicolás López de Yrarraga and Francisco Cava, on the basis of their instructions from the authorities of Honduras-Higueras before their departure for Castile with Alvarado in 1536, made the following requests during the next two years. They sought relief from taxes and import duties. They asked that, since the deposits of gold and silver which had thus far been discovered in Higueras lay in the district of San Pedro, refining should be carried out in that town; that any license hitherto granted to colonists of Guatemala to exploit such deposits in Higueras be revoked. Permission to pay only a tenth of precious metals to the Crown rather than the normal royal fifth was requested for a period of years. The Crown was asked to permit enslavement of Indians captured in war and to prevent Indians of pueblos of Honduras-Higueras which Alvarado had assigned in encomienda from being taken outside the province to serve for labor or burden-bearing elsewhere. The procuradores likewise petitioned the Crown to forbid arms, horses, or slaves from being taken from individual citizens for indebtedness.

Freedom from imposts and payment to the Crown of a tenth rather than the legal fifth of precious metals were of more than ordinary importance to a province such as Honduras-Higueras. A diezmo would allow the colonists to have a greater share of gold and silver for themselves during the first years of colonization. The geographical isolation of Honduras-Higueras meant that

---

[32] For the exact nature of these petitions and the measures which the Crown adopted, which will be discussed in the following paragraphs, see various cedulas issued 1537–39 in AGI, Guatemala 402.

few ships arrived; this fact, combined with the difficulty of transport within the province, caused a scarcity of commodities from overseas and high costs for everything. Easier and less costly procurement of imports would obviously contribute to greater stability and aid in developing the province.

Since the colonists naturally regarded mining as their greatest immediate source of wealth, all measures directed toward the increase of that activity were considered fundamental to their well-being. The procuradores and the treasurer García de Celís, as Montejo, desired that the riches of Honduras-Higueras should be exploited exclusively by the colonists of the province. Likewise they did not wish the Indians of Honduras-Higueras to be employed elsewhere. In these matters García de Celís, the procuradores of Honduras-Higueras, and Montejo were of one mind, and for the same reasons.

The Crown granted most of the petitions which García de Celís and the procuradores presented during 1537 and 1538. Furthermore, the residue from the smelting of gold and silver for six years, and an additional sum of 50,000 maravedises a year for two years from fines assessed for the Crown, were granted for the construction and support of hospitals. However, the Crown not only refused to approve the procuradores' petitions to permit extensive enslavement of Indians, as well as requests for authorization for limited enslavement which Montejo later made, but stringently prohibited any such action through cedulas issued to Montejo.

One of the major causes advanced to explain the constant internal political turmoil which had existed in Honduras from the founding of the colony was the annual election by each city and town of alcaldes ordinarios, regidores, alguaciles, and other municipal officials. These yearly elections, which were traditional Castilian constitutional practice, led to factionalism, jealousy, and strife among the colonists, who formed rival parties and quarreled violently not only among themselves but also with the higher provincial officials. García de Celís and the procuradores brought this situation to the attention of the Crown in 1537 and petitioned that, to provide a remedy, the Crown should henceforth appoint *regidores perpetuos,* or "perpetual councilmen," to the cabildos of Honduras-Higueras. Regidores perpetuos held office for life by direct appointment by the King and were consequently lifted out of election bickering and the vagaries of local conditions. They were expected to rise above petty factionalism and provide a stable, independent element in municipal government which could do much to allay disorder and eliminate the evil effects of party rivalries. It was also anticipated that regidores perpetuos would constitute a valuable, permanent policy-forming body and that they would tend to prevent the governor from controlling the municipal councils in his own interests. Many governors did everything in their power to dominate the cabildos, and such policy frequently produced dissension and impaired the orderly processes of government.

The Crown heard these petitions with favor and soon appointed regidores perpetuos to the cabildos of Honduras-Higueras, selecting both royal treasury officials and colonists for the posts. Appointment of the already independently situated royal treasury officials as regidores perpetuos was common because as officers responsible only to the Crown they could readily exert a stabilizing influence. The factor Juan de Lerma, who for many years had collaborated with Montejo, and the veedor Alonso de Valdés were appointed regidores of the city in which the governor would reside, Gracias a Dios in this case. Hernán Sánchez de Alvarado, a relative of Pedro de Alvarado, and Francisco Cava were named regidores perpetuos of Gracias a Dios; López de Yrarraga was appointed a regidor perpetuo of San Pedro.

In the summer of 1539, Licenciado Cristóbal de Pedraza was elected procurador to represent Honduras-Higueras at Court by all the cabildos except that of Trujillo, which looked to the influential Bartolomé de las Casas to make known its needs to the Crown. Pedraza, as chief prelate of Honduras-Higueras and judge of the controversy between Alvarado and Montejo, enjoyed high prestige among the colonists, especially Alvarado's partisans, and was well regarded by Alvarado himself after Montejo yielded in mid-1539. Pedraza had decided to return to Castile in connection with the ecclesiastical affairs of the province and to hasten his appointment as bishop which he had expected before first coming to the province in 1538.[33] The petitions which Pedraza was to present to the Crown well illustrate the measures which the municipal governments and most of the colonists themselves considered best calculated to bring stability and prosperity to the colony. They reflect the "public opinion" of the time.

As procurador, Pedraza was to give the Crown a full account of the developments in Honduras-Higueras which had led to Montejo's relinquishment of office to Alvarado and was to present a series of petitions on behalf of the cabildos. The cabildo of Gracias a Dios, especially, gave Pedraza detailed instructions. He was to request the Crown to give permanent validity to the agreement between Montejo and Alvarado by which Alvarado became governor of Honduras-Higueras and Montejo received the governorship of Chiapas.

[33] See Document regarding Pedraza's mission to Court (n.d.), AGI, Guatemala 968B; Designation of Cristóbal de Pedraza as Procurador of Gracias a Dios, July 7, 1539, AGI, Guatemala 965; Cabildo of Gracias a Dios to the Crown, August 10, 1539, AGI, Guatemala 44; Pedraza to the Crown, Badajoz, September 16, 1541, AGI, Guatemala 164. See also Cabildo of Comayagua to the Crown, September 5, 1539, AGI, Guatemala 43, and Juan de Lerma to the Crown, San Pedro, October 31, 1539, AGI, Guatemala 49, and various cedulas issued by the Crown between 1540 and 1543 in answer to petitions presented at Court on behalf of Honduras-Higueras, AGI, Guatemala 393, 402, and 965.

He was to make known the need permanently to incorporate Honduras-Higueras with Guatemala, since, it was then held, the colonists of Honduras-Higueras themselves did not have sufficient resources to suppress a general native revolt. Knowledge among the natives that immediate support from Guatemala would be available for Honduras-Higueras would of itself give the Indians pause, it was thought. If a revolt did occur, the cabildo maintained, the colonists of united Guatemala and Honduras-Higueras would be in a position to suppress the movement through their combined resources and would not have to request aid from the Crown or any other source.

Further petitions Pedraza was to lay before the Court were in the main similar to those presented earlier on behalf of Honduras-Higueras and concerned measures the local authorities and colonists considered necessary for the economic and political advancement of the colony. He was to request that the privilege of turning over to the royal treasury only a tenth of precious metals be extended for ten years more, and, likewise, that freedom from import and export duties, which had been granted for four years, be also further prolonged for ten additional years.

To make possible the increased output of precious metals, the Crown was asked to permit the employment of Indian household servants, natives captured in warfare, and Indians enslaved by other natives under their own customs, for labor in the mines, since the colonists lacked slaves and sufficient resources to purchase them in large numbers from any source. The Spaniards declared that unless mining was expanded, they would remain perpetually poor and discontented, and, furthermore, royal incomes would not reach the desired level. Pedraza was also to request that 500 more negro slaves be sent to the province for the mining of gold—these to be apportioned among the colonists, who would pay for them. More slaves, it was stated, would add significantly to both royal revenues and private incomes by increasing the output of gold.

At the behest of the authorities of Gracias a Dios, Pedraza was further to petition the Crown to direct that the casa de fundición originally established at San Pedro, should be transferred to Gracias a Dios, or to any other municipality where the governor and royal treasury officials might reside. The authorities of San Pedro had requested that the Crown order all refining for the province to be carried out in that town, but the officials of Gracias a Dios maintained that their city was more centrally located and that any continued refining of precious metals at San Pedro would be to the serious disadvantage of Gracias a Dios.

Pedraza was likewise to request the Crown to direct the royal treasury officials of Honduras-Higueras to establish a well-constructed warehouse at Puerto de Caballos to facilitate the loading and unloading of ships, serve as a storage place for merchandise, and make the port itself more attractive to merchants and ships' captains.

Confirmation was to be asked of encomienda grants as they stood after Alvarado had readjusted them following Montejo's removal from office. Pedraza was also to request that they be made into hereditary holdings, which, it was declared, would cause the encomenderos to deal with the natives more justly and would lead to the more rapid conversion of the Indians to Christianity. More important, if the encomenderos were assigned their pueblos as hereditary holdings, they would have more incentive to remain in the province and foster its development.

The *penas de cámara,* or court fines, it was held, should be applied to the construction and maintenance of public works in the cases of municipalities which possessed no *propios,* or public lands, from which they could derive revenues. All general privileges of a political and economic nature which the Crown had granted to the municipalities of New Spain and Guatemala were also to be requested for Honduras-Higueras.

In 1540 or 1541, after changes had taken place in the governmental structure of the province, the municipalities of Honduras-Higueras elected another procurador, Bernardo de Cambranes,[34] to represent them at Court. Among other things, Cambranes was to repeat the petitions for an extension of the period during which only a tenth of precious metals was to be paid the Crown and for prolonged exemption from import and export duties. These latter petitions were eventually granted by the Crown. Another royal decree, quite in contrast to what the cabildo of Gracias a Dios desired, provided that refining of precious metals for the province should be carried out at San Pedro, and that a smelter should remain there.[35]

ECONOMIC DEVELOPMENTS

The authorities of Honduras-Higueras also took steps on their own initiative to better conditions in the province. Roads had remained inadequate, despite Montejo's efforts to improve communications during his first period as governor. Lack of a good, permanent road between San Pedro and Puerto de Caballos was still a great handicap to the commercial development of the province.

[34] See a Royal Cedula of October 26, 1541, AGI, Guatemala 402, which indicates the selection of Cambranes as a procurador by the cabildos and colonists of Honduras-Higueras.
[35] See various cedulas issued in 1541, AGI, Guatemala 402.

Merchants and masters of ships continued to hesitate to put in at Puerto de Caballos largely because they realized the difficulty of transporting their goods inland. Importing even a minimum of the articles which the province needed was a problem. Commerce in the true sense remained almost non-existent. Authorities and colonists, realizing that such a situation had to be remedied, came to an agreement with Alonso Ortiz, one of the lieutenants of the Guatemalan officials while Honduras-Higueras was still under the authority of that province, through which Ortiz guaranteed to construct and maintain a road between San Pedro and Puerto de Caballos. The expenses of this important enterprise were to be borne by the colonists of Higueras.[36]

In connection with the importance which Puerto de Caballos possessed as a port to serve both Honduras-Higueras and Guatemala—and San Salvador, San Miguel, and northern Nicaragua as well—the Crown in 1541 directed the authorities and royal treasury officials of the province to construct a strong fortress there for its defense. It considered such a fortress necessary because of possible attack on the coasts of the New World by the French in view of the prolonged and bitter Habsburg-Valois wars. Natives of the region were to be employed in this construction.[37]

There were several visitas generales carried on in Honduras-Higueras during the period between Alvarado's assumption of office in 1539 and the installation of the Audiencia de los Confines. The object of such visitas was to improve administration in general, inspect municipal government, initiate or improve public works, hear complaints of governmental injustices either from Spaniards or Indians, and safeguard the welfare of the natives.

The first of these visitas was carried out by Alvaro de Paz, whom the authorities of Guatemala had sent to Honduras-Higueras to reassert their jurisdiction after Alvarado's death but whom the interim coadministrators persuaded to accept the office of visitador general under their authority. Paz sought to safeguard the welfare of the Indians and promulgate ordinances to establish reforms with respect to the labor of negro slaves in the gold mines of the Valley of Olancho and the area of the Guayape. He also strongly recommended that an adequate, permanent road be finally established between San Pedro and Puerto de Caballos. Paz later served as a lieutenant of Pérez de Cabrera.[38]

After Maldonado had been accepted as governor at Gracias a Dios at the turn of 1542–43, he and the Guatemalan Bishop Marroquín, in view of the assignment to the latter of temporary superior spiritual oversight in Honduras-

---

[36] Cedula of December 27, 1542, AGI, Guatemala 402.
[37] Cedula of October 27, 1540, AGI, Guatemala 402.
[38] Probanza of Alvaro de Paz, 1559, AGI, Patronato 62-13.

Higueras pending the designation of a bishop there, made a joint visita of the territory which Maldonado controlled. Marroquín was, of course, concerned with ecclesiastical matters as well as civil during this visita. Both he and Maldonado envisaged permanent basic reforms to improve the situation of the Indians, the continued building and improvement of roads, and the progressive development of the harbor of Puerto de Caballos. Marroquín was greatly disturbed by incontestable evidence of the decrease in Indian population.[39] In view of earlier cedulas ordering Pedraza and Montejo to establish an official, fixed taxation of the tributes which the Indians were to give their encomenderos, Maldonado and the bishop must also have sought to lay the basis for such an assessment. The jurisdictional problems and administrative confusion which then existed, however, prevented them from making effective to any great degree the more important general measures which they planned, especially since Pérez de Cabrera then controlled the coastal area and refused to give up his authority. It was in the course of this visita that Maldonado, accompanied by Marroquín, had gone to San Pedro in his unsuccessful effort to obtain acceptance as governor there.

As acting spiritual head of Honduras-Higueras, Marroquín made a second visita of the province, with Montejo's co-operation, a few months before the latter relinquished authority to the Audiencia de los Confines in the spring of 1544. This visita was obviously concerned mainly with church affairs. Marroquín remained in Honduras-Higueras until the establishment of the audiencia and continued his visita after that tribunal took office.[40]

Commerce slowly developed after 1544; more ships began to come to the province than during the preceding years. Montejo, Maldonado, Marroquín, and apparently also Pérez de Cabrera, as well as the local authorities, were throughout unanimous in their desire to develop Puerto de Caballos as a principal port and to establish a permanent road from San Pedro to Puerto de Caballos, the building of which had finally been assigned to Alonso Ortiz. A town again came into existence at Puerto de Caballos, and by 1542 there was a sufficient number of settlers there—a population which temporarily increased when ships arrived with merchandise—to cause the authorities of San Pedro to petition the Crown for authority to designate an alcalde each year to exercise civil and criminal jurisdiction at Puerto de Caballos. This measure was sanctioned by the Crown, which directed that appeals from action taken by the alcalde thus elected should go before the lieutenants whom the governors of the province placed in San Pedro. The size and condition of this

[39] Bishop Francisco de Marroquín to the Crown, San Pedro, January 15, 1543, AGI, Guatemala 156.
[40] Bishop Francisco de Marroquín to the Crown, Gracias a Dios, March 15, 1545, AGI, Guatemala 156.

revived settlement at Puerto de Caballos in its earliest period is obscure, although it was clearly at first subordinate to San Pedro.[41]

During his last periods as governor, Montejo issued decrees carefully regulating the period of storage and conditions of the sale of goods which arrived from Castile at Puerto de Caballos and San Pedro in an effort to promote commerce, even though this measure was in opposition to regulations which San Pedro itself had established to govern such traffic.[42] As more ships came to the province, merchants set themselves up in the several towns and cities, although some of them, finding that conditions were not as favorable as they had hoped, soon passed on in search of more profitable fields. Merchandise from overseas long remained scarce and high priced despite slowly increasing trade, for

with the scarcity of everything from Castile which exists, what is worth one maravedí there costs four to eight maravedises here, and what is valued there at a *cuarto* is worth a *real* here, and what values a real there is worth a *peso de oro* here. . . . Merchants do not wish to bring goods [to this province] unless they can gain two hundred or three hundred per cent, and even then they curse the land and go away, saying that they will never come back. . . .[43]

Even though there was a gradual improvement, regardless of all handicaps, and even though Puerto de Caballos increased in importance, trade did not begin to approach the volume which Montejo and others had envisaged in their plans to make Honduras-Higueras a great commercial province on the route between Castile, the West Indies, and Peru. All in all, development of the province in this respect proved a slow, though nevertheless expanding, process.

Mining continued to improve after 1539, especially on the discovery of gold in the Valley of Olancho and the finding of the rich placer deposits of the Guayape. The total number of pesos de oro netted between August 1540 and March 1542 seems to have been 100,000. Of this total, 10,000 pesos went as the royal diezmo. While Honduras-Higueras was still united to Guatemala, another 100,000 pesos de oro were mined by cuadrillas owned by authorities and colonists of Guatemala and were taken to that province. In 1540 the figures for refinement in Gracias a Dios were 5000 pesos, for San Pedro 9000, and for Trujillo 10,000. In March 1542, 30,000 pesos' worth of gold was reported ready for refining in San Pedro and 15,000 pesos' worth in Trujillo.

[41] See Cedulas of June 6 and 16, 1543, AGI, Guatemala 393.
[42] Residencia of Montejo for Honduras-Higueras, 1544, AGI, Justicia 300.
[43] Bishop Cristóbal de Pedraza to the Crown, Trujillo, December 22, 1548, AGI, Guatemala 164.

Silver production in the region of Comayagua in 1541 was some 2,050 marcos.[44] In 1560, the treasurer of Guatemala, Francisco de Castellanos, wrote of the heavy gold production of the region of the Guayape:

. . . up until the time [I write] a great sum in pesos de oro has been taken from [the Río de Guayape], from which have come to His Majesty as his royal quintos more than 350,000 pesos de oro. . . .[45]

If Castellanos' statement is correct, it would mean that by 1560 gold to the value of 1,750,000 pesos had been obtained from the rich deposits of the Guayape area.

With respect to agriculture and grazing, the Spaniards from the first had introduced European trees, plants, and domestic animals and fowls. As colonization progressed they built up haciendas, many of them large, on which they bred livestock. The Spaniards trained Indians to care for and breed these animals. Wheat, possibly introduced by Montejo during his first governorship between 1537 and 1539, grew well in the Valley of Comayagua. Spanish efforts to grow wheat succeeded there, whereas they failed in many parts of the Indies because of adverse climate. The Spaniards taught the natives how to cultivate this staple and by the middle of the century it was an important article of tribute in the district of Comayagua.[46]

The natives, on the other hand, continued their own agriculture and simple industry. As before, they raised great quantities of maize, cotton, beans, and, in the lowlands, cacao; they wove cloth and made pottery. From these products they gave tribute to the Crown and their encomenderos and tithes to the Church.[47] In fact, the very tribute requirements tended in many ways to stimulate native industry and agriculture, as well as to enrich both through the addition of European elements.

Despite the universal understanding that a network of adequate roads among the several municipalities of Honduras-Higueras and with other provinces was essential for military security and economic development, and notwithstanding all plans and efforts to develop such a system, communications in general remained poor when the Audiencia de los Confines took office. Wheeled vehicles could pass over the existing roads in only a few places, and

[44] Treasury accounts of Honduras-Higueras, 1540, AGI, Indiferente General 1206; Accounts for the smelting of precious metals at Gracias a Dios and San Pedro 1539–41, AGI, Patronato 180-74; Diego García de Celís to the Crown, San Pedro, March 14, 1542, AGI, Guatemala 49.

[45] Probanza of Francisco de Castellanos, 1560, AGG, Papers from the Archivo Colonial.

[46] See Residencia of Montejo for Honduras-Higueras, 1544, AGI, Justicia 300; Residencia of Alonso Maldonado, President of the Audiencia de los Confines, and of the oidores of the Audiencia, 1548, AGI, Justicia 299; Taxation of the tributes and services of the Indians and native pueblos of the district of the Audiencia de los Confines, 1548–52, AGI, Guatemala 128.

[47] Ibid.

in many localities it was difficult for even pack animals to move over them. Roads and trails remained virtually impassable during the rainy season and, as before, there were very few if any bridges over the streams, which became torrents when the rains came. The results of Montejo's efforts to build and improve roads between 1537 and 1539 had largely disappeared and conditions were worse than at the close of his first period in office. The uncertain political situation which arose because of the triangular jurisdictional controversy between Montejo, Maldonado, and Pérez de Cabrera had made effective progress impossible in that field as well as in others.

The magnitude of the problem of communications is made clear by the distances between the municipalities of Honduras-Higueras as they were calculated at that time. These distances, calculated on the basis of routes existing in 1547, were given as fourteen leagues from Puerto de Caballos to San Pedro, thirty-five leagues from San Pedro to Gracias a Dios, twenty-five leagues from Gracias a Dios to Comayagua, twenty to thirty leagues from Comayagua to San Jorge de Olancho, thirty leagues and more from San Jorge de Olancho to the recently founded town of Nueva Salamanca, and about forty leagues from Nueva Salamanca to Trujillo. It was a good forty leagues by sea from Trujillo to Puerto de Caballos. There was still no ready overland way between those two points. Alonso López de Cerrato, second president of the Audiencia de los Confines, who succeeded Maldonado in 1548, finally established more permanent roads from San Pedro to Gracias a Dios and Comayagua, so that those two interior municipalities at length enjoyed better communications with San Pedro and, over the new permanent road from San Pedro to Puerto de Caballos, with the north coast.[48]

ENCOMIENDA PROBLEMS

The encomienda problem again came acutely to the fore between 1542 and the installation of the Audiencia de los Confines, because of both continued alarming decreases in the native population and the repeated assignment and reassignment of encomiendas by Montejo, Pérez de Cabrera, and Maldonado.[49] The largest encomiendas now numbered less than 200 *tributarios,* or tribute-paying Indians, and many encomiendas did not have more than

[48] *Ibid.;* Royal cedulas issued between 1540 and 1550 regarding roads in Honduras-Higueras, AGI, Guatemala 402; Alonso López de Cerrato to the Crown, Santiago de Guatemala, January 26, 1550, AGI, Guatemala 9. The distances cited were given by Pedraza in a letter to the Crown from Trujillo, dated May 1, 1547 (AGI, Guatemala 164). The official Spanish land league was 5000 varas.

[49] Residencia of Montejo for Honduras-Higueras, 1544, AGI, Justicia 300; Residencia of Alonso Maldonado, President of the Audiencia de los Confines, and of the oidores of the Audiencia, 1548, AGI, Justicia 299; Residencia of Juan Pérez de Cabrera, 1544, AGI, Justicia 63; Action of Ambrosio de Palencia, Judge of Commission with respect to encomienda holdings in Honduras-Higueras by authority of the Audiencia de los Confines, 1544, AGI, Guatemala 965.

thirty. Small encomiendas tended to cause abiding dissatisfaction among conquistador-colonists, and new colonists would not be attracted by grants which
they deemed inadequate. As Montejo well knew, "naturally no settlers will
come when there are no [more] Indians to be given in encomienda. . . ." [50]
Reassignments of encomiendas after 1542 led to confused claims and counterclaims both among encomenderos and between colonists and the governors,
as was inevitable in the jurisdictional uncertainty arising from the simultaneous
presence of three claimants to the governorship. Altogether, the current problems of encomienda grants threatened serious consequences.

On his return to Honduras-Higueras in 1542 Montejo had taken for himself
encomiendas once held by Alvarado and fallen vacant after his death. Montejo's annexation of Yamala, a pueblo the Crown had ordered to be placed
under its protection—"in the Crown"—naturally caused him legal difficulties.
His earlier assignment to a colonist of Honduras-Higueras of a pueblo lying
in disputed territory between that province and Guatemala and held by Cristóbal de la Cueva, formerly an important official of Guatemala, brought him
into further litigation. [51] When governor of the districts of Gracias a Dios and
Comayagua, Maldonado made a number of changes in encomienda assignments there and in his turn created discontent among the ousted colonists.
During his last period in office, Montejo removed some of these pueblos from
Maldonado's grantees and reassigned them to others, including his daughter,
Doña Catalina, and his stepson, Juan de Esquivel. Charges were soon preferred
against Montejo by the dispossessed. [52]

Pérez de Cabrera both appropriated for himself and reassigned encomiendas
in the coastal districts under his control, in disregard of instructions from
the Audiencia of Santo Domingo, and was promptly sued, especially by encomenderos of San Pedro. [53] Upon confirming Montejo as governor, the Audiencia of Santo Domingo directed him to take jurisdiction over all suits against
Pérez de Cabrera. Montejo then revoked all the latter's grants and instructed
his lieutenant in San Pedro, the comendador Buyca, to hear complaints from
all aggrieved encomenderos. On the basis of his findings Montejo reassigned
encomiendas in the district of San Pedro as he saw fit. [54] The authorities of
San Pedro, however, sent a representative, Francisco de Escobar, to protest
Montejo's measures to the Audiencia of Santo Domingo. The tribunal at
length forbade him to make any further readjustments in that district. This

[50] *Ibid.*
[51] *Ibid.*
[52] *Ibid.*
[53] *Ibid.*
[54] *Ibid.*

decree, presented to Montejo early in 1544 by a specially designated judge of commision, Ambrosio de Palencia, was carefully obeyed.[55]

Fortunately for Montejo, his encomienda policy after 1542 was less disturbing than that of 1537–39, but he nevertheless passed on an involved and delicate encomienda problem to the Audiencia de los Confines when that tribunal took office. With its new royal powers and legal knowledge, the audiencia was able eventually to unravel the complicated question of legal titles to encomiendas and to establish an orderly system of holdings.

INDIAN POLICIES

The welfare and protection of the natives and the effective application of royal legislation for their benefit remained a vitally important problem for the authorities of Honduras-Higueras between 1539 and the installation of the Audiencia de los Confines. The alarming decreases in the Indian population demanded action to halt the decline. Protective measures, however, were just as difficult to enforce as in earlier years, because self-seeking colonists were determined to exploit the natives regardless of effects on the Indians or on the ultimate economic development of the colony.

From the moment he arrived in Honduras-Higueras in the autumn of 1538, Pedraza, as Protector of the Indians, was ready to enforce royal legislation designed to foster the welfare of the Indians. Although he and Montejo had co-operated closely on such measures before Alvarado's return in 1539, the colonists hoped to have a free hand when Alvarado again became governor. But cruel and short-sighted exploitation of the natives, almost universal in the early period of conquest and colonization, was by this time being increasingly restricted through more effective application of royal policy, to the disappointment of the colonists of Honduras-Higueras. Pedraza renewed the prohibition against employment of free and household Indians in the mines, a measure instituted by Montejo between 1537 and 1539 but ignored after Alvarado's return. To protect the Indians from overwork Pedraza issued an ordinance on October 19, 1539, stringently regulating the use of natives in all types of economic activity. Pedraza took a strong stand against enslavement of Indians under any circumstances, in compliance with royal decrees.[56]

Pedraza also forbade the citizens of San Pedro to sell, lease out, give, loan,

[55] Ibid.
[56] Bishop Cristóbal de Pedraza to the Crown, Gracias a Dios, May 1, 1547, AGI, Guatemala 164; Cabildo of San Pedro to the Crown, November 1, 1539, AGI, Guatemala 44; Diego García de Celís to the Crown, Puerto de Caballos, July 30, 1540, AGI, Guatemala 49; Probanza regarding promulgation of measures in defense of the Indians drawn up by Cristóbal de Pedraza, San Pedro, 1539, AGI, Indiferente General 1206; Summary of a letter from Cristóbal de Pedraza to the Crown regarding measures to protect the Indians (n.d.), AGI, Indiferente General 1206.

or exchange any Indians held in encomienda. He considered this measure necessary both to conserve the native population and to protect the Indians from mistreatment and abuses by Spaniards who contracted for them with encomenderos for labor service, whether in mines or on haciendas. These abuses, forbidden by Montejo in application of royal cedulas during his first governorship, had again been permitted by Alvarado. Such treatment had deleterious effects everywhere but seems to have harmed particularly the Indians of the district of San Pedro.[57]

One of Pedraza's objections to Alvarado's monetary claims against Montejo during their quarrel over the governorship was Alvarado's illegal employment of free Indians for forced labor in the mines. Pedraza refused to admit that claims in connection with gold or silver produced by natives forced to labor in contravention of royal ordinances were valid, an indication of his sincerity.[58]

Like the better officials and other churchmen, Pedraza was a strong advocate of a policy basically contradictory from the purely humanitarian viewpoint: employing numerous negro slaves to relieve the burdens on the Indians who with their special legal status as wards of the Crown could not be enslaved at first except under specific circumstances and later not at all. Montejo, Pedraza, and other officials of Honduras-Higueras had recommended that negro slaves, valued much higher as workers than Indians, should be imported. Therefore, at Lisbon, on his way to Castile, Pedraza in 1540 contracted for 165 negroes. These slaves eventually reached Honduras, where 54 were assigned to citizens of Gracias a Dios, 57 to those of San Pedro, and 54 to those of Comayagua. The individual colonists receiving these slaves, destined for employment in the mines and for general labor purposes, were expected to pay for them. During his final period as governor Montejo recommended that even more negroes be sent to the province. By 1545 there may have been as many as 1500–2000 in Honduras-Higueras.[59]

Before departing for Castile late in 1539 or early in 1540, Pedraza continued to maintain his school for the sons of caciques and other Indian boys in his dwelling in Gracias a Dios. There he instructed them in the Faith and the elements of European education. The school was supported, as from the first, by the revenues from the pueblo of Talva, which Montejo had set aside for its maintenance in accordance with the royal decree authorizing the establishment of the school. When Pedraza left for Castile he placed one of his fellow priests of Gracias a Dios in charge of his colegio. It unfortunately went out of existence shortly after Pedraza departed, for the original success was the

[57] *Ibid.*
[58] Montejo *v.* Pedraza, 1539, AGI, Justicia 129-2.
[59] See Maldonado to the Crown, San Pedro, January 15, 1543, DII, 24:351.

result of Pedraza's careful nurture and Montejo's support until Alvarado assumed authority over Honduras-Higueras in 1539.[60]

Pedraza's efforts to protect the Indians and enforce royal ordinances which favored them aroused the same kind of opposition that similar measures by Montejo had evoked.[61] The cabildo of Gracias a Dios even instructed Pedraza, as procurador of Honduras-Higueras at Court, to petition royal measures permitting employment of Indians in the mines, contrary to his own regulations. Then, after he had left for Castile, the royal treasury officials strongly denounced his policies to the Crown. They declared that Pedraza had seized their letters of protest against his policies, that he had represented conditions among the natives as much worse than they actually were, and that, through his protective measures, he had hindered the development of mining. They went so far as to request the Crown to ignore Pedraza as a procurador until the despatches and documents drawn up by Montejo against Pedraza as a result of his removal from office in Honduras-Higueras in 1539, and other protests from the cabildos, had been carefully examined at Court.[62] The royal treasury officials repeated the old arguments that the Indians gave little tribute in Honduras-Higueras as compared with other provinces and that the mines were the only real source of Crown revenues and individual wealth for the colonists. They consequently emphasized, by implication, the close relationship between mining and the permanence of the colony as they saw it, and advocated freer use of the Indians in exploitation of precious metals. The Crown, however, firmly supported Pedraza's measures.[63]

The status and welfare of the natives were of special concern to Montejo, Maldonado, and the Guatemalan Bishop Marroquín after Pedraza left for Castile.[64] The question of illegal forced labor in the mines and burden-bearing persisted as a most acute problem. In the absence of adequate roads over which vehicles and pack animals could readily pass, it was impossible to relieve the natives from the heavy task of transport. The system of burden-bearing, or tamemes, had perforce to be legally sanctioned, although measures were taken to bring it under official control and to eliminate the most flagrant abuses, regulatory steps initiated by García de Celís when coadministrator.

[60] Bishop Cristóbal de Pedraza to the Crown, Trujillo, May 1, 1547, AGI, Guatemala 164.
[61] Bishop Cristóbal de Pedraza to the Crown, Trujillo, May 1, 1547, AGI, Guatemala 164; Cabildo of San Pedro to the Crown, November 1, 1539, AGI, Guatemala 44; Diego García de Celís to the Crown, Puerto de Caballos, July 30, 1540, AGI, Guatemala 49; Probanza regarding promulgation of measures in defense of the Indians drawn up by Cristóbal de Pedraza, 1539, AGI, Indiferente General 1206; Summary of a letter from Cristóbal de Pedraza to the Crown regarding measures to protect the Indians (n.d.), AGI, Indiferente General 1206.
[62] Ibid.
[63] Ibid.
[64] See Residencia of Montejo for Honduras-Higueras, 1544, AGI, Justicia 300, and Residencia of Alonso Maldonado, President of the Audiencia de los Confines, and of the oidores of the Audiencia 1548, AGI, Justicia 299.

This regularization, well-intentioned though it was, in actuality was little more than formalization of practices which had started soon after the Spaniards first entered the province. Even under official supervision, the encomenderos themselves were now permitted to employ their encomienda Indians for transport and to hire them out under contract at arranged prices to any other Spaniards. The regularized system loaned itself to the same abuses as had earlier uncontrolled practices. Subjection to unfamiliar climates still claimed victims. Indians were required to carry burdens over great distances, sometimes as many as sixty leagues. Neglect, ill-treatment, exhaustion, and disease continued to take a heavy death toll. In this connection, it is significant to emphasize that the Crown had ordered the building of roads adequate for vehicles and pack animals for the purpose of lightening hardships on the natives as well as for improving communications and promoting economic development. Both Montejo and Maldonado promulgated ordinances between 1542 and 1544 providing that, to safeguard the health of the Indians, no Spaniard should send natives of the higher, cooler, and mountainous sections of the district of Gracias a Dios to the hot coast as burden-bearers. Although Montejo, who had issued somewhat similar decrees during his first governorship from 1537 to 1539, was accused of having disregarded his own regulation on certain occasions, he stoutly denied such charges.[65] Shortly after its installation the Audiencia de los Confines took further regulatory steps, providing that only a specified number of tamemes from each pueblo should serve each year, under close official regulation.[66]

Encomenderos also continued to hire out their Indians under contract for labor on the haciendas despite efforts to prevent it. This action, like burden-bearing, also meant the transfer of natives to unaccustomed climate and terrain, with the same pernicious results. Forced labor in the mines was also difficult to eradicate. The death rate among the Indians employed here remained high, despite the good intentions of the Crown and the provincial governors.[67]

These problems were so persistently difficult of solution because the practices involved were inseparable from the essential economic structure of the province and were therefore almost impossible wholly to eliminate, despite the efforts of Montejo and Maldonado. Much more effective measures were later taken by the Audiencia de los Confines, in application of legislation by the Crown. The system of tamemes, which the audiencia itself found it necessary to accept at first and finally formalized, was eventually abolished as a legalized institution. Furthermore, under provisions of the New Laws, the audiencia

---

[65] *Ibid.*
[66] Residencia of Alonso Maldonado, President of the Audiencia de los Confines, and of the oidores of the Audiencia, 1548, AGI, Justicia 299.
[67] *Ibid.*; Residencia of Montejo for Honduras-Higueras, 1544, AGI, Justicia 300.

prevented the taking of Indian slaves under any circumstances whatsoever and freed slaves taken earlier.[68]

The audiencia also took another very important step which the Crown had ordered as early as 1538 but which warfare in Honduras-Higueras and subsequent confusion had prevented Montejo, Pérez de Cabrera, and Maldonado from effectuating. This measure was the legal establishment of a fixed schedule of the tributes and services which the Indians were to give to their encomenderos. Service for the encomendero, whether on his haciendas or in his home, was now permitted only with specific permission from the audiencia and was limited to a designated number of Indians from the encomendero's pueblo, from two to ten at most. The encomendero was required to provide these natives with food while they were in service. Encomienda Indians were no longer to carry tributes to the municipality in which the encomendero resided unless the encomendero himself provided them with carts or other means of transport. Furthermore, ploughing of land for the planting of wheat was not required of Indians unless the encomendero provided oxen. Under this official assessment only stipulated amounts and types of tributes were to be provided, and only at specified intervals. On the agricultural side, maize, wheat, cotton, beans, chickens, peppers, honey, and cacao were principal kinds of tribute; on the native handicraft side, cotton cloth, rush mats, pottery, and stone implements for the grinding of grain. Fish were given as tribute by pueblos on the coast and by those living on the shores of lakes and along rivers. No gold or silver was included in tributes, since employment of encomienda Indians in the mines had long been forbidden by law. These official taxations were placed in full effect by the Audiencia de los Confines between 1548 and 1552.[69]

[68] *Ibid.;* Residencia of Alonso López de Cerrato, President of the Audiencia de los Confines, and of the oidores of the Audiencia, 1553, AGI, Justicia 301 and 302.

[69] Taxation of tributes and services of the Indians and native pueblos of the district of the Audiencia de los Confines, 1548–52, AGI, Guatemala 128. For the beginnings of official taxation on a general basis see Residencia of Alonso Maldonado, President of the Audiencia de los Confines, and of the oidores of the Audiencia, 1548, AGI, Justicia 299. The form of the official taxation of tributes is illustrated by the following assessment for the pueblo Guaxaquira in the district of Comayagua (AGI, Guatemala 128):

". . . 100 indios: Juan de Monguía (encomendero).

"En la ciudad d. sanctiago dla. provia. de guatimala en primero dia del mes d. março año dl. nacismio. de nro. salvador ihu. xpo. d. mill e quias. e quarenta y nueve años los señores presidente e oidores dl. audia. y chancilleria rreal d. su magd. q. en la dha. ciudad rreside se taso el pueblo d. guaxaquiro ques. en los terminos e juron. dla. villa de comaiagua y esta encomendado en juan de monguia vezino della madose. a los naturales dl. dho. [pueblo] q. es en el valle de la dha. villa le syembren en cada un año en dos sementeras· quatro hanegas d. mahiz e ma. de frisoles y lo beneficien cojan y encierren en la millpa donde se sembrare y lo q. dellos se cogiere sy su encomendero les diere carreta y harria se lo lleven a la dha. villa y le sienbren y venefficien el el dho. valle cada año una hanega de algodon y de lo q. dello se cogiere den quarenta toldillos cada año y le siembren el el dho. pueblo y le den cada pascua dos dozenas de gallinas de castilla q. son por año seis dozenas y le den cinco cantaros de miel cada año y seis petates pequenas para barbacoas y seis cantaros y seis ollas y seis comales y cinco indios de servio. ordinarios en la dha. villa con q. sea obligado a darles. d. comer todo el tpo. que le sirvieren y enseñarles la dotrina xpiano. no an de dar otra cosa ni se les a de llevar los dhos. yndios por ninga. via que sea ni comuta ninga. cosa de un tributo en otro so las penas contenidas en las leies y ordenancas por su mt. hechas para la buena governon. de las yndias el licendo. cerrato el licendo. pero rramirez el licendo. rrogel."

THE CHURCH

The Crown intended that Honduras-Higueras should constitute a bishopric a number of years before the province actually became an independent diocese.[70] It has already been seen that a bishop, Fray Alonso de Guzmán, had been designated before 1535 but had not taken office.[71] Pedraza was then, in 1538, named acting ecclesiastical head of the province, apparently with the clear understanding that he would later become bishop.[72] Meanwhile, first in 1538 and again in October 1541, pending Pedraza's actual appointment during his visit to Castile, the Crown assigned to the Bishop of Guatemala superior ecclesiastical jurisdiction over Honduras-Higueras. Marroquín was also directed to make an ecclesiastical inspection tour of Honduras-Higueras. It was on the basis of this authorization that he had made the joint visita general of the province with Maldonado in 1543 and his own visita the following year.[73]

Meanwhile, at Court Pedraza worked to hasten his appointment as Bishop of Honduras-Higueras [74] and sought the adoption of measures for its religious advancement. He was eventually so designated and obtained a number of decrees to strengthen the Church within the province, including the appointment of more clerics. Also, at his own initiative and expense, he contracted with a group of carpenters and masons to accompany him to his new bishopric to build churches and acquired the necessary materials and tools. He purchased a ship at Seville to carry all these and himself back to Honduras-Higueras, presumably in mid-1542.[75] Just as he was about to sail, the Crown ordered a delay.[76]

The royal order which halted Pedraza grew out of charges which Montejo's chaplain and legal counselor, Bachiller Juan Alvarez, had placed before the Consejo de Indias in connection with Pedraza's removal of Montejo from

[70] See Cedula designating Montejo Governor of Honduras-Higueras, March 1, 1535, AGI, Guatemala 402.

[71] Ibid.

[72] Cedulas designating Cristóbal de Pedraza spiritual head of Honduras-Higueras, January 29, 1538, AGI, Guatemala 402.

[73] See Cedulas of February 12, 1538, AGI, Guatemala 393, and of October 26, 1541, AGI, Guatemala 402.

[74] See Cedula of June 26, 1539 (issued in Toledo), AGI Guatemala 402, for the approximate time the confirmation of Pedraza as Bishop of Honduras and Higueras began to take definite form. This cedula begins: "Por quanto vos geronimo ytaliano y pantales de negro estantes en esta corte aveis encargado del despacho de las bulas del obspado. de la provincia de ygueras y cavo de honduras . . ." Instructions concerning the despatch of the Bulls follow.

[75] For Pedraza's action at Court and elsewhere in Castile see Documents concerning Pedraza, "El Obispo de Honduras" (n.d.), AGI, Guatemala 968B; Pedraza to the Crown, Seville, July 8, 1543, AGI, Guatemala 164; Pedraza to the Crown, Seville, December 16, 1544, AGI, Guatemala 164; Pedraza to the Crown, Seville, July 28, 1544, AGI, Guatemala 164; Undated documents regarding Pedraza, AGI, Indiferente General 1380.

[76] Cedula of June 9, 1542, AGI, Indiferente General 1380; Cedula of August 8, 1542, AGI, Contratación 5010.

office in Honduras-Higueras in 1539. It will be recalled that Alvarez had initiated action against Pedraza and Alvarado before the Viceroy and Audiencia of New Spain just after Montejo's removal and that he failed to make any progress in the City of Mexico toward Montejo's reinstatement in the governorship. Then, following Montejo's instructions, which were in violation of the article of his compact with Alvarado providing that litigation regarding their controversy should be halted, Alvarez had sailed for Castile to plead Montejo's case at Court.[77]

Alvarez embarked at Vera Cruz in January 1540, on the same ship which was carrying Hernán Cortés to Spain. At la Habana Alvarez had encountered his enemy Pedraza, then also on his way to Castile. Pedraza determined to find some way to delay Alvarez' voyage and appealed to Cortés, who was fully conversant with the quarrel over Honduras-Higueras and whom Pedraza persuaded to prevent Alvarez' continuing the voyage on the same ship. Pedraza then sailed on with Cortés, while Alvarez had to await another ship.[78] Nevertheless, Alvarez finally reached Court, where he presented Montejo's case against Alvarado and Pedraza and sought to have the Crown vindicate Montejo. He leveled particularly bitter charges against Pedraza, declaring that he had usurped royal jurisdiction in depriving Montejo of office in Honduras-Higueras and that the colonists of that province "cry to God and the Crown because of the grievances which they suffer at Pedraza's hands." Despatches from Montejo arrived at Court to strengthen Alvarez' hand.[79] Meanwhile the controversy between Montejo and Alvarado had become a closed issue through Alvarado's sudden death in 1541; but Alvarez' charges were so skillfully presented and Montejo's arguments in his despatches were so telling that the Crown finally decided on an investigation of Pedraza's conduct as judge in the quarrel between Alvarado and Montejo.

Pedraza at length cleared himself of Alvarez' charges, but it was not until well into 1545, long after the Audiencia de los Confines had been installed at Gracias a Dios, that he again reached Honduras-Higueras.[80] On his voyage he had stopped at Santo Domingo, where he enlisted the services of several priests.[81] He reached Trujillo on August 9, 1545, where, as he wrote:

. . . I was very well received by everyone in the city, both old and young, all of whom rejoiced greatly at my arrival. . . . And on the next day . . . I

---

[77] Montejo *v.* Pedraza, 1539, AGI, Justicia 129-2; Montejo *v.* Alvarado, 1541, AGI, Justicia 134-3; Juan Alvarez to the Crown, la Habana, February 14, 1540, AGI, Santo Domingo 116; Undated documents concerning Pedraza, AGI, Indiferente General 1380; Residencia of Montejo for Honduras-Higueras, 1544, AGI, Justicia 300.

[78] *Ibid.*

[79] *Ibid.*

[80] *Ibid.*

[81] Bishop Cristóbal de Pedraza to the Crown, Trujillo, August 21, 1545, AGI, Guatemala 164.

presented my bulls and the royal provision of Your Majesty . . . and took office as Bishop, to the gratification and satisfaction of the citizens and authorities, and of all others who were present, whether churchmen or laymen. When this ceremony was concluded I put on my vestments and said Mass. . . .[82]

Pedraza established the first seat of the Bishopric of Honduras in Trujillo. About fifteen years later, after Pedraza's death, it was transferred to Comayagua, which had achieved city status and had become the political capital of the province.

Until 1541, few if any churches of lasting construction had been erected in Higueras, although the older city of Trujillo, in Honduras, had permanent churches. In Higueras other public or private buildings, including Montejo's dwelling in Gracias a Dios, were at first used for divine services. The procurador Cambranes so informed the Crown, which directed that permanent buildings be constructed. By 1542 a permanent church had been built in Gracias a Dios, and others followed rapidly.[83]

The Church in Honduras-Higueras was far from wealthy for many years. Tithes given by the Spaniards and Indians in kind were neither great nor productive of large incomes. During the conquest of Higueras between 1537 and the first part of 1539 such tithes as could be collected were applied to the war. For the remainder of 1539 they amounted to only 100 pesos. In Gracias a Dios, in fact, no one cared to take a contract for collecting tithes during 1539. Unsettled political conditions and the dislocation of native population inevitably hampered collection for several years more. However, as conditions became stable, as more churchmen arrived, and as the organization of the Church grew in strength, ecclesiastical finances improved, keeping pace with progress in civil administration.

THE POPULATION

At the opening of 1542 Gracias a Dios is said to have had 28 citizens, fewer than the city had several years before; San Pedro had 32 and Comayagua 39.[84] Trujillo now had from 20 to 25, soon increased to 50. The citizen body of Gracias a Dios, however, before long grew measurably. It is not known how many Spaniards other than "citizens" were present in these municipalities at this time, but there must have been a considerable number. Neither is there available information on the population of Nueva Salamanca or of San Jorge

[82] *Ibid.*
[83] Bishop Cristóbal de Pedraza to the Crown, Trujillo, May 1, 1547, AGI, Guatemala 164; Residencia of Montejo for Honduras-Higueras, 1544; AGI, Justicia 300; Cedula of November 29, 1541, AGI, Guatemala 402.
[84] See Document concerning apportionment of negro slaves to citizens of Honduras-Higueras, 1542, Guatemala 965.

de Olancho, although the latter remained with 25 or so citizens following its reinforcement by Anaya in 1542–43. The number of settlers in Puerto de Caballos is uncertain, but this town must have reached considerable proportions, for its citizens resented subordination to San Pedro and in 1543 sent two representatives to Court to petition independent municipal status. These emissaries were to request full municipal status for the town so that it should no longer be subordinate in any way to San Pedro. The Crown later directed the Audiencia de los Confines formally "to found" a municipality at Puerto de Caballos to facilitate commerce, but the town's relationship to San Pedro could depend on the tribunal's discretion.[85] During this period, too, San Pedro sought to assume city status, as an honorary step upward from its town status and in recognition of its increasing importance. As already indicated, Comayagua, known also as Nueva Valladolid during these years,[86] after the middle of the century became both the political and ecclesiastical capital, with full city status, just as Montejo and others had planned.

It is difficult to estimate accurately the Indian population when the Audiencia de los Confines assumed authority in 1544. In 1547, however, Bishop Pedraza drew a dreary picture: "The land is so ruined and depopulated of Indians because of the great destruction wrought by past governors, that in some districts one can pass for thirty leagues without seeing a pueblo. . . ."[87] According to one report, there were 5786 tribute-paying Indians in all Honduras-Higueras in 1600, distributed as follows in the districts of the following cities and towns: Valladolid (or Comayagua) 1666, Gracias a Dios 1888, San Jorge de Olancho 464, Trujillo 500, San Pedro 376, and Puerto de Caballos 104.[88] There was, of course, a large number of *mestizos,* or persons of mixed Spanish and Indian blood, in the province by this time, who were not counted as Indian tribute payers. Assuming a maximum of five other Indians for each tribute payer, the combined native population, as indicated by this census, was less than 36,000, a startling contrast with the Spaniards' estimate when they first came to Honduras-Higueras.

CONCLUSION

As last royal governor of Honduras-Higueras, Montejo could in 1544 proudly turn over to the new Audiencia de los Confines a province in which the Spaniards held firm sway and which was now more stable, law-abiding, and

---

[85] See Cedula of December 27, 1542, AGI, Guatemala 402; Cedulas of June 6, 1543, and June 16, 1543, AGI, Guatemala 393.

[86] See Bishop Cristóbal de Pedraza to the Crown, Trujillo, May 1, 1547, AGI, Guatemala 164, for a general statement regarding the status of the several municipalities of Honduras-Higueras and their respective citizen bodies.

[87] Bishop Cristóbal de Pedraza to the Crown, Trujillo, May 1, 1547, AGI, Guatemala 164.

[88] Report on the route between Puerto de Caballos and the Bahía de Fonseca, ca. 1590, AGI, Mexico 257.

politically mature then ever before. The major problems which had torn the province from the first years of its existence were largely solved; progress was now possible. That such a situation had materialized after so many years was largely due to Montejo's military achievements. His administrative talents and broad vision had also made their contributions.

Montejo's removal from office in Honduras-Higueras and Chiapas in 1544 upon the installation of the Audiencia de los Confines was of course a heavy personal blow. His plans to build a wider adelantamiento of Yucatan were shattered. Indeed, in view of royal policy to bring the colonies of the Indies under ever-increasing control, such aspirations as Montejo's were utterly unattainable, as he should have realized. Enduring personal control of territory or individual influence was the last thing which the Crown would now permit. His next loss was the Higueras section of the territory between the Río de Copilco and the Río de Ulua, of which the Crown had made him royal governor in 1533. Despite his protests, the Audiencia de los Confines denied him any authority whatsoever in the southeastern portions of these wide lands, which included the town of San Pedro, and denied his claim that the Crown had ever actually united that territory with Yucatan. However, influenced by his recent marriage to Catalina de Montejo, Maldonado, as president of the audiencia, permitted his father-in-law to retain jurisdiction for a while longer over Tabasco, which made up the extreme northwestern section of his Río de Copilco–Río de Ulua grant.[89]

Montejo underwent residencia for Honduras-Higueras on departure from office, and after that process was concluded he remained in Gracias a Dios for some months. In 1546 he went to Ciudad Real de Chiapas to undergo a similar investigation for his governorship of Chiapas, as well as for Yucatan and Tabasco. Each residencia was conducted by an oidor of the audiencia.

After his residencias in Chiapas were finished, Montejo at last returned to Yucatan, very late in 1546, assuming the general administration of the province after an absence of more than a decade. He went back to a Yucatan which had been conquered by his son, his nephew, and other captains, and in which the City of Mérida in the northwest, the towns of San Francisco de Campeche on the west coast, Valladolid in the eastern interior, and Salamanca de Bacalar far to the south, had been founded. Just as he returned to his first province, however, the Spaniards of Yucatan were about to meet a final test. The Indians of the central eastern and southern districts rose in a sudden and fanatical revolt, which the Spaniards suppressed after several months of furious fighting. This left the Yucatecan Maya too exhausted for further uprisings.

[89] For Montejo's final years as a conquistador and administrator see Chamberlain, 1948.

Montejo's aspirations for a wider adelantamiento were soon further dashed. He founded a town not far from the western end of the Golfo Dulce in a region which he believed was advantageous for the development of commerce for Guatemala and Honduras-Higueras as well as for Yucatan, but Maldonado's successor in the presidency of the Audiencia de los Confines, Alonso López de Cerrato, objected. So too did the Dominicans who were now carrying out the "peaceful reduction" of Vera Paz under rigid royal protection. The Crown then ordered Montejo to withdraw from the Golfo Dulce area. In this way his territory was further reduced. López de Cerrato, with royal approval, also terminated Montejo's authority over Tabasco.

Thus by 1549 Montejo was left with only the peninsula of Yucatan. Even this was soon taken away from him, for the Crown ordered his residencia and removal from office there, despite the royal patent of 1526 which made him lifetime governor. As the royal treasury officials of Honduras-Higueras had written to the Crown about Montejo on an earlier occasion, it was "a great pity that in his old age he should be so crushed and afflicted, and so poverty stricken."

Montejo went to the City of Mexico after removal from office in Yucatan and then returned to Castile to seek vindication and recognition for his services at the hands of his sovereign. As he was about to sail from New Spain, he received a final signal honor: the viceroy appointed him to command the treasure fleet of 1551 from Vera Cruz to la Habana, where his ships united with those from Panama commanded by Captain-General Sancho de Viedma for the voyage across the Atlantic. At Court Montejo lost no time in seeking redress for all his grievances before the Consejo de Indias. He succeeded in regaining a certain amount of favor but died in the autumn of 1553 before his claims had been finally settled. Death overtook him in his native city of Salamanca, where he was buried. Thus ended the life of the true conqueror of Higueras and a man who had envisaged farseeing plans for the development of Honduras-Higueras as a whole. In many respects he was the real founder of the colony.

Meanwhile the Audiencia de los Confines had brought royal authority firmly to its Central American provinces and Honduras-Higueras entered into a period of relative administrative tranquility and order which permitted it to take its place among the well-ordered New World realms of the Crown of Castile. Gone were the turbulent earlier days of Honduras-Higueras which Pedraza described in these words:

I do not know, Your Holy Catholic Majesty, what evil fortune it can be which pursues this land, nor what saturnine planet reigns over it, for since the Christians first came to conquer, pacify and settle it, dissession and mutinies have never ceased among the governors who until this time have held authority, as is clear from that which befell under Cristóbal de Olid, who was the captain who went to the conquest, and then what befell under Diego López de Salcedo and a nobleman who was called Saavedra, whom the Marqués del Valle [Hernán Cortés] had left in the land as his lieutenant. Likewise that which happened to Vasco de Herrera and Diego Méndez [de Hinostrosa]. Because Diego Méndez wished to hold power, he had Vasco de Herrera, who then governed, killed, and then forced everyone to obey himself as governor. [Diego Méndez] governed until the blood of Vasco de Herrera called out for vengeance to God, who was pleased to have the Christians who were in Trujillo at that time elect the Contador Cerezeda as governor and chief officer of justice in name of Your Majesty. And the majority of the Christians joined together and took Méndez and quartered him, and hanged, flogged and cut off the hands and feet of many of his partisans. A little while later the Treasurer Diego García de Celís arrived in the province. . . , and as soon as he came he began to quarrel with Andrés de Cerezeda, who then governed, so that rival parties formed just as though they were citizens of Cáceres and Trujillo [in Castile]. The Treasurer [García de Celís] and others who joined him ridiculed Cerezeda, and scarcely wished to obey him in that which he ordered. Those who followed the Treasurer desired that he [alone] should govern and that the other [Cerezeda] should be destroyed. Then they tried to destroy [the Contador], for [the Treasurer] came back to Castile and placed many charges against him before the Royal Council. . . . At the time I went out to the province I went there with the Treasurer [García de Celís, who was then returning from Castile], and upon my arrival there the first thing which I did was to set myself to the task of making [García de Celís and Cerezeda] friends. Afterward [I composed a quarrel between] the Adelantados Montejo and Alvarado. [Quarrels] such as these have caused much destruction in the land and have led to the dispersal of its Indians, for upon observing the killings, disorders and harm which came down upon [all Indians] many of those who still remained in their pueblos fled to the mountains, where they have stayed to this very time. . . .[90]

With conquest and colonization achieved and with the province more chastened and mature by 1544, the Audiencia de los Confines and the Spaniards of Honduras-Higueras could henceforth look forward to a period of normal development. Nevertheless, Honduras-Higueras and Gracias a Dios did not long remain the administrative center of the Central American provinces, as its municipal officials and colonists wished. After Alonso López de Cerrato replaced Maldonado as president in 1548, the seat of the audiencia was transferred to Santiago de Guatemala, and the tribunal eventually came to be known as the Audiencia of Guatemala. Santigo de Guatemala henceforth, except for

[90] Bishop Cristóbal de Pedraza to the Crown, Seville, December 16, 1544, AGI, Guatemala 164.

a brief five-year period ending in 1570, was the political capital of colonial Central America, with Honduras-Higueras as one of the provinces of the district of the audiencia—also known as the Reino de Guatemala.[91] Symbolic of the transition from the rough, harsh and desperate period of conquest and initial colonization to one in which these major tasks were completed and stability and progress could be anticipated, the jurists of the audiencia, steeped in Roman law and unquestioning servants of an absolute monarch, had, in 1544, replaced the daring, truculent, and unbending soldiers who first brought Castilian dominion to the land.

[91] As finally constituted, after a number of changes in policy and territorial assignments, the district of the Audiencia of Guatemala was made up of Guatemala, Honduras-Higueras, San Salvador, Chiapas, Nicaragua, and Costa Rica. Briefly outlined, shifts in territory were as follows: after transfers between the districts of the Audiencia of Guatemala and the Audiencia of New Spain, Yucatan was finally assigned to the Audiencia of New Spain in 1560; Tabasco was also finally assigned to New Spain; Panama was transferred between the districts of the Audiencias of Guatemala and Peru until in 1567, it was placed within the Viceroyalty of Peru, with a new, but subordinate, audiencia. A potentially major change in the center of gravity and territorial changes within the Central American provinces came with the transfer of the seat of the Central American audiencia from Santiago de Guatemala to Panama in the mid-1560's. Chiapas and Guatemala were now assigned to the district of the Audiencia of New Spain, and the Central American tribunal had jurisdiction over Honduras-Higueras, Nicaragua, Costa Rica, and the west coast of New Granada. However, the Audiencia moved back to Santiago de Guatemala by 1570, with authority over Guatemala, Chiapas, Honduras-Higueras, San Salvador, Nicaragua, and Costa Rica. See Haring, 1947, pp. 81–82, 90–91.

Bibliography

COMMENTS ON SOURCES

THE HISTORY of Honduras-Higueras from its first colonization until mid-1539 has been recorded in early chronicles, published documents, and the works of modern writers, especially Bancroft in his *History of Central America,* Milla in the *Historia de la América Central* . . . , and Durón in his *Bosquejo de historia de Honduras.* . . . Manuscript sources such as despatches, residencias, legal suits, and probanzas of merits and services in the Archivo General de Indias de Sevilla and the Archivo General del Gobierno, in Guatemala City, however, add important elements which are not available in published form, and make possible new interpretations and reevaluations. Among the chroniclers, Herrera, Gómara, Bernal Díaz, and Oviedo give detailed narratives of the course of events in Honduras-Higueras through 1536, the Fifth Letter of Relación of Hernán Cortés is an important source for that great conquistador's intervention, and the *Colección de documentos inéditos . . . de Indias* (DII) include many documents of fundamental value, such as documents concerning Andrés de Cerezeda and letters of Pedro de Alvarado and Francisco de Montejo. Herrera gives the only available account of the rise of the great native leader Lempira and of his assassination at the siege of the Peñol of Cerquin, even though many published and unpublished documents tell in detail of the "War of Cerquin." The full story of the final conquest of Higueras by Montejo has been made available only through the collation of information contained in a great number of published and unpublished documents.

The controversy between Montejo and Alvarado for jurisdiction over Honduras-Higueras in 1539 is dealt with briefly by Herrera and Oviedo, but the details are made clear only by the voluminous suits Montejo versus Pedraza, 1539 (AGI, Justicia 129-2) and Montejo versus Alvarado, 1541 (AGI, Justicia 134-3), and unpublished letters of Montejo and other officials which are found in the Archivo General de Indias de Sevilla.

The history of Honduras-Higueras from the time Alvarado forced Montejo from the governorship in the summer of 1539 until the installation of the Audiencia de los Confines at Gracias a Dios in the spring of 1544 is almost in its entirety a hitherto unknown chapter in Spanish colonial history and depends wholly on manuscript sources from the Archivo General de Indias de Sevilla, along with a few supporting documents from the Archivo General del Gobierno, Guatemala City. The documents which reveal this unknown chapter are multitude. They consist of residencias, documents originating in the Audiencias of New Spain and Santo Domingo and in the cabildos of the cities and towns of Honduras-Higueras, legal suits, correspondence of governors and other officials, royal cedulas, and probanzas of merits and services. The separation of Honduras-Higueras from Guatemala after Alvarado's death is revealed mainly by the record of the choice of Diego García de Celís and Juan López de Gamboa as co-administrators of Honduras-Higueras by the cabildos of the province itself (AGI, Guatemala 965) and the Residencias of Montejo for Honduras-Higueras and Chiapas, 1544 and 1546 (AGI, Justicia 300). The complex and significant constitutional situation in which Montejo, Juan Pérez de Cabrera, and Alonso Maldonado found themselves as rival contestants for authority over Honduras-

Higueras between 1542 and 1544 is revealed by the mentioned residencias of Montejo, the Residencia of Juan Pérez de Cabrera, 1544 (AGI, Justicia 63), the suit Fiscal *v.* Juan Pérez de Cabrera, 1566 (AGI, Justicia 286-4-1), and to a lesser degree the Residencia of Maldonado, 1548 (AGI, Justicia 299). A great number of other manuscripts add further details to the history of this hitherto unknown period.

TABLE OF BIBLIOGRAPHICAL ABBREVIATIONS

A. Manuscript Sources

AGG—Archivo General del Gobierno, Guatemala City.

AGI—Archivo General de Indias de Sevilla. Upon citation of legajos which are divided into números and ramos, subdivisions will be indicated by appropriate numbers separated by hyphens: e.g. AGI, section of Patronato, legajo 1, número 1, ramo 1, would be Patronato 1-1-1. Except in unusual cases "section of" and "legajo" will be omitted in citing manuscript sources, whether from the Archivo General de Indias or elsewhere.

B. Published Documents

DII—Colección de documentos inéditos relativos al descubrimiento, conquista y colonización de las antiguas posesiones españoles en América y Oceanía, sacados de los archivos del Reino, y muy especialmente del de Indias.

C. Chronicles and Secondary Works

Bancroft—Bancroft, H. H. The works of Hubert Howe Bancroft.

Herrera—Herrera y Tordesillas, Antonio de. Historia general de los hechos de los Castellanos en las islas i tierra firme del Mar Océano. Citation is made to decada, libro, and capítulo, e.g. Herrera, 1601–15, 1-1-1.

Oviedo—Fernández de Oviedo y Valdés, Gonzalo. Historia general y natural de las Indias, isla y tierra firme del Mar Océano. Citations are made to libro and capítulo, e.g. Oviedo, 1851–55, 1-1.

Remesal—Remesal, Antonio de. Historia de la Provincia de S. Vicente de Chyapa y Guatemala de la Orden de nro. glorioso Padre Sancto Domingo. Citations are made to libro, and capítulo, e.g. Remesal, 1619, 1-1.

A. General Bibliography, Historiography, and Bibliographical Aids

ANTONIO, NICOLÁS
1783–88 Biblioteca hispana nova hispanorum scriptorum qui ab anno MD ad MDCLXXXIV flouere notitia. 2 vols. Madrid.

HARISSE, H.
1866 Biblioteca americana vetustissima: description of works published between the years 1492 and 1551. New York.

JONES, C. K.
1942 A bibliography of Latin American bibliographies. Washington.

KENISTON, H.
1920 List of works for the study of Hispanic-American history. New York.

LEÓN PINELO, ANTONIO DE
1629 Epitome de la biblioteca oriental i occidental nautica i geográfica. Madrid.

SÁNCHEZ ALONSO, B.
1927 Fuentes de la historia española e hispano-americana: ensayo de bibliografía sistemática de impresos y manuscritos que ilustran la historia política de España y sus antiguas provincias de ultramar. 2 vols. Madrid.

TORIBIO MEDINA, J.
1897–1907 Biblioteca hispano-americana (1493–1810). 7 vols. Santiago de Chile.

WEBER, F.
1911 Beiträge zur charakteristik der alteren geschictsschreiber über Spanisch-Amerika. Leipzig.

B. Guides to Archives and Libraries

GROPP, A. E.
1941 Guide to libraries and archives in Central America and the West Indies, Panama, Bermuda, and British Guiana. New Orleans.

PARDO, J. JOAQUÍN
1945 Indice de los documentos existentes en el Archivo General del Gobierno, Tomo I. Guatemala.

RODRÍGUEZ MARÍN, P.
1916–26 Guía histórica y descriptiva de los archivos, bibliotecas y museos arquelógicos de España que están a cargo del Cuerpo Facultativo del Ramo. 2 vols. Madrid.

TORRES LANZAS, P.
1900 Relación descriptiva de los mapas, planos, etc. de México y Florida existentes en e Archivo General de Indias. 2 vols. Sevilla.

1903 Relación descriptiva de los mapas, planos, etc. de la Audiencia y Capitanía de Guatemala . . . existentes en el Archivo de Indias. Madrid.

VILLACORTA C., J. ANTONIO
1944 Bibliografía guatemalteca. Guatemala.

C. Geography

ALCEDO, ANTONIO
1786 Diccionario geográfico histórico de las Indias Occidentales o América. Madrid.

C. Geography (*continued*)

CARLSON, F. A.
  1944 Geography of Latin America. New York.
JAMES, P. E.
  1942 Latin America. New York.
LÓPEZ DE VELASCO, JUAN
  1884 Geografía y descripción universal de las Indias. Madrid.
VÁZQUEZ DE ESPINOSA, ANTONIO
  1942 Compendium and description of the West Indies. (Translated by Charles Upson
     Clark.) Washington.

D. Law

CARRO, V. D.
  1944 La teología y los teólogos-juristas españoles ante la conquista de América. 2 vols.
     Madrid.
ESCHRICHE Y MARTÍN, J.
  1874–76 Diccionario razonado de legislación y jurisprudencia. 2 vols. Madrid.
  1847–51 Los códigos españoles, concordados y anotados. 12 vols. Madrid.
PUGA, VASCO DE
  1563 Provisœs, cédulas, instrucciones de Su Magestad. México.
SOLÓRZANO PEREIRA, JUAN DE
  1776 Política Indiana. . . . Madrid.
SPAIN
  1681 Recopilación de leyes de los Reynos de las Indias. 4 vols. Madrid.
SPAIN, CONSEJO DE INDIAS
  1596 Libro primero (segundo) de provisiones, cédulas, capítulos de ordenanças y
     cartas, librados y despachados en diferentes tiempos por los Reyes Católicos; con
     acuerdo de los señores presidentes y de su consejo, tocantes al govierno de las
     Indias (edited by Diego de Enzinas). Madrid.
  1893 The New Laws of the Indies for the good treatment and preservation of the
     Indians promulgated by the Emperor Charles the Fifth, 1542–1543. London.

E. Manuscript Sources

ARCHIVO GENERAL DEL GOBIERNO, GUATEMALA CITY (cited as AGG)
  Cedulas (register books).
  Probanzas of Merits and Services:
    Gonzalo de Cartagena, Santiago de Guatemala, 1570.
    Alonso de Funés, Comayagua, 1549.
  Papers from the Archivo Colonial, Guatemala City:
    Cedulas, originals and copies, and register books.
    Probanzas of Merits and Services:
      Luis de Aguilar, Nueva Salamanca, Section of Honduras, leg. 57, exp. 1.
      Gonzalo de Armenta, San Miguel de la Frontera, 1564.
      Juan Bardales, Trujillo, 1544, Section of Honduras, leg. 72, exp. 2.
      Benito Carrasco, San Jorge de Olancho, 1544, Section of Honduras, leg. 27, exp. 1.
      Miguel de Casanos, Nueva Salamanca, 1548, Section of Honduras, leg. 62, exp. 1.

E. Manuscript Sources (continued)

   Francisco de Castellanos, Tesorero of Guatemala, Xérez de la Frontera, 1560, Section of Guatemala, leg. 268, exp. 1.

   Alvaro de Fuentes y de la Cerda, 1624, Section of Guatemala, leg. 344, exp. 9.

   Andrés Francisco, Valladolid del Valle de Comayagua, 1560.

   Pedro de Garro, Santiago de Guatemala, 1541.

   Pedro Gómez de Rueda. Santiago, 1553.

   Melchor Hernández, Santiago de Guatemala, 1556, Section of San Salvador, leg. 193, exp. 1.

   Francisco Méndez, Gracias a Dios, 1548, Section of Honduras, leg. 13, exp. 1.

   Juan Rodríguez, Gracias a Dios, 1548, Section of Guatemala, leg. 411, exp. 2.

   Juan Ruíz de la Vega, Comayagua, 1548.

   Miguel de Trujillo, San Miguel de la Frontera, 1548.

   Section of San Salvador, leg. 121, exp. 21.

   Antonio de Vergara, Comayagua, 1543.

 Papers from the Archivo Municipal of Guatemala City:

   Cartas antiguas de particulares.

   Cartas antiguas escritas a esta Ciudad de Guatemala.

   Cartas de agentes.

   Cartas de ciudades y villas.

   Libro de consultas.

   Cartas de personas Ylustres.

   Ynstruciones y cartas.

   Reales cédulas, lib. 4.

 Papers from the Archivo de Protocolos Colonial, Guatemala City:

   Cedulas concerning Honduras-Higueras (originals).

   Libro de la tesoria de su magested de la quenta y razon q. della tiene yo el tesorero franco. de castellanos, tesorero en esta provincia, de guatemala desdel año de mdxxix que comenzo . . . en adelante (1524–1558).

   Libro de votos de las causas y pleitos qe. començo en el mes de julio de 1545 hasta el de 1564.

   Probanza of merits and services of Alonso de Funés, Comayagua, 1549.

ARCHIVO GENERAL DE INDIAS, SEVILLE (cited as AGI)

Audiencia de Guatemala

   Leg. 1. Consultas originales correspondiente al distrito de la Audiencia de Guatemala. 1586–1637.

   Leg. 9. Audiencia de Guatemala: Cartas y expedientes del presidente y oidores de dicha Audiencia: año de 1529 a 1573.

   Leg. 39. Cartas y expedientes de los gobernadores de Costa Rica y Honduras. 1526–1699.

   Leg. 43. Cartas y expedientes de los cabildos seculares de León de Nicaragua, San Salvador y Comayagua. 1539–1689.

   Leg. 44. Cartas y expedientes de varios cabildos seculares del distrito de la Audiencia. 1530–1695.

E. Manuscript Sources (continued)

Leg. 49. Cartas y expedientes de oficiales reales de Valladolid de Comayagua en Honduras. 1530–1697.

Leg. 52. Cartas y expedientes de personas seculares del distrito de la Audiencia de Guatemala. 1526–1561.

Leg. 53. Cartas y expedientes de personas seculares del distrito de la Audiencia de Guatemala. 1562-1571.

Leg. 97. Confirmaciones de encomiendas de indios en el distrito de la Audiencia. 1564–1611.

Leg. 110. Ynformaciones de oficio y parte del distrito de la Audiencia. 1526–1551.

Leg. 111. Ynformaciones de oficio y parte del distrito de la Audiencia. 1552–1569.

Leg. 112. Ynformaciones de oficio y parte del distrito de la Audiencia. 1570–1571.

Leg. 128. Un libro de tasaciones a los naturales de las Provincias de Guatemala, Nicaragua, Yucatan y Comayagua. 1548–1551.

Leg. 156. Cartas y expedientes de los Obispos de Guatemala. 1536–1639.

Leg. 161. Cartas y expedientes de los Obispos de Chiapa. 1541–1699.

Leg. 162. Cartas y expedientes de los Obispos de León de Nicaragua. 1544–1685.

Leg. 163. Cartas y expedientes des los Obispos de Vera Paz. 1570–1604.

Leg. 164. Cartas y expedientes de los Obispos de Valladolid de Comayagua en Honduras. 1541–1700.

Leg. 168. Cartas y expendientes de personas eccas. del distrito de dicha Audiencia. 1532–1570.

Leg. 173. Cartas y expedientes de personas eccas. del distrito de dicha Audiencia. 1600–1605.

Leg. 386. Registros de oficio: reales ordenes dirigidos a los authoridades del destrito. 1551–1647.

Leg. 393. Registros de partes: reales ordenes dirigidos a los autoridades corporaciones y particulares del destrito. 1529–1551.

Leg. 402. Registros: Honduras e Higueras: reales ordenes dirigidos a los autoridades y particulares de aquella provincia. 1525–1605.

Leg. 965. Papeles por agregar. 1527–1577.

Leg. 966. Papeles por agregar. 1578–1599.

Leg. 968A, 968B. Papeles por agregar.

Leg. 971. Papeles por agregar.

Audiencia de México

Leg. 68. Cartas y expedientes del presidente y oidores de Méjico vistos en el Consejo. 1533–1571.

Leg. 1098. Registros de oficio y partes: reales ordenes dirigidos a los autoridades y particulares de Nueva España. 1548–1552 and 1566–1569.

Leg. 2999. Registros: reales ordenes dirigidos a los autoridades y particulares. 1531–1604.

Audiencia de Santo Domingo

Leg. 49. Cartas y expedientes remitidos por la Audiencia de Santo Domingo. 1530–1561.

E. Manuscript Sources (continued)

Leg. 71. Tres libros de cartas de los autoridades personas eclesiásticas y seculares de esta isla: 1534–1574.

Leg. 116. Cartas y expedientes de los cabildos seculares de Cuba y Habana. 1527–1612.

Leg. 168. Cartas.

Leg. 172. Cartas.

Contaduría

Leg. 1. Cuentas de los gastos de varias comisiones conferidas a diferentes sugetos por encargos particulares. 1514–1547.

Leg. 661. Cuentas de los tesoreros de Nueva España. . . . 1544–1553.

Leg. 662A. Cuentas de los tesoreros de Nueva España. . . . 1533–1543.

Leg. 987. Cuentas de Real Hacienda de los años de 1527 a 1529 y 1533 a 1556.

Contratación

Legs. 3281, 4948A, 5009, 5010, 5103. All cited legajos include important materials on Honduras-Higueras.

Escribanía de Cámara

Leg. 1006A. Dn. Franco. Montejo, conqor. Adelantado y governor. de las Provs. de Yucatan, con el sor. Fiscal sre. el despojo qe. se le hizo del govierno y approvechamto. de los tributos de yndios qe. posehya. . . . 1552. Cited as Montejo *v*. Fiscal over removal from office, 1552.

Indiferente General

Leg. 415. Registros, Asientos y Capitulaciones. 1508–1605.

Leg. 737. Consultas del Consejo y Cámara. 1529–1556.

Leg. 857. Papeles y borradores del Consejo.

Leg. 1206. Expedientes, Ynformaciones y Probanzas. 1539–1541.

Leg. 1207. Expedientes, Ynformaciones y Probanzas. 1547–1549.

Leg. 1380. Peticiones y Memoriales.

Leg. 1382A. Peticiones y Memoriales.

Leg. 2984. Reales resoluciones sobre consultas, breves y expediéntes. 1523–1559.

Justicia

Leg. 63. Residencia tomada el año de 1544 a Dn. Juan Perez de Cabrera Govor. que fue de la provincia de Honduras; por Dn. Alonso de Valdez juez nombrado para este efecto. 1544. Cited as Residencia of Juan Pérez de Cabrera, 1544.

Leg. 129, núm. 2. El Adelantado Dn. Franco. Montejo Govor. de las provincias de Yucatan Higueras y Honduras, con el Protector de Yndios Licdo. Dn. Cristobal de Pedraza sre. haverle este embargado los bienes y suspendido de sus empleos. 1539. Cited as Montejo *v*. Pedraza, 1539.

E. Manuscript Sources (continued)

Leg. 134, núm. 3. Dn. Franco. de Montejo Govor. y capn. General de la prova. de Yucatan, con el Adelantado Dn. Pedro de Alvarado, sre. el derecho a una encomienda de yndios. 1541. Cited as Montejo *v.* Alvarado, 1541.

Leg. 204, núm. 2, ramo 1. El Adelantado Dn. Franco. de Montejo con el Fiscal de S. M. sre. la suplicacion que interpone de una cedula dada sre. el Pueblo de Escupuçalco: Mexico. Año de 1556.

Leg. 244. Relacion de la Residencia q. tomo el doctor blas cota al adelantado Montejo (1549–1550). Cited as Residencia of Montejo for Yucatan and Tabasco, 1549–1550.

Leg. 280, núm. 4. Dn. Diego de Alvarado vezino de la Ciudad de Gracias a Dios, con Juan de Castriqui de la propia vecindad sobre la pertenencia a la mitad de los pueblos de yndios Coloma Yarnaynia y Chandeque. 1546.

Leg. 281, núm. 2. Alvaro de Paz vecino de la Ciudad de Sn. Pedro en la governacion de Higueras con Alonso y Lorenzo Dorrego hermanos vecinos de la Ciudad de Gracias a Dios sobre derecho al pueblo de yndios de Macholoa. 1547.

Leg. 282, núm. 1. Elena de Chaves vecina de la Ciudad de Gracias a Dios, con Luis de Barrasco de la propia vecindad, sre. que este la devolviese los pueblos de yndios Tambla Tenambla Cuzuyegua. 1549.

Leg. 272, núm. 3. Francisco de Alvarado vecino de la Ciudad de Gracias a Dios con Franco. Lievana de la propia vecindad sobre derecho a los pueblos Lepaera y Tocuyuco. 1549.

Leg. 286, núm. 1. Juan Vasco de Plasencia, contador de la prova. de Onduras con el Fiscal de S. M. sre cierta condenacion. . . . 1550.

Leg. 286, núm. 4, ramo 1. Fiscal con Juan Perez de Cabrera Governador que fue de la provincia de Honduras sre. el pago de los sueldos que le correspondian el tiempo que servia el govierno de la Nueva Cartago. 1556. Cited as Fiscal *v.* Juan Pérez de Cabrera, 1556.

Leg. 295, 296. Residencia tomado et año de 1535 al Adelantado Dn. Pedro de Alvarado Governador que fue de la provincia de Guatemala y a sus tenientes por el Licdo. Alonso Maldonado oidor de la Audiencia de Mexico. 1535. Cited as Residencia of Alvarado, 1535.

Leg. 299. Residencia tomada el año de 1547 a los Licdos. Alonso de Maldonado, Pedro Ramirez de Quiñones, Diego Herrera y Juan Rogel, Presidente y Oidores de la Audiencia de Guatemala, por el Licdo. Lopez Cerrato juez nombrado para este efecto. 1547. Cited as Residencia of Maldonado 1547 (1548).

Leg. 300. Audiencia de Guatemala: Residencia tomado a el Adelantado Dn. Francisco Montejo Governador que fue de las provincias de Chiapa Yucatan Tabasco y Cozumel y a sus tenientes, por el Licdo. Juan Rogel Oidor de la Audiencia de Guatemala, juez nombrado para este efecto. 1553. Residencia q. tomo el Licendo. Rogel al adelantado Montejo de la governacion de Honduras . . . (1544). Cited as Residencia of Montejo for Honduras-Higueras, 1544. Residencias of Montejo for Honduras-Higueras, Chiapas, Yucatan, and Tabasco, 1544–1550. Residencias of Montejo for Chiapas, Yucatan and Tabasco, 1546–1550.

E. Manuscript Sources (*continued*)

Leg. 301, 302. Residencia tomada el año de 1553 a los Licdos. Alonso Lopez Cerrato, Tomas Lopez, Diego Herrera y Juan Rogel, Presidente y oidores de esta Audiencia de Guatemala, por el Don Antonio Rodriguez de Quesada Oidor de la Nueva España, juez nombrado para este efecto. 1553.

Leg. 1005, núm. 3, ramo 1. El Adelantado D. Francisco Montejo Governor de las provincias de Yucatan con Dn. Pedro de Alvarado sobre el derecho a los terminos del Rio de Grijalva que dho. Montejo havia conquistado y pacificado a su costa. 1533. Cited as Montejo *v.* Alvarado, 1533.

Leg. 1008, núm. 3, ramo 3. Andres Nuñez, vecino de la villa de Comayagua, con Alonso Aleman y Hernando de Baeza vecinos de Sevilla sobre fianzas de unas mercaderias. 1543.

Leg. 1021, núm. 3, ramo 2. El Adelantado Dn. Franco. de Montejo, Govor. de la Prova. de Yucatan, con el Fiscal de S. M. sre. el pago de su salario y otras cosas. 1552. Cited as Montejo *v.* Fiscal over salaries, 1552.

Leg. 1031, núm. 2. Dn. Cristobal de Pedraza, Protector de Yndios de la Gobernacion de Honduras, con el Br. Juan Alvarez Clerigo sobre ciertos desordenes cometidos en cuanto a la observancia de las reales provisions. 1540.

Leg. 1032, núm. 1, 2, 3. Suits between citizens of Puerto de Caballos and citizens of other town over Indian pueblos. 1541–1544.

Leg. 1032, núm. 2. Martin de Villarubia, vezno. de la Ciudad de Sn. Pedro de Puerto de Caballos, con Cristoval Gallegos vecino de dha. ciudad sre. dro. a los pueblos de yndios de Petoa y Cuchivite en la Provincia de Honduras. 1543.

Leg. 1032, núm. 4, ramo 1. Alonso Garcia, vecino de la Ciudad de Gracias a Dios, con el Adelantado Dn. Francisco Montejo, Governador de la provincia de Higueras, sre. haverele despolado del pueblo de yndios de Yamala. 1545.

Leg. 1033, núm. 2, ramo 1. Dn. Cristobal de la Cueva, vecino de la Ciudad de Xérez de la Frontera, con el Adelantado dn. Francisco Montejo sobre derecho a los tributos del pueblo de yndios de Tecurucelo. 1553.

Leg. 1035, núm. 2, ramo 2. El Señor Fiscal: con el Adelantado Dn. Pedro de Alvarado, governador de Goathemala, sre. que se le manda apremiar al dho. Adelantado a q. vuelva en persona a su governacion a dar residencia del tiemp qe. ha servido en ella. 1537. Cited as Fiscal *v.* Alvarado, 1537.

Leg. 1035, núm. 3, ramo 1. Fiscal con . . . García de Celís, tesorero de la provincia de Honduras, sobre escesos cometidos en su oficio. 1537. Cited as Fiscal *v.* Diego García de Celís, 1537.

Leg. 1037, núm. 2, ramo 2. Fiscal con el Licdo. Alonso Maldonado, Presidente que fue de la Audiencia de Guatemala, sobre derecho al pueblo de yndios Azapuçalco. 1550.

Patronato

Leg. 20.
Leg. 56. Merits and Services of Conquistadores. 1540–1543.
Leg. 58. Merits and Services of Conquistadores. 1548.
Leg. 60. Merits and Services of Conquistadores. 1552–1556.

E. Manuscript Sources (continued)

   Leg. 62. Merits and Services of Conquistadores. 1559.

   Leg. 63. Merits and Services of Conquistadores. 1560.

   Leg. 71. Merits and Services of Conquistadores. 1571.

   Leg. 72. Merits and Services of Conquistadores. 1572.

   Leg. 74. Merits and Services of Conquistadores. 1575-1576.

   Leg. 180. Papeles sobre el buen gobierno de Nueva Espana. 1519–1540.

   Leg. 181. Papeles sobre el buen gobierno de Nueva Espana. 1541–1560.

   Leg. 184. Papeles sobre el buen gobierno de Nueva Espana. 1525–1572.

   Leg. 275. Son copias de minutes de Reales Cedulas, de sentencias en varias residencias, de despachos y provisiones de enplazamiento despachados por el Consejo y Camara de Yndias pertenecientes al buen gobierno de aquellos dominios. 1511–1586.

   Leg. 278. Minutas de cedulas . . . [sobre] buen gobierno de las Yndias. 1539–1540.

F. Published Documents

ARBITRAJE DE LIMITES

   1932   Arbitraje de limites, Guatemala y Honduras: Anexos. Washington.

CEDULARIO HERÁLDICO

   1933   Cedulario heráldico de conquistadores de Nueva España. México.

COLECCIÓN DE DOCUMENTOS

   1864–84   Colección de documentos inéditos relativos al descubrimiento, conquista y colonización de las antiguas posesiones españoles en América y Oceanía sacados de los archivos del Reino y muy especialmente del de Indias. 42 vols. (Cited as DII.) Madrid.

   1934   Libro viejo de la fundación de Guatemala. Guatemala.

GAYANGOS, PASCUAL DE

   1866   Cartas y relaciones de Hernán Cortés al Emperador Carlos V. Paris.

RÚJULA Y DE OCHOTERENO, JOSÉ DE, and ANTONIO DEL SOLAR Y TABOADA

   1931   Francisco de Montejo y los Adelantados del Yucatán, geneología de los Condes y Duques de Montellano: notas y documentos biográficos y genealógicos. Badajoz.

SPAIN, MINISTERIO DE FOMENTO

   1877   Cartas de Indias. Madrid.

SPAIN, MINISTERIO DE TRABAJO Y PREVISIÓN

   1930   Catálogo de pasajeros a Indias durante los signlos XVI, XVII y XVIII. Madrid.

G. Chronicles, Early Histories, and Secondary Works

AGUADO, PEDRO DE

   1916–17   Historia de Santa Marta y Nuevo Reino de Granada. 2 vols. Madrid.

AITON, A. S.

   1936   Antonio de Mendoza, first viceroy of New Spain. Durham, N. C.

ALVARO, HECTOR, and TITO PÉREZ ESTRADA

   1936   Homenaje a la Ciudad de Gracias a Dios en el CD aniversario de su fundación, 1536–1936. San Pedro Sula.

G. Chronicles, Early Histories, and Secondary Works (continued)
ANGHIERA, PETER MARTYR D'
1912 De orbe novo, the eight decades of Peter Martyr D'Anghiera. Translated by F. A. MacNutt. 2 vols. New York and London.
BANCROFT, H. H.
1883–87 The history of Central America. 3 vols. San Francisco.
CASAS, BARTOLOMÉ DE LAS
n.d. Historia de las Indias. 3 vols. Madrid.
1646 Brevíssima relación de la destruyción de las Indias. Barcelona.
CHAMBERLAIN, R. S.
1940 The lineage of the Adelantado don Francisco de Montejo and his will and testament. *Rev. Hist. de América*, no. 8, pp. 53–56. México.
1943 La controversia entre Cortés y Velázaquez sobre la gobernación de la Nueva España, 1519–1522. *Anales Soc. Geog. e Hist. de Guatemala*, 19: 23–56. Guatemala.
1945a Un documento desconocido del Licenciado Cristóbal de Pedraza, Protector de los Indios y Obispo de Honduras. *Anales Soc. Geog. e Hist. de Guatemala*, 20: 33–38. Guatemala.
1945b El último testamento de don Francisco de Montejo, Adelantado de Yucatán, 1553. *Anales Soc. Geog. e Hist. de Guatemala*, 20: 83–90. Guatemala.
1945c Ensayo sobre el Adelantado don Francisco de Montejo y sus proyectos para el desarrollo económico de la Provincia de Honduras e Higueras. *Anales Soc. Geog. e Hist. de Guatemala*, 20: 209–217. Guatemala.
1946a The founding of the City of Gracias a Dios, first seat of the Audiencia de los Confines. *Hispanic Amer. Hist. Rev.*, 26: 2–18. Durham.
1946b Plan de siglo xvi para abrir un camino de Puerto Caballos a la Bahía de Fonseca en sustitución de la ruta de Panamá. *Anales Soc. Geog. e Hist.* 21: 61–65. Guatemala.
1947a The early years of San Miguel de la Frontera. *Hispanic Amer. Hist. Rev.*, 27: 633–646. Durham, N.C.
1947b The governorship of the Adelantado Francisco de Montejo in Chiapas, 1539–1544. *Carnegie Inst. Wash.*, Pub. 574, Contrib. 46. Washington.
1947c Proyectos de conquista pacífica formulados por el Licdo. Cristóbal de Pedraza, Protector de los Indios y Prelado de Honduras e Higueras, y por el Licenciado Juan de Arteaga, Obispo Electo de Chiapas. *Honduras Maya,* año 2, números 2 y 3, pp. 12–18. Tegucigalpa.
1948 The conquest and colonization of Yucatan, 1527–1550. *Carnegie Inst. Wash.,* Pub. 582. Washington.
DIAZ DEL CASTILLO, BERNAL
1904 Historia verdadera de la conquista de la Nueva España (Genaro García, editor). 2 vols. México.
1933–34 Verdadera y notable relación del descubrimiento y conquista de la Nueva España y Guatemala. 2 vols. Guatemala.
DIFFIE, B. W.
1945 Latin American civilization: colonial period. Harrisburg, Pa.

G. Chronicles, Early Histories, and Secondary Works (continued)

DURÓN, R. E.

   1927   Bosquejo de historia de Honduras de 1502 a 1921. San Pedro.

FERNÁNDEZ DE OVIEDO Y VALDÉS, GONZALO

   1851–55   Historia general y natural de las Indias, Islas y Tierra-Firme del Mar Océano. 4 vols. Madrid.

FERNÁNDEZ PIEDRAHITA, LUCAS

   1688   Historia general de las conquistas del Nuevo Reino de Granada. Amberes.

FUENTES Y GUZMÁN, FRANCISCO ANTONIO

   1882–83   Historia de Guatemala, o Recordación Florida. 2 vols. Madrid.

   1932–33   Recordación Florida. . . . 3 vols. Guatemala.

GONZÁLEZ BARCÍA, ANDRÉS

   1749   Historadores primitivos de las Indias Occidentales. 3 vols. Madrid.

GROOT, J. M.

   1889–93   Historia eclesiástica y civil de Nueva Granada. 5 vols. Bogotá.

GUATEMALA, COMISIÓN DE LÍMITES

   1929   Cartografía de la América Central. Guatemala.

HANKE, LEWIS

   1949a   The Spanish struggle for justice in the conquest of America. Philadelphia.

   1949b   Bartolomé de las Casas, pensador político, historiador, antrópologo. La Habana.

HARING, C. H.

   1947   The Spanish empire in America. New York.

HELPS, A.

   1900–04   The Spanish conquest in America. 4 vols. London and New York.

HERRERA Y TORDESILLAS, ANTONIO DE

   1601–15   Historia general de los hechos de los Castellanos en las Islas i Tierra Firme del Mar Océano. Madrid.

ICAZA, F. A.

   1923   Conquistadores y pobladores de Nueva España. 2 vols. Madrid.

IPSILANTI, GEORGE

   1943   Escudos de armas de la Provincia de Honduras. *Boletín de la Biblioteca y Archivo Nacionales,* Año 3, Número 6, pp. 131–156. Tegucigalpa.

JUARROS, DOMINGO

   1857   Compendio de la historia de la Ciudad de Guatemala. 2 vols. Guatemala.

KELLY, J. E.

   1932   Pedro de Alvarado, conquistador. Princeton.

LEHMANN, W.

   1920   Central-Amerika. Teil I. 2 vols. Berlin.

LÓPEZ DE GÓMARA, FRANCISCO

   1554   La historia general de las Indias con todos los descubrimientos y cosas notables que han acaecido en ellas dende que se ganaron hasta agora. Anvers.

LUNARDI, F.

   1941–42 Descubrimiento de la gran metrópoli Maya en el Valle de Comayagua, Republic de Honduras. *Revista del Archivo y Biblioteca Nacionales,* vols. 19, 20. Tegucigalpa.

G. *Chronicles, Early Histories, and Secondary Works (continued)*

1942–43   Lempira, el héroe de la epopeya nacional de Honduras. *Revista del Archivo y Biblioteca Nacionales,* vols. 20, 21. Tegucigalpa.

1943   Los misterios Mayas del Valle de Otoro. *Revista Geográfica Americana,* vol. 20, no. 118. Buenos Aires.

1945a   Choluteca: ensayo histórico-etnográfico. Tegucigalpa.

1945b   Iglesia y convento de San Francisco: El Valle de Comayagua: *Documentos para la historia:* no. 3. Tegucigalpa.

1946a   El Tenguax y la primera iglesia catedral de Comayagua: El Valle de Comayagua. *Documentos para la historia:* no. 1. Tegucigalpa.

1946b   La fundación de la Ciudad de Gracias a Dios y de las primeras villas y ciudades de Honduras. Tegucigalpa.

MacNutt, F. A.

1909   Bartholomew de las Casas: his life, his apostolate, and his writings. New York and London.

Mendieta, Gerónimo de

1870.   Historia eclesiástica indiana. México.

Merriman, R. B.

1918–1937   The rise of the Spanish Empire in the Old World and in the New. 4 vols. New York.

Milla, José, and Agustín Gómez Carrillo

1879–1897   Historia de la América Central desde el descubrimiento del País por los españoles (1502) hasta su independencia de España (1821). 4 vols. Guatemala.

Morison, S. E.

1942   Admiral of the Ocean Sea: a life of Christopher Columbus. Boston.

Pardo, J. Joaquín

1944   Efemérides para escribir la historia de la Muy Noble y Muy Leal Ciudad de Santiago de los Caballeros del Reino de Guatemala. Guatemala.

Peralta, M. M. de

1883   Costa Rica, Nicaragua, y Panamá en el siglo xvi: su historia y sus límites.

Plaza, J. A. de

1850   Memorias para la historia de la Nueva Granada desde su descubrimiento hasta el 20 de julio de 1810. Bogotá.

Ramos, M. A.

1929   Divulgaciones militares. Tegucigalpa.

Remesal, Antonio de

1619   Historia de la Provincia de S. Vicente de Chyapa y Guatemala de la Orden de nro. glorioso Padre Sancto Domingo. Madrid.

1904   Revista del Archivo y Biblioteca Nacional de Honduras. vol. 1.

Roys, R. L.

1943   The Indian background of colonial Yucatan. *Carnegie Inst. Wash.,* Pub. 548. Washington.

Salgado, Felix

1931   Elementos de historia de Honduras. Tegucigalpa.

G. Chronicles, Early Histories, and Secondary Works (continued)

SANDOVAL, PRUDENCIO DE
1681 Historia de la vida y hechas del Emperador Carlos V: Máximo Fortíssimo. 2 vols. Amberes.

SANTA CRUZ, ALONSO DE
1920–27 Crónica del Emperador Carlos V. 5 vols. Madrid.

SCHOLES, F. V., and R. L. ROYS
1948 The Maya Chontal Indians of Acalan-Tixchel. *Carnegie Inst. Wash.*, Pub. 560. Washington.

SIMÓN, PEDRO
1627 Conquista de Tierra Firme. Cuenca.
1882–92 Noticias historiales de las conquistas de Tierra Firme en las Indias Occidentales. 5 vols. Bogotá.

SPINDEN, H. J.
1928 Ancient civilizations of Mexico and Central America. New York.

SQUIER, E. G.
1855 Notes on Central America; particularly the States of Honduras and San Salvador. New York.

STONE, D. Z.
1940 The Ulua Valley and Lake Yojoa. *In* The Maya and their Neighbors, pp. 386–94. New York.
1941 Archaeology of the north coast of Honduras. *Mem. Peabody Mus. Harvard Univ.*, vol. 9, no. 1. Cambridge.

STRONG, W. D.
1935 Archaeological investigations in the Bay Islands. *Smithsonian Misc. Coll.*, vol. 92, no. 14. Washington.
1940 Anthropological problems in Central America. *In* The Maya and their Neighbors, pp. 377–85. New York.

——, A. KIDDER II, and A. J. D. PAUL, JR.
1938 Preliminary report on the Smithsonian Institution. Harvard University archaelogical expedition to northeastern Honduras, 1936. *Smithsonian Misc. Coll.*, vol. 92, no. 14. Washington.

TORQUEMADA, JUAN DE
1723 Monarquía Indian. 3 vols. Madrid.

VALLE, RAFAEL HELIODORO
1948 Cristóbal de Olid, conquistador de México y Honduras. México.

VÁZQUEZ, FRANCISCO
1714–16 Chrónica de la Provincia del Santíssimo Nombre de Jesús de Guatemala de el Orden de No. Seráphico Padre San Francisco en el Reyno de la Nueva España. 2 vols. Guatemala.

WINSOR, J.
1884–89 Narrative and critical history of America. 8 vols. Boston and New York.

ZAVALA, S.
1945 Contribución a la historia de las instituciones coloniales en Guatemala. *Jornadas*, no. 36. México.